SPSS:
A Minimalist Approach

Glenn E. Meyer
Lewis and Clark College

Harcourt Brace Jovanovich College Publishers
Fort Worth Philadelphia San Diego New York Orlando Austin San Antonio
Toronto Montreal London Sydney Tokyo

ISBN: 0-03-055392-X

Address editorial correspondence to:
301 Commerce Street, Suite 3700
Fort Worth, TX 76102

Address orders to:
6277 Sea Harbor Drive
Orlando, FL 32887
1-800-782-4479 outside Florida
1-800-433-0001 (inside Florida)

PRINTED IN THE UNITED STATES OF AMERICA

3 4 5 6 7 8 9 0 1 2   066   9 8 7 6 5 4 3 2 1

SPSS™: A Minimalist Approach
[With SPSS/ PC + ™ 4.0]
Glenn E. Meyer

Table of Contents

Chapter 1: The Archetypal Minimalist SPSS™ Setup
The style of the book & SPSS basics

Chapter 2: System Issues

SPSS/ PC + ™ 4.0

SPSS® 4.0 for the Unix ™

SPSS® for the Macintosh ®

Chapter 3: Frequency distributions (FREQUENCIES)

Creating & interpreting frequency distributions, getting descriptive statistics & various graphic outputs.

Chapter 4: Descriptive Statistics (DESCRIPTIVES)

Calculation of various descriptive statistics

Chapter 5: Z-scores (DESCRIPTIVES+ SAVE SUBCOMMAND)

Using DESCRIPTIVES to calculate Z-scores, printing & saving them

Chapter 6: Boxplots & Stem-Leaf diagrams (EXAMINE)

Production of Boxplots & Stem and Leaf Diagrams

Chapter 7: One Sample t-test (DESCRIPTIVES & MANOVA)

Difference of a sample mean from a population mean

Chapter 8: Two Sample t-test (T-TEST)

Difference of one sample mean from one group from the sample mean of another independent group

Chapter 9: Paired-Sample t-test (T-TEST)

Difference of one mean from another with matched or paired samples

Chapter 10: Chi-Square Test of Independence (CROSSTABS)

Chi square test for independence of one classification variable vs. a second classification variable

Chapter 11: Chi-Squares for a Population Set of Frequencies (NPAR Tests)

Chi-square test for a set of frequencies vs. an hypothesized or given set of frequencies

Chapter 12: Pearson's Correlation Coefficient (CORRELATIONS)

Calculation of Pearson's Product Moment Coefficient (r)

Chapter 13: Scattergrams & Regression lines (PLOT)

Production of Scattergrams & Linear Regression Equations

Chapter 14: Oneway Analysis of Variance (ONEWAY)

Comparison of means for independent groups, trend analysis

Chapter 15: Between Groups Factorial Anova (MANOVA)

Factorial Anova for Independent Groups & Interactions

Chapter 16: Repeated Measure Anovas, Latin Squares & Analysis of Covariance (MANOVA)
Anova designs with repeated trials or matched groups or covariates

Chapter 17: Multiple Regression & Partial Correlation
(REGRESSION, PARTIAL CORR)

Prediction of a Y score from a set of X variables (X_1 to X_k) & Partial Correlation

Chapter 18: Assorted Multivariate Statistics
(DISCRIMINANT, FACTOR, MANOVA)

Examples of Several Popular Multivariate Procedures

Chapter 19: Nonparametric Statistics

Assorted Nonparametric Statistics (used for Ranks, Categorical Data or when Measurement Data doesn't meet the assumptions)

Chapter 20: Data Manipulation

Various ways of manipulating, printing, entering & saving data

CHAPTER 1: THE ARCHETYPAL MINIMALIST SPSS SETUP

THE STYLE OF THE BOOK & SPSS BASICS

SUMMARY OF A GENERAL SPSS SETUP

set width = 80 .
data list *list* / *name name name* . *
variable labels *name 'label'* / *name 'label'* .
value labels *name value 'label' value 'label'* /
            name value 'label' value 'label' .
missing values *name (value,value,value)* / *name (value,value,value)* .
begin data .
\#   \#   \#   \#
\#   \#   \#   \#
\#   \#   \#   \#
\#   \#   \#   \#
\#   \#   \#   \#
end data .
specific analysis .
finish .

* SPSS/PC+™4.0 uses : data list *free* / *name name name* .

REAL WORLD EXAMPLE USING *FREQUENCIES*

set width = 80 .
data list list / sex test1 test2 test3. *
variable labels sex 'sex of student' .
value labels sex 1 'female' 2 'male' 3 'missing' /
            test1 test2 test3 -1 'missing' .
missing values test1 test2 test3 (-1) /
            sex (3) .
begin data .
1 70 80 50
1 67 80 56
1 77 89 90
1 68 67 99
1 45 67 -1
2 89 67 89
2 56 84 20
2 77 98 55
2 55 99 34
2 66 88 68
3 45 78 99
end data .
frequencies variables = sex test1 test2 test3 .
finish .

* SPSS/PC+™ 4.0 uses data list free / sex test1 test2 test3

I. Introduction to SPSS

SPSS is a very powerful system with a lot of bells and whistles. It can run on many different systems and environments. These distinctions can be daunting to the beginner. Luckily for the user or the teacher, the current version of SPSS maintains a common language and syntax across its different platforms. The setups that you see in this book are written in a style such that they should work across the different systems and computers on which you may find SPSS. They are all congruent with the language descriptions in the SPSS® Reference Guide, which holds for all systems. These systems are SPSS® for the Macintosh®, SPSS® for Unix™, SPSS/PC+™ 4.0, SPSS® for OS/2™, SPSS® for IBM® MVS™, SPSS® for IBM® CMS™, and SPSS® for VAX/VMS®.

We will discuss particulars of these systems in Chapter 2. If there turns out to be some difference in the language and setups, we will try to document for the systems we tested. Specifically, we have tested our setups with SPSS® for the Macintosh®, SPSS® for Unix™, and SPSS/PC+™ 4.0 .

It is usually the case that the minor differences in command language are between SPSS/PC+™ 4.0 and all the other versions. One major difference that you will see again and again is that for all versions of the SPSS except SPSS/PC+™ 4.0 the data list command is:

data list *list / name name name* .

For SPSS/PC+™ 4.0, the command is

data list *free / name name name* .

Don't worry, we will explain this command in a minute. For DOS users, remember the difference. It will be footnoted at the beginning of each chapter as a reminder.

When you purchase SPSS for a PC, Mac, or PS/2, you will probably get the manuals for that system. If working on a main frame or minicomputer version, you may not want to purchase the full manual set. This book can substitute if you want documentation on how to use your system. Note that SPSS can be implemented with a base set of procedures. You may need to purchase or your institution may need to supply access to the Advanced Statistics modules, which can be added to the base versions of SPSS. For example, to do factorial analyses of variance you need the Manova programs. This procedure is an add-on depending on your systems.

The book emphasizes some of the most common analyses and manipulations that students and the 'average' researcher use. By the time, you are skilled enough statistically to use the more esoteric procedures, you probably can dive right into the full set of advanced manuals that you can purchase from SPSS, Inc. These manuals can be intimidating to the beginner and thus we offer this one. We have tried to write it so each analysis is done clearly and presented with an archetypal example and the most common variants of setups. We have also tried to interpret the results for you. Many people can get lost in the massive amount of information that a package like SPSS can produce. For people who only want to "Dear God, let me pass Stats" or "Get this analysis done by Thursday!" , it can be frightening.

However, for those just using it for occasional analyses or wanting an introduction, there is a very straightforward template which can be used for the most common tasks. We've tried to make it easy, generic and use the easiest data entry format.

II. SPSS SETUPS AND AN ARCHETYPAL ANNOTATED EXAMPLE

SPSS setups can be considered as having three major parts that are linked in order:

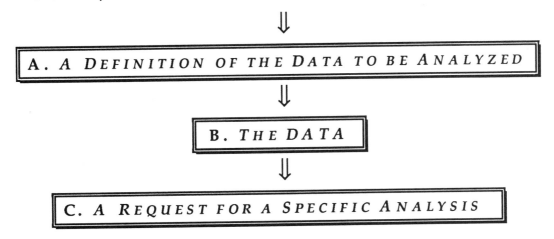

Without going into detailed rules (yet), let's look at a simple task (and then explain the details). The task we will use is creating a frequency distribution using the SPSS program called **FREQUENCIES**.

FREQUENCIES

In this example, we have:

1. A set of students (in this case, 11 students). Each will be on one line of data.

2. Some are male, some are female (in this case, 5 of each). For one student this information is unknown.

3. Each student has taken 3 exams. There are 4 variables per subject (sex and three test scores). They will be noted as **SEX**, **TEST1**, **TEST2** and **TEST3**.

4. We want to get a set of frequency distributions. We want one for the sex of the students and one for each test.

5. Each student will be typed on one line. First will be their sex with a **1** indicating a female and a **2** indicating a male.

6. If the value of **SEX** is unknown, a **3** will be typed. If a test score is missing a **-1** be will be typed.

The following setup will produce the frequency distributions for each test and for the breakdown of the students' sex. *This example is only to identify the major parts of a setup. The frequency program will be described in detail later.* The setup as it would be typed into the computer would look as follows:

```
set width = 80 .
data list list / sex test1 test2 test3.   [Note: data list free / etc. for SPSS/PC+]
variable labels  sex 'sex of student' .
value labels sex 1 'female' 2 'male'  3 'missing' /
                 test1 test2 test3 -1 'missing' .
missing values test1 test2 test3 (-1) /
                sex (3) .
begin data .
1 70 80 50
1 67 80 56
1 77 89 90
1 68 67 99
1 45 67 -1
2 89 67 89
2 56 84 20
2 77 98 55
2 55 99 34
2 66 88 68
3 45 78 99
end data .
frequencies variables =  sex test1 test2 test3 .
finish .
```

The following figure breaks down the setup into its major constituent subgroups.

Data Definition Commands

```
set width = 80 .
data list list / sex test1 test2 test3 .
variable labels  sex 'sex of student' .
value labels sex 1 'female' 2 'male'  3 'missing' /
                    test1 test2 test3 -1 'missing' .
missing values test1 test2 test3 (-1) /
                    sex (3) .
```

```
begin data .
1 70 80 50
1 67 80 56
1 77 89 90
1 68 67 99
1 45 67 -1
2 89 67 89
2 56 84 20
2 77 98 55
2 55 99 34
2 66 88 68
3 45 78 99
end data .
```

Data Section:
   Bounded by Begin Data & End Data Commands .

```
frequencies variables =  sex test1 test2 test3 .
```

```
finish .
```

Request for Frequency Distributions

This set up will produce frequency distributions. Below is the one for the Variable **SEX**. The full output for this program (FREQUENCIES) will be explained in Chapter 3 but we can use this to see important facets of the output as they compare to the setup. These facets are noted by numbered superscripts.

    1. The variable being charted is **SEX**

    2. Five were men. Five were women.

    3. One subject's sex is unknown.

```
SEX          sex of student  1


                                               VALID     CUM
      VALUE LABEL  2          VALUE  FREQUENCY  PERCENT  PERCENT  PERCENT

   female                      1.00      5       45.5     50.0     50.0
   male                        2.00      5       45.5     50.0    100.0
   missing  3                  3.00      1        9.1    MISSING
                                       -------  -------  -------
                             TOTAL      11      100.0    100.0

VALID CASES      10      MISSING CASES     1  3
```

For interpreting the output fully, see Chapter 3.

III. A BREAKDOWN OF THE THREE BASIC SECTIONS

NOTES ON HOW TO ARRANGE AN SPSS COMMAND LINE:
Line Length and Continuing a Command to the Next Line

There are several general rules about writing the commands we will be using:

1. Start command in column one and **end the command with a period (.)** .
2. Don't type lines longer than 80 characters (off the end of your screen).
3. If a line needs to be continued (it's longer than 80 characters), then start the continuation on the next line but indent it by at least one column. More than one is fine; you can do what looks nice. **Remember the period after the end of the command. DON'T EVER USE THE TAB KEY FOR SPACING IN SPSS SETUPS! THE PROGRAM MAY NOT REGARD THEM AS BLANK SPACES!**

4. In some setups we start with a **set width = 80** command. This is useful when working with screen output or 8 [1]/2 by 11 inch paper. If the command is left out, some SPSS output can run off the right side of the screen or paper. There are other useful **set** commands that control output (see Chapter 2)

A. DATA DEFINITION

We are going to describe 4 basic setup commands. They are the **DATA LIST**, **VARIABLE LABELS**, **VALUE LABELS**, and **MISSING VALUES** statements. Only the **DATA LIST** is mandatory. The remaining are optional but very useful.

DATA LIST

1. General Layout

The DATA LIST command is the most important command of your setup. If it is incorrect, the setup will not run and will produce seemingly endless unfriendly error messages or even more insidiously nice looking but totally incorrect results.

SPSS has a wide variety of very sophisticated manners of data entry, and the DATA LIST command can become very complicated. We have chosen to present one style in our setups which experience has demonstrated to be the easiest for casual or beginning users to use. Once familiar with the system, the manuals explain other very useful and versatile layouts. We are gaining simplicity at the loss of considerable power. For this, our data must be setup as follows:

> a. Each subject can only have **one line of data** (80 total columns).
> b. The data can **only be numbers.** There can be no alphanumerics or "$", etc. We can't type the subjects' names (unless you want to put them after the data on a line. However, SPSS will be unable to use this information).
> c. Each bit of data must be **separated by at least one blank** space. However, more than one blank doesn't hurt. Each column of data must have its own name (i.e. sex, test1, test2, test3). **DON'T EVER USE TABS!**
> d. Thus, your **data** can be considered as **matrix** with one **row** across representing an individual **subject** and the *columns* separated by blanks representing the value of a specific *variable* for that subject.

It is possible to arrange your data in many ways, as in the manual, but we're taking a simple and hard to screw up approach.

Thus some sample data lines for our subjects in the preceding example looked as follows:

	sex	test1	test2	test3
subject # 1	1	70	80	50
subject # 2	1	67	80	56

First came their sex, then a blank, then a test score, a blank, etc.

This simple arrangement is conveyed to SPSS by the data list command. For our examples:

    a. It *must* be the *first command* in your setup.

    b. It *must* start in the *first column* as you type.

    c. Its form is:

        data list list / {variable names} .

It seems silly to say **list list**. There is a reason, but that's just the way it is! Thus the **DATA LIST** command is generally written as for most SPSS versions:

    data list list / ········ *list of variable names* ········· **.**

Again for SPSS/PC+™ 4.0, the commands is :

    data list free / ········ *list of variable names* ········· **.**

2. Variable Names

There are easy rules for variable names if you don't want to use all the nuances of SPSS. The rules are:

    a. Each variable must have a unique name (i.e. sex, test1, etc.).

    b. Make all names eight letters or numbers or less.

    c. Don't start with a number or punctuation sign.

    d. Avoid reserved words. These are used by SPSS for its commands. Don't use: **TO, BY, WITH, THRU, INTO** for variable names.

    d. Most versions of SPSS don't care if the name is in lower or UPPER CASE.

Use of the "to" Shortcut

There is one easy shortcut which is worthwhile learning. In our example we had three test scores. It wasn't hard to type test1, test2, and test3. This would get tedious if the subject had taken *10* exams and we had to type test1, test2, test3, test4, test5, test6, test7, test8, test9, test10.

SPSS lets you use a shortcut. We could have typed a data list as follows:

data list list / sex test1 to test3 . *

> ***** at this point, we will stop noting the 'free' usage for SPSS/PC every time.

In the case of ten exams, we could have entered:

data list list / sex test1 to test10 .

SPSS will respond as if you type in all the variables individually. Later you can keep referring to the whole set as **test1 to test3**, or you can refer to any separate one, such as **test8**, in the case where you established ten exams. Thus the general form would be:

var1 to var#

where the **#** represents the last variable using the prefix. You can also have more than one such list on a data list card. If our subjects had also take four chemistry tests, we could have typed:

data list list / sex test1 to test3 chem1 to chem4 .

This example also demonstrates why you can't use **to** for a variable. SPSS thinks it is part of this command. **Be careful not to separate the number part of the name. Don't type test_1 to test_3 (the underlying just notes the blank spaces). It will have dire consequences.**

VARIABLE LABELS

Variable names can be ambiguous. While **SEX** seems to stand for the subjects' gender, it doesn't have to. It might mean "the sex of the preferred sex partner," or it might mean "the sex of your oldest sibling." It is very common to end up with variable names that you don't remember anymore. A name like WT16X as compared to HT17X will make little sense the next day. It's better to have SPSS print an explanatory label when it gives you output.

The general form then of the command is:

variable labels *name 'label' / name 'label'* .

You give a variable name and then in single quotes you get to write an up to **120 character label** explaining what the variable means. It is better to be brief and succinct. In our beginning example, the command we used was:

variable labels sex 'sex of student' .

This lead to this label being used in the output as highlighted below:

SEX	sex of student				
VALUE LABEL		VALUE	FREQUENCY	PERCENT	VALID PERCENT	CUM PERCENT
female		1.00	5	45.5	50.0	50.0
male		2.00	5	45.5	50.0	100.0
missing		3.00	1	9.1	MISSING	
		TOTAL	11	100.0	100.0	

If there are more than one **VARIABLE LABELS**, then they are separated by a slash and continued on the next line if room is need. Assume in our example, we wanted to label each test as follows:

test1	=	First test
test2	=	Midterm
test3	=	Final exam.

The command would look as follows:

variable labels   sex 'sex of student' /
test1 'First test' /
test2 'Midterm' /
test3 'Final' .

VALUE LABELS

Just as variable names can be ambiguous, so can the values of the variable. In our example we coded females as '1', males as '2' and entered a '3' if the sex of the student was unknown. This is an arbitrary scheme. We could have used any numbers. Thus, we get output. It would be nice if we could label the values such that we know what is happening. It is a classic problem to have a set of codes (i.e. 1 = female, 2 = male) written on a piece of yellow paper which is then lost, soaked in coffee, eaten by the dog, scribbled on by a child, ripped up or burned by a disgruntled employee, boyfriend, girlfriend, etc. I have seen this happen. Because of this, it would be nice if we could get SPSS to document our codes. It also gives nice print outs and charts.

The command is **value labels** and the general form is:

value labels *name name ... value 'label' value 'label' /
name value 'label' value 'label' .*

Each label can be 40 characters, but limits in the size of SPSS output suggest you should stick with **8 characters for labels** if you can.

For our example, we wanted to identify the males, females and missing values for the variable **SEX**. For the test scores, we want to identify '-1' as missing. Thus the command looked as follows:

value labels **sex 1 'female' 2 'male' 3 'missing' /
test1 test2 test3 -1 'missing' .**

We can see the labels that are being used in the output as underlined below. Without the value labels statement, the labels "female", "male" and "missing" would not be in the output and you wouldn't know that a '1' should for a female, etc.

OUTPUT WITH VALUE LABELS

```
sex          sex of student


                                               VALID      CUM
     VALUE LABEL            VALUE  FREQUENCY  PERCENT  PERCENT  PERCENT

  female                    1.00       5        45.5     50.0     50.0
  male                      2.00       5        45.5     50.0    100.0
  missing                   3.00       1         9.1   MISSING
                                    -------  -------  -------
                           TOTAL      11       100.0    100.0
```

MISSING VALUES

It is common for data to be missing. Sometimes, the subject doesn't know the answer, sometimes you forget to write it down, sometimes the subject doesn't answer for some reason. Given the format of the data that we are using, you can't just leave it blank (you could with other types of SPSS setups; see manual). Thus, you need to fill in some "fake" value. However, you don't want this computed in your statistics. For example, if we computed the mean of test3, note below that the subject has a '-1' instead of a score. The last person has a '3' for sex.

```
1    70    80    50
1    67    80    56
1    77    89    90
1    68    67    99
1    45    67    -1     ⇨⇨   TEST3 SCORE IS MISSING
2    89    67    89
2    56    84    20
2    77    98    55
2    55    99    34
2    66    88    68
3    45    78    99     ⇨⇨   SEX IS MISSING
```

You don't want a '-1' computed into the average. Thus we need a command that tells SPPSX to note for us the number of missing values and not to use it in statistical computations. The general form of the command is:

missing values *name name ... (value, value, value) /*
name (value, value, value) .

The specific instance in our example is:

**missing values test1 test2 test3 (-1) /
sex (3) .**

This lead to the value '3' being marked as missing in the output as seen below:

```
sex          sex of student


                                              VALID      CUM
     VALUE LABEL          VALUE  FREQUENCY  PERCENT   PERCENT   PERCENT

     female                1.00       5      45.5      50.0      50.0
     male                  2.00       5      45.5      50.0     100.0
     missing               3.00       1       9.1    MISSING
                                    -------   -------   -------
                          TOTAL      11     100.0     100.0

VALID CASES        10    MISSING CASES        1
```

Note that *VALID PERCENT* does not include this person. That is the purpose of a missing value command.

If you want to have more than one value specified as missing for a given variable, these can be listed in the parentheses. Assume we wanted the values '3' and '4' to be missing for sex. Then the command would look as follows:

missing values test1 test2 test3 (-1) /

sex (3, 4) .

B. SPECIFYING AN ANALYSIS

The rest of the book is about specifying analyses. Thus we won't spend a lot of time discussing this now. The important point is that of placement. The rules are as follows:

1. Put the first analysis you want to conduct after the data description commands and after the data section (ending with the **end data** command).
2. If you want to do another analysis, just put it after the first.

In our example we used **FREQUENCIES** so it was typed in its appropriate position as below:

```
set width = 80 .
data list list / sex test1 test2 test3 .
variable labels  sex 'sex of student' .
value labels sex 1 'female' 2 'male'  3 'missing' /
             test1 test2 test3 -1 'missing' .
missing values test1 test2 test3 (-1) /
             sex (3) .
begin data .
1 70 80 50
1 67 80 56

    etc.


end data .
frequencies variables =   sex test1 test2 test3 .
finish  .
```

Let's say we also wanted to do another analysis (a Pearson's Correlation between all the test scores, which will be explained in detail later). The setup would look as follows (note the **boldfaced** placement of the analyses).

```
data list list / sex test1 test2 test3  .
variable labels  sex 'sex of student' .
value labels sex 1 'female' 2 'male'  3 'missing' /
                test1 test2 test3 -1 'missing' .
missing values test1 test2 test3 (-1) /
                sex (3) .
begin data .
1 70 80 50
1 67 80 56
1 77 89 90
1 68 67 99
1 45 67 -1
2 89 67 89
2 56 84 20
2 77 98 55
2 55 99 34
2 66 88 68
3 45 78 99
end data .
```
frequencies variables =   sex test1 test2 test3 .
correlations test1 to test3 .
```
finish.
```

Note that the second analysis (CORRELATIONS) must come after the END DATA command!

C. DATA

The data are placed before the first analysis. As described above we are using one line per subject with blanks between variables. The important point is that the data set has to be bounded by a **begin data** and **end data** command. Leave these out and you have trouble. Thus the general form is:

begin data .

\# \# \# \#

\# \# \# \#

\# \# \# \#

\# \# \# \#

\# \# \# \#

end data .

The specific example we are using looks as follows with the data in **boldface**.

```
data list list / sex test1 test2 test3  .
variable labels  sex 'sex of student' .
value labels sex 1 'female' 2 'male'  3 'missing' /
             test1 test2 test3 -1 'missing' .
missing  values  test1  test2  test3  (-1) /
             sex (3) .
begin  data .
1  70  80  50
1  67  80  56
1  77  89  90
1  68  67  99
1  45  67  -1
2  89  67  89
2  56  84  20
2  77  98  55
2  55  99  34
2  66  88  68
3  45  78  99
end  data .
frequencies variables =  sex test1 test2 test3 .
finish  .
```

IV. ENDING THE SETUP

This is very easy. When you are all done type **finish.** All our setups have included a **FINISH** command. This was deliberate; if you leave it out, you may not exit SPSS when the analysis is completed but instead enter the Menu systems specific to your computer as described in Chapter 2. If you want to avoid this little trick, make sure to use the **FINISH** command.

V. YOUR SYSTEM

The next chapter will give details on how to use several versions of SPSS. You can skip the sections for other machines other than your own. In Chapter 2, we will be using a very simple setup for examples. As you will see, it uses the DESCRIPTIVES procedure to calculate the mean, standard deviation, minimum and maximum scores for the variable X. DESCRIPTIVES itself will be described in more detail later.

S P S S / P C +™ 4 . 0

```
set width = 80 .
data list free / x .
begin data .
1
2
3
end data .
descriptives x .
finish .
```

All Other SPSS Versions

```
set width = 80 .
data list list / x .
begin data .
1
2
3
end data .
descriptives x .
finish .
```

CHAPTER 2: SYSTEM ISSUES

SPSS/PC+™ 4.0

SUMMARY OF COMMANDS [1]

c:\> spsspc/re file.set

Invokes Review editor and setup saved in file.set. Does not do analyses - just an editor.

c:\> spsspc file.set

Instructions in **file.set** submitted in Batch Mode to SPSS. Listing of results, error messages sent to **spss.lis**.

c:\> rename spss.lis file.ans

Renames your results to file.ans. Otherwise might be replaced by another run.

c:\> spsspc file.set > file.ans

Instructions in **file.set** submitted in Batch Mode to SPSS. Listing of results, error messages sent to **file.ans**.

c:\> spsspc

Starts up the REVIEW Menu system.

c:\> spsspc; Then an *F10*; Then an *Exit to Prompt*

Starts up the Menu system, then sends you to *Command Prompt* mode.

SPSS/PC+™ 4.0 FILE CONTROL COMMANDS

set listing= 'file.ans' .

Saves your listing (analyses) if saved in file.ans.

set log = 'gm.set' .

Saves your setup (commands and data) in gm.set . For use in Command Prompt Mode and REVIEW Menus.

include 'filename' .

Inserts the text file 'filename' into your SPSS set up. Useful for Command Prompt Mode or REVIEW Menus.

dos 'command' .

Executes a DOS command from inside of SPSS. ' dos . ' leaves SPSS for DOS prompt (c:\>). 'exit' returns you to SPSS.

set runreview manual .

Insert in 'spssprof.ini' file if want program always to startup in Command Prompt Mode. (use '**review**.' to call up REVIEW Menu when in Command Prompt Mode).

---

[1] File names are examples.

F - KEY COMMANDS FOR MINI-MENUS
Choose with Cursor and <return> or Type Bold-Faced Letter

F1 : info:	Review help	Menus	File list	Glossary	menu HIP off
F2 : windows:		Switch	Change size	Zoom
F3 : files:	Edit different file		Insert file	
F4 : lines:	Insert after	insert Before	Delete	Undelete
F5 : look:	Forward find	Backward find	fOward change	bAckward change
F6 : go to:	Output pg			
F7 : mark/unmark area of:	Lines	Rectangle	Command	
F8 : area:	Copy	Move	Delete	Round
F9 : file:	write Whole file		Delete	
F10 : run:	Exit to prompt			
	or			
F10 : run:	run from Cursor	run from marked Area	Exit to prompt	

NAVIGATING IN THE REVIEW MENUS
Generating Commands

```
┌─────────────────── Guide to Menu Commands ───────────────────┐
│ ENTER (←┘)   Paste Selection & Move Down One Level in Menu    │
│ TAB or →     Temporarily Paste Selection & Move Down One Level│
│ ESC or ←     Remove Last Temporary Paste & Move Up One Level  │
│ Alt-ESC      Jump to Main Menu (also Ctrl-ESC)               │
│ Alt-K        Kill All Temporary Pastes                        │
│ Alt-T        Get Typing Window                                │
│ Alt-E        Switch to Edit Mode                              │
│ Alt-M        Remove Menus                                     │
│ Alt-V        Get Variables Window                             │
│ Alt-C        Run from Cursor                                  │
└──────────────────────────────────────────────────────────────┘
```

Motion Commands

```
┌──────────────────────────────────────────────────────────────┐
│  Short Distance                    Long Distance              │
│  Home    ↑   PgUp    Tab     Ctrl-Home    Ctrl-PgUp           │
│  ←           →      ↑Tab     Ctrl-←           Ctrl-→          │
│  End     ↓   PgDn    ←┘      Ctrl-End     Ctrl-PgDn           │
└──────────────────────────────────────────────────────────────┘
```

INTRODUCTION TO DOS AND SPSS/PC+™ 4.0

We hope you know some DOS. You really don't need too much. In Section I, we give a list of simple commands that you might use. There are three ways to use SPSS on a DOS system. They are Batch Mode, Command Prompt Mode, and the REVIEW Menus . We will explain and give examples of each. The question for the beginner is which one to use. This is of course your own personal preference. In Batch Mode you create a complete SPSS/PC+™ 4.0 setup in a word processor or editor program, submit it to SPSS/PC+™ 4.0, and then check your listing. In Command Prompt Mode you will call up the SPSS/PC+™ 4.0 program in a way that it will give you a prompt (SPSS/PC:). At the prompt you will enter SPSS/PC+™ 4.0 commands. Mistakes in syntax will be immediately flagged and you can correct them. The setup so generated can be saved for later Batch runs. In the REVIEW Menu Mode, you call up a menu that enables you to import an already created file or create a new one and save it.

We have found that it is easiest to use the Batch or Command Prompt Mode once you have some familiarity with the structure of the SPSS language. Going through the REVIEW Menus for each command is time consuming and for the novice, the menu system can be intimidating. You can get stuck in its different levels and panic. Menus are hot in the design of computer-human interfaces (the author gives a seminar on the topic). However, for the DOS version and the novice, the minimalist suggestion is to use Batch or Command Prompt Modes. We will explain each.

I. BATCH MODE OR USING ALREADY CREATED SETUPS
A. GETTING STARTED WITH DOS:

You need to understand something about DOS, the operating system for your PC. Please excuse me if you already know these fundamentals.

1. DOS Prompt:

DOS is the system that runs your computer. When you start your computer it gives you a prompt such as:

C:\>

At this prompt, you type commands for your computer.

The C refers to the drive I am using. Drives are either the floppy drives (⊜) on your machine (the toaster slots in which you stick a floppy disk 🖫) or your machine's hard drive. Your machine boots off one drive and you see its prompt.

If you want to change drives you type :

C:\ >d :

Your prompt will change to

D:\ > .

When I started my system, I see the C:> prompt; I then changed to the D drive, It goes as follows

MS-DOS Ver. 3.30

☞ [DOS GAVE ME THIS, WHEN I BOOTED THE SYSTEM]

C:\>

C:\>d: ☞ [I TYPED THE ' d: ']

D:\>   ☞ [THE PROMPT CHANGES TO 'D']

2. Your directories and files:

Directories are groups of files. Files are stored data, text, programs, or even weirder things. You don't have to worry about the latter. Each drive can contain different directories, each of which is full of files. We will not discuss directory structure and subdirectories in great depth as we want to keep this simple.

Files have an up to eight-character file name and then a period and then an up to three-character extension, such as

filename.ext

Be careful with extensions. Stay away from : com, exe, sys, bat, cpi.

These are defined by DOS to mean something special. Use things like : dat [for data], or txt [for text] for innocuous extensions. Thus a file might be named : test2.gm.

You see your directory or list of files with a **dir** command like so:

```
C:\>dir

 Volume in drive C is INSIGNIA
 Directory of  C:\

COMMAND   COM     25276     2-03-88     2:31p
DOS             <DIR>       2-08-88     7:45p
INSIGNIA        <DIR>       2-08-88     7:51p
AUTOEXEC  BAT       137     3-17-88     3:53p
CONFIG    SYS        56     7-15-91     5:11p
SPSS            <DIR>       7-16-91     3:04p
         6 File(s)     77824 bytes free

C:\>
```

A line with an extension such as COMMAND.COM is a file. It is full of information, programs or commands. A line with a 'name & <DIR> is a directory and contains more files. So my **SPSS <DIR>** contains my files for using SPSS/PC+™ 4.0.

A directory is noted by a backslash (\ ) before the name. This is called "the path".

There are many commands to use directories and you really should refer to some DOS manual. You can move into a directory with the **cd** command. Thus, if I typed:

C:\ > cd SPSS

I would move down into my SPSS directory. If I typed a **dir** command, I would get a list of whatever files were in that directory such as:

```
C:\SPSS>dir

 Directory of  C:\SPSS

SPSSE    MSG    325632   9-29-90   12:57p
SPSS     LOG        66   8-12-91    4:58p
SPSS     LIS       112   8-12-91    4:58p
SPSSL    OVL    256976   9-26-90    6:59p
SPSSA    EXE     95872   9-26-90    4:46p
SPSSA    OVL    139392   9-26-90    7:26p
SPSSF    OVL    541728   9-26-90    6:51p
SPSSL    EXE     83072   9-26-90    4:42p
SPSSPC   COM     24576   4-15-91    2:22p
SPSSTR   EXE     68384   9-26-90    4:29p
SPSSTR   OVL     40160   9-26-90    5:39p
SPSSTR   RES      3875   9-26-90    5:40p
SPSSPROF INI        19   1-30-91    4:24p
SPSSF    EXE     77056   9-26-90    4:38p
        14 File(s)    1605632 bytes free

C:\SPSS>
```

These are some of my SPSS files.

If I wanted to move back up out of the SPSS directory (\SPSS), I would type at the prompt:

cd ..

The two periods (..) are needed. Type them! You will return to the parent directory (the directory above or in this case the C hard drive). An example looks like so:

```
SPSSTR    OVL      40160    9-26-90    5:39p
SPSSTR    RES       3875    9-26-90    5:40p
SPSSPROF INI         19    1-30-91    4:24p
SPSSF     EXE      77056    9-26-90    4:38p
         14 File(s)     1605632 bytes free
```

C:\SPSS>cd ..   ☞ **[I typed cd ..]**

C:\>   ☞ **[I'm back at the level of the C
drive]**

Thus, files are referred to by three things:

1. the drive
2. the directory
3. the filename

An example would be:

c:\ *spss* <u>test2.gm</u>

This refers to a file named <u>test2.gm</u> that is in my *directory SPSS* that is on my hard drive C.

AN IMPORTANT NOTE: Make sure that you know what drive and directory contains the SPSS program files. If you attempt to use the program from another directory, you'll get an error message. You can arrange it so SPSS is accessible from other directories. Our examples will assume this has been done.

A setup is constructed in a word processor such as Microsoft® Word, Wordperfect™ or using SPSS's REVIEW editor, saved and transferred to your directory (your set of files on your system). This file is then submitted to SPSS/PC+4.0™ using SPSS commands, run and you then examine your listing.

You will need to learn one of these word processors. If you make a mistake you correct the errors in the original file and then run it again. DOS commands that are helpful for the novice are:

alt-c - stops ongoing process (this is at DOS level)
cd directory name - changes to a subdirectory
cd .. - brings you back up to the parent directory
copy filename1 filename2 - copies first file and gives it
    the name filename2

dir - shows directory

del filename - remove file

print filename - prints file

rename filename1 filename2 - changes the name of filename1
   to filename2. Remember this one for later. We'll use it
   with the SPSS.LIS and SPSS.LOG files.

type filename - displays entire file on
   screen

It would be a good idea to buy a simple introduction to DOS book, if you are a novice. The other manuals aren't that comprehensible to beginners.

B. CREATING THE FILE AND USING EDITORS:

Assume I want to create a simple setup containing the commands:

```
set width = 80 .
data list free / x .
begin data .
1
2
3
end data .
descriptives x .
finish  .
```

How do I go about it? It depends if you want to use a word processor program, SPSS/PC+4.0™ 's Review editor, or DOS's EDLIN. In all cases, I will name this file **test.gm** .

1. WORD PROCESSORS:

If you are using PCs, you are probably aware that there are very powerful word processing programs available, such as Microsoft® Word, Wordstar™ , etc. If I were doing a big setup, I would use one of these because of their power. However, such programs usually save their files full of special formatting characters or in a specially coded fashion. You need a setup file that is:

- ASCII
- Has no line longer than 80 characters
- Each line ends with carriage-return, line-feed
- No special codes
- Ends with a <ctrl - z> - typical of most DOS files.

Most word processors can store a file in this fashion. You will need to check the manuals and look for how to save files as standard ASCII files, text with line breaks or something of that fashion.

Let me give you a cautionary example and show you how to check a file. I created a file in Microsoft Word which held the sample setup. However, I saved it in Word's own format in on my E drive with the name **test.chr**. Then I displayed it on my screen using the type command. The result is below. The file has the commands plus a whole lot of really weird characters. They are Word's format structure for fonts, paragraphs, etc. As you might imagine, SPSS would get rather excited if it tried to use this file.

```
E:\>type test.chr
1┘      ½          8    ♣ ♦ ♦ ♣ ↑ ↑ NORMAL.STY
                                              set width = 80 .
data list free / x .
begin data .
1
2
3
end data .
descriptives x .
finish .

█m‖    ¶ ♦|⊥
                    █mÇ   γ   w  8   t
                                                    8  ℮♦  ¶8Ç   Æ   m
¿     '  ‖    ' ┙     ' ┘    '  ┐    '  ┌    '       ' γ   ' 8  S Ω  S              ♀<
<♦♣   '‖8   ¿ ‖8δ▲┰8α=⊥/  á‡áL¦ 8‖8▶;⊥8  ⊥8 −¦Ç8    ∆ⁿ ▶        H   H      8 8 8
  ♦>D    █m    ♦|⊥   8Ç                        ♦|⊥       8   i     8  j
8Ç                    └ ♦|⊥ ♦    ♦>p    ♦Edit   ¶ ♦|⊥
                                                    8α8Ç█m   ¶ ♦|⊥
                                                               Ç8Ç8△
 △ ‖█   < ♦|⊥ ♠L¦Ç8   ∆ⁿ ▶        H   H      8 8 8    ♦>L   ‖█   └ ♦|⊥ ‡
♦>p    ♦Font    $ ♦|⊥    ♦>L ♦>┐ ♦>┤   ♦>L┐U┐U┐U┐U   < ♦|⊥       8
E:\>_
```

Thus, if you use the type command and you don't use just the plain old set of commands, be careful and check the file. You may have to convert it or resave it. Check your word processor manual.

2. USING THE SPSS/PC+4.0™ REVIEW EDITOR:

SPSS/PC+4.0™ contains its own editing program called REVIEW. It is a standard word processor and fairly easy to use. You evoke it with the command **spsspc/re *filename*.** If the file exists already, REVIEW will open it and you can edit it. If the file does not exist, REVIEW will save your setup under that name.

a. Creating a new file called test.gm.

First I will check my directory as follows (again we are assuming SPSS is accessible from this directory).

```
C:\>dir

 Directory of  C:\

 .              <DIR>       1-01-80     2:17p
 ..             <DIR>       1-01-80     2:17p
 TEST    CHR      896       8-14-91    11:17a
         7 File(s)   20685312 bytes  free
```

It does not contain the file I want. TEST.CHR is the one with all the weird stuff. To create the file I want I would type the command:

```
C:\>spsspc/re test.gm
```

This would put me into SPSS/PC+4.0™ 's REVIEW editor and a logo screen would appear that looks as follows (we have added some explanatory graphics in gray for you):

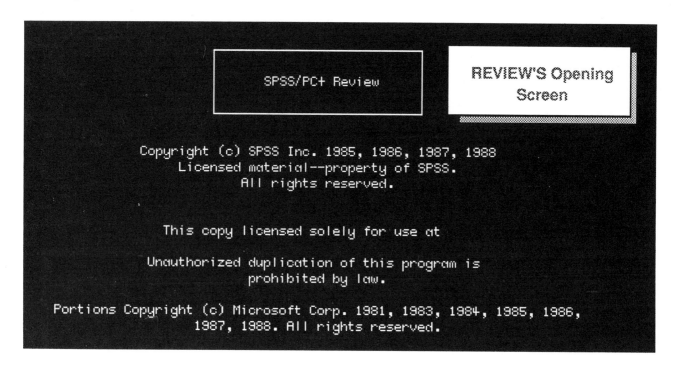

Next would appear a window in which I could type my setup. In this screen, I have typed my setup.

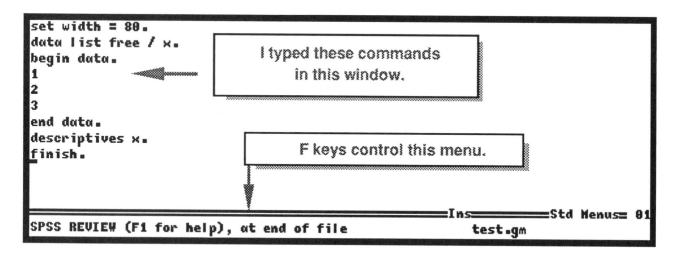

I edit in this setup by navigating with the cursor keys and can then insert or delete. I also can use more powerful editing commands by using menus chosen with the F keys. I also use these menus to save and exit the REVIEW editor.

Major points for using REVIEW menus are:

1. You can navigate with your cursor keys and thus delete text or insert text.

2. You can also use more powerful editing commands evoked by the F keys as follows:

```
F1 : info:              Review help    Menus    File list    Glossary    menu HIP off
F3 : files:          Edit different file        Insert file
F4 : lines:          Insert after          insert Before    Delete    Undelete
F5 : look:            Forward find    Backward find    fOward change    bAckward change
F6 : go to: Output pg
F7 : mark/unmark area of:    Lines    Rectange    Command
F8 : area functions
F9 : file:              write Whole file    Delete
F10 : run:    Exit to prompt
```

You choose the subcommand by moving with your cursor and hitting return. You can also type the **boldface letter** - for example the **W** in "write **W**hole file". For explanations of each subcommand, you should refer to your SPSS/PC+4.0™ manual although some of them are simple. If you don't like the command you are in or want to change command, hit <esc> and then another function key.

3. To save the setup that I just entered, I would hit **F9**. **The following screen will appear with the F9 menu at the bottom:**

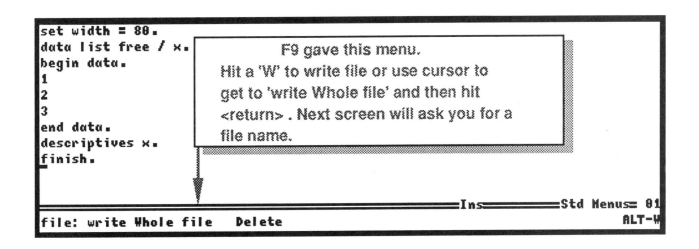

At this point if I type 'W' or use my cursor to get to **"write Whole file"** and then hit <return>, the next screen will appear and ask me to confirm the file name.

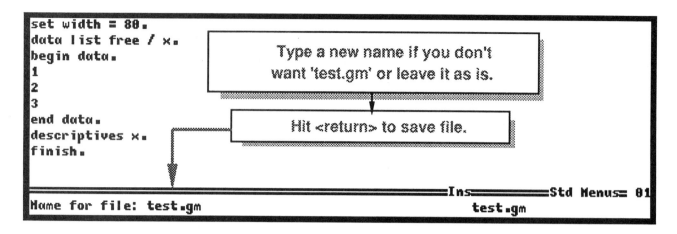

4. Next you want to exit. You exit by hitting function key **F10.** You will be asked if you want to Exit. Type a 'y' if you want to exit. The screen will look as follows:

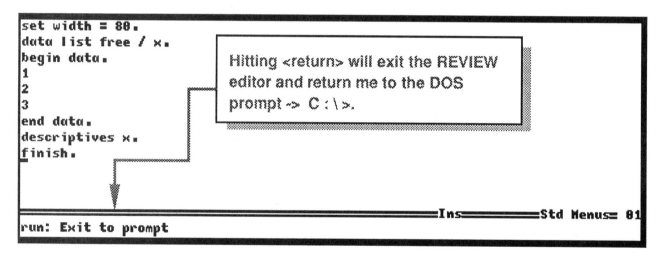

You will go the the prompt and your directory will now contain the file **test.gm** as follows:

```
C:\>dir

 Directory of  C:\

.              <DIR>        1-01-80    2:17p
..             <DIR>        1-01-80    2:17p
TEST    CHR        896      8-14-91   11:17a
TEST    GM          97      8-14-91    5:06p
        8 File(s)   20685312 bytes  free
```

I can now submit this file to SPSS in several fashions.

3. USING EDLIN TO CREATE YOUR SETUP:

DOS supports a fairly primitive editor program called EDLIN which you can use to create a setup. EDLIN is old-fashioned, as you have to type different letter commands (noted in **bold face**) to edit. The file is marked by line numbers. The following is an EDLIN session to create **test.gm** along with some annotations. You can find more in the DOS manuals. It may not be worth the time.

```
C:\>edlin test.gm    ☞ [Starts creation of test.gm]
New file
*i                   ☞ ['i' starts text entry]
        1:*set width = 80 .
        2:*data list free / x.
        3:*begin data .
        4:*1
        5:*2
        6:*2
        7:*end data .
        8:*descriptives x.
        9:*finish.^C  ☞ [^C = <ctrl-c> ends text entry]
*e                   ☞ ['e' exits EDLIN]

C:\>                 ☞  [test.gm is now saved]
```

I can now submit this file to SPSS in several fashions.

C. SUBMITTING AND RUNNING THE SETUP:

I would submit this job to SPSS/PC+4.0™ by typing the following command at the Unix prompt (the system gives you the C :\ >):

c:\> spsspc **test.gm**

The setup will be run and the listing (containing analyses or error messages) will be put in my directory as **spss.lis.** First you will see the SPSS logo, then your setup, then your analyses. What follows is such a session :

Screen 1 [The LOGO]

Version 4.0

Copyright (c) SPSS Inc. 1984 - 1990
Licensed material--property of SPSS.
All rights reserved.

This copy licensed solely for use at

Unauthorized duplication of this program is
prohibited by law.

Portions Copyright (c) Microsoft Corp. 1981, 1983, 1984, 1985, 1986
1987, 1988. All rights reserved.

Screen 2
[The Setup is Brought In]

```
                                                    CASE  #      0
set automenu off.

End of Profile.
INC 'test.gm'
set width = 80.
data list free / x.
begin data.
end data.
     3 cases are written to the compressed active file.

This procedure was completed at 15:17:14
descriptives x._
```

Screen 3 [The Analysis]

```
                                                              MORE

Number of Valid Observations (Listwise) =          3.00

Variable    Mean    Std Dev   Minimum   Maximum    N  Label

X           2.00     1.00      1.00      3.00      3
```

IMPORTANT NOTE ABOUT "M O R E" : In the upper right hand corner of Screen 3, you see the word "M O R E.". Your flow of output will stop at this point. If you want it to continue, hit <return> or <space bar> to continue your output.

C. EXAMINING, PRINTING AND PROTECTING YOUR RESULTS:

At this point, you will return to the DOS prompt (c:\>). You may wonder if your analysis has been saved and it is the file **spss.lis**. It appears in your directory.

```
Directory of  C:\
SPSS     LIS     951   8-15-91   3:18p
TEST     GM       97   8-14-91   5:06p
TEST     BAK      97   8-14-91   3:21p
```

Now you can look at spss.lis on your screen with the **type** command .

```
C:>\type spss.lis

           SPSS/PC+ The Statistical Package for IBM PC      8/15/91
set automenu off.
INC 'test.gm'
set width = 80.
data list free / x.
begin data.
end data.
     3 cases are written to the compressed active file.

This procedure was completed at 15:18:24
descriptives x.
```

```
-----------------------------------------------------------------
Page    2                       SPSS/PC+                     8/15/91


Number of Valid Observations (Listwise) =        3.00

Variable       Mean    Std Dev   Minimum   Maximum     N  Label

X              2.00      1.00      1.00      3.00       3
-----------------------------------------------------------------
Page    3                       SPSS/PC+                     8/15/91

This procedure was completed at 15:18:39
finish.
End of Include file.
```

It would be an excellent idea at this point to rename the **spss.lis** file, because if you don't the next time you run the program, the listing will be in **spss.lis**. The DOS command would be as follows.

$$C:\backslash >r\ e\ n\ a\ m\ e\ \ s\ p\ s\ s\ .l\ i\ s\ \ g\ m\ .a\ n\ s$$

You may print **spss.lis** or whatever you name it with **print** *filename* as in:

$$C:\backslash >p\ r\ i\ n\ t\ \ s\ p\ s\ s\ .l\ i\ s$$

You may want to edit **spss.lis** to remove extraneous material and then print it or incorporate it into another document. If you have made a mistake or series of mistakes, **spss.lis** contains the annotated error messages. You will need to edit **test.gm** and make the appropriate corrections before rerunning the job.

D. ANOTHER WAY OF RENAMING YOUR RESULTS:

If you don't want to go through the bother of renaming your file in DOS, you can do it in SPSS itself. You will need to use the **set listing** command. It has the form of:

$$s\ e\ t\ \ l\ i\ s\ t\ i\ n\ g\ =\ 'f\ i\ l\ e\ n\ a\ m\ e'\ .$$

Note that the filename should conform to DOS naming rules and it is always inside single quotes ('). You would insert this command in your setup like so:

```
set listing = 'gm.ans'
set width = 80 .
data list free / x .
begin data .
1
2
3
end data .
descriptives x .
finish  .
```

If I ran this job, my listing would be saved as **gm.ans**, not as spss.lis.

Once you understand SPSS/PC+4.0™ , it's very easy to run in Batch Mode. If you are doing a major setup, you probably want to create the setup in an editor or word processor. Working directly in SPSS/PC+4.0™ would be way to cumbersome and perhaps risky. Word processors have better backup capabilities. Also, even if your setup is incorrect, you won't loose it. Working with menus or command lines can be exciting for the novice. If you have typed a big setup and it's going nuts on output or you are stuck in some command, you might want to crash the job. If you do, you might loose all the setup you have typed. In Batch Mode, its still on your directory.

E. YET ANOTHER WAY OF RENAMING YOUR RESULTS! :

There is another way of renaming your listing file and it might be the easiest. If you had used the following DOS command:

c:\> spsspc file.set > file.ans

then **file.set** will be run and the answer stored immediately in **file.ans**. In our case we might type

c:\ > spsspc test.gm > gm.ans .

F. WARNING ABOUT THE FINISH LINE:

All our setups have included a **FINISH** command. This was deliberate; if you leave it out, you won't exit SPSS when the analysis is completed but instead enter the Menu system described in Section III. If you want to avoid this little trick, make sure to use the **FINISH** command.

II. COMMAND PROMPT MODE (SPSS/PC:)

Command Prompt Mode is a very easy way to work. In Command Prompt Mode you will call up the SPSS/PC+™ 4.0 program in a way that it will give you a prompt (SPSS/PC:). At the prompt you will enter SPSS/PC+™ 4.0 commands. Mistakes in syntax will be immediately flagged and you can correct them. The setup so generated can be saved for later Batch runs. Some of us here think it is the easiest for small to medium jobs. For big ones, work in Batch. You only have to watch out for files and periods (end each command with a period - to continue a command, just hit return).

A. GETTING STARTED:

To enter Command Prompt Mode, there are some nuances. It depends if you want to modify your SPSS/PC+™ 4.0 system to always enter the prompt mode (**2.**) or whether you want to enter the prompt mode through the menu system (**1.**).

1. ENTERING THROUGH THE REVIEW MENUS:

To enter the Command Prompt system you will:

Step 1: At the DOS prompt type 'spsspc' like so

c:\> spsspc

Step 2: The SPSS logo screen appears:

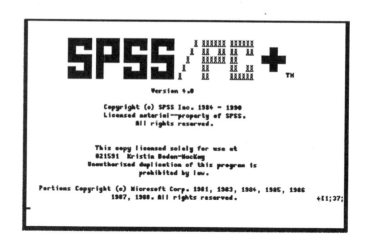

and then the SPSS REVIEW menu screen appears:

```
   SPSS/PC+ The Statistical Package for IBM PC          7/31/91
set automenu off.



─────────────────────────────────────────────────────────────


                                              ═Ins═══════Std Menus═ 01
User profile has executed.                         scratch.pad
```

Then hit the **F 1 0** key. On the bottom of the screen, choices will appear.

```
   SPSS/PC+ The Statistical Package for IBM PC          7/31/91
set automenu off.



─────────────────────────────────────────────────────────────


                                              ═Ins═══════Std Menus═ 01
run: run from Cursor   Exit to Prompt
```

Step 3: Choose *Exit to Prompt*:

You choose **Exit to Prompt** with the cursor keys and a <return> or by typing an E

You will exit to the SPSS/PC: prompt.

2. SETTING THE PROGRAM TO ALWAYS START IN THE COMMAND PROMPT MODE:

You can set SPSS/PC+™ 4.0 so that it always starts up in Command Prompt Mode. When the program starts to run, the first thing it does is execute commands saved in a

DOS file named **s p s s p r o f . i n i**   This file comes with the system. Look for it in an abridged version of my directory:

```
                      etc.

SPSSTR     RES      3875      9-26-90      5:40p
SPSSF      EXE     77056      9-26-90      4:38p
TEST       GM         97      8-14-91      5:06p
GM         ANS        624     8-16-91      9:11a
GM1        ANS        624     8-16-91      9:14a
SPSSPROF   INI         42      8-16-91      2:00p
REVIEW     TMP        183     8-12-91      3:07p
TEST       ANS       2659     8-16-91     10:55a
SPSS       LIS        132     8-16-91      2:00p
SPSS       SY1       2048     8-16-91     11:12a
           39 File(s)    1597440 bytes free
```

If I examine this directory as I first started to use the program, it only contained one command (set automenu off). Look:

```
C:\ >t y p e   s p s s p r o f . i n i
s e t   a u t o m e n u   o f f . *
```

* For the curious, this command controls whether a large set of menus appear in the Output window whenever the program starts up. This setting prevents that. Once the program starts up, you can turn on the menus if you want with an <alt-m>

In any case,   I edit the file **spssprof.ini**   and   add   the   command **"set runview manual."** . Recall you can edit the file with a word processor, REVIEW or EDLIN. Now the file would look as follows if I typed it:

```
C:\ >t y p e   s p s s p r o f . i n i
s e t   a u t o m e n u   o f f .
s e t   r u n r e v i e w   m a n u a l .
```

Now whenever I start SPSS with the DOS command **'spsspc'** , I will go immediately to the **SPSS/PC:** prompt. If you want to bring up the Review Menu while in a prompted session, type the command **review** at the SPSS/PC: prompt like so:

```
S P S S / P C : r e v i e w   .
```

The REVIEW menu will appear.

3. A PROMPTED SESSION:

Below I have begun a hypothetical session. I have just evoked SPSS with the **SPSS/PC:** prompt. At this prompt I can start typing SPSS commands and seeing results. Remember to end commands with a period (.) .

```
SPSS/PC:set listing = 'test.ans' .  ☞ [Type commands after prompt]

SPSS/PC:set width = 80 .

SPSS/PC:data list free / x.

SPSS/PC:begin data .    ☞ [When I typed begin data, SPSS expects me to
                            type in the data and end with END DATA.]
Enter END DATA to signal end of data input.

1
2                       ☞ [Type data, one number per lines]
3
end data.

    3 cases are written to the compressed active file.

SPSS/PC:descriptives x.

This procedure was completed at 10:50:18
                                                                MORE
          ☞ [When you see MORE, hit <return> to continue output]

Number of Valid Observations (Listwise) =          3.00

Variable     Mean     Std Dev   Minimum   Maximum    N  Label

X            2.00      1.00      1.00      3.00      3

SPSS/PC:finish.    ☞ [Returns me to DOS prompt]
C:\>:
```

B. WHERE ARE COPIES OF THE SETUP AND ANSWER?

OK! But what about my answer! It just went by on the screen! How about saving the setup? Is it gone? (Excuse the use of the vernacular-power computer types and stuffy professors should go get a life at this point).

There is no need to worry! SPSS automatically saves your setup in a special file called **spss.log**. The output has been saved in a file called test.ans. **This must be requested. We did it in the setup with the set = listing 'test.ans' command.** Remember:

spss.log   = a setup made of your commands and data
test.ans   = your statistics.

There are other ways to save your answer. If I did not use the **set listing =** **'test.ans'** command then the listing would have been automatically saved in a file named spss.lis as happens in Batch Mode.

Also, if you want to keep the setup or listings and they are saved under spss.log and spss.lis respectively you had better change their names using the "rename" command. If you run another job, a new spss.log and spss.lis file will be created over your old ones. They're history. You could:

`C:\ >rename spss.log filename2` – copies setup and

gives it the name filename2 (please don't be literal and always use filename2!).

C. TYPOS IN COMMAND MODE.

You type a command, ending with a period (.). If you make a mistake, an error message is printed and you have the chance to make a correction. For example

```
SPSS/PC:data lust free / x.      ☞ [My mind wandered & I typed this.]


ERROR        1, Text: DATA LUST   ☞ [SPSS asks for correction.]
INVALID COMMAND-Check spelling. If it is intended as a continuation of a
previous line, the terminator must not be specified on the previous line.
If a DATA LIST is in error, in-line data can also cause this error.
This command not executed.

SPSS/PC:data list free / x.      ☞ [A new prompt is issued & I retype
                                    the command.]
```

If there are logical mistakes, meaning the command is OK but you don't want to do that, you'll need to retype or go into the spss.log file and fix it as a batch job.

D. OTHER NEAT TRICKS.

1. Help:

If you need help in Command Prompt Mode, type help at the prompt:
SPSS/ PC:help
The program will provide instruction for the help mode as follows:

```
                        HELP
Use the Help windows in REVIEW for help on SPSS/PC+
commands.  For help on a specific command or subcommand:
Type "REVIEW." to enter REVIEW.  Clear the menus (if they are
present) with Alt-M.  Type the command and, if appropriate,
the subcommand for which you want help.  Raise the menus with
Alt-M.
```

2. DOS inside a SPSS command session.

If you want to use unix commands inside spss, type

S P S S / P C : d o s ' c o m m a n d ? ' .

Now don't actually type 'command?', type the command you want:

S P S S / P C : d o s ' t y p e t e s t . g m ' .

After the DOS command is carried out you go back to the S P S S / P C : prompt. If you type just: S P S S / P C : d o s ., you are out of SPSS and back in DOS, however your SPSS process is still active and you can return with DOS 'exit' command.

III. USING THE REVIEW MENUS

The menu mode is difficult for a beginner as you need to be knowledgeable about the menu system and the language of SPSS. While menus are supposed to be user friendly, I would be reluctant to use these unless I was a touch sophisticated. I recommend Command or batch for the beginner. Interestingly, once you are really skilled, users may also prefer Batch as why go through many menus when you already know what to type. But be brave and give the menus a try. Don't do it on an important data set at first. Also, we can't go through every nuance. If you want to use the menu system, you should read the *SPSS/PC+™ 4.0 Base Manual* .

We will present two scenarios. The first is bringing in an already done file and running it. The second is using the menu manager to create a setup. Note that you start the same way for both tasks. Note that if we put '< >' around a key sequence, you just use the keys. Don't type the "less than' (<) and 'greater than signs' (>). So if you see <F 10>, the < > are just artistic notes common in computer books.

A. BRINGING AN ALREADY CREATED SETUP

1. GETTING STARTED IN REVIEW MENU MODE.

The first steps are similar to those used for entering Command Prompt Mode (**Section II A**). At the DOS prompt type 'spsspc' :

c : \ > s p s s p c

This will bring up two screens as follows:

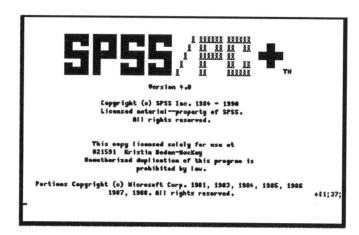

and then the SPSS REVIEW menu screen appears (we've annotated some of the parts of the screen):

Output and Menus for Generating Commands Appear Here.

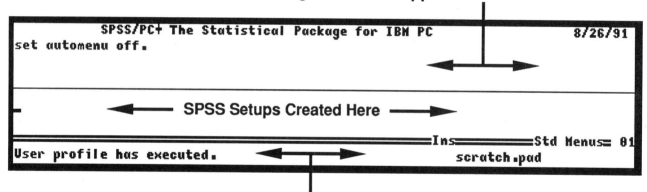

Mini-Menus Produced by F - Keys Appear Here.

As you see above, the window has three parts:

❑   1. Output and Menus to Generate Commands

❑   2. Area to Edit Commands

❑   3. Small Menus with Choices evoked by F - keys. Watch for these in
       following examples.

2. BRINGING IN A FILE (< F 3 >)

You navigate in menus by using alt-key combinations (< alt key >) and function keys. These are given in the Base Manual. We will tell you the relevant ones for the operations we demonstrate. The file we will bring in is called 'test.gm'. We created it with a word processor or the REVIEW editor and it is in our DOS directory.

To bring in an already created setup, type: < F 3 > (the F3 function key). The following menu appears. At the bottom is the request for the file you wish to use.

```
         SPSS/PC+ The Statistical Package for IBM PC              8/26/91
set automenu off.




_
                                                        Ins           Std Menus= 01
files: Edit different file    Insert file
```

Hit return if Edit different file name is highlighted. It it isn't or type E or use the cursor to get to Edit different file name and then return. You will be asked for the file name at the File to edit : line.

Now type the file with the setup (our case 'test.gm') as seen in the menu below:

```
         SPSS/PC+ The Statistical Package for IBM PC              8/26/91
set automenu off.




                                                        Ins           Std Menus= 01
File to edit: test.gm_
```

Hit < return > and 'test.gm' appears in the window as was typed in our directory.

```
       SPSS/PC+ The Statistical Package for IBM PC              8/26/91
set automenu off.


set width = 80.
data list free / x.
begin data.
1
2
3
end data.
descriptives x.
finish.    ..................................................

                                          ═Ins═          ═Std Menus═ 01
                                               test.gm
```

Note the cursor (⊨) below the "f" in finish. This marks your cursor position in the setup.

2. EXECUTING THE COMMANDS (< F 10 >).

Use the cursor keys to get to top of the setup (you'll see the ⊨ is now at the top). Press **<F 10>** to get the | r u n   f r o m   C u r s o r | command. If the highlighting is not on | r u n   f r o m   C u r s o r |, use your cursor keys to move to it or you can type the letter C.

```
       SPSS/PC+ The Statistical Package for IBM PC              8/26/91
set automenu off.


set width = 80.
data list free / x.
begin data.
1
2
3
end data.
descriptives x.
finish.

                                          ═Ins═          ═Std Menus═ 01
run: run from Cursor    Exit to prompt                        ALT-C
```

Hit return and your analysis will be started. One warning, make sure the cursor is at the command where you want to start executing. If you don't, you start executing at the cursor point.

Your answer flashes by on the top of the window. Recall it is being saved in **'spss.lis'** because of our set listing command. Also your setup is being saved in **spss.log** (as in Command Prompt Mode). Remember we could change these assignments with the **'set listing '** and **'set log '** commands as explained earlier.

Since the setup contains a **'finish'** command, we exited SPSS and went back to DOS. If the setup did not contain the **'finish'**, we would stay in the REVIEW menu system and your analyses would be available for examination.

Thus, assume we ran the setup but had removed the **'finish'** command. We would see the following screen (you may have to hit <return>, when you seen the word 'MORE' at the top of the screen.

```
Number of Valid Observations (Listwise) =        3.00

Variable      Mean      Std Dev    Minimum    Maximum    N  Label

X             2.00      1.00       1.00       3.00       3
-------------------------------------------------------------------------
Page    3                      SPSS/PC+                          8/27/91

This procedure was completed at 11:36:00
-------------------------------------------------------------------------
Page    4                      SPSS/PC+                          8/27/91




-




                                              =Ins=========Std Menus= 01
SPSS REVIEW (F1 for help), empty file              scratch.pad
```

You can look at your answer without exiting the program. Your analyses are in the top of the screen in the Output window. You can navigate in that window using the cursor keys or a set of search commands found in the Base Manual. However, you will have to move the cursor into the top window by pressing **< F 2 >. This will bring up a mini-menu at the bottom of the screen that allows you to move the cursor to the top screen if you choose** SWITCH **with the cursor and press <return>**

or you type an 'S'. You can return to the input window on the bottom with another **< F 2 >.** The bottom mini-menu looks as follows:

```
═══════════════════════════════════════════════════Ins═══════════Std Menus═ 01
windows: Switch     Change size     Zoom                                 ALT-S
```

If you want to exit the program press **F 10** and you will be given an exit option.

4. DOING MORE ANALYSES(**< F 10 >**)

If you had not typed a 'finish.' command as we did then you could type in more analyses (such as a **frequencies x** .) and continue. You would just need switch to the input window (**< F 2 >**) and type the new command and **< F 10 >**. This will give you the `run from Cursor` prompt and you can continue. Again make sure you move the cursor to the level of the command you want to execute. In other words if you type a few lines and then `run from Cursor`, you are below the lines you want to execute. Remember to move up. If you try to `run from Cursor` and haven't moved up - you will miss some commands. Also if you try the cursor keys to move up, once you have selected `run from Cursor`, the cursor keys wont work. Again. if you typed 'finish.', the program wants you to exit if you give it an **< F 10 >** and choose **E X I T** .

B . CREATING A SETUP USING THE MENUS

You can have SPSS create the commands line by line using the Menu Manager. The general principle is to go to a command in the menu, select it and enter it using <tabs> and <returns>. To be quite honest, I find it easy to just type the commands in Batch Mode files or in Command Mode. With a little skill, it's much faster. However, the REVIEW Menu does have the advantage of rather full explanations of the command if you are not familiar with it. In our example, we will create a DATA LIST statement.

1. GETTING THE MAIN MENU (**< alt M >**).

Enter the SPSS system from DOS (with c:\> spsspc) and the two initial screens :

SPSS LOGO: FIRST SCREEN

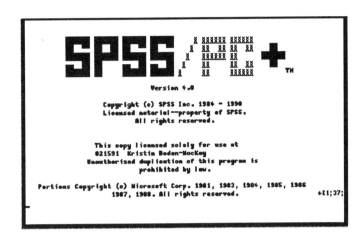

SPSS REVIEW MENU: SCREEN 2

```
         SPSS/PC+ The Statistical Package for IBM PC          7/31/91
set automenu off.




⌐

                                                   Ins        Std Menus  01
User profile has executed.                      scratch.pad
```

Type an **< alt M >**. This brings up the below **MAIN MENU** which enables you to generate commands. The commands will be placed in the input window at the cursor (⌐).

Main Menu From < Alt-M >

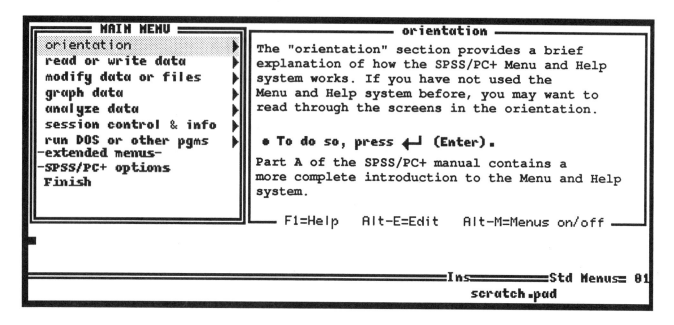

2. CHOOSING A COMMAND (**Tabs and Returns**).

To enter the data list command, use the cursor keys to go to **read or write data** line as seen in the below menu.

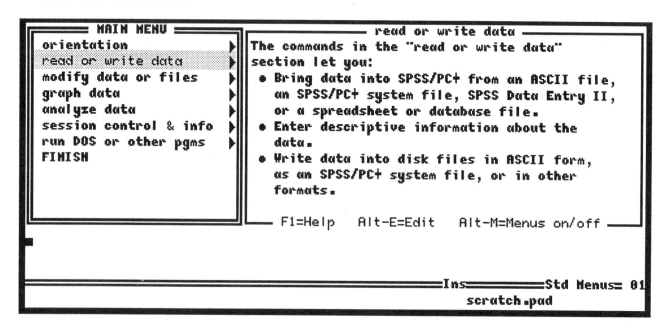

If you do this, then hit **< tab >**. The next menu will follow. **If you see an▶** , then **hitting < tab > will bring up the next set of menu selections.**

So now I hit a < tab > and the next menu appears.
< TAB >

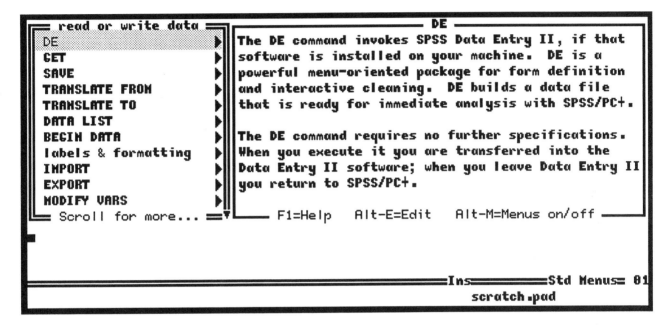

```
═ read or write data ═                    ──────── DE ────────
DE                         ▶   The DE command invokes SPSS Data Entry II, if that
GET                        ▶   software is installed on your machine.  DE is a
SAVE                       ▶   powerful menu-oriented package for form definition
TRANSLATE FROM             ▶   and interactive cleaning.  DE builds a data file
TRANSLATE TO               ▶   that is ready for immediate analysis with SPSS/PC+.
DATA LIST                  ▶
BEGIN DATA                 ▶   The DE command requires no further specifications.
labels & formatting        ▶   When you execute it you are transferred into the
IMPORT                     ▶   Data Entry II software; when you leave Data Entry II
EXPORT                     ▶   you return to SPSS/PC+.
MODIFY VARS                ▶
 Scroll for more... ═▼     ── F1=Help   Alt-E=Edit   Alt-M=Menus on/off ──


                                                    Ins══════Std Menus═ 01
                                                        scratch.pad
```

I used the cursor key to move down from **D E** so that **D A T A   L I S T** is now highlighted.

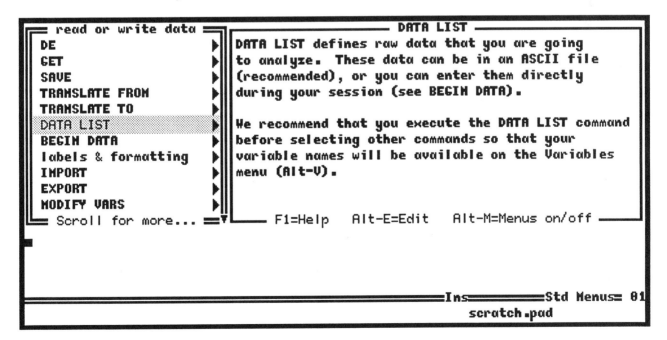

```
═ read or write data ═                    ──────── DATA LIST ────────
DE                         ▶   DATA LIST defines raw data that you are going
GET                        ▶   to analyze.  These data can be in an ASCII file
SAVE                       ▶   (recommended), or you can enter them directly
TRANSLATE FROM             ▶   during your session (see BEGIN DATA).
TRANSLATE TO               ▶
DATA LIST                  ▶   We recommend that you execute the DATA LIST command
BEGIN DATA                 ▶   before selecting other commands so that your
labels & formatting        ▶   variable names will be available on the Variables
IMPORT                     ▶   menu (Alt-V).
EXPORT                     ▶
MODIFY VARS                ▶
 Scroll for more... ═▼     ── F1=Help   Alt-E=Edit   Alt-M=Menus on/off ──


                                                    Ins══════Std Menus═ 01
                                                        scratch.pad
```

If I type a **< return >**, then the command **DATA LIST** is entered in the Input Window as seen below and menu options for DATA LIST appear.

Next Screen with DATA LIST entered.

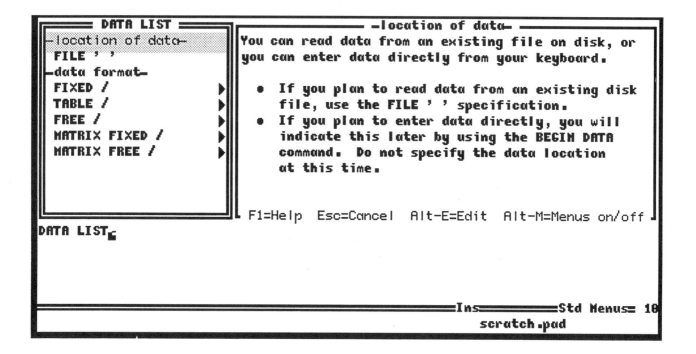

I could now :

a. Type some information myself (the rest of the setup). Type **< alt E >** to start to type at position of the cursor (◄).

b. Continue choose menu options (i.e. use the cursor to go to **FREE** / . If I pressed return, the word FREE would appear so I had a DATA LIST FREE (as we use in our setups) and then I would be asked for variables.

   If I was done with the DATA LIST command, I would type **< esc >** to return up the menus. This would take me up the menus step by step. Or I could type **< alt esc >** and return to the main menu and start with a new command. I could select an analysis or transformation. Once I was done, I would **< F 10 >** to move to **run from Cursor** and execute my analyses.

   Thus each command can be built from the menu manager. If you know the SPSS language, it might be easier to type them straight off. However, the manager is helpful if you forget syntax or want to use its help facilities and explanations.

To Repeat the steps for Building a Command:

1. Enter from DOS using c : \ > s p s s p c .
2. **< alt m >** to get to Main Menu.
3. Use cursor keys to pick command topic.
4. **< Tab >** takes you down to the next level if present.
5. **< Return >** enters the command in Input Window.
6. You can type more information now (use **< alt e >** to enter edit mode if necessary).
7. Return up the menu with **< alt esc >** for Main Menu.
8. When ready **< F 10 >** to run job.
9. Buy the Base Manual and use the help screens if necessary.

IV. Differences between Spss/pc+ ™ 4.0 and Other System Versions of SPSS.

It is obviously annoying to have inconsistencies between SPSS/PC+™ 4.0 and the other versions of SPSS that run on other systems and computers. We have documented the differences for the programs that we use in the following chapters. However, we want to repeat some points already made and make some others.

The First Big Difference:

- All SPSS versions except for SPSS/PC+™ 4.0 can use the

    data list list / *variables names , etc.
  command structure.

- SPSS/PC+™ 4.0 must use the

    data list free / *variable names , etc.*
  command structure.

The Second Big Difference:

All SPSS versions except for   use descriptions of commands found in the SPSS® Reference Guide (1990). SPSS/PC+™ 4.0 commands may have a slightly different style.

The difference is usually in the use of **options** and **statistics** commands in SPSS/PC+™ 4.0   which differs from SPSS. The latter uses key words exclusively.

SPSS/PC+™ 4.0 , however, may use numbers for these. It is a relic of older versions of SPSS.

For example, an SPSS **descriptives** command might look like:

descriptives choc dep / **statistics = mean stddev variance range** .

while the equivalent SPSS/PC+™ 4.0 command would be:

descriptives choc dep / **statistics = 1 , 5, 6, 9 .**

Note the use of numbers rather than names. We have documented these differences in the chapters that follow. For the programs we document, the following are the ones with these style variances:

SPSS/PC+™ 4.0 Programs that Vary from SPSS in Use of Options And Statistics Numbers

ANOVA

CORRELATION

DESCRIPTIVES

DISCRIMINANT

MEANS

NPAR TESTS

ONEWAY

T-TEST

There may be some other features in SPSS that SPSS/PC+™ 4.0 does not have. These will not affect your setups because they are not crucial to our approach.

SPSS® 4.0 FOR UNIX™ *

* These examples were produced on a SunOS 4.1.1 using a Sun 4/490 .

SUMMARY OF UNIX COMMANDS*
*FILE NAMES ARE EXAMPLES

% spss -m < file.set > *file.ans*

Instructions in **file.set** submitted in Mode to SPSS. Listing of results, error messages sent to **file.ans***.

% spss -m < file.set > file.ans &

Instructions in **file.set** submitted in Batch Mode to SPSS. Listing of results, error messages sent to **file.ans**[†]. "&"makes job run in background so you can still work in Unix.

% spss -m < file. set

Instructions in file.set submitted in Batch Mode to SPSS. Listing of results sent to screen and not saved.

% spss -m

Command Line Mode gives you SPSS> prompt. Type a command at the prompt. Listing to screen. Commands saved in spss.jnl[†].

%spss -m -t file.ans OR %spss - m > file.ans

Command Line Mode gives you SPSS> prompt. Type a command at the prompt. Listing to file.ans. Commands saved in spss.jnl[†].

%cp spss.jnl filename2

Copies setup and gives it the name filename2 (Please don't be literal and always use filename2!).

%spss

Starts up the Menu Manager system.

%lpr file.ans

Print your listing (analyses) if saved in file.ans.

[†] Note you might use the 'set listing' command instead , see below.

SPSS FILE CONTROL COMMANDS

set listing file.ans .

Saves your listing (analyses) if saved in file.ans.

set journal gm.set .

Saves your setup (commands and data) in gm.set. For use in Command Line Mode and Menu Manger Mode.

include filename .

Inserts the text file 'filename' into your SPSS set up. Useful for Command Line Mode or Menu Manager.

NAVIGATING IN THE MENU MANAGER
Generating Commands

	Guide to Menu Commands
ENTER	Paste Selection & Move Down One Level in Menu
TAB	Temporarily Paste Selection & Move Down One Level
ESC ESC	Remove Last Temporary Paste & Move Up One Level
ESC J	Jump to Main Menu
ESC K	Kill All Temporary Pastes
ESC T	Get Typing Window
ESC E	Switch to Edit Mode
ESC M	Remove Menus
ESC Y	Switch between Standard and Extended Menus

ESCAPE KEY MINI-MENUS
Choose with Cursor and <return> or Type CAPITAL Letter

<esc - 1>: info:	manageR help	Menus	File list	Glossary	syntaX
<esc - 2>: windows:	Switch	Change size	Zoom		
<esc - 3>: files:	Edit different file		Insert file		
<esc - 4>: lines:	Insert after	insert Before	Delete	Undelete	
<esc -5>: look:	Forward find	Backward find	fOward change	bAckward change	
<esc - 6>: go to:	Output pg				
<esc -7>: mark/unmark area of:		Lines	Rectangle	Command	
<esc - 8>: area:	Copy	Move	Delete	Round	
<esc - 9>: file:	write Block	write Whole file		Delete	Append block
<esc -0>: run:	run from Cursor	run marked Area		Exit	autoviewNew off
<esc> <esc>	**Type this if you want to get out of the mini-menu!**				

INTRODUCTION TO UNIX COMMANDS AND SPSS

We hope you know some Unix. You really don't need too much. We will give a list of simple commands that you might use. There are three ways to use SPSS on a Unix system. They are Batch Mode, Command Line Mode and the Menu Manager Mode. We will explain and give examples of each. The question for the beginner is which one to use. This is, of course, your own personal preference. In Batch Mode you create a complete SPSS setup in a word processor or editor program, submit it to SPSS and then check your listing. In Command Line Mode you will call up the SPSS program in a way that it will give you a prompt (SPSS >). At the prompt you will enter SPSS commands. Mistakes in syntax will be immediately flagged and you can correct them. The setup so generated can be saved for later Batch runs. In the Menu Manager Mode, you call up a menu that enables you to import an already created file or create a new one and save it.

We have found that it is easiest to use the Batch or Command Line Mode once you have some familiarity with the structure of the SPSS language. Going through the menus for each command is time consuming and for the novice the menu system can be intimidating. You can get stuck in its different levels and panic. Menus are hot in the design of computer-human interfaces (the author gives a seminar on the topic). However, for the Unix version and the novice, the minimalist suggestion is to use Batch or Command Line Modes. We will explain each.

One note, we won't explain directory and subdirectory usage in great detail. Simply, your directory is the list of files that are associated with you. If you understand Unix directories then you are already a pro compared to the novice. If you want to manipulate directories and refer to subdirectories, be sure that you put single quotes (') around file descriptions. For example: set listing 'home/f/meyer/file.ans'. If this means nothing to you, don't worry.

Below you will find Unix commands that are helpful for the novice:

```
cat filename - displays entire file on screen.
control-c - stops ongoing process (this is at Unix level).
cp filename1 filename2 - copies first file and gives it
    the name filename2.
help - help files for Unix commands.
jove filename - starts up Jove editor to create new file or
    to edit a file if it already exists.
logout (or control-d) - disconnects (or logs you out) from
    the computer.
```

lpr filename - prints file.

ls - shows directory.

mail - use it to send messages.

more filename - shows file on screen (press space bar to see more).

rm filename- remove file.

To use a Unix system, you will need to learn how to:

1. Log on the system using your account name and password.

2. Manipulate files and directories using commands such as the ones listed above.

3. Use an editor such as Jove to create your setups if you want to work in Batch Mode.

4. Start the SPSS program.

Details of logging on your system are best left to your site. However, once you log on - you will receive a Unix prompt (%). This means Unix is waiting for a command. For example, we will present below (with annotations) how I logged on my system. listed my directory, and displayed an SPSS setup on my screen:

```
SunOS UNIX (sun)

login: meyer        ☞ [I typed 'meyer'.]
Password:           ☞ [I type my password but it is not shown on screen]
Last login: Tue Aug 27 13:04:57 from annex-mr2

Welcome to  SunOS 4.1.1 on Sun 4/490!


% ls ☞ [I  type the  'ls'  and Unix  directory is  displayed]
commando       meyer.ans    valdesc.sps     valplot.sps     value.sps
file.ans       spss.jnl     valfmt.sps      valrpt.sps
file.set       test.ans     valfreq.sps     value.BAK
krs            testset      valmeans.sps    value.dat
sun% cat file.set         ☞ [I ask for 'file.set' to be displayed]
set width = 80.
data list list / x.
begin data .
1
2                                     ☞ [The Contents of 'file.set']
3
end data .
descriptives x.
finish.
%           ☞ [Enter another Unix Command.]
```

To create a file, I would use the Jove editor; I find it easy for novices to use. Jove is a "hot keypad" editor. Whatever you type gets inserted into the file at the current "point". To create **file.set**, I typed **jove file.set** at the Unix prompt as follows:

% jove file.set

This causes the Jove screen to appear. You type in the window.

You can navigate in the window using cursor keys or commands. For small setups, it is easy to make corrections and insertions just by moving to the area and adding or deleting over the material. You can also use control < ctrl > characters to give commands and move around. A small set of other useful Jove commands is as follows:

```
                    J o v e   C o m m a n d s

Ctrl-A              Move to the beginning of the line.
Ctrl-E              Move to the end of the line.
Ctrl-V              Move down one page/screen.
Ctrl-Z              Move up one page/screen.
Esc <               Move to the beginning of the buffer.
Esc >               Move to the end of the buffer.

Ctrl-X Ctrl-R       Read file.  Prompts for file name.
Ctrl-X Ctrl-W       Write file.  Prompts for file name.
Ctrl-X Ctrl-C       Exit Jove.
Ctrl-X Ctrl-Z       Exit Jove and save changes before leaving.
Ctrl-K              Kill to the end of the line.

Esc K               Kill to end of sentence.
Ctrl-O              Insert a line above.
Ctrl-Y              Yank (re-insert) last killed text.

Ctrl-\[text]        Search forwards for text.
Ctrl-R[text]        Search backwards for text.
```

Again, you can use other editors if you wish.

I. BATCH MODE OR USING ALREADY CREATED SETUPS

A setup is constructed in a word processor such as Jove or VI on the Unix system or created on a personal system and transferred to your Unix directory. (Make sure you don't have formatting characters in the file. See the example in the SPSS/PC section.) This file is then submitted to SPSS using Unix commands, and you then examine your listing. You will need to learn one of these word processors. If you make a mistake you correct the errors in the original file and then run it again.

A. Getting Started and Using Unix to Direct Output

Assume I have created using the simple SPSS setup containing the commands:

```
set width = 80 .
data list list / x .
begin data .
1
2
3
end data .
descriptives x .
finish  .
```

The setup is put into my directory with the name **file.set**. You can see it in my directory below (using the **ls** command):

```
% ls
commando       meyer.ans       valdesc.sps      valmeans.sps      value.BAK
file.set       spss.jnl        valfmt.sps       valplot.sps       value.dat
krs            test.ans        valfreq.sps      valrpt.sps        value.sps
```

I would submit this job to SPSS by typing the following command at the Unix prompt (the system gives you the %):

$$\% \ \text{spss -m} < \textbf{file.set} > \textit{file.ans}$$

file.set contains the spss setup created by a word processor such as Jove or VI. The command sends your listing to *file.ans*. This file contains your statistical output. Your directory should now look like:

```
% ls
commando       meyer.ans       valfmt.sps       valrpt.sps
file.ans       spss.jnl        valfreq.sps      value.BAK
file.set       test.ans        valmeans.sps     value.dat
krs            valdesc.sps     valplot.sps      value.sps
```

Now you can look at file.ans on your screen with the **cat** or **more** commands. You may print **file.ans** with **lpr file.ans**. You may want to edit file.ans to remove extraneous material and then print it or incorporate it into another document. If you have made a mistake or series of mistakes, file.ans contains the annotated error messages. You will need to edit file.set and make the appropriate corrections before rerunning the job.

We find two other versions of Batch Mode entry to be useful.

% s p s s - m < f i l e . s e t > f i l e . a n s &

Now the Batch Mode job runs in background. In other words, after a <return> is typed, the system works on job but you are given a Unix prompt (%) to do other work. Otherwise you would have to sit and wait for the job to complete before you could use your terminal or computer. Your run is assigned a job number. Use jobs command to check the progress of your job.

You can also run a job in Batch Mode without saving the output:

% s p s s - m < f i l e . s e t

Your answers or mistakes flash by on the screen. It's useful for debugging small jobs or looking for simple typos before saving.

Once you understand SPSS, it's very easy to run in Batch Mode. If you are doing a major setup (as I do for surveys with 3500 subjects and 550 variables per subject), you probably want to create the setup in an editor or word processor. Working directly in SPSS would be way too cumbersome and perhaps risky. Word processors have better backup capabilities. Also, even if your setup is incorrect, you won't loose it. Working with menus or command lines can be exciting for the novice. If you have typed a big setup and it's going nuts on output or you are stuck in some command, you might want to crash the job. If you do, you might loose all the setup you have typed. In Batch Mode, it's still on your directory.

If you have creating file.ans, you can see it on the screen with:

%m o r e f i l e . a n s
or:

%c a t f i l e . a n s
You can print your listing with:

%l p r f i l e . a n s

B. USING THE SET COMMAND TO DIRECT OUTPUT:

It is also possible to direct output listings without using the Unix command:

% spss -m < file.set > file.ans

In your setup itself, SPSS can control the filename used for the listing of results and error messages using the **set** command. The command would be :

set listing filename .

This command will send the listing to the specified file. For example, I want to send my answer to a file to be called **meyer.ans**. My setup would now be:

```
set listing meyer.ans .
set width = 80 .
data list list / x .
begin data .
1
2
3
end data .
descriptives x .
finish  .
```

I would use the Unix command;

% spss -m < file.set

and my answer would be found in my directory as **meyer.ans**. It wouldn't flash by on the screen. Again, if you are using a full directory specification - use single quotes around it.

II. COMMAND LINE MODE

Command Line Mode is a very easy way to work. In Command Line Mode you will call up the SPSS program in a way that it will give you a prompt (SPSS >). At the prompt you will enter SPSS commands. Mistakes in syntax will be immediately flagged and you can correct them. The setup so generated can be saved for later Batch runs. Some of us here think it is the easiest for small to medium jobs. For big ones, work in Batch. You only have to watch out for files and periods (end each command with a period - to continue a command, just hit return).

A. GETTING STARTED AND A SESSION TRANSCRIPT:

To enter Command Line Mode, you simply type at the prompt (%):

% spss - m

Below I have an hypothetical session. I have just looked at my directory with an ls and then typed **spss -m**. This evokes SPSS which gives me some SPSS ads and info and the SPSS > prompt. At this prompt I can start typing SPSS commands. The session starts with an **ls** and is as follows:

Session Transcript

```
% ls
commando        valfreq.sps     valrpt.sps      value.sps
krs             valdesc.sps     valmeans.sps    value.BAK
meyer.ans       valfmt.sps      valplot.sps     value.dat


% spss -m

Try the new SPSS Release 4.0 features: ☞ [SPSS gives me this output.]


* LOGISTIC REGRESSION procedure        * CATEGORIES Option:
* EXAMINE procedure to explore data    *   conjoint analysis
* FLIP to transpose data files         *   correspondence analysis
* MATRIX Transformations Language       * GRAPH interface to SPSS Graph


See the new SPSS documentation for more information on these new features.


SPSS>set listing test.ans .   ☞ [SPSS gave the prompt. I typed the rest.]
SPSS> set width = 80 .
SPSS> data list list / x .
SPSS> begin data .          ☞ [When I typed begin data, SPSS gave me
DATA> 1                            the DATA > prompt. I type the data.]
DATA> 2
DATA> 3
DATA> end data .            ☞ [I typed end data & get an SPSS > prompt]


Preceding task required .02 seconds CPU time;   7.44 seconds elapsed.


SPSS> descriptives x . ☞ [I typed descriptives x & output follows]

There are 199,712 bytes of memory available.
The largest contiguous area has 199,264 bytes.

76 bytes of memory required for the DESCRIPTIVES procedure.
4 bytes have already been acquired.
72 bytes remain to be acquired.
☞  [HERE'S THE ANSWERS]
Number of valid observations (listwise) =        3.00
                                                      Valid
Variable    Mean     Std Dev   Minimum   Maximum    N  Label

X           2.00     1.00      1.00      3.00       3

Preceding task required .02 seconds CPU time;   .02 seconds elapsed.


SPSS> finish .              ☞ [I am done so I typed finish.]

    9 command lines read.
    0 errors detected.
    0 warnings issued.
    0 seconds CPU time.
   64 seconds elapsed time.
      End of job.
```

B. WHERE ARE COPIES OF THE SETUP AND ANSWER?

OK! But what about my answer? It just went by on the screen! How about saving the setup? Is it gone? (Excuse the use of the vernacular-power computer types and stuffy professors should go get a life at this point).

There is no need to worry! SPSS automatically saves your setup in a special file called **spss.jnl**. The output has been saved in a file called **test.ans**. This must be requested. We did it in the setup with the **set listing test.ans** command. There is another way to do which we will explain later. However, if you don't do one of these, your answer wasn't saved. Hope you can remember an ANOVA table. In any case, after the above session my directory would contain the following new files (compare it to the previous directory):

```
% ls
commando        spss.jnl        valfmt.sps      valplot.sps     value.dat
krs             test.ans        valfreq.sps     valrpt.sps      value.sps
meyer.ans       valdesc.sps     valmeans.sps    value.BAK
```

Remember:

spss.jnl = a setup made of your commands and data

test.ans = your statistics

There are other ways to save your answer. You could start SPSS by

%spss -m -t file.ans OR %spss -m > file.ans

Both work in Command Line Mode and send statistical analyses to file.ans. You would not have to type the **set listing file.ans** command. However, if you prefer could still use the set listing command later in a session to change the file for each analysis so that after starting and doing some work, the output file changes:

SPSS >set listing *filenext.ans* .

This will send the next listings to filenext.ans.

Also, if you want to keep the setup you had better change its name. If you run another job, a new spss.jnl file will be created over your old one. It's history. You could:

%cp spss.jnl filename2

which copies setup and gives it the name filename2 . (Please don't be literal and always use filename2!)

You could also start your setup with a **set journal command**. This will send your setup to the file specified in a manner similar to the **set listing** command. Thus

$$SPSS > set\ journal\ gm.set\ .$$

would save the setup to **gm.set**.

C. TYPOS IN COMMAND MODE.

You type a command, ending with a period (.). If you make a mistake, an error message is printed and you have the chance to make a correction. For example:

```
SPSS> data lust lust / x .      ☞ [My mind wandered and I typed this]

>Error # 1.  Command name: DATA      ☞ [SPSS asks for correction]
>Text appearing in the first column is not recognized as a command.  Is it
>spelled correctly?  If it was intended as a continuation of the previous
>command, the first column must be blank.
>This command not executed.

SPSS> data list list / x.           ☞ [I retype the command]
```

If there are a logical mistakes, meaning the command is OK but you don't want to do that, you'll need to retype or go into the **spss.jnl** file and fix it as a batch job.

D. USING AN ALREADY CREATED SETUP IN COMMAND MODE (INCLUDE COMMAND)

It is also possible to bring in an already created file into a Command session. If **file.set** already exists, it is possible to bring it into a prompted session. The directory below indicates that **file.set** has been created.

```
% ls
commando      meyer.ans      valdesc.sps      valmeans.sps      value.BAK
file.set      spss.jnl       valfmt.sps       valplot.sps       value.dat
krs           test.ans       valfreq.sps      valrpt.sps        value.sps
% spss -m    ☞ [I enter Command Mode.]

Try the new SPSS Release 4.0 features:

* LOGISTIC REGRESSION procedure        * CATEGORIES Option:
* EXAMINE procedure to explore data    *    conjoint analysis
* FLIP to transpose data files         *    correspondence analysis
* MATRIX Transformations Language      * GRAPH interface to SPSS Graph

See new SPSS documentation for more information on these new features.

SPSS> include file.set .☞ [I typed the INCLUDE FILE.SET.]
    1  set width = 80.
    2  data list list / x.          ☞ [These seven lines are inserted &
```

```
    3  begin data .                      executed which gives the output]
    6  end data.
    7  descriptives x.

There are 199,712 bytes of memory available.
The largest contiguous area has 199,264 bytes.

76 bytes of memory required for the DESCRIPTIVES procedure.
4 bytes have already been acquired.
72 bytes remain to be acquired.

Number of valid observations (listwise) =          3.00

                                                 Valid
Variable        Mean    Std Dev   Minimum   Maximum    N   Label

X               2.00     1.00      1.00      3.00      3

Preceding task required .02 seconds CPU time;   .02 seconds elapsed.

    8  finish.
     8 command lines read.
     0 errors detected.
     0 warnings issued.
     0 seconds CPU time.
     7 seconds elapsed time.
       End of job.
  % ☞ [Note that if I didn't have a finish command I would return to
           the SPSS> prompt.]
```

If you have an error, you are alerted of the fact and the processing stops at that command. In other words, you don't see the rest of **file.set**. See the following example with a mistyped **data list list**:

```
SPSS> include file.set .
    1  set width = 80.
    2  data list lust / x.☞ [O O P S ! ]

>Error # 4100 on line 2 in column 11.  Text: LUST
>Unrecognized text appears on the DATA LIST command in the file
>specification section.  This text will be ignored.
>This command not executed.

>Note # 214
>Due to an error, INCLUDE file processing has been terminated & the active
>file has been lost. You may either redefine your data or leave SPSS.
  ☞ [I'm in trouble and need to edit file.set so I type finish.]
SPSS> finish
     4 command lines read.
     1 errors detected.
     0 warnings issued.
     0 seconds CPU time.
    21 seconds elapsed time.
       End of job.
```

E. OTHER NEAT TRICKS.

1. Help:

If you need help in Command Line Mode, type help at the prompt:

SPSS>help

The program will give you a pretty reasonable help menu. You could also type a question mark and then the command you can't comprehend:

SPSS>? regression

The help documentation for that command will appear and you will also be in Help Mode.

2. Unix inside a SPSS command session.

If you want to use unix commands inside spss, type

SPSS> host command?

Now don't actually type 'command?' - type the command you want:

SPSS> host mail mooney
or:

SPSS> host ls setup *

After the Unix command is carried out, you go back to the SPSS > prompt.

If you type just **SPSS> host**, you are out of SPSS and back in Unix, however your SPSS process is still active and you can return with a Control-D.

III. USING THE MENU MANAGER

The Menu Mode is difficult for a beginner, because you need to be knowledgeable about the menu system and the language of SPSS. While menus are supposed to be user friendly, I would be reluctant to use these unless I was a touch sophisticated. I recommend Command or Batch for the beginner. Interestingly, once you are really skilled, users may also prefer Batch, because why go through many menus when you already know what to type. But be brave and give the Unix menus a try. Don't do it on an important data set at first. Also, we can't go through every nuance. If you want to use the menu system, you should read the *SPSS® for Unix™: Operations Guide*.

We will present two scenarios. The first is bringing in an already done file and running it. The second is using the menu manager to create a setup. Note that you start the same way for both tasks. Note that if we put **< >** around a key sequence, you just use the keys. Don't type the less-than (**<**) and greater-than signs (**>**). So if you see **<esc j>**, the **< >** are just artistic notes common in computer books.

A. BRINGING IN AN ALREADY CREATED SETUP

1. GETTING STARTED IN MENU MODE: At the Unix prompt type 'spss', e.g.:

%s p s s

This will bring up the first menu which looks as follows (we've annotated some of the parts of the screen):

Output and Menus for Generating Commands Appear Here.

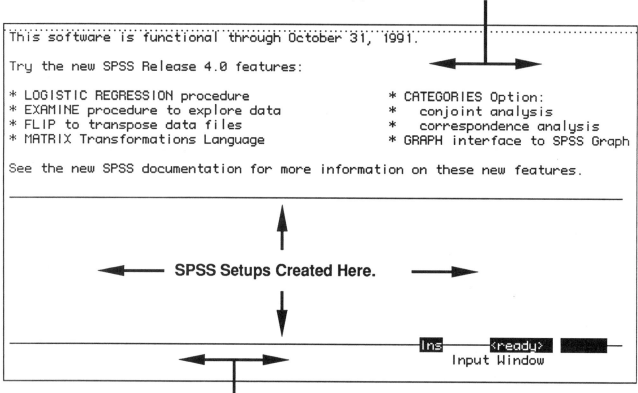

```
This software is functional through October 31, 1991.

Try the new SPSS Release 4.0 features:

* LOGISTIC REGRESSION procedure          * CATEGORIES Option:
* EXAMINE procedure to explore data      *    conjoint analysis
* FLIP to transpose data files           *    correspondence analysis
* MATRIX Transformations Language        * GRAPH interface to SPSS Graph

See the new SPSS documentation for more information on these new features.
```

SPSS Setups Created Here.

```
                                         Ins        <ready>
                                              Input Window
```

Mini-Menus Produced by <esc-number> Appear Here.

As you see above, the window has three parts:

❑ 1. Output and Menus to Generate commands.

❑ 2. Area to Edit Commands.

❑ 3. Small Menus with Choices evoked by <esc-number>. Watch these in following examples.

2. BRINGING IN A FILE (<esc 3>)

You navigate in SPSS Menu Mode by using control (<ctrl>) and escape key combinations (<esc>) . These are given in the Operations Guide. We will tell you the relevant ones for the operations we demonstrate. The file we will bring in is called 'testset' . We created it with Jove and it is in our Unix directory.

To bring in an already created setup, type: **<esc 3>** (the escape key and the number 3). The following menu appears. Highlighted at the bottom is the request for the file you wish to use.

```
This software is functional through October 31, 1991.

Try the new SPSS Release 4.0 features:

* LOGISTIC REGRESSION procedure        * CATEGORIES Option:
* EXAMINE procedure to explore data    *    conjoint analysis
* FLIP to transpose data files         *    correspondence analysis
* MATRIX Transformations Language      * GRAPH interface to SPSS Graph

See the new SPSS documentation for more information on these new features.
_____




                                                          Ins      ready
_____
files: Edit different file    Insert file
```

Hit **<return>** if Edit different file name is highlighted. If it isn't, type **E** or use the cursor to get to | **Edit different file** | name and then return. You will be asked for the file name at the | **File to edit:** | line.

There is another way to bring in a file. That is to use the **INCLUDE** command as shown above. However, I don't recommend it for the Menu Manager because if you use the statement, it brings in the commands and executes them. However, you cannot edit the commands. They're not in the window.

Now type the file with the setup (our case **testset**) as seen in the menu below:

```
This software is functional through October 31, 1991.

Try the new SPSS Release 4.0 features:

* LOGISTIC REGRESSION procedure        * CATEGORIES Option:
* EXAMINE procedure to explore data    *    conjoint analysis
* FLIP to transpose data files         *    correspondence analysis
* MATRIX Transformations Language      * GRAPH interface to SPSS Graph

See the new SPSS documentation for more information on these new features.
_____




_____
                                               Ins        ready
File to edit: testset
```

Hit <return> and **testset** appears in the window as was typed in our directory.

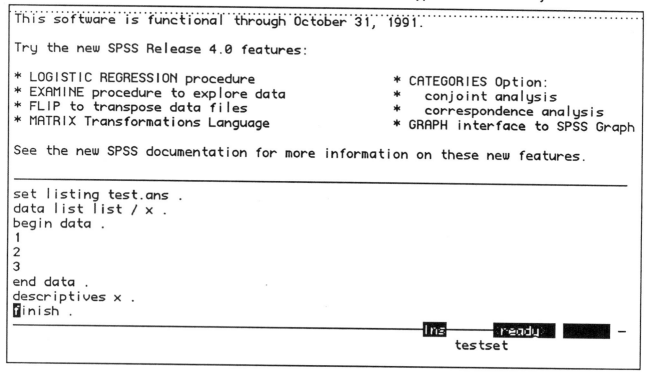

```
This software is functional through October 31, 1991.

Try the new SPSS Release 4.0 features:

* LOGISTIC REGRESSION procedure        * CATEGORIES Option:
* EXAMINE procedure to explore data    *    conjoint analysis
* FLIP to transpose data files         *    correspondence analysis
* MATRIX Transformations Language      * GRAPH interface to SPSS Graph

See the new SPSS documentation for more information on these new features.
_____
set listing test.ans .
data list list / x .
begin data .
1
2
3
end data .
descriptives x .
finish .
_____
                                               Ins       ready          -
                                                 testset
```

Note the cursor (■) over the **f** in finish. This marks your cursor position in the setup.

3. EXECUTING THE COMMANDS (<esc 0>).

Use the cursor keys to get to top of setup (set listing command-recall this is to send output to **test.ans**). You'll see a ▌ or other to mark the cursors position. I'd probably add a set width = 80 command. Type **<esc 0>** (**zero** not the letter O - Oh!) to get the $\boxed{\text{run from Cursor}}$, command.

If the highlighting is not on $\boxed{\text{run from Cursor}}$, use your cursor keys to move to it or you can type the letter **C.**

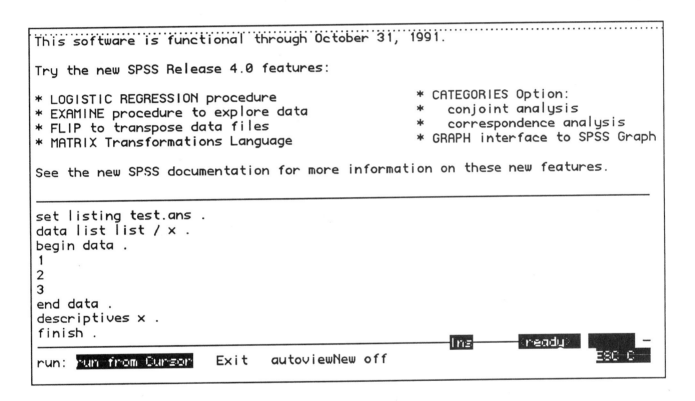

Hit **<return>** and your analysis will be started. One warning, make sure the cursor is at the command where you want to start executing. If you don't, you start executing at the cursor point.

Your answer flashes by on the top of the window. Recall that it is being saved in **test.ans** because of our set listing command. Also your setup is being saved in **spss.jnl** (as in Command Line Mode) Here's your answer. We zoomed the window with an **<esc z>.**

You can look at your answer without exiting the program. You will see that the cursor is now on top in the Output window. You can navigate in that window using the cursor keys or a set of search commands found in the Operations Guide. You can return to the input window on the bottom with an **<esc s>**. If you want to exit the program type **<esc 0>** and you will be given an exit option.

4. DOING MORE ANALYSES(**<esc 0>**)

If you had not typed a **finish** command as we did then you could type in more analyses (such as a **frequencies x .**) and continue. You would just need to switch to the input window (**<esc s>**) and type the new command and **<esc 0>**. This will give you the ⌐run from Cursor⌐ prompt and you can continue. Again make sure you move the cursor to the level of the command you want to execute. In other words if you type a few lines and then ⌐run from Cursor⌐, you are below the lines you want to execute. Remember to move up. If you try to ⌐run from Cursor⌐ and haven't moved up - you will miss some commands. Also if you try the cursor keys to move up, once you are at ⌐run from Cursor⌐-they don't work. Again. if you typed **finish.**, the program wants you to exit if you give it an **<esc 0>**.

You can also expand the size of your output viewing area with an **<esc z>** as below. As highlighted, you can get back to the regular window with **<esc> <esc>**

```
Number of valid observations (listwise) =          3.00
                                            Valid
Variable     Mean     Std Dev   Minimum   Maximum    N  Label

X            2.00      1.00      1.00      3.00      3
2
13:41:07  Lewis & Clark College SPSS      Sun-4/490           SunOS 4.1.1


Preceding task required .00 seconds CPU time;   .14 seconds elapsed.

->      finish .

     9 command lines read.
     0 errors detected.
     0 warnings issued.
     0 seconds CPU time.
   224 seconds elapsed time.
       End of job.


                                               Ins     FINISH
ZOOMview: press ESC ESC to unZOOM.                   Output Window
```

B. CREATING A SETUP USING THE MENUS

You can have SPSS create the commands line by by line using the Menu Manager. The general principle is to go to a command in the menu, select it, and enter it using <tabs> and <returns>. To be quite honest, I find it easy to just type the commands in Batch Mode files or in Command Line Mode. With a little skill, it's much faster. However, the Menu Manager does have the advantage of rather full explanations of the command if you are not familiar with it. In our example, we will create a data list statement.

1. GETTING THE MAIN MENU (<esc M >).

After entering the SPSS system from Unix (with %spss) and seeing the initial screen, type an **<esc M>**. This brings up the **MAIN MENU,** which enables you to generate commands. The commands will be placed in the input window at the cursor (▌).

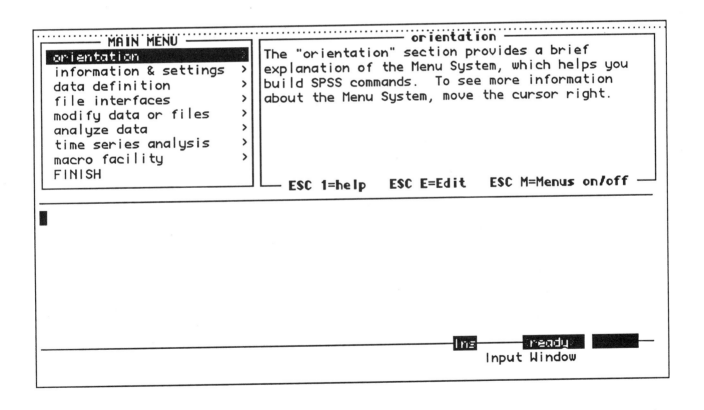

2. CHOOSING A COMMAND (**Tabs and Returns**).

To enter the data list command, use the cursor keys to go to **data definition** line, as seen in the below menu. If you do this, then hit **<tab>**. The next menu will follow. If you see an **>**, then hitting **< tab>** will bring up the next set of menu selections.

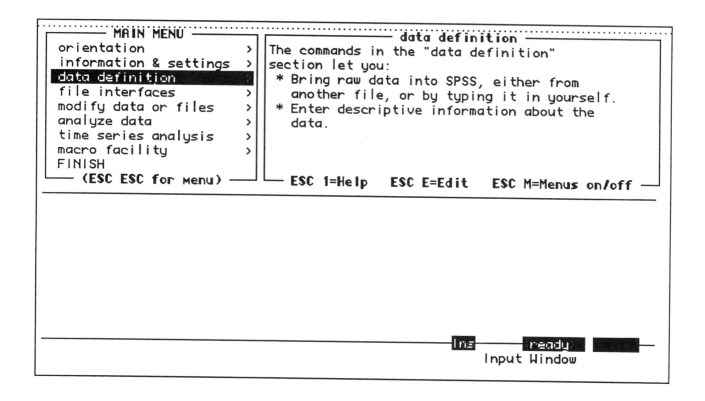

So now I hit a tab and the next menu appears.

< TAB >

3. ENTERING A COMMAND.

DATA LIST is now highlighted.

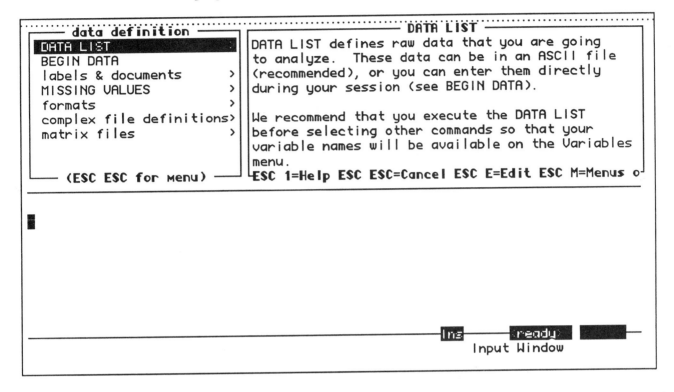

If I type a **<return>**, then the command **DATA LIST** is entered in the Input Window. I could now:

a. type some information myself (the rest of the setup).

b. continue to choose menu options (i.e. use the cursor to go to **LIST** / . If I pressed <return>, the word LIST would appear so I had a DATA LIST LIST (as we use in our setups) and then I would be asked for variables.

See the Next Screen with DATA LIST entered.

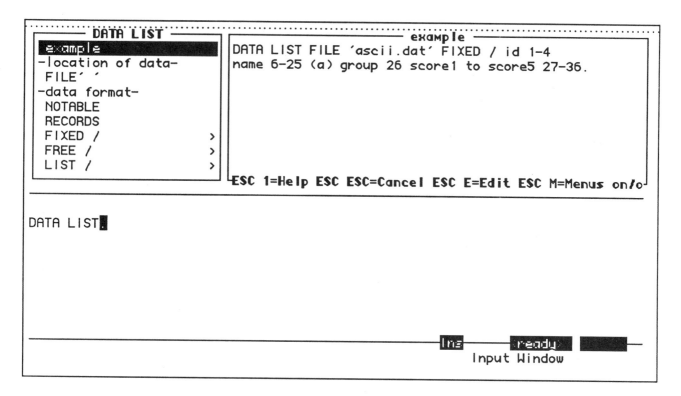

If I was done with the Data list command, I would type **<esc esc>** to return up to the menus. This would take me up the menus step by step. Or I could type **<esc j>** and return to the main menu and start with a new command. I could select an analysis or transformation. Once I was done, I would **<esc 0>** to move to **run from Cursor** and execute my analyses.

Thus each command can be built from the Menu Manager. If you know the SPSS language it might be easier to type them straight off. However, the manager is helpful if you forget syntax or want to use its help facilities and explanations.

SUMMARY OF STEPS FOR BUILDING A COMMAND:

1. Enter from Unix using % s p s s .
2. **<esc m>** to get to Main Menu.
3. Use cursor keys to pick command topic.
4. **<Tab>** takes you down to the next level if present.
5. **<Return>** enters the command in Input Window.
6. You can type more information now (use **<esc e>** to enter Edit Mode if necessary).
7. Return up the menu with **<esc esc>** or <esc j> for Main Menu.
8. When ready use **<esc 0>** to run job.
9. Buy the Operations Guide and use the help screens if necessary.

SPSS® for the Macintosh® *

* These examples were produced on a Macintosh II using System 6.07. They have also run under 7.0. However, this won't affect our following discussion.

INTRODUCTION TO SPSS® FOR THE MACINTOSH®

We hope you have some experience with the Macintosh interface. You really don't need too much. In fact, this interface is very easy to learn. We suspect that if you are using this version of SPSS, you already are familiar with the basics of the Macintosh desktop. If not, your Macintosh has some excellent instructional demonstrations and training files (Guided Tours). If you haven't tried them, you should. It is much easier to use the Macintosh interface than those for DOS and Unix (although this can be argued by fanatics/believers/users of all three operating systems). The SPSS® for the Macintosh® Operations Guide is quite understandable for the Mac user.

There are three ways to generate SPSS setups on a Macintosh system. They are: 1) Using SPSS editing functions in its INPUT WINDOW; 2) Using a word processor; and 3) Using the COMMAND GENERATOR mode. We will explain and give examples of each. The question for the beginner is which one to use. This is, of course, your own personal preference. In the first mode, you can type in your setup using SPSS editing functions (which are typical Mac-like) and easy to use. In the second mode, you create a complete SPSS setup in a word processor or editor program, insert it into SPSS and then check your output. In the COMMAND GENERATOR mode, you call up a menu to create a new setup by using menu selections and pasting the selection into the INPUT WINDOW. In all three cases, you can save your setup after it has been run.

We have found that it is easiest to use the first two methods once you have some familiarity with the structure of the SPSS language and some familiarity with word processors. For a large setup, I would rather use a word processor because they are more powerful than SPSS' own editing functions. For small jobs, I would use the INPUT WINDOW directly. We will give an example of each.

Going through the COMMAND GENERATOR for each command is time consuming and for the novice the menu system can be intimidating. You can get stuck in its different levels and panic. Menus are hot in the design of computer-human interfaces (the author gives a seminar on the topic). First, we will explain a little about the Macs and then how to use SPSS on them.

THE MACINTOSH DESKTOP METAPHOR

Macs come in different varieties. There are Classics, Pluses, LCs, SEs, IIs of various configurations, Portables, Powerbooks and Quadras. There may be more by the time you read this. They all have one thing in common, they use the desktop metaphor. Simply, your desktop is the operating system for your Mac. You may be using a version of System 6.0 or 7.0 to run SPSS. The desktop is presented as a set of windows containing a set of files that are stored on your hard drive or on floppies. They appear as icons of various shapes and color. These files may be programs or data. They may be saved in folders that look like actual file folders scattered on a desk (hence the desktop metaphor). You navigate in the desktop with your mouse. The following set of illustrations will point out the Mac, the desktop, the mouse, and the appearance of folders and icons (we will use the SPSS icons).

MAC COMPUTERS, SCREENS AND MICE

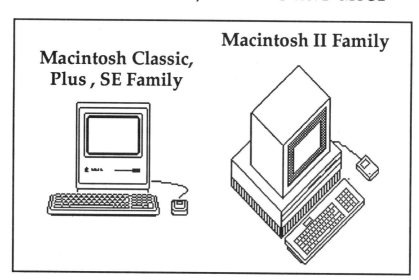

You will need a Mac with at least 4MB of memory to run SPSS under Multifinder. I would suggest more. We have not extensively explored System 7.0, but as it needs much memory, the more the merrier. Also, you need a fair amount of disk space. All of SPSS takes up 15 MB. You can run the basics with 6MB of disk space. One never can have enough disk space.

The reason to use the Mac II family, Quadras, or Mac LCs is to have better screens and easier availability of color. In fact, if you just bought a Mac Classic, you might find that some programs cost as much as your machine.

A Mac with a Desktop on the Screen

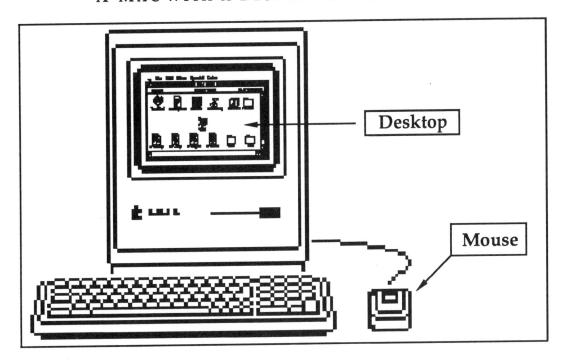

As seen above, the Macintosh screen is filled with little pictures or icons. These represent data, program, or folders (containing more data and programs). Using your mouse, you move and select folders. This makes much more sense if you do one of the Apple-supplied Guided Tours that come with the system. To open a folder, you move the mouse cursor to the folder and double-click on it. To call up or start a program, you also double-click on the icon of the program. The icon for SPSS is:

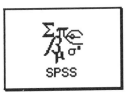

You will find it in the center of the window entitled **mac spss**. I chose the name **mac spss** for this window, you could pick another. :

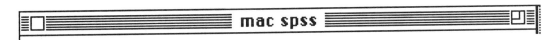

The other files and folders are part of the SPSS package.

This is illustrated in the next figure.

THE MACINTOSH DESKTOP WITH SPSS FOLDER OPENED

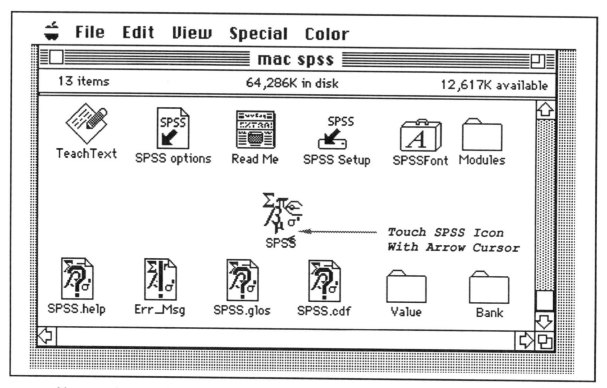

You need to touch the central icon with the arrow cursor controlled by your mouse, as noted above, and then double-click on it as follows:

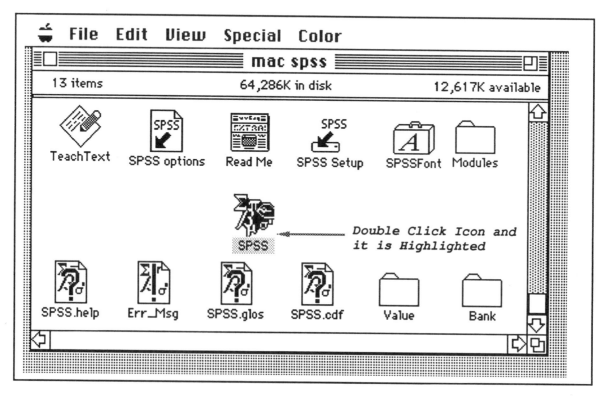

Double-clicking on the SPSS icon, causes it to be highlighted and then the SPSS windows will appear on the screen looking as follows:

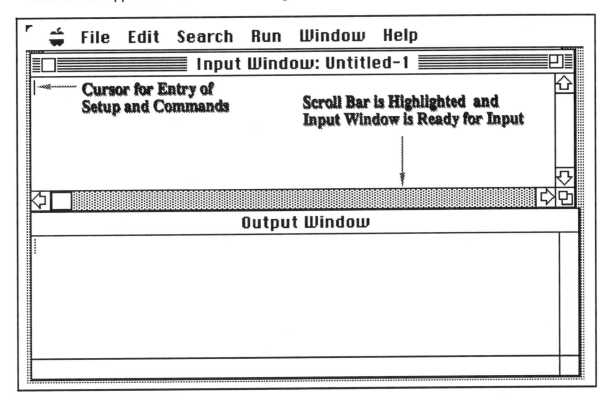

I. USING THE INPUT WINDOW

GETTING STARTED AND ENTERING THE SETUP
INTO THE INPUT WINDOW:

Assume I want to input the simple SPSS setup containing the commands:

```
set width = 80 .
data list list / x .
begin data .
1
2
3
end data .
descriptives x .
finish  .
```

I would click the **INPUT WINDOW** to be sure it is active (if it was not already active). Remember that an active window has the highlighted or gray scroll bars. A cursor appears as a vertical line (|). If you start to type, the setup will entered into the **INPUT WINDOW**. It would look as follows:

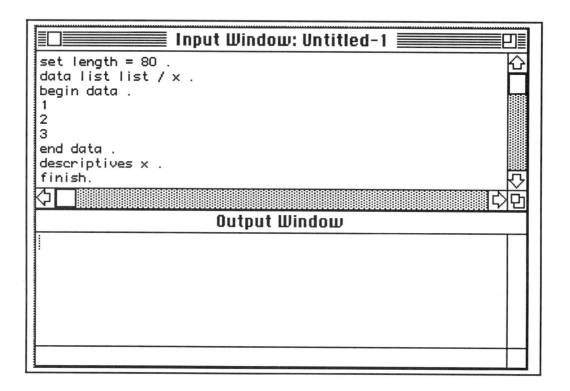

Editing and correcting the setup is rather easy and Mac-like. If you have used a Mac word processor before, it is quite similar. You use the cursor to move the insertion point. You can **cut** and **paste**. If you double-click a word, it is highlighted, etc. The best practice for this, is some familiarity with one of the many Mac word processors.

Once you run a setup (see below), you can click back into the INPUT WINDOW and correct mistakes and rerun the setup. You can also enter new commands or data by using the INPUT WINDOW.

II. USING A WORD PROCESSOR FOR SETUP CREATION

It is possible to create a setup in a word processing program such as Microsoft® Word or Wordperfect™. There are two ways to enter the setup in the INPUT WINDOW such that it can be run :

A. USING THE CLIPBOARD.

Select the setup commands in the Word Processor's Window, copy the selection and then paste in into the SPSS INPUT WINDOW. This particularly easy to do with short setups and if you are running Multifinder with System 6.0X or using System 7.0. Below is a Microsoft® Word setup where we have selected and then copied our little setup.

Setup Written in Microsoft® Word, Selected & Copied

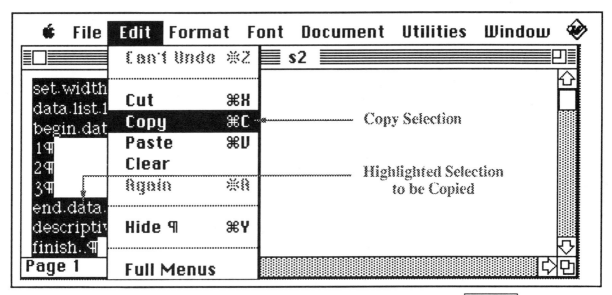

The setup is saved in the CLIPBOARD where we can now choose ⌜PASTE⌟ and insert it into the SPSS **INPUT WINDOW** as shown below.

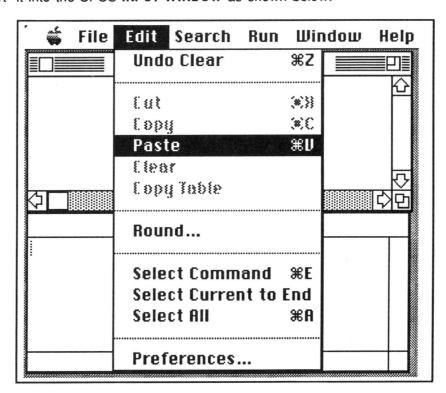

The setup will appear in the **INPUT WINDOW** and can be selected and run.

B. OPENING THE WORD PROCESSOR'S FILE FROM SPSS.

If you saved the file as plain text (without formatting and line breaks, etc), you can use the Open command from the File menu in SPSS. Only files that are compatible (plain text) will appear in the file menu, where they can be opened. The setup will appear in the **INPUT WINDOW**. In the following example, we have created our setup in Microsoft® Word and saved it in a file named **S2**. Clicking on Open will cause the setup to appear in the **INPUT WINDOW**.

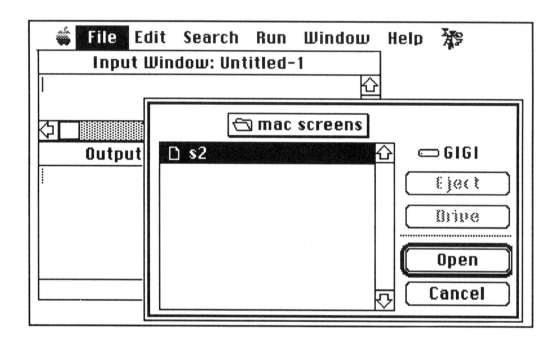

III. USING THE COMMAND GENERATOR

The COMMAND GENERATOR menu mode is difficult for a beginner as you need to be knowledgeable about the menu system and the language of SPSS. While menus are supposed to be user friendly, I would be reluctant to use these unless I was a touch sophisticated. Interestingly, once you are really skilled, users may also prefer to type setups directly or with a word processor because why go through many menus when you already know what to type. But be brave and give the Macintosh menus a try. Don't do it on an important data set at first. Also, we can't go through every nuance. If you want to use the menu system, you should read the *SPSS® for Macintosh™: Operations Guide*.

A. GETTING STARTED IN COMMAND GENERATOR MENU MODE:

Pull down the ⟨WINDOW⟩ menu to ⟨COMMAND GENERATOR⟩ and release as follows:

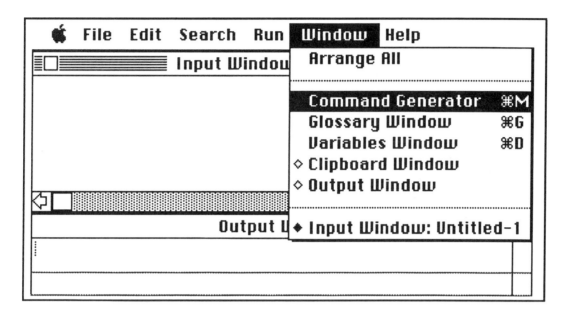

This will bring up the first menu, which looks as follows:

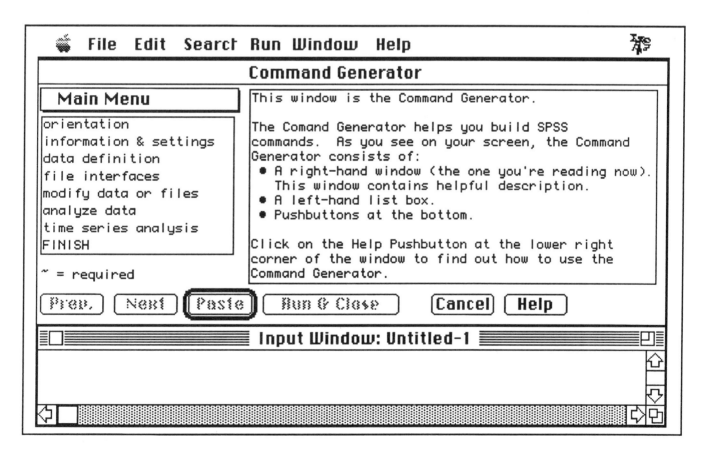

As you see above, the window has three parts:

☐ 1. INPUT WINDOW where the commands appear.

☐ 2. MAIN MENU used to pick command and paste in the INPUT WINDOW.

☐ 3. COMMAND GENERATOR WINDOW to explain commands and give help.

B. ENTERING THE COMMANDS

The general principle is to go to a command in the menu, select it and enter it using PASTE. To be quite honest, I find it easy to just type the commands in Batch Mode files or in Command Line Mode. With a little skill, it's much faster. However, the COMMAND GENERATOR does have the advantage of rather full explanations of the command if you are not familiar with it. The general method is to find a command in the MAIN MENU WINDOW and then paste it into the INPUT WINDOW. In our example, we will create a **DATA LIST** statement.

1. CHOOSING A COMMAND

To enter the **DATA LIST** command, use the mouse to go to DATA DEFINITION line as seen in the below menu. If you do this, then double-click DATA DEFINITION or click on NEXT.

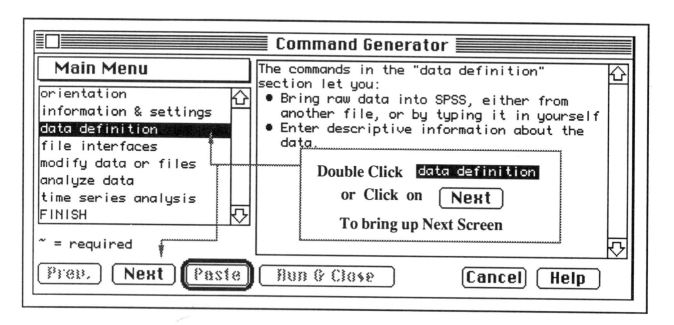

The Next Menu Appears.

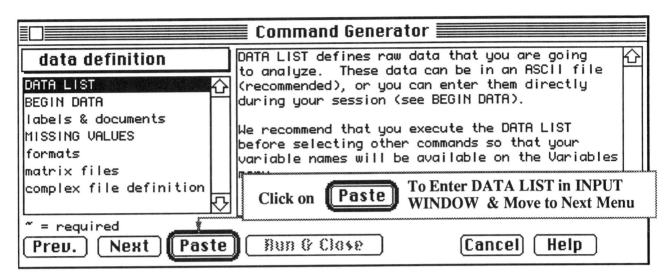

The Next Menu Appears & 'DATA LIST' is Pasted in
Input Window:Untitled-1.

The command **DATA LIST** is entered in the **INPUT WINDOW**.

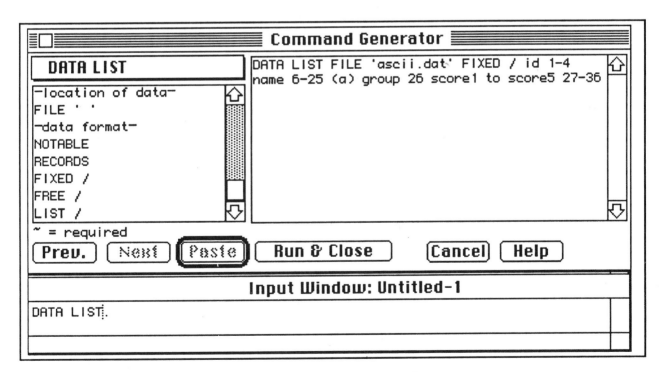

I could now:

a. type some information myself (the rest of the setup).

b. continue to choose menu options (i.e. use the cursor to go to **LIST**/ . If I click PASTE , the word LIST would appear so I had a DATA LIST LIST (as we use in our setups) and then I would be asked for variables.

c. After creating this command, I could return up the menus by use of the Previous button (**Prev.**) and find the next command or procedure that I want and paste those until the set up is complete and ready to run.

IV. RUNNING THE SETUP

It is very easy to run this setup. There are two steps:

1. Select the parts of the setup, you wish to run. There are two ways to do this:

a. Highlighting by holding down the mouse key and dragging down across the parts you want (see below):

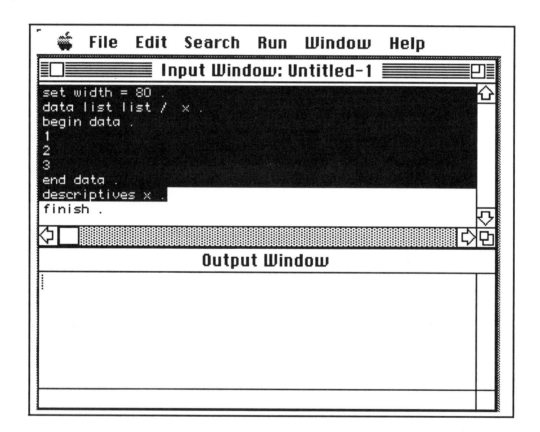

b. Using the Select Commands under the Edit Menu as seen below:

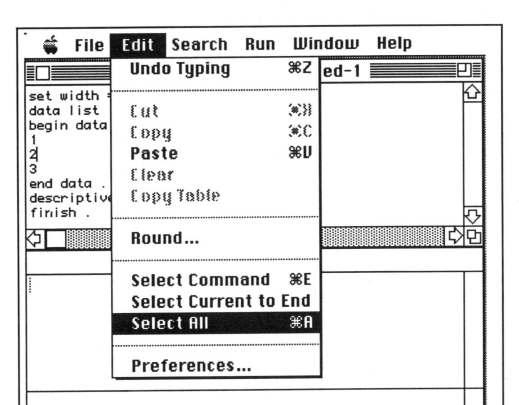

After using either method to select the whole setup or parts you want to run, you would next pull the Run menu and release it. The screen would appear as follows:

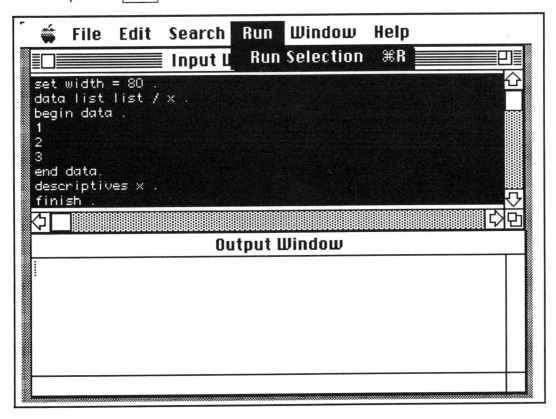

Your output would appear in the **OUTPUT WINDOW** to be discussed later. If you are creating the setup from scratch you can now save the setup. This also will be discussed later.

V. VIEWING THE OUTPUT.

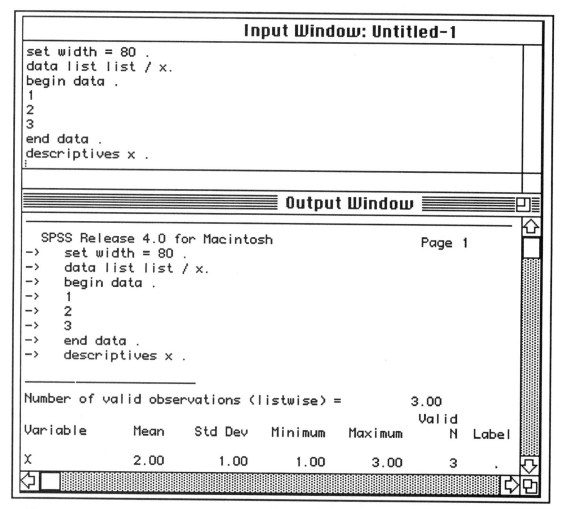

Your output appears in the **OUTPUT WINDOW**. You can scroll up and down in the window. You can highlight selections and cut and paste so that sections of the output can be insert via the Clipboard into other documents. You can also type in the window at the point indicated by the mouse cursor.

VI. SAVING THE OUTPUT

Once an output is completed, you might want to save it. There are three methods of saving your output.

A. SELECT THE PART OF THE OUTPUT YOU WANT AND COPY IT USING

1. the ⌘C keyboard command.

2: [Copy] from the [Edit] menu as seen below:

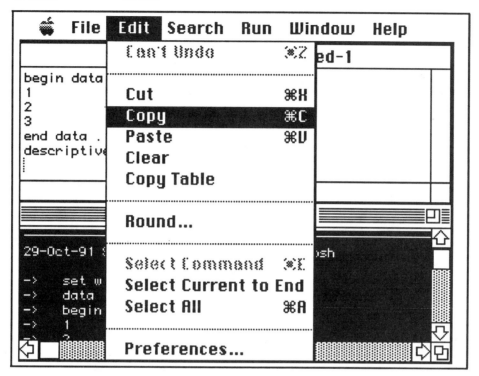

The highlighted part is in the CLIPBOARD and can be pasted into another document.

B. USE THE [Save] COMMAND FROM THE [File] MENU.

1. Click on the Output window (Scroll bars are gray) so it is active.
2. Pull down [File] Menu to [Save As...] and release as seen below.

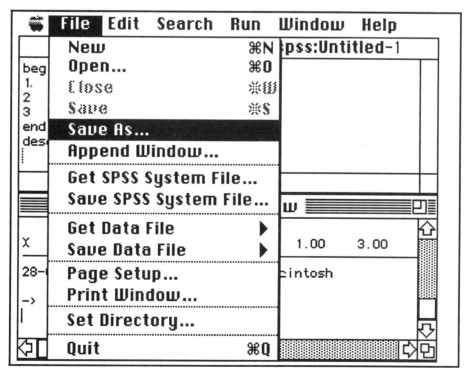

The following menu will appear to save the output. I typed in **Setup Answer** as the filename.

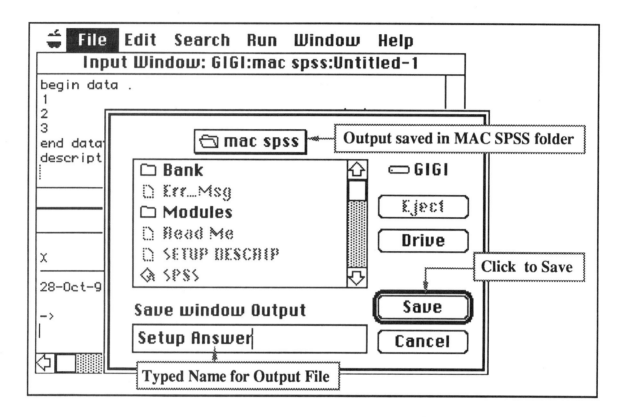

Setup Answer nows appears in the **mac spss** folder as seen below.

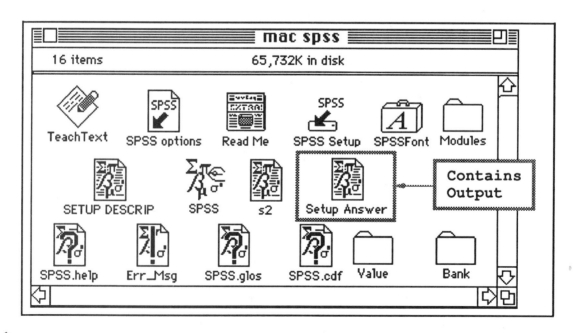

VII. SAVING THE SETUP

If the Input Window is active, pull down the File menu to Save As... and release:

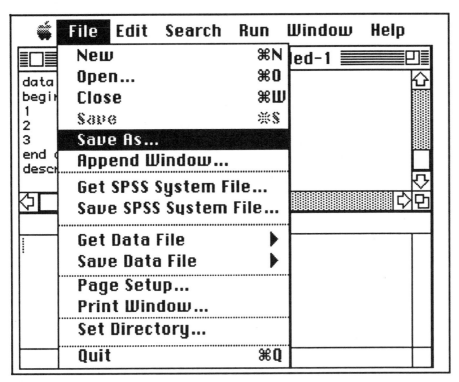

A menu to save the setup will appear. The setup is saved in the **mac spss** folder:

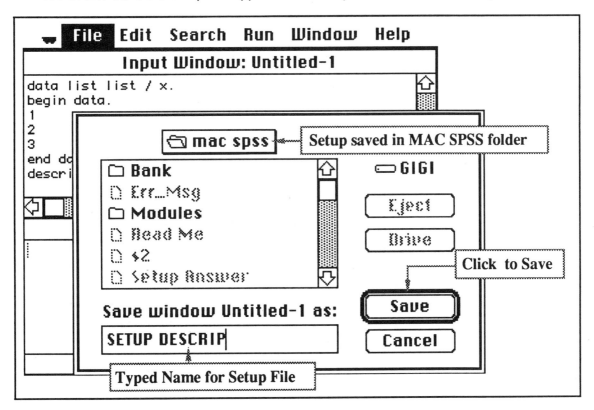

SETUP DESCRIP holds our setup.

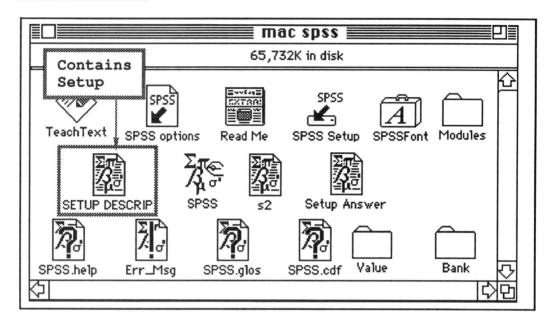

If you double-click on **SETUP DESCRIP** you will launch SPSS and a window will appear that contains our setup. You can edit and run it. Below is how the screen would appear if I double-clicked on **SETUP DESCRIP:**

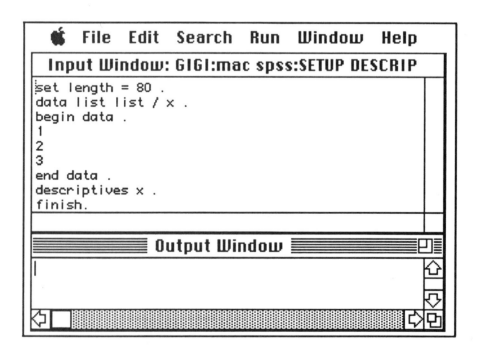

Note that the INPUT WINDOW is now titled **mac spss: SETUP DESCRIP** since that is the file containing our setup.

VIII. QUITTING SPSS AND THE FINISH COMMAND

A. Setups Containing the Finish Statement

Our setup contained a **finish** statement at its end. If we ran the setup, this statement would cause SPSS to quit. However, before it quits, the program throws up a warning window and ask if you want to save your output. If you click on **OK**, the file saving menu appears as we presented before. You can now type in a name for the output.

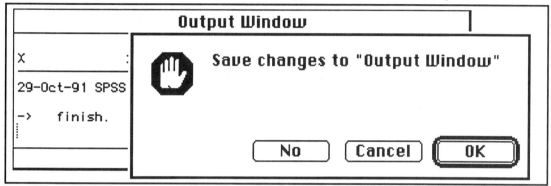

If you click on **Cancel** then you return to SPSS where you can open another setup or start a new INPUT WINDOW by using **New** under the **File** Menu.

B. Quitting From the ▮File▮ Menu

You can quit at any time by going to the ▮File▮ menu and pulling down to **Quit ⌘Q** and releasing, as seen below. You can also just type ⌘Q :

File Edit Search Run
New   ⌘N
Open...   ⌘O
Close   ⌘W
Save   ⌘S
Save As...
Append Window...
Get SPSS System File...
Save SPSS System File...
Get Data File   ▶
Save Data File   ▶
Page Setup...
Print Window...
Set Directory...
Quit   ⌘Q

If you have not saved your setup and outputs, you will be asked if you want to do this. We have already shown the warning that appears for saving Output. The warning to save your setup is quite similar as seen below:

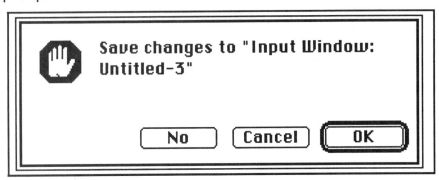

If you click on **OK**, then the menu used to name and save files will appear as shown before.

IX. PRINTING WINDOWS

You may want to print one of your windows (INPUT, OUTPUT, etc.). This is done by selecting the window by clicking on (scroll bars are gray). Next you choose Print Windows... from the File menu as seen below:

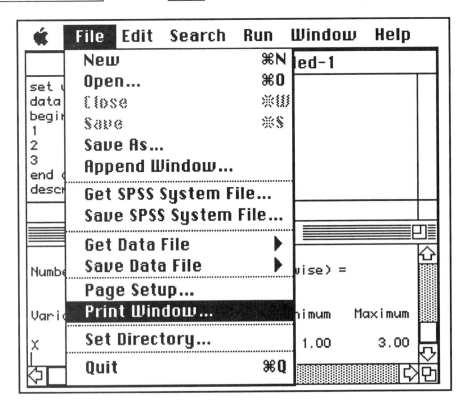

This will bring up the typical Mac print window that appears as follows:

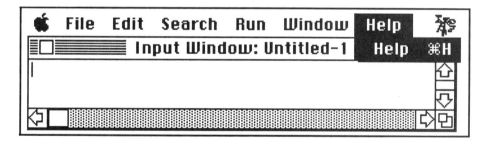

Clicking **OK** will initiate printing. You should make yourself familiar with Mac printing options and the nuances of the printer that you are using.

X. HELP AND THE GLOSSARY

There are two useful ways to get on-line help during a session. The first is the
HELP. This menu can bring up definitions of an SPSS term or command from a set controlled by a scroll bar. To evoke, the Help facility, you need to pull down the **Help** command or type a **command H (⌘ H)**. This is shown below:

EVOKING HELP

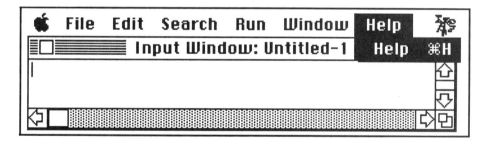

Next, we scroll down to a command (Correlations) and click on it. The complete specifications appear in the window.

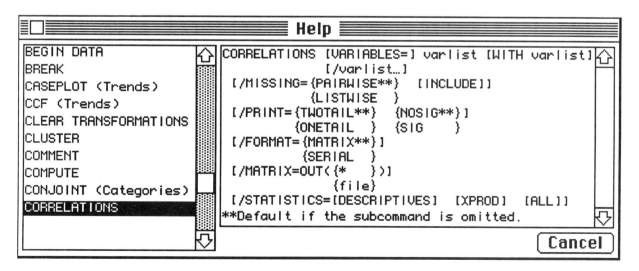

You can scroll and select another term or command. **Cancel** closes the window.

The second useful facility is the **Glossary Window**. If you aren't sure of a term in a setup or output, you can select the term and then pull down the glossary window or type ⌘ **G**. The selected term, if available, will be defined in the window. You can even paste the definition into the window you have open. This useful if using the SPSS output as part of a report. In the following example, we have : 1. Run our standard setup; 2. Selected the term Std Dev for definition by clicking or highlighting it ; 3. Opened the Glossary Window.

SELECTING A TERM & OPENING THE Glossary Window

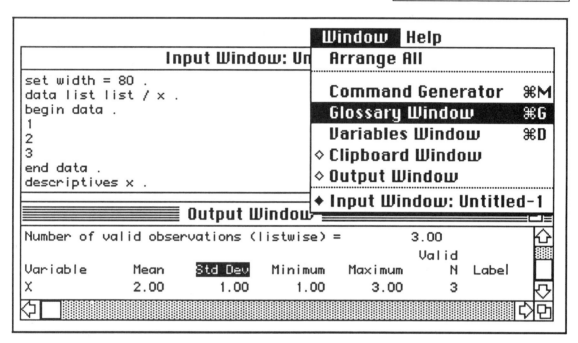

DEFINITION APPEARS IN Glossary Window

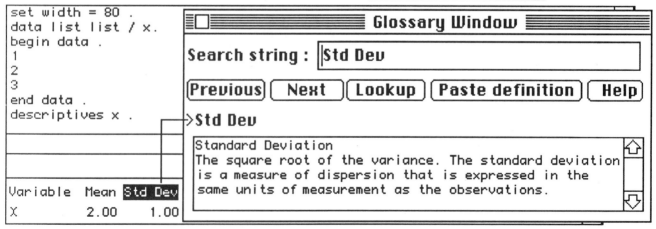

We could now | **Paste** | the definition into the output window, ask for another term to be defined by selecting it, or typing it in the glossary window. You don't have to always select a term to use the glossary. You can just open the window and type the term.

CHAPTER 3: FREQUENCIES

CREATING & INTERPRETING FREQUENCY DISTRIBUTIONS, GETTING DESCRIPTIVE STATISTICS & VARIOUS GRAPHIC OUTPUTS

SUMMARY OF SPSS SETUPS

```
set width = 80 .
data list list / x y z .1
begin data .
        .
        .
      data
        .
        .
end data .
frequencies  variables = x y z
         / optional statistics and chart requests .
finish .
```

REAL WORLD EXAMPLE

```
set width = 80 .
data list list /   major sex gpa sat .
begin data .
 2 0    3.5 460
 2 1    3.7 800
 1 1    3.2 610
 2 1    3.5 490
 2 0    3.4 470
 2 0    3.9 610
 1 0    2.8 580
 2 1    2.7 410
 1 1    3.8 630
 2 1    4.0 790
 3 1    3.4 490
 2 0    3.1 400
 2 1    3.8 610
 1 1    3.3 610
 1 1    3.7 500
 2 1    3.4 430
 3 1    3.1 540
 1 1    3.7 610
 2 1    2.7 400
 3 1    3.4 390
 1 0    3.0 490
end data .
frequencies variables = major sex gpa sat.
finish .
```

Produces Frequency Distributions of the Variables:
major (in college), *sex* (male, female), *gpa* (grade point average) and *sat* (SAT score) for 21 subjects (one per line of data.

---

[1] Use '**data list free / x y z** .' for **SPSS/PC+' 4.0.**

PURPOSE OF THE PROCEDURE AND STATISTICS:

The purpose of the Frequencies program is to print frequency distributions. It can also produce descriptive statistics, bargraphs and histograms.

HOW TO DO FREQUENCIES ON SPSS

Example 1 : Basic Setup

In this example we have four variables per subject. The first is their major. The second is their sex. The third is the subjects' GPA and the fourth is an SAT score. Thus our data look as follows:

<u>major</u>   <u>gpa</u>

2   1   **3.6** 410

2   **1**   2.7 **390**

<u>sex</u>   <u>sat</u>

Each line represents one subject.

Our goal is to get frequency distributions for all of the variables (major, sex, gpa, and sat). The setup and output are as follows:

BASIC SETUP

```
set width = 80 .
data list list / major sex gpa sat .
begin data .
 2 1    3.6 410
 2 1    2.7 390
 2 1    3.5 510
 3 1    2.9 430
 2 1    3.1 600
 3 1    3.5 610
 1 0    3.2 610
 2 1    3.6 560
 3 1    3.8 700
 2 0    3.8 460
 2 0    3.6 590
 3 0    3.1 500
 1 1    3.1 410
 2 1    3.5 470
 2 1    3.4 210
 2 0    3.4 610
 2 0    3.8 510
 3 0    3.7 600
 2 1    3.0 470
 2 0    3.5 460
 2 1    3.7 800
 1 1    3.2 610
 2 1    3.5 490
 2 0    3.4 470
 2 0    3.9 610
 1 0    2.8 580
 2 1    2.7 410
 1 1    3.8 630
 2 1    4.0 790
 3 1    3.4 490
 2 0    3.1 400
 2 1    3.8 610
 1 1    3.3 610
 1 1    3.7 500
 2 1    3.4 430
 3 1    3.1 540
 1 1    3.7 610
 2 1    2.7 400
 3 1    3.4 390
 1 0    3.0 490
end data .
frequencies variables = major sex gpa sat.
finish .
```

RELEVANT OUTPUT AND INTERPRETATIONS

```
 1    0  set width = 80 .
 2    data list list /  major sex gpa sat .
 3    begin data.
44    end data .
45    frequencies variables = major sex gpa sat.
```

MAJOR

VALUE LABEL	VALUE	FREQUENCY	PERCENT	VALID PERCENT	CUM PERCENT
	1.00	9	22.5	22.5	22.5
	2.00	23	57.5	57.5	80.0
	3.00	8	20.0	20.0	100.0
	TOTAL	40	100.0	100.0	

VALID CASES   40   MISSING CASES   0

- -

SEX

VALUE LABEL	VALUE	FREQUENCY	PERCENT	VALID PERCENT	CUM PERCENT
	.00	13	32.5	32.5	32.5
	1.00	27	67.5	67.5	100.0
	TOTAL	40	100.0	100.0	

VALID CASES   40   MISSING CASES   0

GPA

VALUE LABEL	VALUE	FREQUENCY	PERCENT	VALID PERCENT	CUM PERCENT
	2.70	3	7.5	7.5	7.5
	2.80	1	2.5	2.5	10.0
	2.90	1	2.5	2.5	12.5
	3.00	2	5.0	5.0	17.5
	3.10	5	12.5	12.5	30.0
	3.20	2	5.0	5.0	35.0
	3.30	1	2.5	2.5	37.5
	3.40	6	15.0	15.0	52.5
	3.50	5	12.5	12.5	65.0
	3.60	3	7.5	7.5	72.5
	3.70	4	10.0	10.0	82.5
	3.80	5	12.5	12.5	95.0
	3.90	1	2.5	2.5	97.5
	4.00	1	2.5	2.5	100.0
	TOTAL	40	100.0	100.0	

VALID CASES   40   MISSING CASES   0

SAT

VALUE LABEL	VALUE	FREQUENCY	PERCENT	VALID PERCENT	CUM PERCENT
	210.00	1	2.5	2.5	2.5
	390.00	2	5.0	5.0	7.5
	400.00	2	5.0	5.0	12.5
	410.00	3	7.5	7.5	20.0
	430.00	2	5.0	5.0	25.0
	460.00	2	5.0	5.0	30.0
	470.00	3	7.5	7.5	37.5
	490.00	3	7.5	7.5	45.0
	500.00	2	5.0	5.0	50.0
	510.00	2	5.0	5.0	55.0
	540.00	1	2.5	2.5	57.5
	560.00	1	2.5	2.5	60.0
	580.00	1	2.5	2.5	62.5
	590.00	1	2.5	2.5	65.0
	600.00	2	5.0	5.0	70.0
	610.00	8	20.0	20.0	90.0
	630.00	1	2.5	2.5	92.5
	700.00	1	2.5	2.5	95.0
	790.00	1	2.5	2.5	97.5
	800.00	1	2.5	2.5	100.0
	TOTAL	40	100.0	100.0	

VALID CASES   40   MISSING CASES   0

INTERPRETATIVE POINTS FOR BASIC SETUP

GPA ← variable name

percentile rank of the score

frequency of score

score

VALUE LABEL	VALUE	FREQUENCY	PERCENT	VALID PERCENT	CUM PERCENT
	2.70	3	7.5	7.5	7.5
	.				
	.				
	3.90	1	2.5	2.5	97.5
	4.00	1	2.5	2.5	100.0
	TOTAL	40	100.0	100.0	

VALID CASES   40   MISSING CASES   0

Example 2 : Setup with Value Labels

In this example we have four variables per subject. The first is their major. The second is their sex. The third is the subjects' GPA and the fourth is a SAT score. Thus our data look as follows:

```
major          gpa
  2 1     3.6 410   ----> Data for One Subject
  2 1     2.7 390
  sex          sat
```

When looking at a frequency distribution, there is a problem of not knowing what the scores represent when using categorical variables such as sex or major. GPA and SAT are self-explanatory. SPSS lets us have labels printed so we know what numerical code is associated with a subject's score. In this example, we will assign the following codes:

Variable	Values	Labels
Sex	0	Male
	1	Female
Major	1	Humanities
	2	Science
	3	Social Science

The cases of the data used before thus represent:

```
major        gpa
  2  1      3.6 410  ----> Case 1, Science major, Female
     sex         sat
```

Our setup will contain identifying labels for the major and sex through use of the **value labels** command. The general format is as follows:

```
value labels  x  score 'label for that score'
                 score 'label for that score'/
              y  score 'label for that score'
                 score 'label for that score' .
```

The example we will use will contain labels for sex and major and looks as follows:

```
value labels sex  0 'male'
                  1 'female' /
           major 1 'humanities'
                 2 'science'
                 3 'social science' .
```

The setup is as follows (the added labels are in **boldface** but recall that they are not typed in boldface):

LABELED SETUP

```
set width = 80 .                          2 1    3.0 470
data list list /  major sex gpa sat .     2 0    3.5 460
value labels sex 0 'male'                 2 1    3.7 800
                 1 'female' /             1 1    3.2 610
              major 1 'humanities'        2 1    3.5 490
                    2 'science'           2 0    3.4 470
                    3 'social science'  . 2 0    3.9 610
begin data .                              1 0    2.8 580
 2 1    3.6 410                           2 1    2.7 410
 2 1    2.7 390                           1 1    3.8 630
 2 1    3.5 510                           2 1    4.0 790
 3 1    2.9 430                           3 1    3.4 490
 2 1    3.1 600                           2 0    3.1 400
 3 1    3.5 610                           2 1    3.8 610
 1 0    3.2 610                           1 1    3.3 610
 2 1    3.6 560                           1 1    3.7 500
 3 1    3.8 700                           2 1    3.4 430
 2 0    3.8 460                           3 1    3.1 540
 2 0    3.6 590                           1 1    3.7 610
 3 0    3.1 500                           2 1    2.7 400
 1 1    3.1 410                           3 1    3.4 390
 2 1    3.5 470                           1 0    3.0 490
 2 1    3.4 210                          end data .
 2 0    3.4 610                          frequencies variables = major sex .
 2 0    3.8 510                          finish .
 3 0    3.7 600    ⇒      ⇒      ⇒
```

INTERPRETATIVE OUTPUT FOR LABELED SETUP.

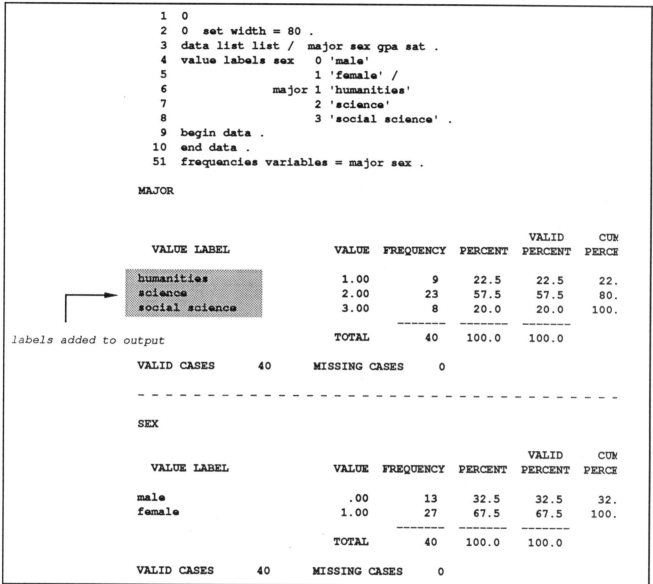

```
      1  0
      2  0   set width = 80 .
      3  data list list /   major sex gpa sat .
      4  value labels sex    0 'male'
      5                      1 'female' /
      6           major 1 'humanities'
      7                 2 'science'
      8                 3 'social science' .
      9  begin data .
     10  end data .
     51  frequencies variables = major sex .
```

MAJOR

VALUE LABEL	VALUE	FREQUENCY	PERCENT	VALID PERCENT	CUM PERCE
humanities	1.00	9	22.5	22.5	22.
science	2.00	23	57.5	57.5	80.
social science	3.00	8	20.0	20.0	100.
		-------	-------	-------	
	TOTAL	40	100.0	100.0	

labels added to output

VALID CASES   40   MISSING CASES   0

- -

SEX

VALUE LABEL	VALUE	FREQUENCY	PERCENT	VALID PERCENT	CUM PERCE
male	.00	13	32.5	32.5	32.
female	1.00	27	67.5	67.5	100.
		-------	-------	-------	
	TOTAL	40	100.0	100.0	

VALID CASES   40   MISSING CASES   0

Example 3 : Setup with Statistics

In this example we have the same four variables per subject. However we can request descriptive statistics by adding a **statistics** subcommand to the setup. The statistics available and their SPSS code are as follows:

STATISTIC	KEYWORD	STATISTIC	KEYWORD
mean	mean	kurtosis	kurtosis
median	median	standard error of kurtosis	seskurt
mode	mode	sum ($\sum X$)	sum
standard deviation	stddev	minimum score	minimum
variance	variance	maximum score	maximum
standard error of mean	semean	range	range
skewness	skewness	all (does all the above)	all
standard error of skewness	seskew		

Our example will request the mean, median and standard deviation of the GPA's.

STATISTICS SETUP

```
set width = 80 .
data list list /  major sex gpa sat .
value labels sex    0 'male'
                    1 'female' /
              major 1 'humanities'
                    2 'science'
                    3 'social science' .
begin data .
 2 1   3.6 410
     .
    etc.
     .
 1 0   3.0 490
end data .
frequencies variables = gpa  /
              statistics = mean median stddev .
finish .
```

INTERPRETATIVE OUTPUT FOR STATISTICS SETUP

GPA

Value Label	Value	Frequency	Percent	Valid Percent	Cum Percent
	2.70	3	7.5	7.5	7.5
	2.80	1	2.5	2.5	10.0
	2.90	1	2.5	2.5	12.5
	3.00	2	5.0	5.0	17.5
	3.10	5	12.5	12.5	30.0
	3.20	2	5.0	5.0	35.0
	3.30	1	2.5	2.5	37.5
	3.40	6	15.0	15.0	52.5
	3.50	5	12.5	12.5	65.0
	3.60	3	7.5	7.5	72.5
	3.70	4	10.0	10.0	82.5
	3.80	5	12.5	12.5	95.0
	3.90	1	2.5	2.5	97.5
	4.00	1	2.5	2.5	100.0
		-------	-------	-------	
	Total	40	100.0	100.0	

Mean	3.385	Median	3.400	Std dev	.353

MISSING VALUES USAGE

1. **Data** are frequently **left out** when individuals make a mistake, refuse to answer, do not know the answer to a question or for other reasons.

2. Such data are called **missing values.**

3. These data are **not** usually **included** in analyses. For example, if estimating the percentage of women versus men in a group or the average (or mean) score for a group, you would want to exclude these cases. However, you would also want to see how many values were missing to see if you have a major problem with the study.

4. SPSS lets you assign **three values** as missing through use of a **missing values** command. It looks as follows:

missing values x (value1, value2, value3)
            y (value1, value2, value3) .

Real examples would be as follows:

missing values sex (3,4) .
or
missing values sex (3,4)
gpa (998, 999) .

In the two examples that follow, see how the missing values affect the frequency distributions and the calculation of statistics. The values of the statistics are based only on the nonmissing cases; check the difference. Note that each SPSS program has various options for utilizing missing values and should be checked individually.

SETUP WITH MISSING VALUES FOR SEX

```
set width = 80 .
data list list / major sex gpa sat .
missing values sex (3,4) .
value labels sex      0 'male'
                      1 'female'
                      3 'missing'
                      4 'not sure' /
         major 1 'humanities'
               2 'science'
               3 'social science' .
begin data .
 2 1   3.6 410
 2 1   2.7 390
 2 1   3.5 510
 3 1   2.9 430
 2 1   3.1 600
 3 1   3.5 610
 1 0   3.2 610
 2 1   3.6 560
 3 1   3.8 700
 2 0   3.8 460
 2 0   3.6 590
 3 0   3.1 500
 1 1   3.1 410
 2 1   3.5 470
 2 1   3.4 210
 2 0   3.4 610
 2 0   3.8 510
 3 0   3.7 600
 2 1   3.0 470
 2 0   3.5 460
 2 1   3.7 800
 1 1   3.2 610
 2 1   3.5 490
 2 0   3.4 470
 2 0   3.9 610
 1 0   2.8 580
 2 1   2.7 410
 1 1   3.8 630
 2 1   4.0 790
 3 1   3.4 490
 2 0   3.1 400
 2 1   3.8 610
 1 1   3.3 610
 1 1   3.7 500
 2 1   3.4 430
 3 1   3.1 540
 1 1   3.7 610
 2 1   2.7 400
 3 3   3.4 390 missing data for sex
 1 4   3.0 490 missing data for sex
end data .
frequencies variables = sex .
finish .
```

INTERPRETATIVE OUTPUT FOR MISSING VALUES
SETUP FOR SEX

```
  1     0
  2     0   set width=80 .
  3     data list list /  major sex gpa sat .
  4     missing values   sex (3,4) .
  5     value labels    sex        0 'male'
  6                                 1 'female'
  7                                 3 'missing'
  8                                 4 'not sure' /
  9                major        1 'humanities'
 10                             2 'science'
 11                             3 'social science' .
 12     begin data.
 42     end data .
 43     frequencies variables =  sex   .
```

SEX

VALUE LABEL	VALUE	FREQUENCY	PERCENT	VALID* PERCENT	CUM† PERCENT
male	.00	12	30.0	31.6	31.6
female	1.00	26	65.0	68.4	100.0
missing	3.00	1	2.5	MISSING	
not sure	4.00	1	2.5	MISSING	
	TOTAL	40	100.0	100.0	

VALID CASES   38   MISSING CASES   2

---

* Percent based on those who correctly answered the question.

† Percentile ranks based on those who correctly answered the question.

Missing Values and Statistics Setup

```
set width = 80 .
data list list /  major sex gpa sat .
missing values sex (3,4) gpa (998, 999) .
value labels sex           0 'male'
                           1 'female'
                           3 'missing'
                           4 'not sure' /
              major        1 'humanities'
                           2 'science'
                           3 'social science' /
              gpa          998 'dnt know'
                           999 'no ans' .
begin data.
 2 1   998 410 -----------> missing data for gpa
 2 1   999 390 -----------> missing data for gpa
 2 1   999 510 -----------> missing data for gpa
 3 1   2.9 430
 2 1   3.1 600
 3 1   3.5 610
 1 0   3.2 610
 2 1   3.6 560
 3 1   3.8 700
 2 0   3.8 460
 2 0   3.6 590
 3 0   3.1 500
 1 1   3.1 410
 2 1   3.5 470
 2 1   3.4 210
 2 0   3.4 610
 2 0   3.8 510
 3 0   3.7 600
 2 1   3.0 470
 2 0   3.5 460
 2 1   3.7 800
 1 1   3.2 610
 2 1   3.5 490
 2 0   3.4 470
 2 0   3.9 610
 1 0   2.8 580
 2 1   2.7 410
 1 1   3.8 630
 2 1   4.0 790
 3 1   3.4 490
 2 0   3.1 400
 2 1   3.8 610
 1 1   3.3 610
 1 1   3.7 500
 2 1   3.4 430
 3 1   3.1 540
 1 1   3.7 610
 2 1   2.7 400
 3 3   3.4 390
 1 4   3.0 490
end data .
frequencies variables = gpa /
          statistics = mean median stddev .
finish .
```

INTERPRETATIVE OUTPUT FOR MISSING VALUES AND STATISTICS SETUP

```
 1  0
 2  0   set width=80
 3  data list list /  major sex gpa sat
 4  missing values sex (3,4) gpa (998, 999)
 5  value labels sex        0 'male'
 6                          1 'female'
 7                          3 'missing'
 8                          4 'not sure' /
 9            major         1 'humanities'
10                          2 'science'
11                          3 'social science' /
12          gpa          998 'dnt know'
13                       999 'no ans' .
14  begin data .
15  end data .
46  frequencies variables = gpa /
               statistics = mean median stddev .
```

GPA

VALUE LABEL	VALUE	FREQUENCY	PERCENT	VALID PERCENT	CUM PERCENT
	2.70	2	5.0	5.4	5.4
	2.80	1	2.5	2.7	8.1
	2.90	1	2.5	2.7	10.8
	3.00	2	5.0	5.4	16.2
	3.10	5	2.5	13.5	29.7
	3.20	2	5.0	5.4	35.1
	3.30	1	2.5	2.7	37.8
	3.40	6	5.0	16.2	54.1
	3.50	4	0.0	10.8	64.9
	3.60	2	5.0	5.4	70.3
	3.70	4	0.0	10.8	81.1
	3.80	5	2.5	13.5	94.6
	3.90	1	2.5	2.7	97.3
	4.00	1	2.5	2.7	100.0
dnt know	998.00	1	2.5	MISSING	
no ans	999.00	2	5.0	MISSING	
	TOTAL	40	100.0	100.0	

MEAN   3.395   MEDIAN   3.400   STD DEV   .347 [*]

VALID CASES   <u>37</u>   MISSING CASES   3

_____

[*] Note that the statistics are based on only the <u>37</u> cases that do not have missing data.

BARCHARTS

SPSS can draw simple barcharts of the data. In reality, there are many more sophisticated graphing packages available on other systems. However, the setup is as follows (note there are several options for format described in the manual):

BARCHART SETUP

```
set width = 80 .
data list list / major sex gpa sat .
value labels sex   0 'male'
                   1 'female' /
            major 1 'humanities'
                  2 'science'
                  3 'social science'.
begin data .
 2 1   3.6 410
 2 1   2.7 390
 2 1   3.5 510
 3 1   2.9 430
 2 1   3.1 600
 3 1   3.5 610
 1 0   3.2 610
 2 1   3.6 560
 3 1   3.8 700
 2 0   3.8 460
 2 0   3.6 590
 3 0   3.1 500
 1 1   3.1 410
 2 1   3.5 470
 2 1   3.4 210
 2 0   3.4 610
 2 0   3.8 510
 3 0   3.7 600
 2 1   3.0 470
 2 0   3.5 460
 2 1   3.7 800
 1 1   3.2 610
 2 1   3.5 490
 2 0   3.4 470
 2 0   3.9 610
 1 0   2.8 580
 2 1   2.7 410
 1 1   3.8 630
 2 1   4.0 790
 3 1   3.4 490
 2 0   3.1 400
 2 1   3.8 610
 1 1   3.3 610
 1 1   3.7 500
 2 1   3.4 430
 3 1   3.1 540
 1 1   3.7 610
 2 1   2.7 400
 3 1   3.4 390
 1 0   3.0 490
end data .
frequencies variables = gpa / barchart /
    statistics = mean median stddev .
finish .
```

INTERPRETATIVE OUTPUT

```
frequencies variables = gpa  / barchart /
       statistics = mean median stddev .

GPA                                              VALID    CUM
  VALUE LABEL      VALUE  FREQUENCY  PERCENT  PERCENT  PERCENT
                   2.70       3       7.5      7.5      7.5
                                            etc.
                   3.80       5      12.5     12.5     95.0
                   3.90       1       2.5      2.5     97.5
                   4.00       1       2.5      2.5    100.0
                          -------  -------  -------
                  TOTAL      40     100.0    100.0

                    ---------------+
       2.70 I               3 I
                    ---------------+
                    I
                    -----+
       2.80 I  1 I
                    -----+
                    I
                    -----+
       2.90 I  1 I
                    -----+
                    I
                    ---------+
       3.00 I        2 I
                    ---------+
                    I
                    --------------------+
       3.10 I                     5 I
                    --------------------+
                    I
                    ---------+
       3.20 I        2 I
                    ---------+
                    I
                    -----+
       3.30 I  1 I
                    -----+
                    I
                    ------------------------+
       3.40 I                         6 I
                    ------------------------+
                    I
                    --------------------+
       3.50 I                     5 I
                    --------------------+
                    I
                    ---------------+
       3.60 I               3 I
                    ---------------+
                    I
                    --------------------+
       3.70 I                   4 I
                    --------------------+
                    I
                    --------------------+
       3.80 I                     5 I
                    --------------------+
                    I
                    -----+
       3.90 I  1 I
                    -----+
                    I
                    -----+
       4.00 I  1 I
                    -----+
                    I

       I........I........I........I........I........I
       0        2        4        6        8
                              FREQUENCY
      MEAN    3.385    MEDIAN    3.400    STD DEV   .353
```

HISTOGRAMS

SPSS can draw simple histograms of the data. In reality, there are many more sophisticated graphing packages available on other systems. However, the setup is as follows (note there are several options for format described in the manual):

SETUP

```
set width = 80 .
data list list /  major sex gpa sat .
value labels sex    0 'male'
                    1 'female' /
            major 1 'humanities'
                    2 'science'
                    3 'social science' .
begin data .
 2 1   3.6 410
 2 1   2.7 390
     etc.
 3 1   3.4 390
 1 0   3.0 490
end data .
frequencies variables =  sat /
            histogram /
            statistics = mean median stddev.
finish .
```

INTERPRETATIVE OUTPUT FOR HISTOGRAM SETUP

```
...etc.
frequencies variables =  sat / histogram/
            statistics = mean median stddev .
```

SAT

VALUE LABEL	VALUE	FREQUENCY	PERCENT	VALID PERCENT	CUM PERCENT
	210.00	1	2.5	2.5	2.5
	390.00	2	5.0	5.0	7.5
	etc.				
	790.00	1	2.5	2.5	97.5
	800.00	1	2.5	2.5	100.0
		-------	-------	-------	
	TOTAL	40	100.0	100.0	

SAT

```
    COUNT  MIDPOINT   ONE SYMBOL EQUALS APPROXIMATELY   .20 OCCURRENCES
      1      215    *****
      0      244
...etc.
      4      389    ********************
      5      418    ************************
      2      447    **********
      6      476    ****************************
      4      505    *******************
      1      534    *****
      1      563    *****
      4      592    *******************
      9      621    **************************************************
      1      708    *****
      2      795    **********
             I....+....I....+....I....+....I....+....I....+....I....+....I
             0        2        4        6        8       10
                          HISTOGRAM FREQUENCY
MEAN        524.250    MEDIAN      505.000    STD DEV      114.665
```

S P S S / P C + ™ 4.0 O U T P U T

It is sometimes the case that the output looks slightly different on personal systems.
SPSS/PC+™ 4.0 histogram and barchart examples are presented below. They are a touch prettier.

H I S T O G R A M

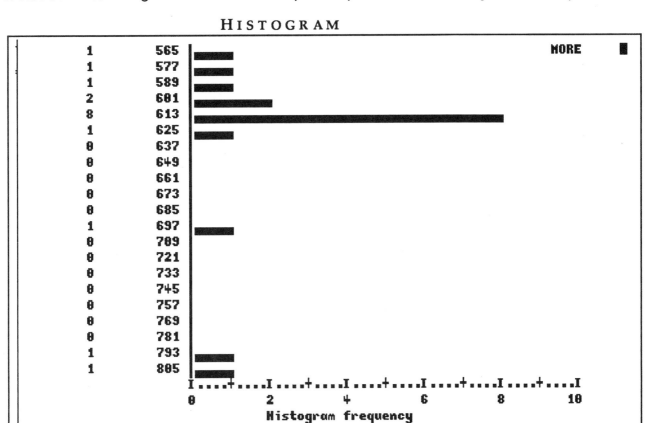

B A R C H A R T

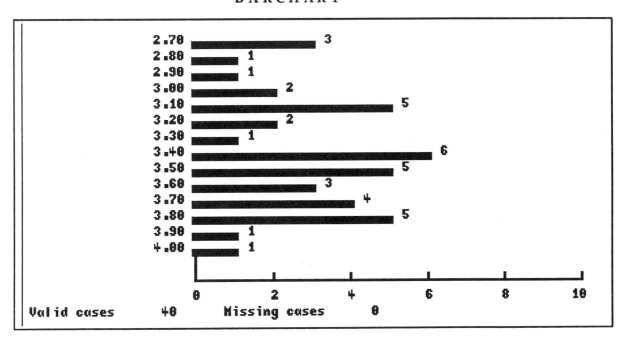

'HISTOGRAMS = NORMAL' AND DONE WITH SPSS®
FOR THE MACINTOSH®

Once FREQUENCIES calculates the mean and standard deviation of a data set, it can print a histogram that superimposes the normal curve over the data. Thus if the data set is somehow not normal, this will be immediately apparent. We present an output from the Macintosh version of SPSS. However, **all** versions can produce this output using the same FREQUENCIES command. We will use our initial setup and present the output from SPSS® FOR THE MACINTOSH® for the variable **sat**. The dots over the histogram represent the interpolate normal curve. The addition is 'histogram = **normal**'.

SETUP

```
set width = 80 .
data list list / major sex gpa sat .
begin data .
 2 1   3.6 410

etc.

 1 0   3.0 490
end data .
frequencies variables = sat /
            histogram = normal /
            statistics = all .
finish .
```

OUTPUT

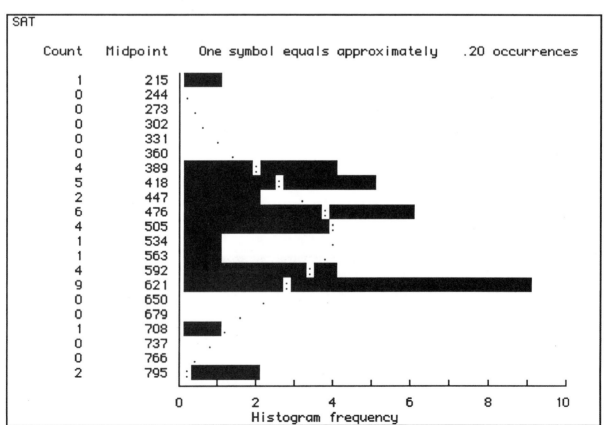

CHAPTER 4: DESCRIPTIVE STATISTICS

CALCULATION OF VARIOUS DESCRIPTIVE STATISTICS

SUMMARY OF SPSS SETUP[1]:

```
set width = 80 .
data list list/ x y .
begin data .
      .
    data
      .
      .
end data .
descriptives x y / statistics = ? . *
finish .
```

*   Note that the italics command is optional-see Example 2 below.

REAL WORLD EXAMPLE

```
set width = 80 .
data list list / dep choc .
variable labels dep 'Depression score'/ choc
    'Amount of Chocolate eaten per week' .
begin data .
4  4
6  7
6  5
8  8
8  7
8  9
9  11
9  10
7  5
7  6
9  9
10 9
11 13
end data .
descriptives dep choc .
finish .
```

Produces Mean, Standard Deviation, Minimum and Maximum Scores of the Variables:
dep (depression score) and *choc* (amount of chocolate eaten) for 13 subjects (one per line of data).

---

[1] **SPSS/PC+**™ **4.0 uses a different command structure; please check the next page.**

SUMMARY OF SPSS/PC + ™ 4.0 SETUP

```
set width = 80 .
data list free/ x y .
begin data .

    data

end data .
descriptives x y / statistics = #, # . *
finish .
```

---

*   Note that the italics command is optional-see Example 2 below.

REAL WORLD EXAMPLE

```
set  width = 80 .
data list free / dep choc .
variable labels dep 'Depression score'/ Choc
    'Amount of Chocolate eaten per week' .
begin data .
1 1
2 2
2 0
2 3
4 5
3 4
4 4
6 7
6 5
8 8
8 7
8 9
9 11
9 10
7 5
7 6
9 9  [Produces :  Mean,  Standard Deviation,  Minimum  &  Maximum]
10 9                       ↓
11 13                      ↓
end data .                 ↓
descriptives choc dep / statistics = 1 , 5, 10, 11 .
finish .
```

PURPOSE OF THE PROCEDURE

Get descriptive statistics for the scores such as the mean, standard deviation, and standard error of the group.

HOW TO DO DESCRIPTIVES

Example One : The basic setup using default statistics

In our example, we have:

1. Two scores per subject. They are:

      a. **dep** - which is an individual's score on a test of depression.

      b. **choc**- which is an individual's report of the amount of chocolate per week.

      Thus our data look as follows:

```
1  1  ---------------      Bob's Depression Score & Chocolate score
2  2  ---------------      Sue's Depression Score & Chocolate score
2  0  ---------------                 etc.
2  3  ---------------                  "
4  5  ---------------                  "
3  4  ---------------                  "
4  4  ---------------                  "
6  7  ---------------                  "
6  5  ---------------                  "
8  8  ---------------                  "
8  7  ---------------                  "
8  9  ---------------                  "
9  11 ---------------                  "
9  10 ---------------                  "
7  5  ---------------                  "
7  6  ---------------                  "
9  9  ---------------                  "
10 9  ---------------                  "
11 13 ---------------                  "
```

2. The setup will contain variables labels to help us identify **dep** and **choc.**

3. The setup will calculate the **mean, standard deviation, minimum** and **maximum** scores.

The setup is as follows:

SETUP

```
set width = 80 .
data list list / dep choc .
variable labels dep 'Depression score'/ choc
    'Amount of Chocolate eaten per week' .
begin data .
1 1
2 2
2 0
2 3
4 5
3 4
4 4
6 7
6 5
8 8
8 7
8 9
9 11
9 10
7 5
7 6
9 9
10 9
11 13
end data .
descriptives dep choc .
finish .
```

SIGNIFICANT PORTIONS OF THE OUTPUT

```
    1  0  set  width = 80 .
    2  data list list / dep choc .
    3  variable labels dep 'Depression score'/ Choc
    4      'Amount of Chocolate eaten per week' .
    5  begin data .
   24  end data .
   25  descriptives choc dep .

Number of valid observations (listwise) =        19.00
```

| | | | | | Valid | |
Variable	Mean	Std Dev	Minimum	Maximum	N	Label
CHOC	6.21	3.49	.00	13.00	19	Amount of Chocolate e
DEP	6.11	3.09	1.00	11.00	19	Depression score

Example Two : Requesting Statistics

Descriptives can also produce a set of statistics which you select. A keyword(s) is(are) added to the setup. The list of key words and their keywords for most versions of SPSS is as follows. Also presented are the numerical codes for SPSS/PC+™ 4.0.

STATISTIC	KEYWORD	SPSS/PC+™ 4.0 No.
mean	mean	1
standard deviation	stddev	5
variance	variance	6
standard error of the mean	semean	2
skewness	skewness	8
kurtosis	kurtosis	7
sum (ΣX)	sum	12
minimum score	min	10
maximum score	max	11
range	range	9
all the above	all	all

The setup which calculates the mean, standard deviation, variance, and range is as follows (note the **boldface** is used to show you the **keywords and output**-you don't have to type it in boldface to the computer nor is the output really in boldface):

SETUP

```
set width = 80 .
data list list / dep choc .
variable labels dep 'Depression score'/ Choc
    'Amount of Chocolate eaten per week' .
begin data .
1 1
2 2
2 0
2 3
4 5
3 4
4 4
6 7
6 5
8 8
8 7
8 9
9 11
9 10
7 5
7 6
9 9
10 9
11 13
end data .
descriptives choc dep / statistics = mean stddev variance range .*
finish .
```

```
*  SPSS/PC+™4.0 -    1: data list free / dep choc .
                     2: descriptives choc dep / statistics = 1, 5, 6 , 9 .
```

SIGNIFICANT PORTIONS OF THE OUTPUT

```
   1  0  set  width = 80 .
   2  data list list / dep choc .
   3  variable labels dep 'Depression score'/ Choc
   4     'Amount of Chocolate eaten per week' .
   5  begin data .
  24  end data .
  25  descriptives choc dep / statistics = mean stddev variance range .

Number of valid observations (listwise) =        19.00
```

Variable	Mean	Std Dev	Variance	Range	Valid N	Label
CHOC	6.21	3.49	12.18	13.00	19	Amount of Chocolate
DEP	6.11	3.09	9.54	10.00	19	Depression score

CHAPTER 5: Z-SCORES

USING DESCRIPTIVES TO CALCULATE Z-SCORES, PRINTING & SAVING THEM

SUMMARY OF SPSS SETUP[1]

```
set width = 80 .
data list list/ x y .
begin data .
     data
end data .
descriptives x y / save .
list variables = zx zy .
   or other commands which use the z-scores *
finish
```

* Note that the commands in italics are optional-see Example 2 below.

REAL WORLD EXAMPLE

```
set width = 80 .
data list list / dep choc .
variable labels dep 'Depression score' /
        choc   'Amount of Chocolate eaten per week' .
begin data .
1 1
2 2
2 0
2 3
4 5
3 4
4 4
6 7
6 5
8 8
8 7
8 9
9 11
9 10
7 5
7 6
9 9
10 9
11 13
end data .
descriptives dep choc / save .
list variables = zchoc zdep .
finish
```

Produces Z-scores, Mean, Standard Deviation, Minimum and Maximum Scores of the Variables: *dep* (depression score) and *choc* (amount of chocolate eaten) for 19 subjects (one per line of data).

---

[1] **SPSS/PC+™ 4.0 uses a different command structure, please check the next page.**

SUMMARY OF SPSS/PC + ™ 4.0 SETUP

```
set width = 80 .
data list free /  x y .
begin data .
    ·
    data
    ·
    ·                          Produces z-scores
end data .                          ↓
descriptives x y / options = 3 /statistics = #, #  *.
finish .
```

---

* *Statistics* **commands is optional.**

REAL WORLD EXAMPLE

```
set  width = 80 .
data list free / dep choc .
variable labels dep 'Depression score'/ Choc
    'Amount of Chocolate eaten per week' .
begin data .
1  1
2  2
2  0
2  3
4  5
3  4
4  4
6  7
6  5
8  7
8  9
9  11
9  10
7  5
7  6
9  9                         Produces   z-scores
10 9                              ↓
11 13                             ↓
end data .                        ↓
descriptives choc dep / options = 3 / statistics = 1 , 5, 10, 11 .
finish .
```

PURPOSE OF THE PROCEDURE

1. Get descriptive statistics for the scores such as the mean, standard deviation, standard error, etc. of the group.
2. Have the z-scores for the variables calculated.

Z-scores are defined as:

$$Z = \frac{X - \overline{X}}{s_X}$$

HOW TO GET Z-SCORES AND THE BASIC COMMAND

Example One : The basic setup using default statistics

In our example, we have:

1. Two scores per subject. They are:

    a. **dep** - which is an individual's score on a test of depression.
    b. **choc**- which is an individual's report of the amount of chocolate per week.

Thus our data look as follows:

```
1     1  --------------- Bob's Depression Score and Chocolate score
2     2  --------------- Sue's Depression Score and Chocolate score
2     0  ---------------            etc.
2     3  ---------------             "
4     5  ---------------             "
3     4  ---------------             "
4     4  ---------------             "
6     7  ---------------             "
6     5  ---------------             "
8     8  ---------------             "
8     7  ---------------             "
8     9  ---------------             "
9    11  ---------------             "
9    10  ---------------             "
7     5  ---------------             "
7     6  ---------------             "
9     9  ---------------             "
10    9  ---------------             "
11   13  ---------------             "
```

2. The setup will contain variable labels to help us identify **dep** and **choc**. These variable labels are optional. They could be omitted from the setup and not alter the results

3. The setup will calculate the **mean, standard deviation, minimum** and **maximum** scores.

4. The setup will calculate and print the **z-scores** for dep and choc by use of the **save** command and the **list** commands.

5. The z-scores are saved as new variables named **zdep** and **zchoc**. These variables are assigned variable labels by adding the variable name for the original variable to **ZSCORE:**. Note that it truncates long ones. Thus, the variable names would be:

Variable Name	Variable Label
ZDEP	ZSCORE: Depression score
ZCHOC	ZSCORE: Amount of Chocolate eaten per w

The setup is as follows (note the **boldface** is used to show you the **keyword** for calculating z-scores and where they appear in the output. You don't have to type it in boldface to the computer, nor is the output really in boldface):

SETUP

```
set width = 80 .
data list list / dep choc .   [data list free / etc. for SPSS/PC + ™ 4.0]
variable labels dep 'Depression score'/
                choc    'Amount of Chocolate eaten per week' .
begin data .
1 1
2 2
2 0
2 3
4 5
3 4
4 4
6 7
6 5
8 8
8 7
8 9
9 11
9 10
7 5
7 6
9 9
10 9
11 13
end data .
descriptives   dep choc /save .  [descriptives dep choc / options = 3 . for SPSS/PC]
list variables = zchoc zdep .
finish .
```

SIGNIFICANT PORTIONS OF THE OUTPUT

```
   1  0  set width = 80 .
   2  data list list / dep choc .
   3  variable labels dep 'Depression score'/
   4                 choc    'Amount of Chocolate eaten per week' .
   5  begin data .
  24  end data .
  25  descriptives variables = dep choc /save .

Number of valid observations (listwise) =        19.00


                                              Valid
Variable   Mean Std Dev  Minimum  Maximum     N   Label

DEP        6.11   3.09     1.00    11.00       19  Depression score
CHOC       6.21   3.49      .00    13.00       19  Amount of Chocolate e

The following Z-Score variables have been saved on your active file:


From       To                                       Weighted
Variable   Z-Score  Label                           Valid N
--------   -------   -----                           -------


DEP        ZDEP      Zscore: Depression score               19
CHOC       ZCHOC     Zscore: Amount of Chocolate eaten per w  19


  26  list variables = zchoc zdep .

      ZCHOC          ZDEP

   -1.49327      -1.65256
   -1.20669      -1.32886
   -1.77986      -1.32886
    -.92010      -1.32886
    -.34692       -.68147
    -.63351      -1.00516
    -.63351       -.68147
     .22625       -.03407
    -.34692       -.03407
     .51284        .61332
     .22625        .61332
     .79943        .61332
    1.37260        .93702
    1.08602        .93702
    -.34692        .28962
    -.06033        .28962
     .79943        .93702
     .79943       1.26071
    1.94578       1.58441
```

OTHER IMPORTANT POINTS ABOUT Z-SCORES

1. The z-scores can be used in other SPSS procedure once they have been created. For example, if you wanted a Frequency distribution of z-scores, you would add a Frequencies command. See the following setup:

```
set width = 80 .
data list list / dep choc .
variable labels dep 'Depression score'/
                choc     'Amount of Chocolate eaten per week' .
begin data .
1 1
2 2
  etc.
10 9
11 13
end data .
descriptives variables = dep choc /save .
list variables = zchoc zdep .
frequencies variables = zchoc zdep .
finish
```

2. The z-scores and other variables can be output to an external file on your system (you need to know how your system works in order to select a filename). For example, if you want to output the z-scores and original scores to an external file (noted as filename), you could use the **file handle, print,** and **execute** commands. See the following setup:

```
set width=80 .
file handle*  .
data list list / dep choc .
variable labels dep 'Depression score'/
                choc     'Amount of Chocolate eaten per week' .
begin data .
1 1
2 2
2 0
    etc.
10 9
11 13
end data .
descriptives variables = dep choc /save .
print  outfile = filename / dep choc zdep zchoc .
execute  .
finish .
```

---

*   The file handle command is specific to the computer that you are using. We hate to be vague but you need to check with your computer center on the specifics for this command or check in the Operations Guide for your system (Macintosh, Unix, OS/2, VAX/VMS, IBM/CMS or MVS™).

Unfortunately, the 'print' command is not available to SPSS/PC+™ 4.0 users. If you want to save the list of z-scores, use the 'list' command and they would be available in your listing and could edited out.

Z-SCORES AND OTHER STATISTICS

In Chapter 4, we presented **DESCRIPTIVES** setups that calculate statistics other than the default ones by use of the **statistics** subcommand. The specifications for different statistics are found in Chapter 4 . This can be done in conjunction with the request for z-scores for both SPSS and SPSS/PC + ™ 4.0 as follows:

SPSS

```
set width = 80 .
data list list / dep choc .
variable labels dep 'Depression score'/
               choc     'Amount of Chocolate eaten per week' .
begin data .
1 1
etc.
10 9
11 13
end data .
descriptives  dep choc / statistics = ?, ? / save .
finish .
```

SPSS/PC + ™ 4.0

```
set width = 80 .
data list free / dep choc .
variable labels dep 'Depression score'/
               choc     'Amount of Chocolate eaten per week' .
begin data .
1 1
etc.
10 9
11 13
end data .
descriptives  dep choc / options = 2 / statistics = #, # .
finish .
```

CHAPTER 6 - BOXPLOTS & STEMLEAF DIAGRAMS [1]

PRODUCTION OF BOXPLOTS & STEM AND LEAF DIAGRAMS

SUMMARY OF BOXPLOT & STEMLEAF SETUP (1 VARIABLE PER PLOT)

```
set width = 80 .
data list list / x y.
begin data
      .
        .
      data
      .

end data .
examine x y.
finish .
```

SUMMARY OF BOXPLOT & STEMLEAF SETUP (1 VARIABLE BROKEN DOWN BY OTHER VARIABLES)

```
set width = 80 .
data list list / x y z.
begin data .
        .
      data
        .
end data .
examine x by y by z .
finish .
```

REAL WORLD EXAMPLE

```
set width = 80 .
data list list /  major sex gpa sat .
begin data .
 2 1   3.6 410
 2 1   2.7 390
 2 1   3.5 510
 3 1   2.9 430
 2 1   3.1 600
 3 1   3.5 610
 1 0   3.2 610
 2 1   3.6 560
 3 1   3.8 700
 2 0   3.8 460
 2 0   3.6 590
 3 0   3.1 500
end data .
examine gpa by major by sex .
finish .
```

Produces Boxplots, Stem and Leaf Diagrams and Descriptive Statistics for the Variable 'GPA ' broken down by 'Major' and by 'Sex'

---

1. Use ' data list **free** / x y z ' for SPSS/PC + ™ 4.0.
   Boxplots & Stemleaf diagrams can also be produced by MANOVA.
   See last page of chapter.

BOXPLOTS & STEM AND LEAF DIAGRAMS

SPSS can construct boxplots and stem and leaf diagrams through use of the EXAMINE program. The former are also called box and whiskers plots. These plots and statistics can be provided for one variable and for the variable as it is broken down into subgroups based on other variables. Boxplots and stem and leaf diagrams are relatively new ways of plotting frequency distributions. It is possible to see central tendency, indications of distribution shape (non-normality) and variability in these plots. The program can also identify extreme and outlier values.

I.   EXAMPLE 1 - ONE VARIABLE PER PLOT

In the following example, we are using the data set from Chapter 3. First, we will request an EXAMINE run for the variable **gpa**.

The command itself is simply:

examine 'variable' , 'variable' .

or in our case as we only want a plot of **gpa**:

examine gpa .

SETUP
set width = 80 .
data list list / major sex gpa sat[1].
begin data .
2 1   3.6 410
2 1   2.7 390
2 1   3.5 510
3 1   2.9 430
2 1   3.1 600
3 1   3.5 610
1 0   3.2 610
2 1   3.6 560
3 1   3.8 700
2 0   3.8 460
2 0   3.6 590
3 0   3.1 500
1 1   3.1 410
2 1   3.5 470
2 1   3.4 210
2 0   3.4 610
2 0   3.8 510
3 0   3.7 600
2 1   3.0 470
2 0   3.5 460
2 1   3.7 800
1 1   3.2 610

↓
2 1   3.5 490
2 0   3.4 470
2 0   3.9 610
1 0   2.8 580
2 1   2.7 410
1 1   3.8 630
2 1   4.0 790
3 1   3.4 490
2 0   3.1 400
2 1   3.8 610
1 1   3.3 610
1 1   3.7 500
2 1   3.4 430
3 1   3.1 540
1 1   3.7 610
2 1   2.7 400
3 1   3.4 390
1 0   3.0 490
end data .
examine   gpa.
finish .

[1] Use 'data list **free** / etc. for SPSS/PC + ™ 4.0.

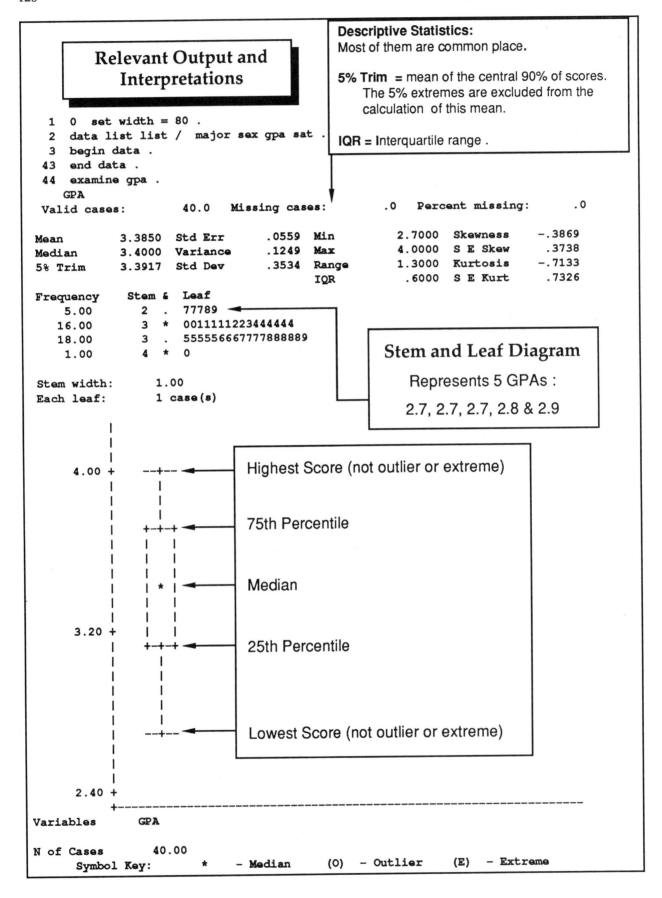

Relevant Output and Interpretations

Descriptive Statistics:
Most of them are common place.

5% Trim = mean of the central 90% of scores. The 5% extremes are excluded from the calculation of this mean.

IQR = Interquartile range .

```
 1   0  set width = 80 .
 2   data list list /  major sex gpa sat .
 3   begin data .
43   end data .
44   examine gpa .
     GPA
Valid cases:        40.0   Missing cases:        .0   Percent missing:        .0
```

Mean	3.3850	Std Err	.0559	Min	2.7000	Skewness	−.3869
Median	3.4000	Variance	.1249	Max	4.0000	S E Skew	.3738
5% Trim	3.3917	Std Dev	.3534	Range	1.3000	Kurtosis	−.7133
				IQR	.6000	S E Kurt	.7326

```
Frequency    Stem &  Leaf
    5.00      2  .  77789
   16.00      3  *  0011111223444444
   18.00      3  .  555556667777888889
    1.00      4  *  0

Stem width:      1.00
Each leaf:       1 case(s)
```

Stem and Leaf Diagram

Represents 5 GPAs :

2.7, 2.7, 2.7, 2.8 & 2.9

```
          |
          |
          |
  4.00  + --+--  ←    Highest Score (not outlier or extreme)
          |   |
          |   |
          |   |
          | +-+-+  ←    75th Percentile
          | | |
          | | |
          | | |
          | | |
          | * |  ←    Median
          | | |
          | | |
  3.20  + | | |
          | +-+-+  ←    25th Percentile
          |   |
          |   |
          |   |
          |   |
          |   |
          | --+--  ←    Lowest Score (not outlier or extreme)
          |
          |
          |
  2.40  +
        +----------------------------------------------------
Variables      GPA

N of Cases      40.00
    Symbol Key:       *   - Median      (O)  - Outlier    (E)  - Extreme
```

1. Each box contains 50 percent of the scores.

2. The upper and lower boundaries of the box mark the 25th and 75th percentiles.

3. The asterisk (*) is the median.

4. The extended lines indicate the highest and lowest scores that are not outliers.

5. Outliers are defined as > 1.5 boxlengths and < 3 boxlengths from the edge of the box and noted with an (O) and a Case number.

6. Extremes are defined as more than 3 box-lengths from the edge of the box and noted with an (E) and a Case number.

II. EXAMPLE 2: OUTLIERS AND EXTREMES (Also an SPSS/PC +™ 4.0 Output)

One major use of the EXAMINE program is to detect extreme scores. Many procedures (e.g., anovas, multiple regression, manova, etc.) can be distorted by scores that are far outside the rest of the distribution. EXAMINE can point out these in its output as we mentioned above. In the next setup, we will look at the SAT scores. We have altered some of the SAT scores so that they will show up as outliers and extremes (see the ones in boldface type). We have also run this setup on SPSS/PC + ™ 4.0. The setups are identical (except for the ubiquitous 'data list free / etc.'. However, the graphics for the PC are nicer.

SETUP WITH OUTLIERS & EXTREMES
(see boldfaced SAT scores)

```
set width = 80 .
data list free / major sex gpa sat ¹
begin data .
  2 1    3.6 800     (#  1)
  2 1    2.7 590
  2 1    3.5 550
  3 1    2.9 530
  2 1    3.1 600
  3 1    3.5 610
  1 0    3.2 610
  2 1    3.6 560
  3 1    3.8 700
  2 0    3.8 560
  2 0    3.6 590
  3 0    3.1 500
  1 1    3.1 510
  2 1    3.5 570
  2 1    3.4 510
  2 0    3.4 610
  2 0    3.8 550
  3 0    3.7 600
  2 1    3.0 470
  2 0    3.5 560
  2 1    3.7 800     (# 21)
                ➡
```

```
  1 1    3.2 610
  2 1    3.5 590
  2 0    3.4 570
  2 0    3.9 610
  1 0    2.8 580
  2 1    2.7 510
  1 1    3.8 630
  2 1    4.0 790     (#  29)
  3 1    3.4 590
  2 0    3.1 500
  2 1    3.8 610
  1 1    3.3 610
  1 1    3.7 500
  2 1    3.4 430
  3 1    3.1 540
  1 1    3.7 610
  2 1    2.7 500
  3 1    3.4 590
  1 0    3.0 200     (# 40)
end data .
examine sat
finish .
───────────────
¹ Use 'data list list / etc. ' for
    SPSS.
```

OUTPUT WITH OUTLIERS & EXTREMES MARKED
(see 'Extremes' ; Cases 1, 21, 29, 40 as Marked Below)

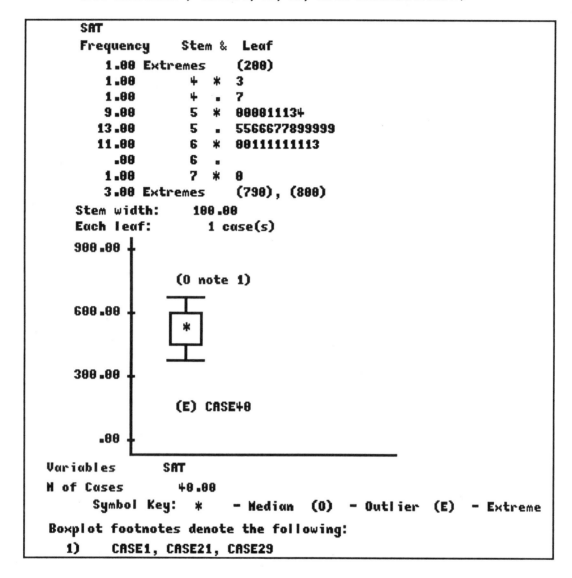

```
SAT
Frequency    Stem &  Leaf
    1.00 Extremes    (200)
    1.00      4  *  3
    1.00      4  .  7
    9.00      5  *  000011134
   13.00      5  .  5566677899999
   11.00      6  *  00111111113
    .00       6  .
    1.00      7  *  0
    3.00 Extremes    (790), (800)
Stem width:    100.00
Each leaf:      1 case(s)
```

```
900.00 |

               (0 note 1)

600.00 |          ┌───┐
                  │ * │
                  └───┘
300.00 |

               (E) CASE40

  .00  |
       └──────────────────────────
Variables        SAT
N of Cases       40.00
       Symbol Key:  *   - Median  (0) - Outlier  (E) - Extreme
Boxplot footnotes denote the following:
   1)    CASE1, CASE21, CASE29
```

III. EXAMPLE 3: MORE THAN ONE VARIABLE

SPSS can construct boxplots and stem and leaf diagrams for one variable as this variable is broken down into subgroups based on other variables. The command structure is quite easy as seen below:

examine Variable$_1$ by Variable$_2$ by Variable$_3$ ... .

In our example we will use GPA broken down by MAJOR and SEX as follows:

examine gpa by major by sex .

We will get descriptive statistics for GPA alone and for the subgroups defined by the six combinations (2 x 3) of MAJOR by SEX. Note if we wanted plots and statistics for GPA by SEX and ignoring MAJOR, we would use the command :

examine gpa by sex . .

SETUP FOR GPA BY MAJOR BY SEX

```
set width = 80 .
data list list /  major sex gpa sat .
variable labels sex 0 'male' 1 'female' /
         major 1 'Human. ' 2 'Science' 3 'Soc. Sci.
' .
begin data .
 2 1   3.6 410
       etc.
 1 0   3.0 490
end data .
examine gpa by sex by major .
finish .
```

ANNOTATED OUTPUT FOR GPA BY MAJOR BY SEX

```
1  0  set width = 80 .
2  data list list /  major sex gpa sat .
3  begin data .

43 end data .
44 examine gpa by major by sex  .
```

GPA ☞ **Descriptive Statistics for GPA Independent of MAJOR and SEX**

Valid cases: 40.0   Missing cases: .0   Percent missing: .0

Mean	3.3850	Std Err	.0559	Min	2.7000	Skewness	-.3869
Median	3.4000	Variance	.1249	Max	4.0000	S E Skew	.3738
5% Trim	3.3917	Std Dev	.3534	Range	1.3000	Kurtosis	-.7133
				IQR	.6000	S E Kurt	.7326

```
Frequency    Stem &  Leaf

    5.00      2  .   77789
   16.00      3  *   0011111223444444
   18.00      3  .   555556667777888889
    1.00      4  *   0
```

```
Stem width:        1.00
Each leaf:         1 case(s)
                  |
                  |
     4.00 +        --+--
                  |    |
                  |    |
                  |    |
                  |  +-+-+
                  |  |   |
                  |  |   |
                  |  |   |
                  |  | * |
                  |  |   |
                  |  |   |
     3.20 +       |  |   |
                  |  +-+-+
                  |    |
                  |    |
                  |    |
                  |    |
                  |    |
                  |  --+--
                  |
                  |
                  |
     2.40 +
                  |
                  +----------------------------------------------------------
```

Variables   GPA
N of Cases   40.00
          Symbol Key: *   - Median   (O) - Outlier   (E) - Extreme

          GPA
By MAJOR   1.00 ☞ **D e s c r i p t i v e   S t a t i s t i c s   f o r   M a j o r = 1   a n d   S e x = 0**
    SEX   .00

Valid cases: 3.0   Missing cases: .0   Percent missing: .0

Mean   3.0000 Std Err   .1155 Min   2.8000 Skewness   .0000
Median   3.0000 Variance   .0400 Max   3.2000 S E Skew   1.2247
5% Trim   .   Std Dev   .2000 Range   .4000 Kurtosis   .
                                       IQR   .4000 S E Kurt   .

Frequency   Stem & Leaf
   1.00   2 . 8
   2.00   3 . 02

Stem width: 1.00
Each leaf: 1 case(s)

          GPA
By MAJOR   1.00 ☞ **D e s c r i p t i v e   S t a t i s t i c s   f o r   M a j o r = 1   a n d   S e x = 1**
    SEX   1.00

Valid cases: 6.0   Missing cases: .0   Percent missing: .0

Mean   3.4667 Std Err   .1229 Min   3.1000 Skewness   -.1148
Median   3.5000 Variance   .0907 Max   3.8000 S E Skew   .8452
5% Trim   3.4685 Std Dev   .3011 Range   .7000 Kurtosis   -2.6584
                                       IQR   .5500 S E Kurt   1.7408

```
Frequency     Stem &  Leaf

    3.00       3  *   123
    3.00       3  .   778

Stem width:      1.00
Each leaf:       1 case(s)
```

etc. for rest of MAJOR by SEX Pairs

```
         GPA
By   MAJOR    3.00    ☞ Descriptive Statistics for Major = 3 and Sex = 1
     SEX     1.00

Valid cases:          6.0   Missing cases:        .0   Percent missing:       .0


Mean        3.3500   Std Err    .1285   Min      2.9000   Skewness    -.1156
Median      3.4000   Variance   .0990   Max      3.8000   S E Skew     .8452
5% Trim     3.3500   Std Dev    .3146   Range     .9000   Kurtosis    -.0765
                                        IQR       .5250   S E Kurt    1.7408


Frequency     Stem &  Leaf

    1.00       2  .   9
    3.00       3  *   144
    2.00       3  .   58
Stem width:      1.00
Each leaf:       1 case(s)
```

☞ GPA Boxplots by MAJOR by SEX

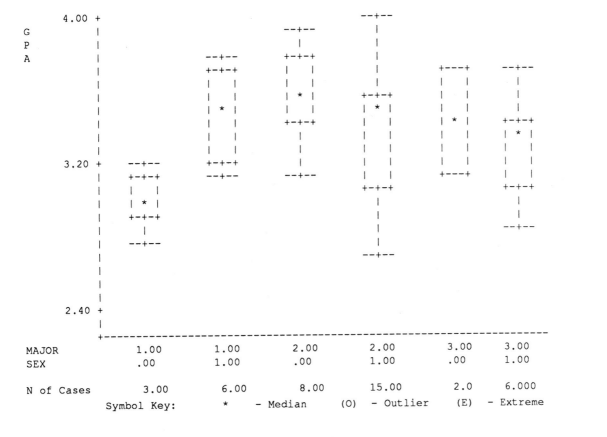

```
MAJOR         1.00      1.00      2.00      2.00      3.00      3.00
SEX            .00      1.00       .00      1.00       .00      1.00

N of Cases    3.00      6.00      8.00     15.00      2.0      6.000
           Symbol Key:       *   - Median    (O)  - Outlier    (E)  - Extreme
```

USE OF MANOVA TO PRODUCE BOXPLOTS

The MANOVA program can also produce the same boxplot and stemleaf output as EXAMINE. However, it is done in context of its ability to conduct anovas, manovas, and other statistics. It is easier to use EXAMINE if this is not desired. MANOVA use for hypothesis testing is described in Chapters 7, 15, and 16. Summary setups are presented below.

SUMMARY OF MANOVA BOXPLOT SETUP

```
set width = 80 .
data list list / x .
begin data .
     x
     x
         data  - one score per line
     x
     x
end data .
manova x /print = cellinfo (means)
         /plot = boxplots .
finish .
```

SUMMARY OF MANOVA STEMLEAF SETUP

```
set width = 80
data list list / x
begin data .
     x
     x
         data  - one score per line
     x
     x
end data .
manova x /print = cellinfo (means)
         /plot = stemleaf .
finish .
```

These commands could be combined in one command:

```
manova x /print = cellinfo (means)
         /plot = stemleaf boxplots .
```

CHAPTER 7: ONE SAMPLE t-TEST

DIFFERENCE OF A SAMPLE MEAN FROM A POPULATION MEAN

SUMMARY OF SPSS SETUPS[1, 2]

```
            1.Descriptives Method

(entails some hand calculation  as described below)

set width = 80 .
data list list/  x .
begin data .
        .
        .
        .
        .
    data
        .
        .
end data .
descriptives x
   /statistics = mean stddev semean .
finish .


    2. Manova method
( ? = μ population mean as described below)


data list list/  x .
compute x = x - ? .
begin data .
        .
        . .
    data
        .
        .
end data .
manova x /print=cellinfo(means)
            signif(univ) /design .
finish .
```

---

[1] SPSS/PC + ™ 4.0 uses a different version of the 'descriptives' command. Check the next page.

[2] Use ' **data list free / x .** ' for SPSS/PC + ™ 4.0 .

REAL WORLD EXAMPLES

Descriptives and Manova Methods

```
set width = 80 .
data list list / iqscore .
begin data .
100
110
125
140
120
130
115
 95
145
120
end data .
descriptives iqscore /statistics = mean stddev semean .
finish .
```

> **Produces Mean, Standard Deviation and Standard Error of the Mean for the Variable IQSCORE such that one can Compute the t-test for Single Samples :**
> There are 10 subjects' IQ scores (one per line of data).

```
data list list / iqscore . *
compute iqscore = iqscore - 100 .
begin data .
100
110
125
140
120
130
115
95
145
120
end data .
manova iqscore / print = cellinfo(means) signif(univ)
               / design .
finish .
```

> **Tests Whether the Mean of the 10 Subjects' IQ Scores (Variable: iqscore) is significantly different from a μ of 100:**
> There are 10 subjects' IQ scores (one per line of data).
>
> *Note; no 'set width' command as this stops the confidence interval from being printed.*

SUMMARY OF SPSS/PC+™ 4.0 DESCRIPTIVES COMMAND

```
set width = 80 .
data list free / iqscore .
begin data .
100--------------------->Bob
110                 ----> Sue
... etc ..
120--------------+
end data .
descriptives iqscore / statistics = 1 , 2 , 5.
finish .
```

PURPOSE OF THE PROCEDURE AND STATISTICS

When conducting the one sample or single t test, you are working with just one group of subjects or observations. You probably want to:

1. Get descriptive statistics for the scores such as the mean, standard deviation, and standard error of the group.

2. Determine if the mean of this single group differs significantly from a known population mean.

The form of the t-test is usually:

$$t = \frac{\text{Sample Mean - Population Mean}}{\text{Standard Error of the Mean}} \quad \text{or} \quad t = \frac{\overline{X} - \mu}{s_{\overline{X}}}$$

The t value is compared against a tabled value with N-1 degrees of freedom. N represents the number of observations in the group.

HOW TO DO THE ONE SAMPLE t-TEST ON SPSS

SPSS does not calculate directly the one sample t-test. There are two strategies you may choose from. The first entails some hand calculation to get the t-score while the second strategy returns an F test rather than the t-score.

In our example, the situation is as follows:

1. There is a group of 10 students (Bob, Sue, ..., Bill, ...) with the following IQ scores: (The names are not needed in the setup, they are to help you orient yourself to how the group should be arranged.)

```
100     <------- Let's call him: Bob
110             Sue,
125             etc.
140              .
120              .
130              .
115              .
 95              .
145     <------- This is Bill who is smart!
120              .
```

2. We want to see if their mean is significantly different from an hypothesized population mean of 100 (the standard for IQ tests).

3. As the mean of the group is 120 and standard deviation is 15.99, there is a significant difference with a sample size of 10, so the printouts should reflect this.

STRATEGY 1: t-TEST THROUGH DESCRIPTIVES

Use the Descriptives program to calculate the mean of the group and standard error. The t-test is then hand computed. Note in this example, the observation is identified as "iqscore."

```
set width = 80 .
data list list / iqscore .
begin data .
100 ---------------->  Bob
110               ---->  Sue
125           |
140           |
120                 +----------------------+
130           ----->  One subject per line |
115                 +----------------------+
 95           |
145           |
120 ----------+
end data .
descriptives iqscore /statistics = mean stddev semean .
finish .
```

RELEVANT SPSS OUTPUT AND ITS INTERPRETATION

```
1  0   set width = 80 .
2  data list list / iqscore .
3  begin data .
14   end data .
15 descriptives iqscore /statistics = mean stddev semean .

Number of Valid Observations (Listwise) =        10.00


                                            Valid
  Variable     Mean   S.E. Mean    Std Dev    N     Label

  iqscore    120.00      5.06       15.99      10
```

The program does not calculate the t-score, so you have to do it as follows:

$$t = \frac{\text{sample mean} - \text{population mean}}{\text{S. E. Mean}} = \frac{120-100}{5.055} = 3.956$$

This **t** value is significant as **p. <.01** with d.f. = 9. Significance is determined by using a standard t-table.

STRATEGY 2: USING MANOVA
USING A COMPUTE & INTERPRETING F - RATIOS

The Manova program is capable of computing whether the group mean is different from the hypothesized population if the following setup is used. Note that:

1. You must include the hypothesized population mean in the setup when you make up the compute card. In our example, the hypothesized population mean ("μ") is 100. Thus the setup has in the data manipulation section:

```
compute  iqscore  =  iqscore  -  100 .
```

2. When the sample mean is reported, the value of the hypothesized population mean must be added back in. In our example the mean is 120. Manova will report 20. You must add the 100. However, the standard deviation is not altered by this. It is all right to use the value reported by the program.

3. The program reports an F value, not a t-score. Note:
   a. It is legitimate to report the F with its degrees of freedom.
   b. If you want to report the t-score, you must take the square root of the F score. In our example, F = 15.65. The square root of 15.65 = 3.956. This is our t-score as calculated in the Descriptives example.
   c. The degrees of freedom for the t-test is N-1 or in our example = 9. This is found in the Manova printout as WITHIN CELL DF.

4. The F value reported is a two tailed test. The significance column (SIG OF F) represents the probability of getting an F score of greater value.

5. The 95 percent confidence interval for the mean is reported in the form[*]:

$$\overline{X} \ \pm \ t_{(.05)} \ \frac{S}{\overline{X}}$$

[*] Important Note: you will only set the confidence interval if you do not use the **set width = 80** . Otherwise the line is too short and you only get the mean and Std. Dev.

However, the hypothesized population mean MUST be added to the reported mean. In example 1, the interval is reported as:

```
95 percent Conf. Interval

8.564      31.436
```

You must add 100 to each to make the interval:

```
108.564 to 131.436
```

These points will be highlighted in the following examples:

    a. Example 1 uses the same data as above and will lead to the same conclusion that there is a significant difference.

    b. Example 2 will present a nonsignificant difference.

    c. Example 3 will present a very significant difference and how to interpret this output.

EXAMPLE 1: SAME DATA SET AS USED IN DESCRIPTIVES

The group mean is 120 and we know that the group differs significantly from a hypothesized mean of 100.

SPSS SETUP FOR MANOVA WITH INTERPRETATIVE NOTATIONS

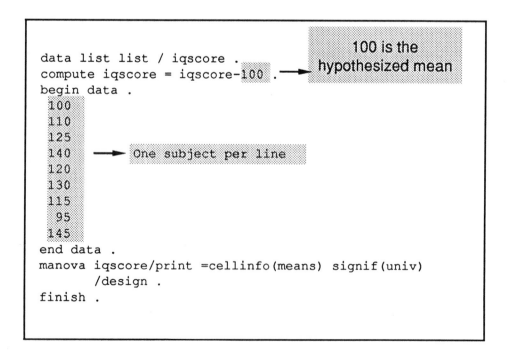

RELEVANT SPSS OUTPUT WITH INTERPRETATIVE NOTATIONS

```
     1   data list list / iqscore .
     2   compute iqscore = iqscore-100 .
     3   begin data .
     4   end data .
    14   manova iqscore/print =cellinfo(means) signif(univ)
    15           /design .

* * * * * A N A L Y S I S   O F   V A R I A N C E * * * * * * * * * * *
        10 cases accepted.
         0 cases rejected because of out-of-range factor values.
         0 cases rejected because of missing data.
         1 non-empty cell.
         1 design will be processed.
- - - - - - - - - - - - - - - - - - - - - - - - - - - - - - - - - - - -
Cell Means and Standard Deviations
Variable .. IQSCORE
                    ┌──┐  Mean    Std. Dev.       N    95 percent Conf. Interval
                    │1.│
                    └──┘
For entire sample       20.000    15.986         10    8.564    31.436

* * * * * A N A L Y S I S   O F   V A R I A N C E -- DESIGN   1 * * * * * * * * *
Tests of Significance for IQSCORE using UNIQUE sums of squares

Source of Variation          SS        DF        MS         F  Sig of F
                                                       ┌──┐            ┌──┐
                                                       │2.│            │3.│
                                                       └──┘            └──┘
WITHIN CELLS              2300.00       9     255.56
 CONSTANT                 4000.00       1    4000.00      15.65    .003
```

IMPORTANT INTERPRETATIVE POINTS OF THE OUTPUT

Point 1: The value of **20** in Gray Box 1 represents the difference between the sample mean and population value. In our case:

$$\bar{X} - \mu = 120 - 100 = 20.$$

Thus if you want the mean of your sample, you must add the population mean (in our case: 100) to the mean reported in 1. Thus 20 + 100 = 120 for the sample mean.

The same addition must be done for the 95 percent confidence interval as the reported:

```
95 percent Conf. Interval

   8.564      31.436
```

becomes :

```
   108.564 to 131.436  .
```

Point 2: In Gray Box 2, the value of $15.65 = 3.96^2$ which is t^2 from same data analyzed by using Descriptives and your own calculation of t. So, if you want to report a t-score rather than the F, just take square root of the F score. The degrees of freedom are 9 (10-1) and is found as the WITHIN CELLS DF

Point 3: The difference is significant as the probability of the F ratio is .003 (Gray Box 3). As this is less than the commonly used values of .05 or .01, you are safe to reject the null hypothesis. The mean of 120 for the group is statistically different from the hypothesized mean of 100.

EXAMPLE 2: NONSIGNIFICANT t, $p > .05$

In this example the data have been changed such that the group mean is now 105. The difference is not significant.

SETUP

```
set width = 80 .
data list list / iqscore .
compute iqscore = iqscore - 100 .
begin data .
        85
        95
       110
       125
       105
       115
       100
        80
       130
       105
end data .
manova iqscore/print = cellinfo (means) signif (univ)
             /design .
finish .
```

RELEVANT SPSS OUTPUT WITH INTERPRETATIVE NOTATIONS

```
  1  0  set width = 80 .
  2  data list list / iqscore .
  3  compute iqscore = iqscore - 100 .
  4  begin data .
  5  end data .
 15  manova iqscore / print = cellinfo ( means) signif (univ)
 16                  /design .

* * * * * * A N A L Y S I S   O F   V A R I A N C E * * * * * *

     10 cases accepted.
      0 cases rejected because of out-of-range factor values.
      0 cases rejected because of missing data.
      1 non-empty cell.
      1 design will be processed.
- - - - - - - - - - - - - - - - - - - - - - - - - - - - - - - - -
Cell Means and Standard Deviations
Variable .. IQSCORE
                               Mean   Std. Dev.         N
                                   1.
For entire sample             5.000   15.986           10
- - - - - - - - - - - - - - - - - - - - - - - - - - - - - - - - -
* * * * * * A N A L Y S I S   O F   V A R I A N C E -- DESIGN  1 * * * * * *

Tests of Significance for IQSCORE using UNIQUE sums of squares
Source of Variation          SS      DF      MS        F   Sig of F

WITHIN CELLS             2300.00      9    255.56
CONSTANT                  250.00      1    250.00      .98 2.   .348 3.
```

IMPORTANT INTERPRETATIVE POINTS OF THE OUTPUT

Point 1: The value of "5" in Gray Box 1 represents the difference between the sample mean and population value. The sample mean = 100+5 = 105. The confidence interval has to be similarly recalculated.

Point 2: In Gray Box 2, $.98 = .9899^2$ which is t^2 from same data. If you want to report the t-score rather than the F, just take square root of the F score.

Point 3: The difference is NOT significant as the probability of the F ratio is .348 in Gray Box 3. As this is much more than the commonly used values of .05 or .01, you FAIL to reject the null hypothesis. The mean of 105 for the group was not found to be statistically different from the hypothesized mean of 100. You can't say the groups are different!

EXAMPLE 3: SIGNIFICANT DIFFERENCE WITH p < .001

In this data set, the sample mean is 140. This produces a significant t-score whose probability is <.001. However, SPSS gives a *p.* = .000. This leads the unsophisticated to conclude that there is no significant difference. This is NOT TRUE. The program didn't have enough decimal places. If the probability was .0005, it would be printed as .000.

SETUP

```
set width = 80.
data list list / iqscore .
compute iqscore = iqscore-100 .
begin data .
     120
     130
     145
     160
     140
     150
     135
     115
     165
     140
end data .
manova iqscore/print = cellinfo(means) signif (univ) / design .
finish .
```

RELEVANT SPSS OUTPUT WITH INTERPRETATIVE NOTATIONS

```
     1   data list list / iqscore .
     2   compute iqscore = iqscore-100 .
     3   begin data .
     4   end data .
    14   manova iqscore/print =cellinfo(means) signif(univ)
    15          /design .
* * * * * A N A L Y S I S   O F   V A R I A N C E * * * * * * * * * * * *
    10 cases accepted.
     0 cases rejected because of out-of-range factor values.
     0 cases rejected because of missing data.
     1 non-empty cell.
     1 design will be processed.
- - - - - - - - - - - - - - - - - - - - - - - - - - - - - - - - - - - - -
Cell Means and Standard Deviations
Variable .. IQSCORE
                          Mean   Std. Dev.        N   95 percent Conf. Inter
For entire sample        40.000    15.986        10     28.564    51.436


* * * * * A N A L Y S I S   O F   V A R I A N C E -- DESIGN   1 * * * * * * *
Tests of Significance for IQSCORE using UNIQUE sums of squares

Source of Variation           SS      DF        MS          F  Sig of F
WITHIN CELLS             2300.00       9    255.56
CONSTANT                16000.00       1  16000.00       62.61    .000
```

1.

Point 1: F is quite large as would be the t of 7.91 (remember the square root). The ".000" should be reported as p<.001. The degrees of freedom are 9 (10 - 1) and are found as the WITHIN CELLS DF.

CHAPTER 8 : TWO SAMPLE *t*-TEST

DIFFERENCE OF ONE SAMPLE MEAN FROM ANOTHER SAMPLE MEAN OF AN INDEPENDENT GROUP

SUMMARY OF SPSS SETUP [1]

```
set width = 80 .
data list list/  group score .
begin data .
  group score
  group score
        .
        .
      data
        .
        .
  group score
end data .
t-test groups = group / variables = score .
finish .
```

REAL WORLD EXAMPLE:

```
set width = 80 .
data list list / group score .
begin data .
  1   100
  1   110
  1   125
  1   140
  1   120
  1   130
  1   115
  1    95
  1   145
  1   120
  2    85
  2    95
  2   110
  2   125
  2   105
  2   115
  2   100
  2    80
  2   130
  2   105
end data .
t-test groups = group / variables = score .
finish .
```

Tests Whether the Mean Score (*Variable: score*) of the 10 Subjects of Group 1 (*Variable: group = 1*) is significantly different from the Mean Score of the 10 Subjects of Group 2 (*group = 2*):
There are 20 subjects' (one per line of data) with the first number indicating their group and the second number being their score.

---

[1] Use ' **data list free / group score** . ' for SPSS/PC + ™4.0 .

PURPOSE OF THE PROCEDURE AND STATISTICS

You are working with two separate groups of subjects or individuals. You want to:

1. Get descriptive statistics for each group such as the mean, standard deviation, and standard errors.

2. Determine if the means of the groups differ significantly from each other.

A version of the formula:

$$ t = \frac{\text{Sample Mean 1} - \text{Sample Mean 2}}{\text{Standard Error of the Difference}} \quad \text{or} \quad t = \frac{\bar{X}_1 - \bar{X}_2}{S_{\bar{X}_1 - \bar{X}_2}} $$

is used (see Howell, 1987, and SPSS Statistical Algorithms, 1983).

HOW TO DO THE TWO SAMPLE t-TEST ON SPSS

SPSS can calculate the two sample t-test. Important points are:

1. How to set up the data and identify the groups.

2. Understand how SPSS deals with equal and unequal size groups.

3. Understand how SPSS deals with unequal group variances and corrects for this (the assumption of homogeneity of variance).

4. Be able to understand the output (this takes some effort). SPSS automatically does a two-tailed test of significance.

Four examples will be presented along with a discussion of the problem of unequal numbers in groups.

EXAMPLE 1: CLASSIC TWO SAMPLE t-TEST WITH A SIGNIFICANT DIFFERENCE

In the following example we have :

1. Two groups of 10 subjects each.

2. The *t* value will be significant.

3. Each case or line of data contains two numbers:

    The first number (the digit 1 or 2) identifies the group the subject belongs to. For example, Group 1 ("1's") could be from New York and group 2 ("2's") could be from California.

4. We have the IQ score from each subject.

5. The data are set up as follows with some interpretative notation. Names will be used to orient you but are not necessary.

DATA

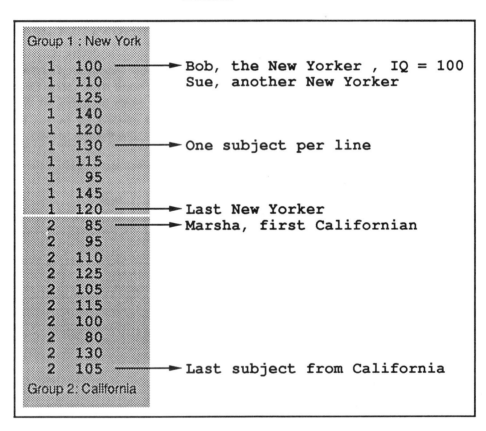

6. The mean of Group 1 is 120 and that of Group 2 equals 105. The difference is significant at the .05 level. Each group has the same standard deviation. The degrees of freedom = 10 + 10 - 2 = 18.

7. A complete set up would look as follows (with some helpful notation):

SPSS SET UP FOR t-TEST WITH INTERPRETATIVE NOTATIONS

```
set width = 80 .
data list list / group score .
begin data
   1   100   ----------------->  New  York  Bob,  etc.
   1   110
   1   125
   1   140
   1   120
   1   130
   1   115
   1    95
   1   145
   1   120
   2    85   ----------------->  Start  of  Group  2
   2    95
   2   110
   2   125
   2   105
   2   115
   2   100
   2    80
   2   130
   2   105
end data .
t-test groups = group / variables = score .
finish    .
```

8. **FOR THIS EXAMPLE ONLY LOOK AT THE OUTPUT IN THE HIGHLIGHTED BOXES! IGNORE OTHER PARTS UNTIL EXPLAINED IN LATER EXAMPLES!!**

RELEVANT SPSS OUTPUT AND INTERPRETATION

```
 1 0 set width = 80 .
  2   data list list/ group score
  3   begin data .
 23   end data.
 24   t-test groups = group / variables = score .
- - - - - - - - - - - - - - - - - - - - - - - - - - - T - T E S T - - - - - -
GROUP 1 - GROUP    EQ      1.00
GROUP 2 - GROUP    EQ      2.00


                                                  *
VARIABLE          NUMBER            STANDARD  STANDARD  *      F    2-TAIL
                 OF CASES    MEAN   DEVIATION   ERROR   *    VALUE   PROB.
-----------------------------------------------------------------------------
SCORE                          1                        *
     GROUP 1     10       120.0000  15.986    5.055     *
                                                        *     1.00  1.000
     GROUP 2     10       105.0000  15.986    5.055     *


--------------------------------------------------------------------------

    POOLED VARIANCE ESTIMATE             SEPARATE VARIANCE ESTIMATE

     T    DEGREES OF  2-TAIL *     T    DEGREES OF  2-TAIL
   VALUE   FREEDOM     PROB. *   VALUE   FREEDOM     PROB.
   ----------------------------------------------------------------
                          *
                        2 *
    2.10      18      0.050 *    2.10     18.00     0.050
                          *
```

IMPORTANT INTERPRETATIVE POINTS OF THE OUTPUT

1. Gray Box 1 contains the means of each group with their standard deviations and standard errors.

> 2. GRAY BOX 2 (POOLED VARIANCE ESTIMATE) CONTAINS THE SIMPLE T-TEST RESULT!
> DON'T EVEN THINK ABOUT THE OTHER PARTS OF THE OUTPUT UNTIL LATER!!

3. This output would be reported as follows:

   a. t = 2.10   b. df = 18   c. p = .05 (this is a two-tailed probability).

There IS a significant difference between the means of Group 1 and Group 2 if you are using the .05 level of significance. Of course, you may work at another level if you choose. SPSS will print out the exact probability which you can compare against your chosen level.

For example, if the output had looked like this:

```
   T      DEGREES OF  2-TAIL

 VALUE     FREEDOM     PROB.

-------------------------------

 2.16      18.00      0.045
```

you might report the difference is significant at the .05 level (as .045 < .05) or not significant at the .01 level (.045 > .01). The choice is yours.

EXAMPLE 2: A CLASSIC t-TEST WITH A VERY LOW SIGNIFICANCE LEVEL (p. <.001)

1. Every thing is the same in this example except that the data of Group 2 have been changed. Group 1 still has a mean of 120 but, Group 2 has a mean of 160. This will give us a very large, negative t-score of -5.60.

2. Again, only look at the output in the boxes for now!

The setup would be as follows with interpretative notation:

```
set width = 80 .
data list list/ group score .¹
begin data .
  1  100     -----> group 1
  1  110
  1  125
  1  140
  1  120
  1  130
  1  115
  1   95
  1  145
  1  120
  2  140     -----> group 2
  2  150
  2  165
  2  180
  2  160
  2  170
  2  155
  2  135
  2  185
  2  160
end data .
t-test groups = group / variables = score .
finish .
```

---

¹ Use ' **data list free / group score .** ' for SPSS/PC + ™4.0 . Assume this for following setups.

RELEVANT SPSS OUTPUT AND INTERPRETATION

```
   1  0   data list list/ group score
   2  0   t-test groups = group / variables = score

   - - - - - - - - - - - - T - T E S T - - - - - -
GROUP 1 - GROUP     EQ      1.00
GROUP 2 - GROUP     EQ      2.00


VARIABLE              NUMBER                  STANDARD     STANDARD  *    F    2-TAIL
                     OF CASES      MEAN      DEVIATION      ERROR    *  VALUE  PROB
-------------------------------------------------------------------------------------
SCORE                                                            1   *
        GROUP 1        10       120.0000      15.986       5.055       *
                                                                       *  1.00  1.000
        GROUP 2        10       160.0000      15.986       5.055       *
                                                                       *
-------------------------------------------------------------------------------------


     POOLED VARIANCE ESTIMATE * SEPARATE VARIANCE ESTIMATE
                              .
     T       DEGREES OF 2-TAIL      T     DEGREES OF  2-TAIL
   VALUE     FREEDOM    PROB.     VALUE    FREEDOM    PROB.
   ---------------------------------------------------------
                                      *
                                 2    *
   -5.60        18      0.000     *   -5.60    18.00    0.000
```

IMPORTANT INTERPRETATIVE POINTS OF THE OUTPUT

1. Gray Box 1 contains the means of each group with their standard deviations and standard errors.

---
2. GRAY BOX 2 (POOLED VARIANCE ESTIMATE) CONTAINS THE SIMPLE T-TEST RESULT!
STILL DON'T THINK ABOUT THE OTHER PARTS OF THE OUTPUT UNTIL LATER!!
---

3. This output would be reported as follows:
   a. $t = -5.60$

The t is negative because Group 1 has a mean smaller than that of Group 2. (120-160 = -40, therefore a negative t-score).
   b. $df = 18$
   c. $p < .001$ (The program reports a two-tailed test.)

Our t-score is so large that the probability of this error occurring by chance is below .001. As SPSS does not print such a small decimal number, the output reads .000!

4. There IS a significant difference between the means of Group 1 and Group 2.

EXAMPLE 3: t-TEST WITH A NONSIGNIFICANT DIFFERENCE.

1. Everything is the same in this example except that the data of Group 2 have been changed. Group 1 still has a mean of 105 but Group 2 has a mean of 100. This will give us a very small t-score and a nonsignificant difference.

2. Again, only look at the output in the boxes for now!

The setup would be as follows with interpretative notation:

SETUP

```
set width = 80 .
data list list/ group score .
begin data .
   1    85 ---> Group 1
   1    95
   1   110
   1   125
   1   105
   1   115
   1   100
   1    80
   1   130
   1   105
   2    80 ---> Group 2
   2    90
   2   105
   2   120
   2   100
   2   110
   2    95
   2    75
   2   125
   2   100
end data.
t-test groups = group / variables = score .
finish .
```

```
              Relevant SPSSX Output and Interpretation

   24  t-test groups = group / variables = score.
- - - - - - - - - - - - - - - T - T E S T - - - - - - -

GROUP 1 - GROUP      EQ        1.00
GROUP 2 - GROUP      EQ        2.00
```

VARIABLE	NUMBER OF CASES	MEAN	STANDARD DEVIATION	STANDARD ERROR	* *	F VALUE	2-TAIL PROB.
SCORE					**1**		
GROUP 1	10	105.0000	15.986	5.055			
						1.00	1.000
GROUP 2	10	100.0000	15.986	5.055			

POOLED VARIANCE ESTIMATE			* * *	SEPARATE VARIANCE ESTIMATE		
T VALUE	DEGREES OF FREEDOM	2-TAIL PROB.	*	T VALUE	DEGREES OF FREEDOM	2-TAIL PROB.
0.70	18	**2** 0.493		0.70	18.00	0.493

IMPORTANT INTERPRETATIVE POINTS OF THE OUTPUT

1. Box 1 contains the means of each group with their standard deviations and standard errors.

---

2. GRAY BOX 2 (POOLED VARIANCE ESTIMATE) CONTAINS THE SIMPLE T-TEST RESULT! STILL DON'T THINK ABOUT THE OTHER PARTS OF THE OUTPUT UNTIL LATER!!

---

3. This output would be reported as follows:

    a. $t = 0.70$

    b. $df = 18$

    c. $p = .493$ (The program reports a two-tailed probability)

4. There is NOT a significant difference between the means of Group 1 and Group 2. This is because the probability value is much greater than .05

EXAMPLE 4: AN EXAMPLE WITH UNEQUAL VARIANCES (INHOMOGENEITY) AND HOW TO INTERPRET THE OUTPUT

1. In this example several things are happening:

a. The means of Group 1 and Group 2 are 120 and 105 respectively.

b. The standard deviation of Group 2 has been increased by a factor of three. Now it is 47.958 rather than the value of 15.986 that it was previously.

This condition is known as inhomogeneity of variance. It is a violation of one of the assumptions of the t-test. SPSS automatically checks for this condition and corrects for it.

We will discuss the importance of this correction after an explanation of the output.

c. Given in this example that there is the "dreaded inhomogeneity of variance" or "violation of the assumptions," we must learn to recognize this in the output. This means we will read the **F-ratio box** and the **Separate variance estimate box**. See the outlines in the example.

SETUP

```
set width = 80 .
data list list/ group score .
begin data .
   1   100     Group  1  (small  variance)
   1   110
   1   125
   1   140
   1   120
   1   130
   1   115
   1    95
   1   145
   1   120
   2    45     Group  2  (LARGE  variance)
   2    75
   2   120
   2   165
   2   105
   2   135
   2    90
   2    30
   2   180
   2   105
end data .
t-test groups = group / variables = score .
finish .
```

Relevant SPSS Output and Interpretation

```
    24   t-test groups = group / variables = score .

GROUP 1 - GROUP       EQ        1.00
GROUP 2 - GROUP       EQ        2.00
```

VARIABLE	NUMBER OF CASES	MEAN	STANDARD DEVIATION	STANDARD ERROR	*	F VALUE	2-TAIL PROB.
SCORE		**1**	**2**		*		**3**
GROUP 1	10	120.0000	15.986	5.055	*		
					*	9.00	0.003
GROUP 2	10	105.0000	47.958	15.166	*		

```
        POOLED VARIANCE ESTIMATE * SEPARATE VARIANCE ESTIMATE
                                  *
        T   DEGREES OF 2-TAIL *   T    DEGREES OF  2-TAIL
      VALUE  FREEDOM   PROB. * VALUE   FREEDOM     PROB.
      ------------------------------------------------------
                                  *
                                  *                          4
       0.94    18    0.361  *  0.94    10.98      0.368
                                  *
```

Important Interpretative Points of the Output

1. Gray box 1 contains the means of each group. Gray box 2 holds the standard deviations and standard errors.

   Note that the means are the same as in Example 1 (Group 1 =120, Group 2 = 105).

2. The standard deviations are quite different! Group 2 has a standard deviation three times that of Group 1 (47.958 versus 15.986).

This difference is known as inhomogeneity of variance and is a violation of the assumptions of the t-test. This is to be feared as it might change your Type 1 error and may lead to the reporting of a difference where none really exists. However, the actual importance of violating the assumptions of the t-test are quite controversial in nature. Also, some suggest that the corrections that SPSS uses may not be the best. It is not our goal to discuss these issues at length in this book. We will explain the intended use of the SPSS output. At the risk of offending some statisticians, such violations might not be very important unless they are major. For a further discussion of when such violations are important and ways to correct, see Howell (1987) and Wilcox (1987).

3. Gray box 3 contains a test of whether the two groups have equal standard deviations or variances (remember that a variance = (standard deviation)^2).

SPSS calculates the **F (df $_{max}$, df $_{min}$)** statistic which equals =

$$\frac{(\text{Bigger SD})^2}{(\text{Smaller SD})^2} \quad .$$

In our example, this fraction =

$$\frac{(47.958)^2}{(15.986)^2} = 9.00$$

Recall **df** is the degrees of freedom for the group and is equal to the number in the group-1 (or N-1).

SPSS then checks this F value for significance. As you see in Gray box 3, this F has **2-TAIL PROB =** .003. This means that the F value **is significant** as its probability < .01 and you do have **inhomogeneity of variance**!

In this case, the powers that be say it would be incorrect to use the standard t-test formulas. A corrected t-value is calculated (see SPSS Statistical Algorithms, 1983) for details. It uses an accepted method but recall this is a controversial area. If you are worried and a novice in statistics, it's best to check with a local expert.

4. In order to report the corrected t-value, you must use the information in Gray box 4 (SEPARATE VARIANCE).

This output would be reported as follows:

　　a. t = 0.94*

* Note that the t value has decreased from that of Example 1 even though the differences (120-105) are the same. This is because the standard error of the difference was increased by the now larger standard deviation of Group 2.

　　b. df = 10.98

* Note that the degrees of freedom are no longer equal to:

$$N_1 + N_2 = 10 + 10 - 2 = 18.$$

They are calculated by a rather imposing looking formula found in the SPSS Statistical Algorithms. Also see Howell (1987) if you want an explanation.

  c. $p = .368$

 The program reports a two-tailed test

d. There **is not** a significant difference between the means of Group 1 and Group 2.

PROBLEM OF UNEQUAL N OR DIFFERENT SIZE GROUPS

 In our examples, both groups always were equal in size and had 10 subjects in each group. If you were calculating a t-test by hand, the formulas would be different if groups were equal or unequal in size (see Howell, 1987). However, if you use SPSS, you need not worry about this. The program automatically uses the correct formula for t and the degrees of freedom.

SUMMARY OF t-TEST EVALUATION

1. Look at t-test output and check *F*-ratio box to see if the *F* has a $p < .05$ (note, you could use .01 also).

2. If $p. > .05$ in F ratio box, use **POOLED VARIANCE** output.

3. If $p. < .05$ in F ratio box, use **SEPARATE VARIANCE** output.

CHAPTER 9: PAIRED-SAMPLE T-TEST

DIFFERENCE OF ONE SAMPLE MEAN FROM ANOTHER SAMPLE MEAN WITH MATCHED OR PAIRED SUBJECTS

SUMMARY OF SPSS SETUP[1]

```
set width = 80 .
data list list/  score1 score2.
begin data .
    score1  score2
    score1  score2
            "
            "
  data
            "
            "
    score1  score2
end data .
t-test pairs = score1 score2 .
finish .
```

REAL WORLD EXAMPLE

```
set width = 80 .
data list list/ score1 score2 .
begin data .
100   116
110   127
125   139
140   153
120   138
130   143
115   130
 95   102
145   158
120   138
end data .
t-test pairs = score1 score2 .
finish .
```

Tests Whether the Mean of Score1 is significantly different from the Mean of Score2 Using a Paired t-test:
There are 10 subjects' (one per line of data) with the first number indicating their score1 and the second number being their score2.

---

[1] Use ' **data list free / score1 score2 .** ' for SPSS/PC + ™4.0 .

PURPOSE OF THE PROCEDURE AND STATISTICS

You are working with paired or matched groups of subjects or observations. This means that a person is tested twice or the observations are in some way matched. You want to:

1. Get descriptive statistics for each group such as the mean, standard deviation, and standard errors.

2. Check to see if the observations have a significant positive correlation.

3. Determine if the means of the groups differ significantly from each other.

HOW TO DO THE PAIRED t-TEST ON SPSS

SPSS can calculate the paired t-test. Important points are:

1. How to set up the data and identify the groups.
2. How to see if the correlation coefficient is significant.
3. How to see if the t is significant so you can state whether or not the difference between the means is significant.

Four examples will be presented:

Example 1: The t-test with paired groups that has a significant correlation and significant difference. This example will also be used to explain the basic setup.

Example 2: A highly significant paired t-test and the interpretation of the significance level.

Example 3: The paired t-test with a nonsignificant difference.

Example 4: The paired t-test with a nonsignificant correlation and a discussion of correlation and the t-test.

EXAMPLE 1: PAIRED t-TEST WITH SIGNIFICANT CORRELATION AND DIFFERENCE BETWEEN MEANS.

In this example :

1. There are ten people (Bob, Sue, etc.).

2. We test their IQ score twice. The first time will be referred to as "score1." The second time is "score2." Thus the data would be arranged as follows:

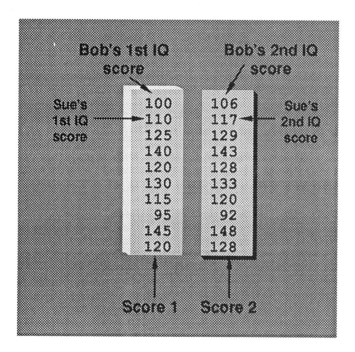

3. We wish to determine if the mean of score1 is significantly different from the mean of score2. To do this we also need to know if there is a positive and significant correlation between score1 and score2.

4. In this example, the mean of score1 is 120 and the mean of score2 is 124.4.

The correlation between score1 and score2 is .981 and is significant (p. <.001). The paired t-test will turn out to be significant.

SPSS SETUP FOR PAIRED t-TEST WITH NOTATION[2]

```
set width = 80 .
data list list/ score1 score2.  ──▶ Established two scores per subject
begin data .
    100   106  ◀──── Bob's two scores
    110   117  ◀──── Sue's two scores
    125   129
    140   143
    120   128
    130   133
    115   120
     95    92
    145   148      Initiates paired t-test for score1 versus score2
    120   128                    │
end data .                       ▼
t-test pairs = score1 score2 .
finish .
```

RELEVANT SPSS OUTPUT WITH INTERPRETATIVE NOTATION

```
 1   0 set width = 80 .
 2   data list list / score1 score2 .
 3   begin data .
13   end data .
24   t-test pairs = score1 score2 .

      - - - t - tests for paired samples - - -
```

Variable	Number of Cases	Mean	Standard Deviation	Standard Error
SCORE1				1
	10	120.0000	15.986	5.055
	10	124.4000	16.621	5.256
SCORE2				

(Difference) Mean	Standard Deviation	Standard Error	Corr.	2-tail Prob.	t Value	Degrees of Freedom	2-tail Prob.
				2			3
-4.4000	3.273	1.035	0.981	0.000	-4.25	9	0.002

---

[2] Use ' **data list free / score1 score2** . ' for SPSS/PC + ™4.0 . Assume for all following setups.

IMPORTANT INTERPRETATIVE POINTS OF THE OUTPUT

1. Gray Box 1 contains the means of score1 and score2, along with their standard deviations and standard errors.

2. Gray Box 2 contains the correlation between score1 and score2. Pearson's correlation coefficient equals .981 and is highly significant as it has a probability of <.001.

3. Gray Box 3 contains the t-score of -4.25. It is interpreted as follows:

    a. the value is negative as score1 is less than score2.

    b. the degrees of freedom = 9 as df = no. of pairs -1 (10-1).

    c. the difference is significant and you reject the null hypothesis because the **2-TAIL PROB.** is less than .05 or .01. It would be reported as p = .002.

    d. the IQ mean for score1 is different from the IQ mean of score2.

EXAMPLE 2: HIGHLY SIGNIFICANT CORRELATION AND DIFFERENCE BETWEEN MEANS

In this example :

1. There are ten people (Bob, Sue, etc.).

2. We test their IQ score twice. The data are arranged as before. So that:

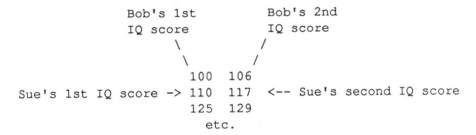

3. We wish to determine if the mean of score1 is significantly different from the mean of score2. To do this we also need to know if there is a positive and significant correlation between score1 and score2.

4. In this example, the mean of score1 is 120 and the mean of score2 is 134.4.

The correlation between score1 and score2 is .981 and is significant with p < .001.

The paired t-test will turn out to be highly significant as the probability of the t-score will be < .001.

SPSS SETUP FOR PAIRED *t*-TEST WITH NOTATION

```
set width = 80 .
data list list/ score1 score2 .   ⇨ ⇨ establishes 2 scores per subject
begin data .
      100   116  ⇨ ⇨ Bob's two scores
      110   127  ⇨ ⇨ Sue's two scores
      125   139
      140   153
      120   138
      130   143
      115   130
       95   102
      145   158
      120   138
end data .
t-test pairs = score1 score2 .   ⇨ paired t-test for score1 vs. score2
finish .
```

RELEVANT SPSS OUTPUT WITH INTERPRETATIVE NOTATION

```
   1   0 set width = 80 .
   2   data list list / score1 score2 .
   3   begin data .
  13   end data .
  24   t-test pairs = score1 score2 .

       - - - t - tests for paired samples - - -
```

Variable	Number of Cases	Mean	Standard Deviation	Standard Error
SCORE1				1
	10	120.0000	15.986	5.055
	10	134.4000	16.621	5.256
SCORE2				

(Difference) Mean	Standard Deviation	Standard Error	Corr.	2-tail Prob.	t Value	Degrees of Freedom	2-tail Prob.
				2			3
-14.4000	3.273	1.035	0.981	0.000	-13.91	9	0.000

IMPORTANT INTERPRETATIVE POINTS OF THE OUTPUT

1. Gray Box 1 contains the means of score1 and score2, along with their standard deviations and standard errors.

2. Gray Box 2 contains the correlation between score1 and score2. Pearson's correlation coefficient equals .981 and is highly significant as it has a probability of <.001. This

is because the probability is less than .001. Since the program only prints 3 decimal places, it prints .000 which is interpreted as < .001.

3. <u>Gray Box 3</u> contains the t-score of -13.91. It is interpreted as follows:

   a. the value is negative as score1 is less than score2.

   b. the degrees of freedom = 9 as df = no. of pairs -1 (9-1).

   c. the difference is significant and you reject the null hypothesis because the **2-TAIL PROB.** is less than .05 or .01. It would be reported as p < .001.

   d. The IQ mean for score1 is significantly different from the IQ mean of score2.

EXAMPLE 3: SIGNIFICANT CORRELATION AND NONSIGNIFICANT DIFFERENCE BETWEEN MEANS.

In this example:

1. There are ten people (Bob, Sue, etc.).

2. We test their IQ score twice. The data are arranged as before. So that:

```
        Bob's 1st          Bob's 2nd
        IQ score           IQ score
               \          /
                100    102
Sue's 1st IQ score -> 110    113  <-- Sue's second IQ score
```

3. We wish to determine if the mean of score1 is significantly different from the mean of score2. To do this we also need to know if there is a positive and significant correlation between score1 and score2.

4. In this example, the mean of score1 is 120 and the mean of score2 is 122.4.

The correlation between score1 and score2 is .894 and **is significant** with p < .001. The probability of the t-score will be = .377. The paired t-test will turn out **not** to be significant.

SETUP

```
data list list/ score1 score2.  ⇨ ⇨ establishes  2  scores  per  subject
begin data .
      100   102    ⇨ ⇨ Bob's  two  scores
      110   113    ⇨ ⇨ Sue's  two  scores
      125   125
      140   139
      120   144
      130   129
      115   116
       95    88
      145   144
      120   124
end data .
t-test pairs = score1 score2 . ⇨ paired  t-test  for  score1  vs.  score2
finish .
```

RELEVANT SPSS OUTPUT WITH INTERPRETATIVE NOTATION

```
     1   0 set width = 80 .
     2   data list list / score1 score2 .
     3   begin data .
    13   end data .
    24   t-test pairs = score1 score2 .
```

```
          - - - t - tests for paired samples - - -
```

Variable	Number of Cases	Mean	Standard Deviation	Standard Error
SCORE1				**1**
	10	120.0000	15.986	5.055
	10	122.4000	18.228	5.764
SCORE2				

(Difference) Mean	Standard Deviation	Standard Error	Corr.	2-tail Prob.	t Value	Degrees of Freedom	2-tail Prob.
				2			**3**
-2.4000	8.168	2.583	0.894	0.000	-.93	9	.377

IMPORTANT INTERPRETATIVE POINTS OF THE OUTPUT

1. Gray Box 1 contains the means of score1 and score2, along with their standard deviations and standard errors.

2. Gray Box 2 contains the correlation between score1 and score2. Pearson's correlation coefficient equals .894 and is highly significant as it has a probability of <.001. Recall how to interpret ".000" as <. 001.

3. Gray Box 3 contains the t-score of -0.93. It is interpreted as follows:

   a. the value is negative as score1 is less than score2.

   b. the degrees of freedom = 9 as df = no. of pairs -1 (9-1).

   c. the difference is not significant and you fail to reject the null hypothesis because the **2-TAIL PROB.** is greater than .05 or .01. It would be reported as p = .377.

   d. the IQ mean for score1 is not different from the IQ mean of score2.

EXAMPLE 4: PAIRED t-TEST WITH A NONSIGNIFICANT CORRELATION AND DIFFERENCE BETWEEN MEANS

In this example:

1. There are ten people (Bob, Sue, etc.) arranged as before. So that:

```
     Bob's 1st          Bob's 2nd
     IQ score           IQ score
            \          /
             100  102
               etc.
```

2. We wish to determine if the mean of score1 is significantly different from the mean of score2. To do this we also need to know if there is a positive and significant correlation between score1 and score2.

3. In this example, the mean of score1 is 120 and the mean of score2 is 123.4. The correlation between score1 and score2 is -.122 and is NOT significant with $p = .738$. Since the correlation coefficient is NOT significant the scientist should rethink the experimental design as the pairing or matching used in the study is not working!

The paired t-test will turn out NOT to be significant. The t equals -.46 and the probability of the t-score will be = .377.

SPSS SETUP FOR PAIRED T-TEST WITH NOTATION

```
set width = 80 .
data list list/ score1 score2 .⇨ establishes  2  scores  per  subject
begin data .
      100 118    ⇨ ⇨ Bob's  two  scores
      110 133    ⇨ ⇨ Sue's  two  scores
      125 110
      140 128
      120 106
      130 102
      115 117
       95 148
      145 143
      120 129
end data .
t-test pairs = score1 score2 .⇨ paired  t-test  for  score1  vs.  score2
finish .
```

RELEVANT SPSS OUTPUT WITH INTERPRETATIVE NOTATION

```
 1  0 set width = 80 .
 2  data list list / score1 score2 .
 3  begin data .
13  end data .
24  t-test pairs = score1 score2 .

    - - - t - tests for paired samples - - -
```

Variable	Number of Cases	Mean	Standard Deviation	Standard Error
SCORE1				1
	10	120.0000	15.986	5.055
	10	123.4000	18.228	4.881
SCORE2				

(Difference) Mean	Standard Deviation	Standard Error	Corr.	2-tail Prob.	t Value	Degrees of Freedom	2-tail Prob.
				2			3
-3.4000	23.353	7.442	-0.122	0.738	-.46	9	.659

IMPORTANT INTERPRETATIVE POINTS OF THE OUTPUT

1. <u>Gray Box 1</u> contains the means of score1 and score2, along with their standard deviations and standard errors.

2. <u>Gray Box 2</u> contains the correlation between score1 and score2. Pearson's correlation coefficient equals -.122 and is not as it has a probability of .738 and greater than .05. The experiment should STOP and think about his or her design as the matching of pairs is not working!

3. <u>Gray Box 3</u> contains the t-score of -0.46. It is interpreted as follows:

   a. the value is negative as score1 is less than score2.

   b. the degrees of freedom = 9 as df = no. of pairs -1 (9-1).

   c. the difference is not significant and you reject the null hypothesis because the **2-TAIL PROB**. is greater than .05 or .01. It would be reported as p = .659.

   d. the IQ mean for score1 is not different from the IQ mean of score2.

CHAPTER 10: χ^2 TEST OF INDEPENDENCE

CHI-SQUARE TEST FOR INDEPENDENCE OF ONE CLASSIFICATION VARIABLE VS. A SECOND CLASSIFICATION VARIABLE

SUMMARY OF SPSS SETUPS: [1]

Scores Entered for Each Person

```
set width = 80 .
data list list/ x y .
begin data .
.
.
.
    xscore yscore
.
.
.
end data .
crosstabs x by y /
        cells = count row column total expected resid /
        statistics = chisq .
finish .
```

XSCORE, YSCORE combination for every subject is entered as data

Frequency Distribution Entered

```
set width = 80 .
data list list/ x y  freq .
weight by freq .
begin data .
.
.
  xscore yscore freq
.
.
.
end data .
crosstabs x by y /
        cells = count row column total expected resid /
        statistics = chisq .
finish .
```

XSCORE, YSCORE combination and frequency of that combination is entered as data

---

[1] Use **data list free/ x y** *etc*. for SPSS/PC+™ 4.0. Assume for all following setups.

REAL WORLD EXAMPLE WITH SCORES ENTERED FOR EACH PERSON *

```
set width = 80 .
data list list / sex fear .  2
value labels sex 1 'male' 2 'female'/
          fear 1 ' yes' 2 'no ' .
variables labels fear 'scared to walk at night' .
begin data .
 1 1
 etc.
 2 1   Compares Percent of Men Versus Women Who Are Scared
 2 2   To Walk at Night. Men are coded as '1' and Women and '2'
 2 2   in the First Column. Being Scared is Coded as a '1' in
 2 2   the Second Column for Each Subject. There is 1 Subject/Line.
 2 2   Chi-square is computed for the data.
 2 2
 1 2
end data .
crosstabs fear by sex / cells = count row column total
    expected resid / statistics .
finish
```

REAL WORLD EXAMPLE WITH FREQUENCY DISTRIBUTION ENTERED *

```
set width = 80 .
data list list / school sex freq .2
value labels school 1 ' Green U.' 2 'Rodney U.'/
          sex 1 'male' 2 'female' .
weight by freq .
begin data .
1 1 650   Compares proportions of Men and Women at Green
2 1 750   University to Rodney University. The four proportions
1 2 950   are marked by SCHOOL in the first column and SEX in
2 2 550   second column. The third column (FREQ) is the number of
end data . students in the combination. Chi-square is computed
crosstabs sex by school /
        cells = count row column total expected resid /
        statistics .
finish .
```

*Note that the value labels are not necessary but added only for clarity of output.

2 Use **data list free/ x y _etc._ .** for SPSS/PC+™ 4.0.

PURPOSE OF THE PROCEDURE AND STATISTICS

The purpose of the **crosstabs** program in this section is to :

1. Give you a crosstabulation of frequencies for two variables under study and the combinations of these two variables. The general form of a crosstabulation is presented below. The data of interest are the frequencies of occurrence of combinations of variables **X** and **Y**.

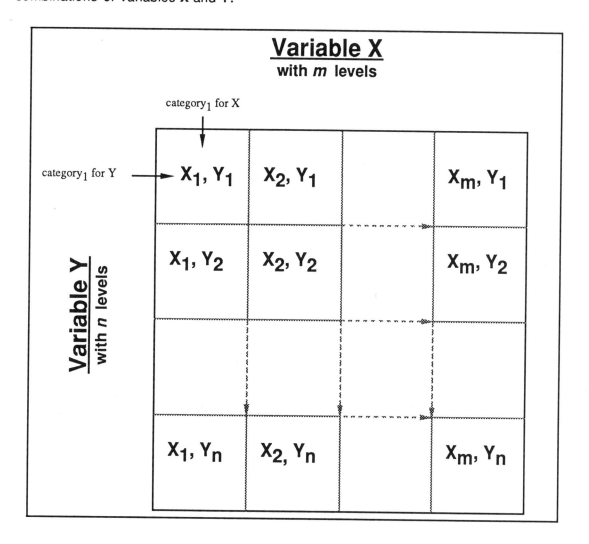

2. Calculate the row, column, and total percents that these frequencies represent.

3. Calculate the chi-square (χ^2) test for independence for your contingency table and test it for significance.

The chi-square statistic (χ^2) is calculated using the standard formula:

$$\chi^2 = \Sigma \; \frac{(O - E)^2 \; *}{E}$$

*Note that the program does calculate the standard corrections (Yates), but this will be discussed in the examples.

Where:

O is the observed frequency. This is from the data.

E is the expected frequency. It is calculated by the formula:

$$\text{Expected (E)} = \frac{\text{Row Total} \; \times \; \text{Column Total}}{\text{Total}}$$

The chi-square statistic (χ^2) is evaluated for significance with a degrees of freedom equal to the:

[NUMBER OF CATEGORIES FOR VARIABLE$_1$ - 1] X [NUMBER OF CATEGORIES FOR VARIABLE$_2$ - 1]

A significant chi-square statistic (χ^2) means that the proportions for the rows (or columns) are not independent of the other variable (column or row) formula.

4. Calculate measures of associations for the contingency table. This will be shown in the examples.

HOW TO DO χ^2 on SPSS

Testing the chi-square test of independence (χ^2) with SPSS entails the use of the **crosstabs** program.

The basic command is:

```
crosstabs x by y /
     cells = count row column total expected resid /
     statistics .
```

Where:

crosstabs	=	the program name
x	=	the first classification variable
y	=	the second classification variable
cells = ...	=	various frequencies and percents requested (see explanation below)
statistics ...		requests chi-square ($\chi2$) be calculated (others can be requested - see below).

However you must make a decision on how you are going to enter the data. There are two ways:

Setup Using WEIGHTed Data

Only the category and the number of people (or whatever) having that score is typed. In other words, you are entering the actual crosstabulated distribution. This is useful if these numbers have been given to you. For example, you are interested if two colleges differ in the proportions of males to females at their schools. One college is Green University (coded as a "1") and the other is Rodney University (coded as a "2"). Assume you code men as "1" and women as "2." The data set will then consist of the possible combinations of scores {1,1}, {1,2}, {2,1}, {2,2} and the frequency of the combination.

The data would look as follows:

SCHOOL	SEX	FREQUENCY	INTERPRETATION
1	1	650 ---->	650 males at Green U.
2	1	750 ---->	750 males at Rodney U.
1	2	950 ---->	950 females at Green U.
2	2	550 ---->	550 females at Rodney U.

The SPSS setup must contain information about the category memberships and the frequencies. This is done in the **data list** and **weight** commands. Variable and value labels can be used at your convenience but are not necessary. For the above situation the following commands describe the data and ask for the crosstabulation and chi-square.

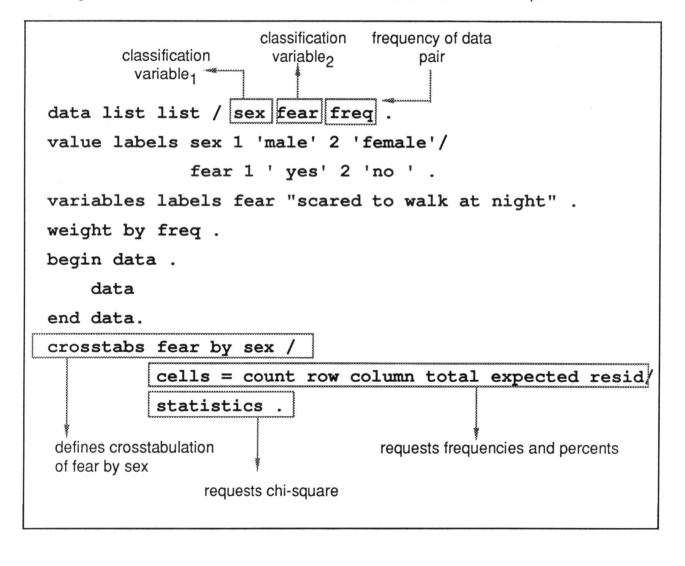

SETUP WITH SCORES FOR EACH SUBJECT

The actual scores for the two categories for each person are typed You have a case for every person indicating their category memberships. For example, let's assume you do a survey where you ask someone their sex and if they are afraid to walk alone at night (see *SPSS*, chapter. 25). If you code men as "1" and women as "2," and whether they are scared walk at night with "1" as "yes" and "2" as "no", your data set is a long list of 1s and 2s for each variable with one pair of scores for each subject. It would look like this

```
Subject's          Response
  Sex             (Yes or No)            Interpretation
   1                   1      --------->   scared male
   2                   2      --------->   brave female
   2                   1      --------->   scared female
   1                   2      --------->   brave male
        etc. -- One line per subject with two scores.
```

For the above situation the following commands describe the data and ask for the crosstabulation and chi-square.

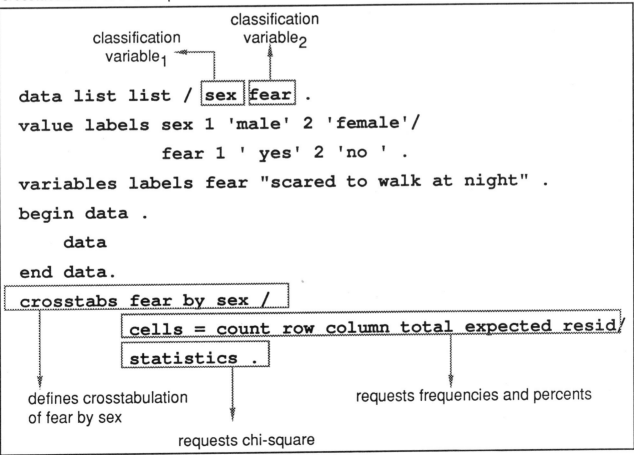

BASIC SETUPS FOR χ^2
WITH FREQUENCIES ENTERED

In this example, we wish to see if the percentages of males and females differ according to the school they attend (Green U. vs. Rodney U.). In other words, does each school have a different male to female ratio. We will enter the data for the number of males at Green U. (650), females at Green (950), males at Rodney (750), and females at Rodney (550) using the **weight** command.

There will be a significant difference as the proportions for each are quite dissimilar. There are 40.6% males and 59.4% females at Green as compared to 57.7% males and 42.3% females at Rodney. Thus, the chi-square statistic (χ^2) will be significant as the probability level will be <.0001.

SIGNIFICANT χ^2 SETUP
WITH FREQUENCIES ENTERED

```
set width = 80 .
data list list / school sex freq . [data list free / etc. for
                                             SPSS/PC+]
value labels school 1 ' Green U.' 2 'Rodney U.'/
             sex 1 'male' 2 'female' .
weight by freq .
begin data .
1 1 650
2 1 750
1 2 950
2 2 550
end data .
crosstabs sex by school /
         cells =count row column total expected resid /
         statistics .
finish .
```

OUTPUT WITH INTERPRETATIVE NOTATIONS

```
   1  0  set width = 80 .
   2  data list list / school sex freq .
   3  value labels school 1 ' Green U.' 2 'Rodney U.'/
   4                sex 1 'male' 2 'female'.
   5  weight by freq .
   6  begin data .
  10  end data .
  11  crosstabs sex by school /
  12            cells = count row column total expected resid /
  13            statistics .

SEX  by  SCHOOL

                  SCHOOL       Page 1 of 1
          Count  |
        Exp Val  |
        Row Pct  |
        Col Pct  | Green U Rodney U
        Tot Pct  |.        .          Row
        Residual|     1.00|     2.00| Total
SEX     --------+--------+--------+
           1.00  |   650  |   750  |  1400
  male           | 772.4  | 627.6  | 48.3%
                 | 46.4%  | 53.6%  |
      1          | 40.6%  | 57.7%  |
                 | 22.4%  | 25.9%  |
                 |-122.4  | 122.4  |
                 +--------+--------+
           2.00  |   950  |   550  |  1500
  female         | 827.6  | 672.4  | 51.7%
                 | 63.3%  | 36.7%  |
                 | 59.4%  | 42.3%  |
                 | 32.8%  | 19.0%  |    2
                 | 122.4  |-122.4  |
                 +--------+--------+
          Column    1600     1300     2900
           Total   55.2%    44.8%   100.0%

       Chi-Square                   Value          DF         Significance
--------------------              -----------     ----        ------------

Pearson                            83.67048         1            .00000
Continuity Correction              82.98833         1            .00000
Likelihood Ratio                   84.02711         1       3    .00000
Mantel-Haenszel                    83.64159         1            .00000

Minimum Expected Frequency -  627.586
```

INTERPRETATIVE POINTS

1. <u>Gray Box 1</u> tells you the variables being analyzed are **sex by school.** The value labels indicate that for **sex** "1" stands for males and "2" stands for females. For **school** "1" stands for *Green University* and "2" stands for *Rodney University*.

The following figure explain the contents of one of the cells of the output.

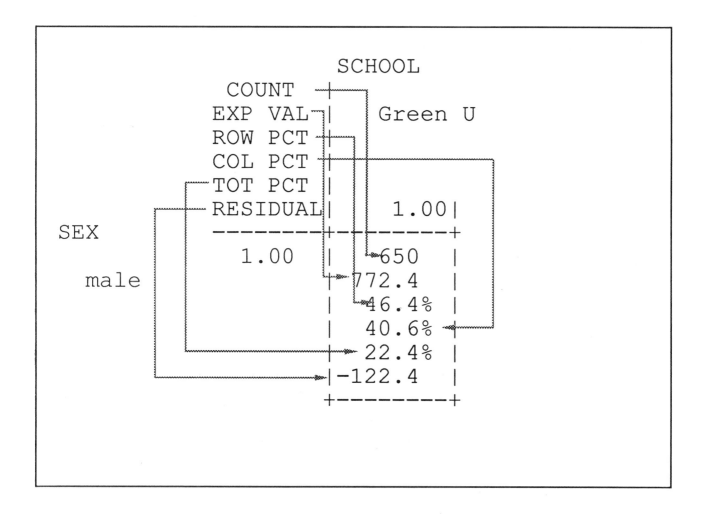

COUNT	=	The number of subjects in that cell. In this case, there are **650 males at Green U.** This is the **O** from chi-square test of independence (χ^2).

EXP VAL	=	**E** (expected from the chi-square test of independence (χ^2)). You would have expected **772.4 males at Green U.** This value is calculated by the formula :

(Row total $\times$ Column Total)/Total

or

(1400 $\times$ 1600) / 2900.

ROW PCT	=	46.4% of the total number of 1400 males are attending Green U.

(650$_{Green\ U.\ Males}$ ÷ 1400$_{Total\ Males}$) x 100.

COL PCT	=	The percent of all the 1600 total students attending Green U. who are male. The percentage is **40.6%** which is

(650$_{Green\ U.\ Males}$ ÷ 1600$_{Green\ U.\ Students}$) x 100.

TOT PCT	=	The percent of 2900 total students question who are attending Green U. and are male. The percentage is **22.4%** which is

(650$_{Green\ U.\ Males}$ ÷ 2900$_{Total\ Students}$) x 100.

RESIDUAL	=	**(O - E)** from the from chi-square test of independence (χ^2). In this cases it is

650-772.4   =   **-122.4.**

2. <u>Gray Box 2</u> contains the row and column frequencies and percents. We see that of the total 2900 students, 1400 (48.3%) are male and 1500 (51.7%) are female. Similarly, 1600 (55.2%) of the total 2900 are attending Green University and 1300 (44.8%) are attending Rodney University .

3. <u>Gray Box 3</u> contains the computed chi-square ($\chi 2$), the degrees of freedom (df), and the significance level. **Please attend to the boldfaced values.** In this example, the **chi-square** is **83.67048**, the **df =1,** and the significance level should be read as **p <.0001**. The 0.0000 in the output represents a **p** that is smaller than the allotted number of decimals. This is a **significant** difference by most standards as **p. < .05 or .01**. Note we will discuss the Yates correction on p. 10.21.

The results are significant because the percentages of males versus females is different for each college and this difference is large enough to be significant. The differences are presented in the figure below which has been extracted from the output above. Note that Green has 40.6% males and 59.4 % females while Rodney has a reversed pattern with 57.7% males and 42.3% males. These are percentages are in opposite directions and very different from the null hypothesis percentages of 48.3% males and 51.7% females found in the **Gray Box 1 (note that we could have made the same analysis based on the rows as well as the columns).**

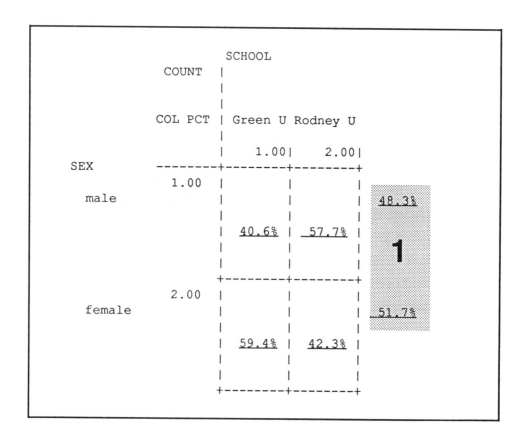

Nonsignificant χ^2 with Frequencies Entered

In this instance, the proportions for men and women at the two schools are very close (65.5% males and 34.5% females for Green versus 63.8% males, 36.2% females for Rodney U.). Thus, the schools do not differ significantly and the probability of the chi-square statistic (χ^2) will be > .05.

Setup

```
set width = 80 .
data list list / school sex freq .
value labels school 1 ' Green U.' 2 'Rodney U.'/
            sex 1 'male' 2 'female' .
weight by freq .
begin data .
1 1 950
2 1 925 ⇨ Frequencies have changed such that
1 2 500    Green and Rodney do not differ significantly
2 2 525    in proportion of males to females.
end data .
crosstabs sex by school /
        cells =count row column total expected resid /
        statistics .
finish .
```

OUTPUT WITH INTERPRETATIVE NOTATIONS

```
 1   0  set width = 80 .
 2  data list list / school sex freq .
 3  value labels school 1 ' Green U.' 2 'Rodney U.'/
 4              sex 1 'male' 2 'female' .
 5  weight by freq .
 6  begin data .
10  end data .
11  crosstabs sex by school /
12          cells =count row column total expected resid /
13          statistics .
```

SEX   by   SCHOOL

```
                     SCHOOL          Page 1 of 1
            Count   |
            Exp Val |
            Row Pct |
            Col Pct | Green U  Rodney U
            Tot Pct |.        .          Row
            Residual|   1.00|    2.00| Total
SEX         --------+--------+--------+
            1.00    |    950 |    925 |  1875
  male              |  937.5 |  937.5 | 64.7%
                    |  50.7% |  49.3% |
                    |  65.5% |  63.8% |------> Note that underlined
                    |  32.8% |  31.9% |        percentages are very close!
                    |   12.5 |  -12.5 |
                    +--------+--------+
            2.00    |    500 |    525 |  1025
  female            |  512.5 |  512.5 | 35.3%
                    |  48.8% |  51.2% |
                    |  34.5% |  36.2% |------> Note that underlined
                    |  17.2% |  18.1% |        percentages are very close!
                    |  -12.5 |   12.5 |
                    +--------+--------+
            Column    1450     1450     2900
            Total     50.0%    50.0%   100.0%
```

Chi-Square	Value	DF	Significance
Pearson	.94309	1	.33148 -> Not Sign.
Continuity Correction	.86915	1	.35119 as > .05
Likelihood Ratio	.94316	1	.33147
Mantel-Haenszel	.94276	1	.33157

Minimum Expected Frequency - 512.500

BASIC SETUP FOR χ^2 WITH SCORES ENTERED

In this example, we wish to see if the percentages of males and females who are afraid to walk alone at night are significantly different We will enter the data for each of the 36 subjects individually with one line of data representing one subject.

There will be a significant difference as the proportions for each are quite dissimilar. There are 80.0% males who are afraid and 20% males who are not afraid. However, only 37.5% of females are afraid, while 62.5% are not afraid. Thus, the chi-square statistic (χ^2) will be significant as the probability level will be =.0093 which is < .01

SETUP

```
set width = 80 .
data list list / sex fear .
value labels sex 1 'male' 2 'female'/
          fear 1 ' yes' 2 'no ' .
variables labels fear
          'scared to walk at night' .
begin data .
 1 1
 1 1    → One line per subject
 1 1
 1 1
 1 1
 1 2
 2 1
 2 1
 2 1
 2 2
 2 2
 2 2
 2 2
 2 2
 1 1
 1 1
 1 1
 1 2
 1 1
 1 1
 1 1
 1 1
 1 1
 1 2
 2 1
 2 1
 2 1
 2 2
 2 2
 2 2
 2 2
 2 2
 1 1
 1 2
 1 1
 1 1
end data.
crosstabs fear by sex /
     cells = count row column total
     expected resid/
     statistics .
finish.
```

OUTPUT WITH INTERPRETATIVE NOTATIONS

```
  1  0  set width = 80 .
  2  data list list / sex fear .
  3  value labels sex 1 'male' 2 'female'/
  4             fear 1 ' yes' 2 'no ' .
  5  variables labels fear 'scared to walk at night' .
  6  begin data .
 42  end data .
 43  crosstabs fear by sex /
 44             cells = count row column total expected resid/
 45             statistics .


FEAR  scared to walk at night  by  SEX


                    SEX          Page 1 of 1
          Count   |
          Exp Val |
          Row Pct |
          Col Pct |male      female
          Tot Pct |                Row
          Residual|   1.00|   2.00| Total
FEAR      --------+--------+--------+
          1.00  |    16 |     6 |    22
   yes          |  12.2 |   9.8 | 61.1%
                |  72.7%|  27.3%|
                |  80.0%|  37.5%|
                |  44.4%|  16.7%|
                |   3.8 |  -3.8 |
                +--------+--------+
          2.00  |     4 |    10 |    14
   no           |   7.8 |   6.2 | 38.9%
                |  28.6%|  71.4%|
                |  20.0%|  62.5%|
                |  11.1%|  27.8%|
                |  -3.8 |   3.8 |
                +--------+--------+
          Column     20      16      36
          Total    55.6%   44.4%  100.0%
```

Note that **80% of males** are fearful as compared to **37.5% of females**. Thus **chi-square is significant**.

Chi-Square	Value	DF	Significance
Pearson	**6.75584**	**1**	**.00934** (< .05)
Continuity Correction	5.08588	1	.02412
Likelihood Ratio	6.92777	1	.00849
Mantel-Haenszel	6.56818	1	.01038

Minimum Expected Frequency -   6.222

NONSIGNIFICANT χ^2 WITH SCORES ENTERED FOR EACH SUBJECT

In this example, we again wish to see if the percentages of males and females who are afraid to walk alone at night are significantly different. We will enter the data for each of the 36 subjects individually with one line of data representing one subject. However, there **will not be a significant difference** as the proportions for each are similar. There are 50% males who are afraid and 50% males who are not afraid; 37.5% of females are afraid, while 62.5% are not afraid. These percentages do not differ enough for significance. Thus, the chi-square statistic (χ^2) will not be significant as the probability level will be =.4533 which is > .05.

SETUP

```
set width = 80 .
data list list / sex fear .
value labels sex 1 'male' 2 'female'/  fear 1 ' yes' 2 'no ' .
variables labels fear 'scared to walk at night' .
begin data .
 1 1
 1 1
 1 2
 1 1
 1 1
 1 2
 2 1
 2 1
 2 1
 2 2
 2 2
 2 2
 2 2
 2 2
 1 1
 1 2
 1 2
 1 2
 1 1
 1 1
 1 2
 1 1
 1 1
 1 2
 2 1
 2 1
 2 1
 2 2
 2 2
 2 2
 2 2
 2 2
 1 1
 1 2
 1 2
 1 2
end data .
crosstabs fear by sex /
              cells = count row column total expected resid/
              statistics = chisq .
finish .
```

OUTPUT WITH INTERPRETATIVE NOTATIONS

```
  1  0  set width = 80 .
  2  data list list / sex fear .
  3  value labels sex 1 'male' 2 'female'/
  4            fear 1 ' yes' 2 'no ' .
  5  variables labels fear 'scared to walk at night' .
  6  begin data .
 42  end data .

FEAR  scared to walk at night  by  SEX


                    SEX            Page 1 of 1
             Count  |
             Exp Val|
             Row Pct|
             Col Pct|male      female
             Tot Pct|                    Row
             Residual|   1.00|    2.00| Total
FEAR         --------+--------+--------+
             1.00  |    10  |     6  |    16
     yes           |   8.9  |   7.1  | 44.4%
                   |  62.5% |  37.5% |
                   |  50.0% |  37.5% |
                   |  27.8% |  16.7% |
                   |   1.1  |  -1.1  |
                   +--------+--------+
             2.00  |    10  |    10  |    20
     no            |  11.1  |   8.9  | 55.6%
                   |  50.0% |  50.0% |
                   |  50.0% |  62.5% |
                   |  27.8% |  27.8% |
                   |  -1.1  |   1.1  |
                   +--------+--------+
          Column       20       16       36
           Total     55.6%    44.4%   100.0%
```

Chi-Square	Value	DF	Significance	
Pearson	.56250	1	.45326	**not significant**
Continuity Correction	.17016	1	.67997	**at p. > .05**
Likelihood Ratio	.56532	1	.45212	
Mantel-Haenszel	.54687	1	.45960	

Minimum Expected Frequency -   7.111

MEASURES OF ASSOCIATION AS ADDITIONAL STATISTICS

After calculating a χ^2, it may be of importance to determine if the association between the two variables is strong. This is similar to evaluating the magnitude of a Pearson's correlation coefficient where as values approach ± 1.0, you achieve better and better prediction. It is possible to do that for the chi-square statistic using the CROSSTABS program. Also, the program can calculate several other measures of association (as these statistics are called) depending on the type of data that you have. Data type refers to the classic distinctions:

categorical / nominal	(**C**)
rank / ordinal	(**R**)
measurement (numeric)	(**N**)

Additional statistics are requested by adding them to the command as follows:

```
crosstabs x by y /
        cells = count row column total expected resid /
        statistics=chisq additional requests .
```

The actual statistics that can be requested, the keyword to use, and the appropriate data type are presented below:

STATISTIC	SPSS KEY WORD	DATA TYPE
Chi-square	chisq	CRN
Phi for 2x2, Cramer's V > 2x2	phi	CRN
Contingency Coefficient	cc	CRN
Lambda, Symmetric & Asym.	lambda	CRN
Uncertainty Coeff., Sym. & Asym.	uc	CRN
Kendall's tau-b	btau	R
Kendall's tau-c	ctau	R
Gamma	gamma	R
Somer's d, Sym. & Asym.	d	R
Eta	eta	IV = C & DV = N
Pearson's correlation coeff. (r)	corr	N
Spearman's correlation	corr	R
Cohen's Kappa	kappa	N
Estimating Risk	risk	C
All the above	all	

The question of which statistic to use depends on the type of data you have. In general, they have values that range from 0 to 1, although Pearson's r can be negative and some statistics have a maximum value that depends on the size of the contingency table (Contingency coefficient). For good discussions of the merits of each, you might refer to the famous 1975 SPSS 2nd edition (red manual) if you can still find one. It's actually quite readable as to how the statistics work. Otherwise, there are many nonparametric texts out there (i.e. Everitt, 1977) that discuss the issue.

The following example demonstrates the issue of the subcommand. We use the same data set analyzing the relationship of SEX and FEAR that led to a significant chi-square. Note that we have added the Uncertainty Coefficient (UC) and the Phi Coefficient to our statistics request. They are highlighted in the command list and the statistical output:

```
  1   0   set width = 80 .
  2   data list list / sex fear .
  3   value labels sex 1 'male' 2 'female'/
  4               fear 1 ' yes' 2 'no ' .
  5   variables labels fear 'scared to walk at night' .
  6   begin data .
 42   end data .
 43   crosstabs fear by sex /
 44       cells = count row column total expected resid/
 45       statistics = chisq uc phi .⇨ ADDITIONAL STATISTICS

FEAR  scared to walk at night   by   SEX

                    SEX              Page 1 of 1
            Count  |
            Exp Val|
            Row Pct|
            Col Pct|male      female
            Tot Pct|                    Row
            Residual|    1.00|    2.00| Total
FEAR .      --------+--------+--------+
            1.00   |    16  |     6  |    22
    yes            |  12.2  |   9.8  | 61.1%
                   | 72.7%  | 27.3%  |
                   | 80.0%  | 37.5%  |
                   | 44.4%  | 16.7%  |
                   |   3.8  |  -3.8  |
                   +--------+--------+
            2.00   |     4  |    10  |    14
    no             |   7.8  |   6.2  | 38.9%
                   | 28.6%  | 71.4%  |
                   | 20.0%  | 62.5%  |
                   | 11.1%  | 27.8%  |
                   |  -3.8  |   3.8  |
                   +--------+--------+
            Column      20        16       36
            Total     55.6%     44.4%   100.0%
```

Chi-Square	Value	DF	Significance
Pearson	6.75584	1	.00934
Continuity Correction	5.08588	1	.02412
Likelihood Ratio	6.92777	1	.00849
Mantel-Haenszel	6.56818	1	.01038

Minimum Expected Frequency - 6.222

Statistic	Value	ASE1	T-value	Approximate Significance
Phi	.43320			.00934 *1
Cramer's V	.43320			.00934 *1
Uncertainty Coefficient :				
symmetric	.14200	.10238	1.38244	.00849 *3
with FEAR dependent	.14399	.10366	1.38244	.00849 *3
with SEX dependent	.14006	.10125	1.38244	.00849 *3

*1 Pearson chi-square probability
*3 Likelihood ratio chi-square probability

YATES CORRECTION

You may have noticed in the output that the chi-square value is given before and after Yates correction as reproduced below:

Chi-Square	Value	DF	Significance	
Pearson	.56250	1	.45326	Before Correction
Continuity Correction	.17016	1	.67997	After Correction
Likelihood Ratio	.56532	1	.45212	
Mantel-Haenszel	.54687	1	.45960	

Yates Correction was developed to correct for problems in determining the significance of chi-square when the data produce small expected values (between 5 and 10). However, there is a large literature suggesting that this correction is inappropriate (see Everitt, 1977; Howell, 1987; for discussion and references). Much current thinking says you need not worry about it so it is permissible and perhaps better to use the first line of output noted as **Pearson**. That is the one that we have highlighted in our discussions.

CHAPTER 11: χ^2 FOR A POPULATION SET OF FREQUENCIES

CHI-SQUARE TEST FOR A SET OF FREQUENCIES VS. AN HYPOTHESIZED OR GIVEN SET OF FREQUENCIES

SUMMARY OF SPSS SETUPS[1]

Scores Entered for Each Person

```
set width = 80 .
data list list / x .
begin data .
category#
category#
.
.
category#
end data .
npar tests chisquare = x
          (category₁ [lo],  categoryₙ [hi]) /
          expected = proportion₁,
          proportion₂, … , proportionₙ .
finish .
```

> **X score is the category membership of each subject .**

Frequency Distribution Entered

```
set width = 80 .
data list list / x freq .
weight by freq   .
begin data .
category₁ , frequency₁
category₂ , frequency₂
.
.
.
categoryₙ , frequencyₙ
end data .
npar tests chisquare = x
          (category₁ [lo],  categoryₙ [hi]) /
          expected = proportion₁,
          proportion₂, … , proportionₙ .
finish .
```

> **X score is category membership #.**
> **FREQ is the number of subjects in catetory.**

---

[1] Use **data list free/ x *etc.*.**   for SPSS/PC+™ 4.0. Assume for all following setups.

Real World Example With Scores Entered for Each Person

```
set width = 80   .
data list list/ sex .
value labels sex 1 'male' 2 'female' .
begin data .
1
1
2
2
2
.
etc
.
1
2
end data .
npar tests chisquare = sex (1,2)/ expected = 55 45 .
finish .
```

> **Tests Whether the Actual Proportion of Men and Women Differs Significantly From 55%f or Men and 45% for Women Using the Chi-Square Statistic:**
> There are any number of subjects (one per line of data) with the number indicating their gender (1 = male, 2 = female).

Real World Example With Frequency Distribution Entered

```
set width = 80 .
data list list / sex freq .
weight by freq .
value labels sex 1 'male' 2 'female' .
begin data .
1 60
2 65
end data .
npar tests chisquare = sex (1,2) /  expected = 55 45 .
finish .
```

> **Tests Whether the Proportion of Men and Women Differs Significantly From 55% Men and 45% Women Using Chi-Square :**
>
> There are 60 males (coded on the first line of data with 1 = male and 60 = frequency) and 65 females (codes on the second line of data with 2= female and 65 = frequency).

PURPOSE OF THE PROCEDURE AND STATISTICS

The purpose of the **npar tests** program in this section is to calculate a chi-square statistic (χ^2) for the frequencies of a set of categories as compared to a given set of population percentages for those categories. These given population percentages must be known ahead of time. The chi-square statistic (χ^2) is calculated using the standard formula:

$$\chi^2 = \sum \frac{(O - E)^2}{E}$$

O is the observed frequency. This is from the data.

E is the expected frequency. This is based on the percentages you have hypothesized.

The chi-square statistic (χ^2) is evaluated for significance with a degrees of freedom equal to the number of categories minus 1 (k-1, if k = number of categories).

HOW TO DO χ^2 ON SPSS

Testing the chi-square statistic (χ^2) with SPSS entails the use of the **npar tests** program. **However you must make a decision on how you are going to enter the data.** There are two ways:

Method 1. The actual score for each person is typed which indicates their category membership. You have a case for every person indicating their category membership. For example, if you code men as "1" and women as "2," your data set is a long list of 1s and 2s with one for each subject. It would look like this:

1
2
1
2
2
etc. -- There is one score per subject

Method 2. Only the category and the number of people (or whatever) having that score is typed. In other words, you are entering the actual frequency distribution. This is useful if these numbers have been given to you. For example, some one tells you there are 80 men and 23 women in your group. Your data would look like this:

1   80

2   23

Depending on which way you set up the data will determine the details of the setup.

In either case the **npar tests** command will look as follows:

```
npar tests chisquare = x (category1,categoryn)/
     expected = percentage1, percentage2,...percentagen .
```

where:

x = the variable name that contains the categories.

$category_1$ = the low score which identifies the categories.

$category_n$ = the high score which identifies the last category.

$percentage_i$ = the hypothesized percentage for the category with the same subscript number.

For example, assume men are coded as "1" and women are coded as "2" for a variable named **sex**. You want to compare the percentages of men (1s) and women (2s) in your data against a hypothesized set of percentages for men and women. Assume that the hypothesized percentage for men is 55% and for women is 45%. The command would be as follows:

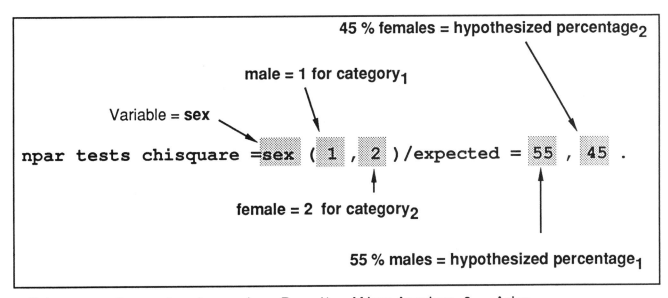

If there were three categories, such as Race (1 = African-American, 2 = Asian, 3 = White), then the command would appear as:

```
npar tests chisquare = race (1,3) / expected = %
     Afro - American, % Asian, % White) .
```

The following examples will use this command with the two different ways of entered the data. Both significant and nonsignificant chi-squares will be presented.

Example 1 : Basic Setup for χ^2 with Scores Entered for Each Subject [2]

In this example we have two categories for the variable **sex** (with "1" indicating male and "2" indicating female). Each individual makes up one case so that in this data set, there is one score per subject and this is their sex. The data would look like this:

$$1 \quad \text{-----------> a male}$$
$$2 \quad \text{----------> a female , etc.}$$

In our example to follow there are 16 males and 4 females. Thus there are 16 "1s" and 4 "2s" typed as a single column. Our goal is to see whether these frequencies are significantly different from an hypothesized set of percentages which are 55% males and 45% females. The chi-square **is** significant as noted in the output.The setup and output are as follows (note that value labels have been added for clarity but are not necessary):

SETUP WITH SCORES FOR EACH SUBJECT & SIGNIFICANT χ^2

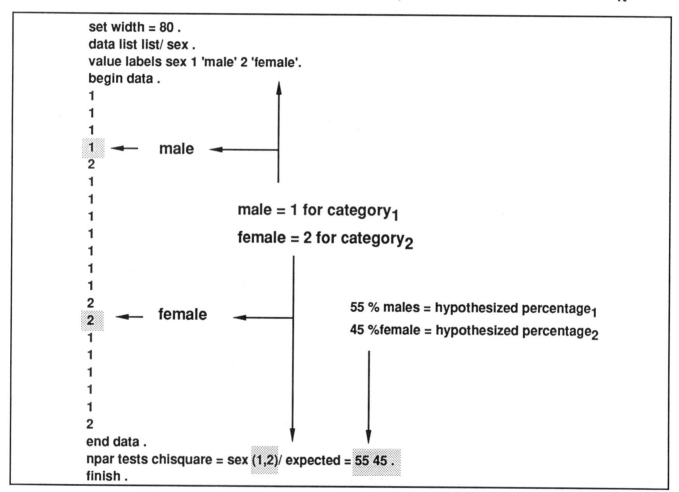

```
set width = 80 .
data list list/ sex .
value labels sex 1 'male' 2 'female'.
begin data .
1
1
1
1          <---   male   <---
2
1
1
1                  male = 1 for category₁
1
1                  female = 2 for category₂
1
1
2
2          <---   female  <---     55 % males = hypothesized percentage₁
1                                  45 %female = hypothesized percentage₂
1
1
1
1
2
end data .
npar tests chisquare = sex (1,2)/ expected = 55 45 .
finish .
```

---

[2] Use ' data list **free** / sex ' for SPSS/PC +™ 4.0 .

Output

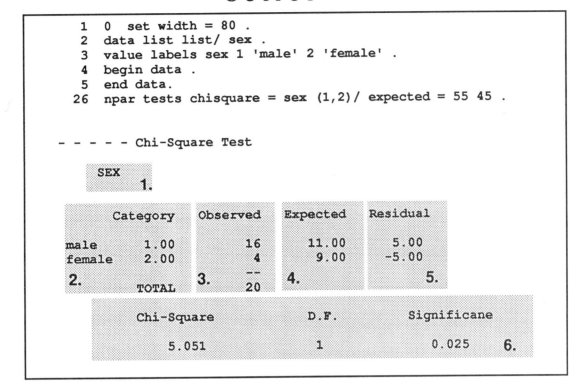

```
     1   0   set width = 80 .
     2   data list list/ sex .
     3   value labels sex 1 'male' 2 'female' .
     4   begin data .
     5   end data.
    26   npar tests chisquare = sex (1,2)/ expected = 55 45 .
```

- - - - - Chi-Square Test

SEX
1.

Category		Observed	Expected	Residual
male	1.00	16	11.00	5.00
female	2.00	4	9.00	-5.00
2.	TOTAL	**3.** -- 20	**4.**	**5.**

Chi-Square	D.F.	Significane
5.051	1	0.025 **6.**

INTERPRETATIVE POINTS

1. Gray Box 1 tells you the variable being analyzed is **sex.**

2. Gray Box 2 again contains the categories.The value labels indicate that "1" stands for males and "2" stands for females.

3. Gray Box 3 tells you how many males and females there were in your data. This is the observed or the **O** in the chi-square equation. Thus, the number of "1s" (males) and "2s" (females) are counted for you.

4. Gray Box 4 contains the expected frequencies based on the percentages that you hypothesized. This is the expected or the **E** in the chi-square equation.

5. Gray Box 5 contains the residual or difference between the observer. This is the **O-E** in the chi-square equation.

6. Gray Box 6 contains the computed chi-square (χ^2), the degrees of freedom (df) and the significance level. In this example, the **chi-square** is **5.051**, the **df** =1 (2-1) and the significance level should be read as **p** =.025. This is a significant difference by most standards as it is below .05 (p. < .05). It would not be significant at the .01 level as p. > .025

NONSIGNIFICANT χ^2 WITH SCORES FOR EACH SUBJECT

In this example, the observed frequencies for males and females are now 8 (42.1%) and 11 (57.9%) respectively. There will not be a significant difference.

```
set width = 80 .
data list list/ sex .
value labels sex 1 'male' 2 'female' .
begin data .
2
2
2
2
2
1
1
2
1
1
1
2
2
1
1
1
2
2
2
end data .
npar tests chisquare = sex (1,2)/ expected = 55 45 .
finish .
```

OUTPUT WITH INTERPRETATIVE NOTATIONS

```
    1   0  set width = 80 .
    2   data list list/ sex .
    3   value labels sex 1 'male' 2 'female' .
    4   begin data .
    5.  end data .
   25   npar tests chisquare = sex (1,2)/ expected = 55 45 .

- - - - - Chi-Square Test

      SEX

                   Cases
          Category  Observed  Expected  Residual

male       1.00        8       10.45     -2.45
female     2.00       11        8.55      2.45
                      --
          Total       19

          Chi-Square           D.F.     Significance
           1.276                1          0.259   --> p.> .05
                                         not significant
```

Example 2: Basic Setups for χ^2 with Frequencies Entered

In this example we have two variables per case (or data line). The first is **sex** (with "1" indicating male and "2" indicating female). The second (**freq**) is the number of that sex we have in the group. Thus our data look as follows:

SEX	FREQ
1	80
2	23

There are 80 males and 23 females. Our goal is to see whether these frequencies are significantly different from an hypothesized set of percentages which are 55% males and 45% females. The chi-square **is** significant as noted in the output. The setup and output are as follows (note that value labels have been added for clarity but are not necessary):

SIGNIFICANT χ^2 WITH FREQUENCIES ENTERED

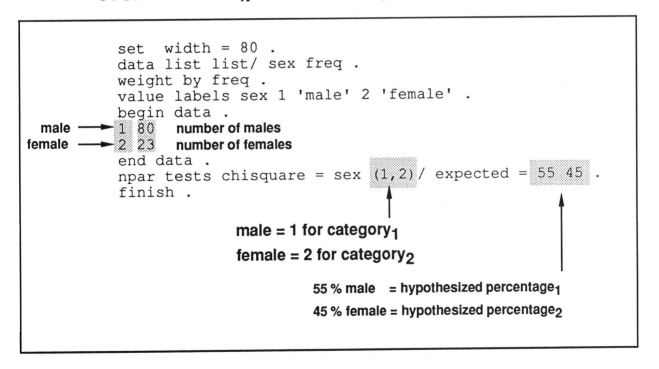

```
            set  width = 80 .
            data list list/ sex freq .
            weight by freq .
            value labels sex 1 'male' 2 'female' .
            begin data .
male   →    1 80    number of males
female →    2 23    number of females
            end data .
            npar tests chisquare = sex (1,2) / expected = 55 45 .
            finish .
```

male = 1 for category_1

female = 2 for category_2

55 % male   = hypothesized percentage_1

45 % female = hypothesized percentage_2

OUTPUT WITH INTERPRETATIVE NOTATIONS

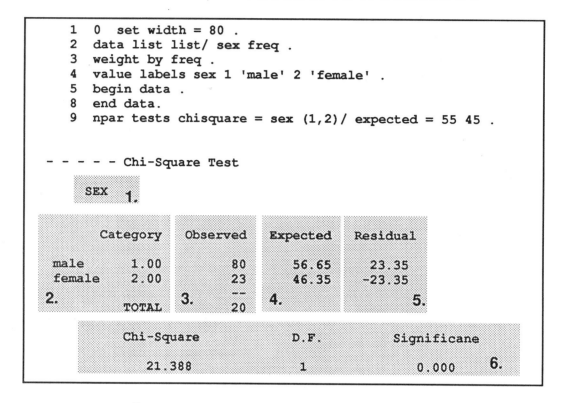

```
      1  0  set width = 80 .
      2  data list list/ sex freq .
      3  weight by freq .
      4  value labels sex 1 'male' 2 'female' .
      5  begin data .
      8  end data.
      9  npar tests chisquare = sex (1,2)/ expected = 55 45 .


- - - - - Chi-Square Test

      SEX   1.


          Category   Observed   Expected   Residual

    male     1.00         80      56.65      23.35
    female   2.00         23      46.35     -23.35
    2.                     --
             TOTAL  3.     20   4.                  5.

          Chi-Square          D.F.        Significane

            21.388             1           0.000     6.
```

INTERPRETATIVE POINTS

1. Gray Box 1 tells you the variable being analyzed is **sex.**

2. Gray Box 2 again contains the categories. The value labels indicate that "1" stands for males and "2" stands for females.

3. Gray Box 3 tells you how males and females there were in your data. This is the observed or the **O** in the chi-square equation.

4. Gray Box 4 contains the expected frequencies based on the percentages that you hypothesized. This is the expected or the **E** in the chi-square equation.

5. Gray Box 5 contains the residual or difference between the observer. This is the **O-E** in the chi-square equation.

6. Gray Box 6 contains the computed chi-square (χ^2), the degrees of freedom (df) and the significance level. In this example, the **chi-square** is **21.388**, the **df =1** (2-1) and the significance level should be read as **p <.001**. This is a significant difference by most standards as it is below .05 or .01.

NONSIGNIFICANT χ^2 WITH FREQUENCIES ENTERED

In this example, the observed frequencies for males and females are now 60 and 65 respectively. There will not be a significant difference.

SETUP

```
set width = 80 .
data list list/ sex freq .
weight by freq .
value labels sex 1 'male' 2 'female' .
begin data .
1 60  ⇨⇨  Frequencies changed to minimize difference
2 65
end data.
npar tests chisquare = sex (1,2)/ expected = 55 45 .
finish .
```

OUTPUT WITH INTERPRETATIVE NOTATIONS

```
  1   0  set width = 80 .
  2   data list list/ sex .
  3   value labels sex 1 'male' 2 'female' .
  4   weight by freq
  5   begin data .
  7.  end data .
  8   npar tests chisquare = sex (1,2)/ expected = 55 45 .

- - - - - Chi-Square Test

      SEX

                    Cases
          Category  Observed  Expected  Residual

male      1.00      60        68.75     -8.75
female    2.00      65        56.25      8.75
                    --
          Total     125

          Chi-Square           D.F.  Significance
            2.475                1       0.116  --> p.> .05
                                                not  significant
```

CHAPTER 12: THE PEARSON PRODUCT MOMENT CORRELATION COEFFICIENT (PEARSON'S *r*)

CALCULATION OF PEARSON'S PRODUCT MOMENT COEFFICIENT (r)

1. SUMMARY OF SPSS SETUP FOR 2 VARIABLES, X AND Y[1]

```
set width = 80 .
data list list / x y .
begin data .
        .
        .
        data
        .
        .
end data .
correlations x y / print = sig / statistics = descriptives .
finish .
```

REAL WORLD EXAMPLE

```
set width = 80 .
data list list/ x y .
begin data .
10    8.04
 8    6.95
13    7.58
 9    8.81
11    8.33
14    9.96
 6    7.24
 4    4.26
12   10.84
 7    4.82
 5    5.68
end data .
correlations   x  y / print = sig / statistics = descriptives .
finish .
```

Computes Correlation Coefficient for variables x and y and tests them for significance (two-tailed). Means and standard deviations are printed. There are 11 subjects with 2 scores each (x , y) with one line per subject.

---

1 SPSS/PC + ™ 4.0 setups are different. See Example 4.

2. SUMMARY OF SPSS SETUP FOR ONE VARIABLE (X) AND A SET OF VARIABLES (Y1 TO Y4)

```
set width = 80 .
data list list / x y1 to y4 .
begin data
        .
        .
        data
        .
        .
end data .
correlations x with y1 to y4 / print = sig / statistics = descriptives .
finish .
```

REAL WORLD EXAMPLE

```
set width = 80 .

data list list/ x y1 to y4 .

begin data .

10     8.04    9.14    7.46    6.58

 8     6.95    8.14    6.77    5.76

13     7.58    8.74   12.74    7.71

 9     8.81    8.77    7.11    8.84

11     8.33    9.26    7.81    8.47

14     9.96    8.10    8.84    7.04

 6     7.24    6.13    6.08    5.25

 4     4.26    3.10    5.39   12.50

12    10.84    9.13    8.15    5.56

 7     4.82    7.26    6.42    7.91

 5     5.68    4.74    5.73    6.89

end data .

correlations  x with y1 to y4 / print = sig / statistics = descriptives

finish .
```

Computes Correlation Coefficients for a variable x with a set of variables (y1 to y5) and tests them for significance (two-tailed). Means and standard deviations are printed. There are 11 subjects with 5 scores each (x, y1, y2, y3, y4) with one line per subject.

3. SUMMARY OF SPSS SETUP FOR A SET OF VARIABLES (X1 TO X5):

```
set width = 80 .
data list list / x1 to x5 .
begin data   .
        .
        .
     data
        .
        .
end data   .
correlations x1 to x5 / print = sig / statistics = descriptives .
finish .
```

REAL WORLD EXAMPLE

```
set width = 80 .
data list list/ x1 to x5 .
begin data .
10     8.04  9.14   7.46   6.58
 8     6.95  8.14   6.77   5.76
13     7.58  8.74  12.74   7.71
 9     8.81  8.77   7.11   8.84
11     8.33  9.26   7.81   8.47
14     9.96  8.10   8.84   7.04
 6     7.24  6.13   6.08   5.25
 4     4.26  3.10   5.39  12.50
12    10.84  9.13   8.15   5.56
 7     4.82  7.26   6.42   7.91
 5     5.68  4.74   5.73   6.89
end data .
correlations  x1 to x5 / print = sig / statistics = descriptives.
finish .
```

Computes Correlation Coefficients for set of variables (x1 to x5) and tests them for significance (two-tailed). Means and standard deviations are printed. There are 11 subjects with 5 scores each (x1, x2, x3, x4, x5) with one line per subject.

4. SUMMARY OF SPSS/PC + ™ 4.0 SETUPS

```
set width = 80 .
data list free / variable list     ( e.g. x y ;
                                     x1 to x5;  x y1 to y4) .
begin data .
      .
      .
      data
      .
      .
end data .
correlations variable list  / options = 5 / statistics = 1 .
finish .
```

REAL WORLD EXAMPLE:

```
set width = 80
data list free / x y1 to y4 .
begin data .
10  8.04  9.14  7.46
etc.
end data.
correlations x with y1 to y4 / options = 5 / statistics = 1.
finish.
```

Calculates Pearson's *r* for X with Y1, Y2, Y3 and Y4 and prints exact two-tailed significance level, mean & standard deviation.

PURPOSE OF THE PROCEDURE AND STATISTICS

The purpose of the Correlations program is to compute the Pearson's Correlation Coefficient. This is an indication of a linear relationship between two quantitative variables. Pearson's correlation coefficient (or **r**) can range from -1 to +1. A value of zero (0.0) indicates that the variables are not related or perhaps more complex or nonlinear relationships. Values close to -1 or +1 indicate strong predicative relationships. The sign indicates the direction of relationship (or its slope). Negative correlations would come from relationships with negative slope. Positive would represent a positive slope.

The correlation coefficient is calculated based on the following formula:

$$r = \frac{\sum Z_x Z_y}{n}$$

The program can also test for statistical significance of the correlation coefficient. It can also produce descriptive statistics (means and standard deviations) for the variables.

HOW TO DO CORRELATIONS ON SPSS

SPSS can calculate the correlation coefficient. Important are:

1. How to set up the data.

2. Requesting a two-tailed test of significance is performed on the correlation correlation.

3. Requesting descriptive statistics (mean and standard deviations).

Three examples are presented:

Example 1: A correlation between two variables (**x** and **y**).

Example 2: A correlation of one variable (**x**) and a set of variables (**y1, y2, y3, y4**).

Example 3: All the correlations among a set of five variables (**x1, x2, x3, x4, x5**). This is called a correlation matrix.

In these examples, some of the correlation coefficients will be positive and some will be negative. It will also be the case that some will be significant and some will not. The basic SPSS command for computing a correlation coefficient or set of coefficients is as follows (with annotations). Note the **variables to be correlated** can take other forms besides **x y** (see examples 2 and 3)*:

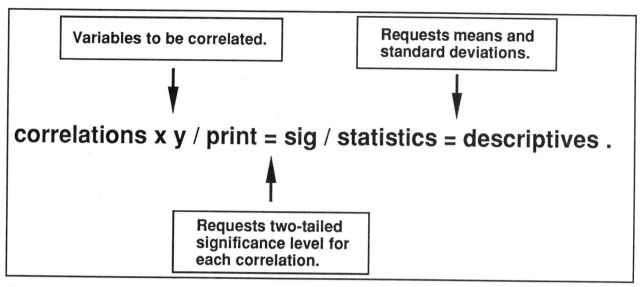

Variables to be correlated.

Requests means and standard deviations.

correlations x y / print = sig / statistics = descriptives .

Requests two-tailed significance level for each correlation.

* [Use '**correlations x y / options = 5 / statistics = 1.**' for SPSS/PC + ™ 4.0]

EXAMPLE 1 : BASIC SETUP FOR TWO VARIABLES (X AND Y)

In this example, the correlation coefficient between the variables **x** and **y** is calculated. It will be positive (.8164) and significant (p = .002, two tailed). There are 11 pairs of scores. Thus, each subject represents one line of data with two scores per line. This is presented below (remember **data list free / x y .** for SPSS/PC +™ 4.0):

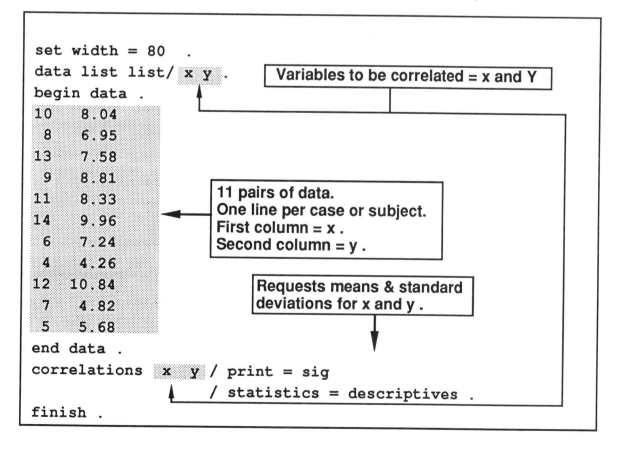

```
set width = 80   .
data list list/ x y .
begin data .
10      8.04
 8      6.95
13      7.58
 9      8.81
11      8.33
14      9.96
 6      7.24
 4      4.26
12     10.84
 7      4.82
 5      5.68
end data .
correlations  x  y / print = sig
                  / statistics = descriptives .
finish .
```

Variables to be correlated = x and Y

**11 pairs of data.
One line per case or subject.
First column = x .
Second column = y .**

Requests means & standard deviations for x and y .

Interpreted Output for Basic Setup for 2 Variables (x & y)

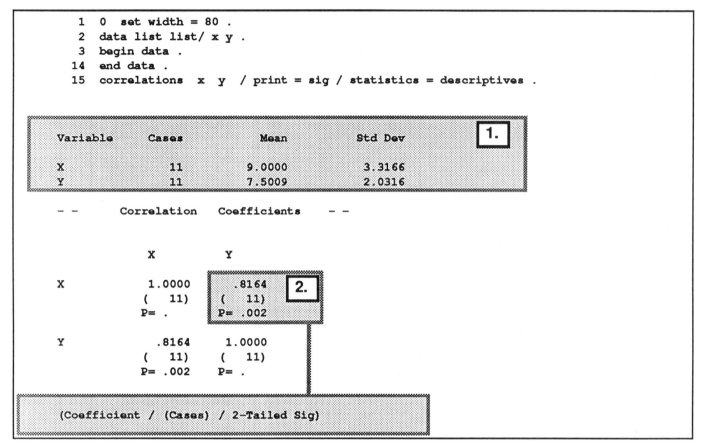

```
 1  0  set width = 80 .
 2  data list list/ x y .
 3  begin data .
14  end data .
15  correlations  x  y  / print = sig / statistics = descriptives .
```

Variable	Cases	Mean	Std Dev	
X	11	9.0000	3.3166	**1.**
Y	11	7.5009	2.0316	

```
- -      Correlation   Coefficients    - -


              X           Y

X         1.0000        .8164      2.
          (   11)       (   11)
          P= .          P= .002


Y          .8164       1.0000
          (   11)       (   11)
          P= .002       P= .
```

(Coefficient / (Cases) / 2-Tailed Sig)

1. <u>Gray Box 1</u> contains the descriptive statistics for **x** and **y**. The number of cases (11), the means for **x** (9.0) and **y** (7.5) and standard deviations for **x** (3.3166) and **y** (2.0316) are reported.

2. <u>Gray Box 2</u> contains the correlation coefficient for **x** and **y** ($r = .8164$), the number of cases used to compute the coefficient and, the two-tailed significance level ($p. = .002$). This would be considered significant by most standards as $.002 < .01$. Note if the <u>p.</u> = .000 it should be reported as ($p. < .001$ as was done for other such reports (see p. 8.8 for example).

3. There are nonshaded areas of the correlations which are not particularly useful. The upper left and lower right corners of the table contain the correlations between **x** versus **x** and **y** versus **y**. These have a value of 1.0 and the probability is not reported. Correlations of a variable with itself is meaningless.

4. The lower left corner is a duplicate of the upper right and reports the correlation between **y** and **x** (which is the same as **x** and **y** in the upper right shaded box). This is somewhat redundant if only two variables are correlated.

EXAMPLE 2 : BASIC SETUP FOR ONE VARIABLE (X) AND A SET OF VARIABLES (Y1, Y2, Y3, Y4) *

In this example, the correlation coefficient between the variables **y** and the variables **x1**, **x2**, **x3**, and **x4** are calculated.

$r_{x,y1}$ is positive (.8164) and significant (*p.* = .002)

$r_{x,y2}$ is positive (.8162) and significant (*p.* = .002)

$r_{x,y3}$ is positive (.8163) and significant (*p.* = .002)

$r_{x,y4}$ is negative (.8164) and **not** significant (*p.* = **.347**)

The means and standard deviations for **x**, **y1**, **y2**, **y3**, and **y4** are also reported.

There are 11 sets of scores. Thus, each subject represents one line of data with five scores per line. This is presented below:

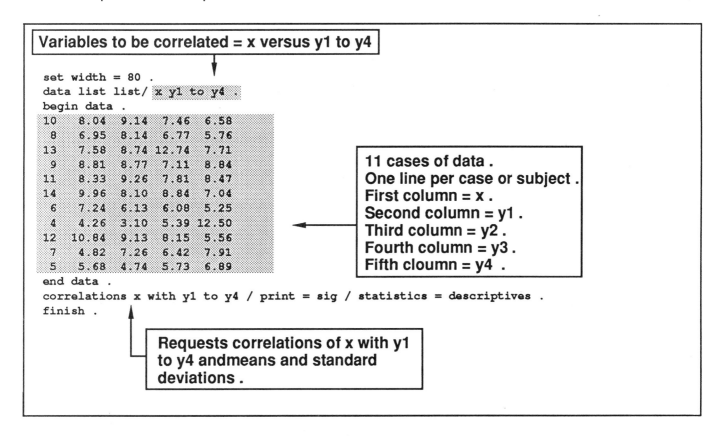

```
                                    Variables to be correlated = x versus y1 to y4

set width = 80 .
data list list/ x y1 to y4 .
begin data .
10    8.04   9.14   7.46   6.58
 8    6.95   8.14   6.77   5.76
13    7.58   8.74  12.74   7.71
 9    8.81   8.77   7.11   8.84
11    8.33   9.26   7.81   8.47
14    9.96   8.10   8.84   7.04
 6    7.24   6.13   6.08   5.25
 4    4.26   3.10   5.39  12.50
12   10.84   9.13   8.15   5.56
 7    4.82   7.26   6.42   7.91
 5    5.68   4.74   5.73   6.89
end data .
correlations x with y1 to y4 / print = sig / statistics = descriptives .
finish .
```

11 cases of data .
One line per case or subject .
First column = x .
Second column = y1 .
Third column = y2 .
Fourth column = y3 .
Fifth cloumn = y4 .

Requests correlations of x with y1 to y4 andmeans and standard deviations .

---

* Use **correlations x with y1 to y4 / options = 5 / statistics = 1.** for SPSS/PC + ™ 4.0 .

Use **data list free / x y1 to y4 .** for SPSS/PC + ™ 4.0.

INTERPRETATIVE POINTS FOR BASIC SETUP FOR ONE VARIABLE (X) AND A SET OF VARIABLES (Y1, Y2, Y3, Y4)

```
 1  0  set width = 80 .
 2  data list list/ x y1 to y4 .
 3  begin data .
14  end data .
15  correlations  x with y1 to y4 / print = sig
                  / statistics = descriptives .
```

Variable	Cases	Mean	Std Dev	
X	11	9.0000	3.3166	**1**
Y1	11	7.5009	2.0316	
Y2	11	7.5009	2.0317	
Y3	11	7.5000	2.0304	
Y4	11	7.5009	2.0306	

- - Correlation Coefficients - -

	Y1	Y2	Y3	Y4	
					2.
X	.8164	.8162	.8163	-.3140	
	(11)	(11)	(11)	(11)	
	P= .002	P= .002	P= .002	P= .347	

(Coefficient / (Cases) / 2-Tailed Sig)

INTERPRETATIVE POINTS

1. <u>Gray Box 1</u> contains the descriptive statistics for **x** and **y1, y2, y3**, and **y4**. The number of cases (11), the means and standard deviations are reported.

2. <u>Gray Box 2</u> contains the correlation coefficient for **x** and **y1, y2, y3** and **y4** ($r_{x,y1}$, $r_{x,y2}$, $r_{x,y3}$, $r_{x,y4}$), the number of cases used to compute the coefficient and the two-tailed significance level. The first three would be considered significant by most standards as .002 < .01. Note if the $p. = .000$ it should be reported as ($p. < .001$ as was done for other such reports (see p. 8.8 for example). The last ($r_{x,y4}$) is noteworthy as it is **negative** (-.314) and **not significant** ($p. = .347 > .05$). **There is a very important point about interpreting the significance levels reported by the program. Each significance test is individual and the probability reported does not**

take into account the increase in Type I error rate due to performing multiple correlations. One should correct for this increased probability. The methodology is outside of the scope of this book. A good reference is Marascuilo and Levin (1983).

EXAMPLE 3 : BASIC SETUP FOR A SET OF FIVE VARIABLES (X1, X2, X3, X4, X5)*

In this example, the correlation coefficients between the set of five variables (**x1, x2, x3, x4, x5**) are calculated. The results are presented as a correlation matrix. Some will be significant and some will not be. The descriptive statistics are presented as they were in the previous examples.

There are 11 pairs of scores. Thus, each subject represents one line of data with five scores per line. This is presented below:

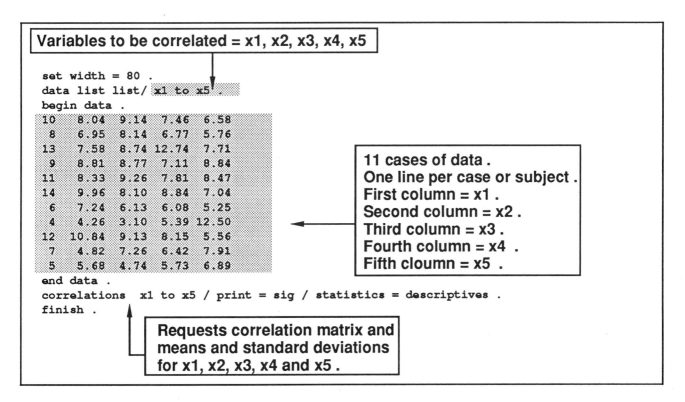

```
set width = 80 .
data list list/ x1 to x5 .
begin data .
10     8.04   9.14   7.46   6.58
 8     6.95   8.14   6.77   5.76
13     7.58   8.74  12.74   7.71
 9     8.81   8.77   7.11   8.84
11     8.33   9.26   7.81   8.47
14     9.96   8.10   8.84   7.04
 6     7.24   6.13   6.08   5.25
 4     4.26   3.10   5.39  12.50
12    10.84   9.13   8.15   5.56
 7     4.82   7.26   6.42   7.91
 5     5.68   4.74   5.73   6.89
end data .
correlations  x1 to x5 / print = sig / statistics = descriptives .
finish .
```

Variables to be correlated = x1, x2, x3, x4, x5

**11 cases of data .
One line per case or subject .
First column = x1 .
Second column = x2 .
Third column = x3 .
Fourth column = x4 .
Fifth cloumn = x5 .**

Requests correlation matrix and means and standard deviations for x1, x2, x3, x4 and x5 .

---

* Use:

data list free / x1 to x5 .

correlations x1 to x5 / options = 5 / statistics = 1.

for SPSS/PC + ™ 4.0 .

INTERPRETATIVE POINTS FOR BASIC SETUP FOR SET OF FIVE VARIABLES (X1, X2, X3, X4, X5)

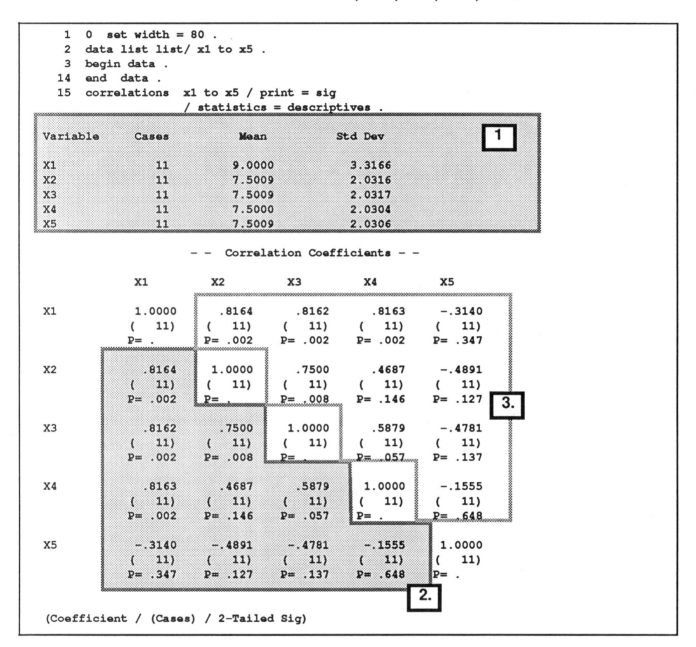

```
 1  0  set width = 80 .
 2  data list list/ x1 to x5 .
 3  begin data .
14  end  data .
15  correlations  x1 to x5 / print = sig
                  / statistics = descriptives .
```

Variable	Cases	Mean	Std Dev	1
X1	11	9.0000	3.3166	
X2	11	7.5009	2.0316	
X3	11	7.5009	2.0317	
X4	11	7.5000	2.0304	
X5	11	7.5009	2.0306	

- - Correlation Coefficients - -

	X1	X2	X3	X4	X5
X1	1.0000	.8164	.8162	.8163	-.3140
	(11)	(11)	(11)	(11)	(11)
	P= .	P= .002	P= .002	P= .002	P= .347
X2	.8164	1.0000	.7500	.4687	-.4891
	(11)	(11)	(11)	(11)	(11)
	P= .002	P= .	P= .008	P= .146	P= .127
X3	.8162	.7500	1.0000	.5879	-.4781
	(11)	(11)	(11)	(11)	(11)
	P= .002	P= .008	P= .	P= .057	P= .137
X4	.8163	.4687	.5879	1.0000	-.1555
	(11)	(11)	(11)	(11)	(11)
	P= .002	P= .146	P= .057	P= .	P= .648
X5	-.3140	-.4891	-.4781	-.1555	1.0000
	(11)	(11)	(11)	(11)	(11)
	P= .347	P= .127	P= .137	P= .648	P= .

3.

2.

(Coefficient / (Cases) / 2-Tailed Sig)

INTERPRETATIVE POINTS

1. <u>Gray Box 1</u> contains the descriptive statistics for **x1, x2, x3, x4**, and **x5**. The number of cases (11), the means and standard deviations are reported.

2. The correlations are presented as a matrix with **x1, x2, x3, x4** and **x5 running across and down the table.** Note the following:

a. This leads to redundancy as Gray Box 2 and Gray Box 3 are mirror images of each other. Only Gray Box 2 will be explained.

b. The diagonal coefficients running from upper left corner to lower right corner are meaningless. These have a value of 1.0 and the probability is not reported. Correlations of a variable with itself is meaningless.

3. <u>Gray Box 2</u> contains the correlation coefficients: $r_{x1,x2}, r_{x1,x3}, r_{x1,x4}, r_{x1,x5}, r_{x2,x3}, r_{x2,x4}, r_{x2,x5}, r_{x3,x4}, r_{x3,x5}, r_{x4,x5}$), the number of cases used to compute the coefficient and the two-tailed significance level. Note the following:

a. The coefficients: $r_{x1,x2}, r_{x1,x3}, r_{x1,x4}, r_{x2,x3}$ would be considered significant by most standards as $p. < .01$. Note if the $p. = .000$ it should be reported as ($p. < .001$ as was done for other such reports (see p. 8.8 for example).

b. The coefficients: $r_{x1,x5}, r_{x2,x4}, r_{x2,x5}, r_{x3,x4}, r_{x3,x5}, r_{x4,x5}$ **are not significant ($p. > .05$).**

c. Note several coefficients are negative.

d. **There is a very important point about interpreting the significance levels reported by the program. Each significance test is individual and the probability reported does not take into account the increase in Type I error rate due to performing multiple correlations. One should correct for this increased probability. The methodology is outside of the scope of this book. A good reference is Marascuilo and Levin (1983).**

CHAPTER 13: SCATTERGRAMS AND REGRESSION LINES

PRODUCTION OF SCATTERGRAMS & LINEAR REGRESSION EQUATIONS

SUMMARY OF SPSS SETUP FOR 2 VARIABLES, X AND Y [1]

```
set width = 80 .
data list list/ x y .
begin data .
     x      y
     x      y
     x      y
     x      y      ←  DATA
     x      y
     x      y
     x      y
end data .
plot / format = regression / plot = y with x by z * .
finish .
     * 'by z'  is optional.
```

REAL WORLD EXAMPLE

```
set  width = 80 .
data list list / x y .
begin data .
1  1
2  2
2  0
2  3
4  5
3  4
4  4
6  7
6  5
8  8
8  7
8  9
9 11
9 10
7  5
7  6
9  9
9  9
8  8
end data .
plot / format = regression / plot = y with x .
finish .
```

---

[1] Use **data list free / x y.** for SPSS/PC + ™ 4.0

Purpose of the Procedure and Statistics

We will use the PLOT program to:

1. Plot a scattergram for two variables (x and y). A visual inspection for nonlinearities, outliers, and subgroups is possible. The regression line is also noted on the graph.

2. Evaluate the existence of a significant linear regression by calculating:

a. Pearson's Correlation Coefficient (r):

This is an indication of a linear relationship between two quantitative variables. Pearson's correlation coefficient (r) can range from -1 to +1. A value of zero (0.0) indicates that the variables are not related or perhaps more complex or nonlinear relationships. Values close to -1 or +1 indicate strong predicative relationships. The sign indicates the direction of relationship (or its slope). Negative correlations would come from relationships with negative slope. Positive would represent a positive slope.

The correlation coefficient is calculated based on the following formula:

$$r = \frac{\sum Z_x Z_y}{n}$$

b. r^2:

Squaring the correlation coefficient results in what is called the coefficient of determination or proportion of explained variance. For example if r = 0.6, the proportion of explained variance = 0.36. If r = -0.7, r^2 = 0.49. Note these could be multiplied by 100 to produce the percent explained variance (36% and 49% respectively).

c. Slope and intercept of the regression line of the form:

$$Y' = Slope * X + Intercept$$

where Y' is the Y score predicted from the X score. Slope and intercept are calculated from the standard formulas (see SPSS Statistical Algorithms).

d. Perform a two tailed test for statistical significance of the correlation coefficient.

e. Calculate the Standard errors of estimate, slope, and intercept (see SPSS Statistical Algorithms).

3. The program can also enable us to plot scattergrams for y and x for different groups on the same scattergram. Unfortunately, the regression statistics cannot be produced for the groups independently.

HOW TO DO SCATTERGRAMS AND REGRESSION LINES ON SPSS

SPSS can produce scattergrams and regression statistics. Important are:

1. How to set up the data.
2. Requesting the regression statistics.
3. Requesting the appropriate graphic format.

Seven examples are presented:

Example 1a: A plot between two variables (**x** and **y**) with a significant and positive linear relationship.

Example 1b: This is the same plot as in **1a** but with labeling of the plot, x axis, and y axis.

Example 2: A plot between two variables (x and y) with a significant inverse or negative relationship.

Example 3: A plot between two variables (x and y) with a nonsignificant relationship.

Example 4: A plot between two variables (x and y) with a nonlinear relationship.

Example 5: A plot between two variables (x and y) which demonstrates that two separate subgroups exit in the data.

The basic SPSS command for producing a scattergram is as follows (with annotations). Note the **variables to be correlated** can take other forms besides **x y** (see examples which follow the annotated one):

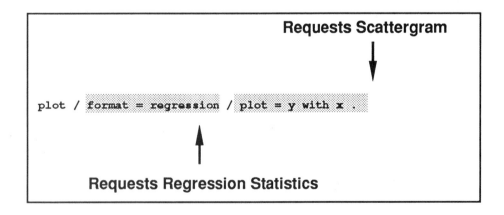

This example will request a scattergram and regression statistics for the variables y and x. The variable **y** will appear as the **vertical axis** and **x** will appear as the **horizontal axis.**

More than one scattergram can be requested. Assume that you have the variables **x1, x2, x3, y1, y2, y3.** The following examples show how to produce multiple plots:

1. All possible combinations:

plot / format = regression / plot = y1 y2 y3 with x1 x2 x3 .

This would plot:

y1 with x1, y1 with x2, y1 with x3
y2 with x1, y2 with x2, y2 with x3
y3 with x1, y3 with x2, y3 with x3

2. Ordered pairs:

plot / format = regression / plot = y1 y2 y3 with x1 x2 x3 (pairs) .

This would plot:

y1 with x1
y2 with x2
y3 with x3

3. Specific pairs:

plot / format = regression / plot = y1 with x 2 ; x2 with x3 .

This would plot:

y1 with x2
x2 with x3

Example 1a: Basic Setup for Two Variables (x & y)

In this example, a scattergram for the variables **x** and **y** is plotted for 19 cases or x,y pairs. There will be a significant correlation (r = .93878, p. < .0001). The coefficient of determination (r^2) will be .88130. The standard error of estimate will be 1.10523. The slope of the regression lines is positive (1.03551) with a standard error of the slope being .09217. The Y intercept of the regression line is -.15666 with the standard error of the intercept being .59957.

Thus there is a strong and significant positive correlation between **y** and **x**. This is seen in the correlation coefficient being close to 1.0. The annotated setup and output are as follows:

FIGURE 1 - SETUP *

```
set  width = 80 .
data list list / x y .
begin data .
     1   1
     2   2
     2   0
     2   3
     4   5
     3   4
     4   4
     6   7
1.   6   5   2.
     8   8
     8   7
     8   9
     9  11
     9  10
     7   5
     7   6
     9   9
     9   9
     8   8
end data .
plot / format = regression / plot = y with x .
finish .
```

↑

Declares Variables x and y

← 1. Column 1 = x scores
  2. Column 2 = y scores

Requests Regression Statistics and Scattergram
↓

FIGURE 2 - OUTPUT NOTATION

```
 1  0  set  width = 80 .
 2  data list list / x y
 3  begin data .
 4  end data .
22  plot / format = regression / plot = y with x .
```

```
Data    Information
        19 unweighted cases accepted.
```

```
Size of the plots
  Horizontal size is 65
    Vertical size is 40
```

Frequencies and symbols used (not applicable for control or overlay plots)

1 - 1	11 - B	21 - L	31 - V
2 - 2	12 - C	22 - M	32 - W
3 - 3	13 - D	23 - N	33 - X
4 - 4	14 - E	24 - O	34 - Y
5 - 5	15 - F	25 - P	35 - Z
6 - 6	16 - G	26 - Q	36 - *
7 - 7	17 - H	27 - R	
8 - 8	18 - I	28 - S	
9 - 9	19 - J	29 - T	
10 - A	20 - K	30 - U	

Numbers reflect multiple occurrences of a pair. Letters are used for frequencies greater than 9. For example: D = 13 occurences of that pair.

* Use **data list free / x y.** for SPSS/PC + ™ 4.0. Assume for all following setups also.

FIGURE 3 - SCATTERGRAM AND REGRESSION STATISTICS

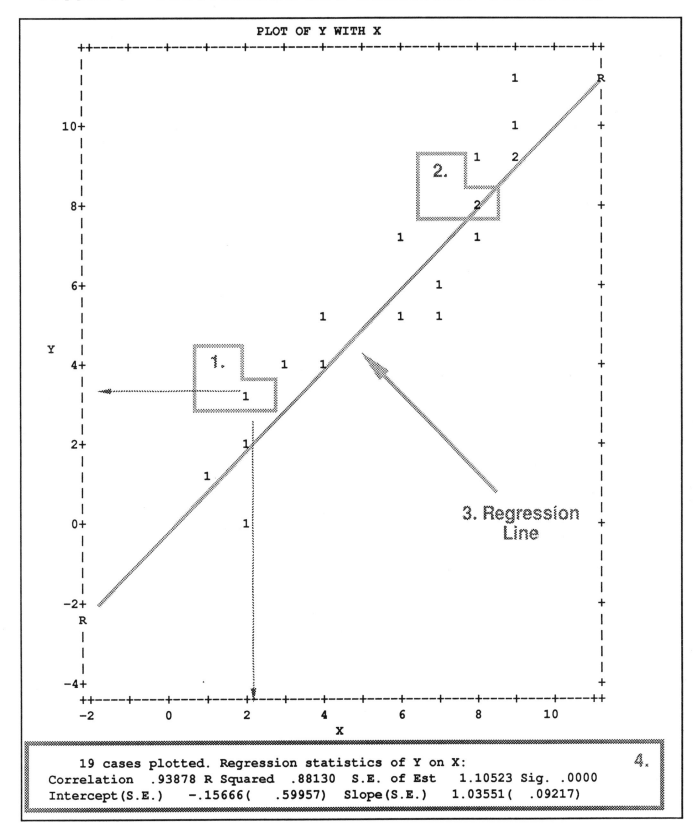

PLOT OF Y WITH X

19 cases plotted. Regression statistics of Y on X:
Correlation .93878 R Squared .88130 S.E. of Est 1.10523 Sig. .0000
Intercept(S.E.) −.15666(.59957) Slope(S.E.) 1.03551(.09217)

1. <u>Gray Box 1</u> represents a plotted point where **x = 2** and **y = 3**. Referring back to the data, this is the fourth subject, for example,

.
.
.

```
begin data .
1  1
2  2
2  0
2  3
```
         .
         .
         .
```
end data .
```

2. <u>Gray Box 2</u> represents that two subjects have the same **x, y** pair of **x = 8** and **y = 8**. Referring back to the data, these are the 10th and 19th subject, for example,

```
begin data .
1  1
2  2
2  0
2  3
4  5
3  4
4  4
6  7
6  5
8  8
8  7
8  9
9  11
9  10
7  5
7  6
9  9
9  9
8  8
end data .
```

3. <u>Note 3</u>. marks how SPSS marks the regression line. Look on the left and right vertical axes for an **R**. **If you connect these points as we have done with the gray line, you can see the actual regression line.**

4. <u>Gray Box 4</u> contains the actual regression statistics. The important information is as follows:

```
19 cases plotted.
```
This is the number of subjects or plotted pairs.

```
Regression statistics of Y on X:
```

```
Correlation  .93878
```
Pearson's r or product moment correlation coefficient

```
R Squared  .88130
```
r^2 or the coefficient of determination. Also the proportion of explained variance.

`S.E. of Est     1.10523`

The standard error of estimate or prediction around the regression line.

`Sig.  .0000`

The correlation is statistically significant. It is calculated as a t-test with df = no. of cases-2. However, *t* itself is not reported by SPSS. You would report significance as *p.* < .001 (see p. 8.8).

`Intercept(S.E.)     -.15666(     .59957)`

The **y** intercept of the regression line (-.15666) and its standard error (.59957).

`Slope(S.E.)     1.03551(     .09217)`

The slope of the regression line (1.03551). It is positive as can be seen in Figure 2. The standard error of the slope = .59957.

Together the slope and intercept of the regression line give an actual equation of

$$Y' = 1.03551 * X + .15666$$

where Y' is the Y score predicted from the X score.

Example 1b: Basic Labeled Setup

It is useful to label the scattergram, vertical (y) and horizontal (x) axes of the scattergram. This is easily done. Let's use the previous example. Assume that we are interested in studying whether depression is related to candy consumption. We survey 19 people and ask how many candy bars they eat per day. We also give them a test of depression. We will use our **x** variable to be their candy consumption and **y** to be their score on the depression test. Higher scores will mean that they are more depressed.

We want our scatterplot to be labeled on top with: **Chocolate versus Depression**

The horizontal or **x** axis should be labeled: **No. of Candy Bars Eaten**

The vertical or **y** axis should be labeled: **Depression Score**

These labels can be added to the plot command as seen below:

```
set width = 80
data list list / x y .
begin data .
1   1
2   2
2   0
2   3
4   5
3   4
4   4
6   7
6   5
8   8
8   7
8   9
9  11
9  10
7   5
7   6
9   9
9   9
8   8
end data .
plot   / format = regression
       / title = '  Chocolate  versus  Depression'
       / horizontal = 'No.  of  Candy  Bars  Eaten'
       / vertical  =  'Depression  Score'
       / plot = y with x .
finish .
```

Each label can contain 40 characters. The output would look as follows with the added labels highlighted for you in gray. We did this, the program doesn't.

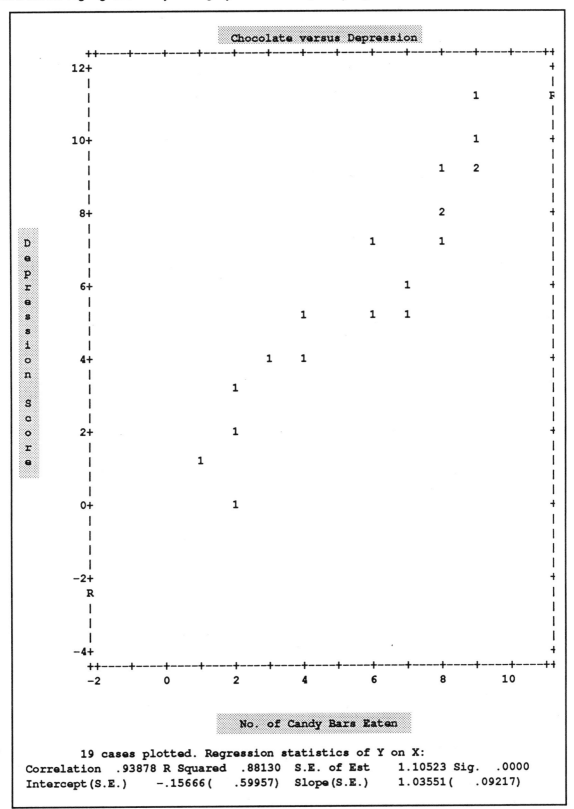

19 cases plotted. Regression statistics of Y on X:
Correlation .93878 R Squared .88130 S.E. of Est 1.10523 Sig. .0000
Intercept(S.E.) -.15666(.59957) Slope(S.E.) 1.03551(.09217)

Example 2: Negative Relationship Between x & y

In this example, the relationship between **x** and **y** is statistically significant but has a negative relationship. When **x** increases, **y** decreases. Pearson's **r = -.89188** which is significant as *p.* < .0001. The coefficient of determination (r^2) will be .79545. **The slope of the regression lines is negative (-1.06479).** The Y intercept of the regression line is 12.22401.

Thus there is a strong and significant negative correlation between **y** and **x. If these were our data, we would conclude that eating chocolate predicts lower depression levels.** The setup is as follows:

S E T U P

```
set  width = 80 .
data list list / x y .
begin data .
1   10
2   12
2   10
2   13
4    5
3    8
4    7
6    5
6    6
8    4
8    5
8    3
9    2
9    0
7    5
7    6
9    3
9    5
8    4
end data .
plot / format = regression
     / title = ' Chocolate versus Depression'
     / horizontal = 'No. of Candy Bars Eaten'
     / vertical = 'Depression Score'
     / plot = y with x  .
finish .
```

RELEVANT OUTPUT & INTERPRETATIVE POINTS

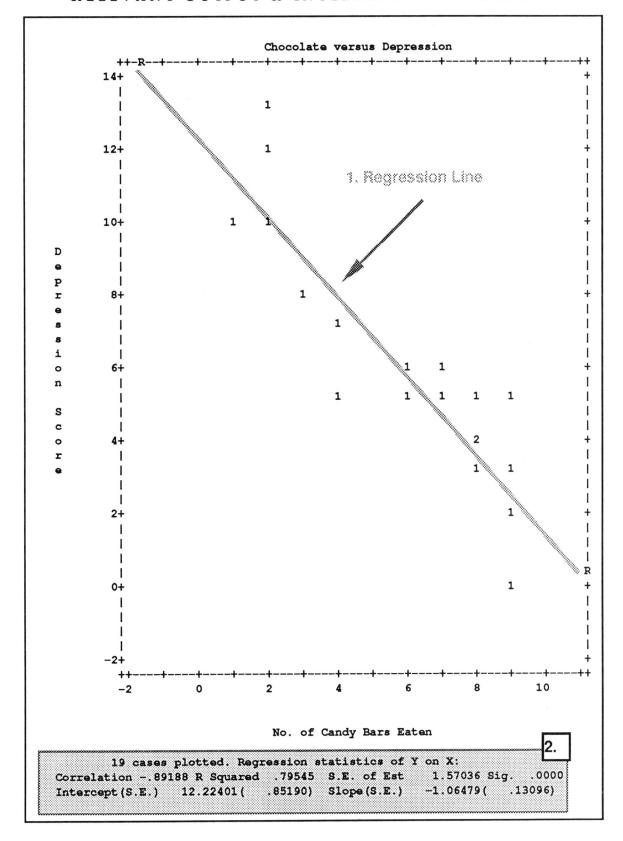

Chocolate versus Depression

1. Regression Line

No. of Candy Bars Eaten

2.

19 cases plotted. Regression statistics of Y on X:
Correlation −.89188 R Squared .79545 S.E. of Est 1.57036 Sig. .0000
Intercept(S.E.) 12.22401(.85190) Slope(S.E.) −1.06479(.13096)

1. Note marks how the SPSS marks the negatively sloped regression line. Look on the left and right vertical axes for an **R. If you connect these points as we have done with the gray line, you can see the actual negatively sloped regression line.**

2. Gray Box 2 contains the regression statistics which indicate the negative relationship between **x** and **y**. The important information statistics to note in this example are:

```
Regression statistics of Y on X:

  Correlation    -.89188
```
Pearson's r or product moment correlation coefficient

```
  Sig.  .0000
```
The correlation is statistically significant.

```
Slope      -1.06479
```
The slope of the regression line (-1.06479). It is negative as can be seen in the figure. The standard error of the slope = .13096.

```
Intercept      12.22401
```

Together the slope and intercept of the regression line give an actual equation of

$$Y' = -1.06479 * X + 12.22401$$

where Y' is the Y score predicted from the X score.

Note that the slope is negative in sign.

Example 3: Nonsignificant Relationship between X and Y

In this example, the relationship between **x** and **y** is not statistically significant. The setup follows. Pearson's $r = .25237$ which is not significant as $p. = .2972$ which is $> .05$. These figures are highlighted in gray on the scattergram Note on the scattergram how the points do not consistently cluster around the gray highlighted regression line (compare this to Example 1a). Since the relationship is not significant the regression line is useless to us.

SETUP

```
set  width = 80 .
data list list / x y .
begin data .
1  1
2  2
2  8
2  3
4  5
3  4
4  4
6  7
6  5
8  2
8  7
8  9
9 11
9  1
7  5
7  6
9  3
9  2
8  8
end data .
plot / format = regression / plot = y with x .
finish .
```

SCATTERGRAM

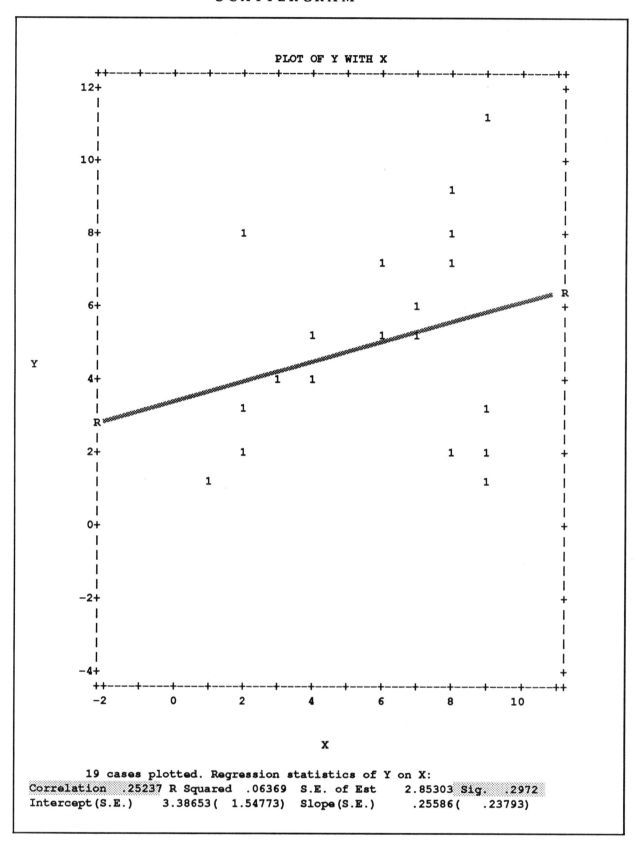

PLOT OF Y WITH X

19 cases plotted. Regression statistics of Y on X:
Correlation .25237 R Squared .06369 S.E. of Est 2.85303 Sig. .2972
Intercept(S.E.) 3.38653(1.54773) Slope(S.E.) .25586(.23793)

Example 4: Nonlinear Relationship between x and y

In this example, the linear relationship between **x** and **y** is not statistically significant. Pearson's r = .11671 which is not significant as $p.$ = .6342 which is > .05. These figures are highlighted in gray on the scattergram (# 3) Note on the scattergram how the points do not consistently cluster around the gray highlighted regression line - No. 1(compare this to Example 1a).

However, there is a nonlinear relationship. We generated the data by using the equation: $y = 1.5\,x^2$. This is highlighted for you by the gray curve (No. 2) which we supplied.

If you see such a scattergram, there are techniques and programs in SPSS which can perform nonlinear regressions (CNLR and NLR). If you are not a sophisticated user, you should seek advice.

SETUP

```
set width = 80 .
data list list / x y .
begin data .
      1.0      1.5
      1.9      5.4
      3.0     13.5
      4.1     25.2
      5.0     37.5
      6.2     57.6
      7.0     73.5
       .5       .3
       .2      0.0
      9.0    121.5
      0.0       .0
      -.5       .3
      -.3       .1
     -2.0      6.0
     -3.0     13.5
     -4.0     24.0
     -5.2     40.5
     -7.0     73.5
     -8.2    100.8
end data .
plot /format = regression / plot = y with x .
finish .
```

SCATTERGRAM

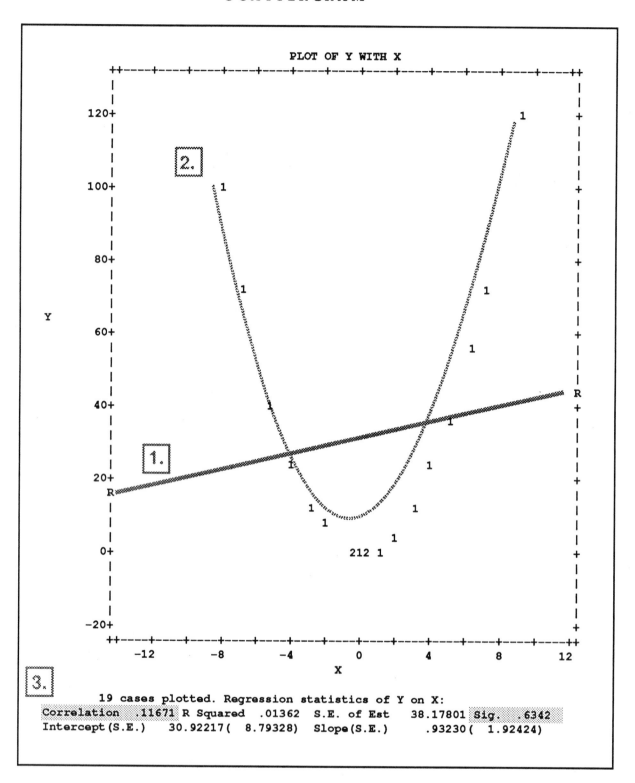

Example 5: Data Subgroups & Use of Control Plots

In this example, we are going to demonstrate SPSS's ability to plot separate subgroups in the same scattergram. The data set is a real one. We obtained people's height in inches, shoe size, and noted their gender. We converted shoe sizes to be on a common scale (as men and women's differ). We then plotted shoe size versus height. You would think that there would be a positive relationship between shoe size and height and a significant correlation. The trick is that there are two groups (men and women). This will make interpretation of the simple scattergram and regression difficult. We will develop these ideas as follows:

1. We will first present the simple regression of shoe size and height.

2. Then we will have SPSS produce the scattergram with the men and women marked separately using a **Control Plot** command in our setup.

3. Last, we will suggest how to deal with the data appropriately.

1. THE SIMPLE REGRESSION OF SHOE SIZE AND HEIGHT.

```
set  width = 80 .
data list list / shoe height sex .¹
value labels sex 1 'female' 2 'male' .²
begin data .
 6   66  1 ³
 5   65  1
 5   63  1
 6   64  1
 9   67  2
10   72  2
 9   72  2
 5   65  1
 6   65  1
 6   66  1
 6   65  1
 6   62  1
 5   64  1      ¹ Subjects' data consists of shoe size, height and gender (sex)
 7   70  1      ² Labels sex as 1 = female, 2 = male.
 5   64  1      ³ Example: shoe size = 6, height = 66 inches, subject is female.
 6   65  1
 3   61  1
 5   68  1
 5   65  1
 9   70  2
 5   66  1
10   67  2
 5   67  1
 4   63  1
 8   68  2
 8   68  2
10   74  2
10   72  2
 9   68  2
end data .
plot / format = regression
     / plot = height with shoe .
finish .
```

SIMPLE SCATTERGRAM OF HEIGHT AND SHOE SIZE

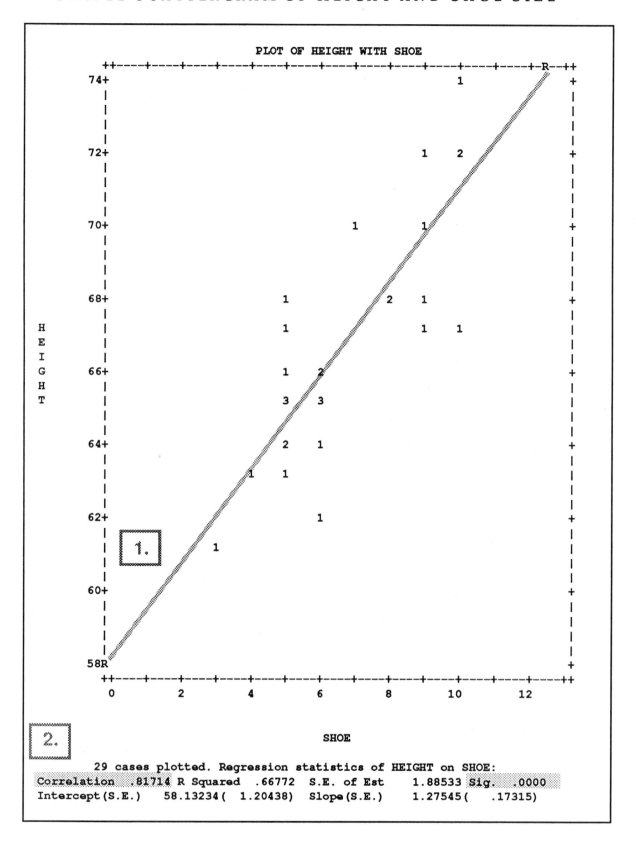

On the surface, this looks like a straight forward linear regression, height and shoe size are strongly related. Pearson's r = .81714 which is significant as *p.* < .0001 . These figures are highlighted in gray on the scattergram (No. 2) Note on the scattergram how the points seem to consistently cluster around the gray highlighted regression line - No. 1.

2. THE CONTROL PLOT FOR SEX

However, the scattergram *lies!* You are being fooled by the existence of two separate groups. The situation is quite different if we look at men and women separately!

This can be shown in SPSS by using what it calls a **Control Plot**. We will slightly alter the setup so that SPSS marks each point on the height/shoe size scattergram by the subjects' membership in a group (in this case: male or female).

For this to occur, we must supply value labels for the grouping or controlling variable. The first letter of the value label will be used for a point on the scattergram. The general form of the PLOT command would be as follows:

plot / format = regression / plot = y with x by z .

The component **by z** requests that the first letters of the value labels for **z** be used in the plot to mark group membership according to **z**. We will **sex** for our group or controlling variable. Our command will thus be:

plot / format = regression / plot = height with shoe by sex

The annotated setup and scattergram are below:

```
set  width = 80 .
data list list / shoe height sex .
value labels sex 1 'female' 2 'male' .  1
begin data
  5  65 1
    etc.
  5  64 1    1 'f' will be used to mark females on scattergram, 'm' for males
  6  66 1
  7  70 1
  5  64 1    2 'by sex' requests that the first letters in 1 mark the points
    etc.
  9  68 2
end data .
plot / format = regression
   / plot = height with shoe by sex . 2
finish .
```

SCATTERGRAM WITH 'm'ALE AND 'f'EMALE INDICATED

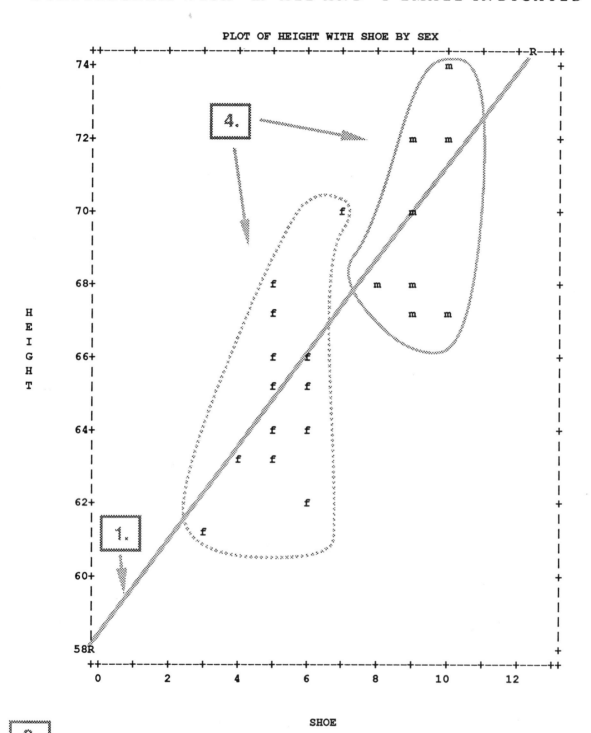

PLOT OF HEIGHT WITH SHOE BY SEX

SHOE

29 cases plotted. Regression statistics of HEIGHT on SHOE:
Correlation .81714 R Squared .66772 S.E. of Est 1.88533 Sig. .0000
Intercept(S.E.) 58.13234(1.20438) Slope(S.E.) 1.27545(.17315)
f:female m:male $:Multiple occurrence

The important points are:

1. The original regression line which is still marked by **R** on the plot.
2. The original regression statistics. They are still the same.
3. The explanation of the **control plot** as female data points are marked by **f** and male points are marked by **m**.
4. We have circled the female and male points. **You can see be visual inspection that the relationship within each group looks weak**.

Point No. 4 is confirmed if we have run separate PLOTs on the males and females (how to do this follows shortly). Below are the regression statistics for each (all 29 subjects, the 19 females as a group, the 10 males as a group). We have boldfaced the important statistics.

All

```
    29 cases plotted. Regression statistics of HEIGHT on SHOE:
Correlation   .81714 R Squared   .66772   S.E. of Est  1.88533 Sig.  .0000
```

Female

```
    19 cases plotted. Regression statistics of HEIGHT on SHOE:
Correlation   .55595 R Squared   .30908   S.E. of Est  1.76842 Sig.  .0134
```

Male

```
    10 cases plotted. Regression statistics of HEIGHT on SHOE:
Correlation   .52339 R Squared   .27393   S.E. of Est  2.28641 Sig.  .1205
```

Note the **Correlations** and **R squared** for the separate groups. For each group, they are much weaker. They are not even statistically significant for the males!

What has happened is the the differences in height between males and females is a confounding variable. This suggested a stronger relationship than actually existed.

The role of confounding variables is complex. They can be dealt with by using multiple regression, partial correlation coefficients, and other techniques. Howell (1987), Marascuilo and Levin (1983), or a whole host of advanced texts discuss this issue. The effects may be better analyzed using multiple regression and/or partial correlations.

You may wonder how we produced the separate statistics for males and females. This was done by using TEMPORARY and SELECT IF commands (see Chapter. 20) in the setup below:

PLOT SETUP USING *SELECT IF* TO PRODUCE SEPARATE SCATTERGRAMS*

```
set  width = 80 .
data list list / shoe height sex .
value labels sex 1 'female' 2 'male'
begin data .
    .
    .
    .
our data set
    .
    .
    .
end data .
plot / format = regression
     / plot = height with shoe by sex .
temporary  .
select if ( sex eq 1) .
plot /  format=regression
     / plot = height with  shoe  .
temporary  .
select if ( sex eq 2) .
plot / format = regression
     / plot= height with  shoe  .
finish .
```

* *Select if* usage will be explained in Chapter 20.

CHAPTER 14: ONEWAY BETWEEN GROUPS ANOVA

COMPARISON OF MEANS FOR INDEPENDENT GROUPS, TREND ANALYSIS

SUMMARY OF SPSS SETUP FOR ONEWAY ANOVA[1, 2]

```
set width = 80 .
data list list / iv dv .
variable labels iv 'Independent Variable' /
                dv 'Dependent Variable' .        → optional
value labels iv, etc. .
begin data
IV₁ DV
IV₂ DV
  DATA                Each Line Represents One Subject
                   IV = Subject's Group; DV = Subject's Score

IVₖ DV
end data
oneway dv by iv (1,k) / statistics = descriptives
                    / other optional commands :polynomial
                                            contrast
                                            ranges
                                            format = labels.

finish .
```

REAL WORLD EXAMPLE

```
set width = 80 .
data list list / major hours .
variable labels hours 'Time spent studying per week' /
                major 'Undergraduate Major' .
value labels major 1 'Humanities' 2 'Soc. Sci.'  3 'Nat. Sci .'
begin data .
1 02
1 08
1 16        Calculates Oneway Anova for Hours By Major:
1 03
1 10        Hours is the Dependent Variable
2 08        Major is the Independent Variable with:
2 06
2 09          1 = Humanities Major (5 students)
2 04          2 = Social Science Major (5 students)
2 11          3 = Natural Science Major (5 students)
3 20
3 19
3 16        The F – ratio is calculated along with group
3 19        means and standard deviations.
3 18
end data .
oneway hours by major (1,3) / statistics = descriptives .
finish .
```

---

[1] There are other programs which calculate anovas. See end of chapter.

[2] SPSS/PC + ™ 4.0 setups differ. See pp. 233,236, 258 . Always use **data list free / etc.**

SUMMARY OF SPSS/PC +™ 4.0 ONEWAY ANOVA SETUP

```
set width = 80 .
data list free / iv dv .
variable labels iv 'Independent Variable' /
                 dv 'Dependent Variable' .          → optional
value labels iv, etc. .
IV₁ DV
IV₂ DV

  DATA                  Each Line Represents One Subject
                        IV = Subject's Group; DV = Subject's Score
IVₖ DV
end data
oneway dv by iv (1,k) / statistics = 1
                      / other optional commands :polynomial
                                                 contrast
                                                 ranges
                                                 format = labels.
finish .
```

REAL WORLD EXAMPLE:

```
set width = 80 .
data list free / major hours .
variable labels hours 'Time spent studying per week' /
                major 'Undergraduate Major' .
value labels major 1 'Humanities' 2 'Soc. Sci.' 3 'Nat. Sci'.
begin data .
1 02
1 08
1 16
1 03
1 10
2 08
2 06
2 09
2 04
2 11
3 20
3 19
3 16
3 19
3 18
end data .
oneway hours by major (1,3) / statistics = 1 .
finish .
```

Purpose of the Procedure and Statistic:

The oneway analysis of variance is used to test for significance between the means of separate groups. Unlike the t-test, there are usually more than two groups of subjects when the anova is performed. Presenting all the formulas for the actual calculations goes beyond the scope of this book. They can be found in standard statistics texts (Howell, 1987; Keppel, 1991; Kirk, 1982; Winer, Brown, & Michels 1991). We will note some of the important equations when appropriate.

We will use the ONEWAY program to:

a. Calculate the F-ratio:

The F-ratio is calculated as :

$$F = \frac{MS \text{ between groups}}{MS \text{ within groups}}$$

The general form of the **MS** or Mean Squares is:

$$MS = \frac{\text{Sum Squares}}{\text{degrees of freedom}}$$

The significance of the F-ratio informs us if there are *any* differences between the groups. *Note that if it is significant, this does not mean that all the groups are significantly different from each other.* Determining which groups are different from each other is done by using planned (CONTRASTS) and unplanned (RANGES)comparisons, as shown later.

b. Descriptive Statistics:

The program will calculate the means, standard deviations, standard error, minimum, maximum, and 95 percent confidence interval for each group.

c. Planned Comparisons (**Contrasts**):

The program allows you to request up to 50 sets of apriori contrasts. These are tested for significance using t-tests.

d. Unplanned comparisons (**Ranges**):

The program allows you to test all possible pairs of means for significant differences using a selection of procedures and alpha levels. Note the SPSS/PC + ™ 4.0 names may be different. The list follows:

PROCEDURE	SPSS NAME (PC+ NAME)	ALPHA LEVELS
Least Significant Difference	LSD	Between 0 & 1, default = .05
Duncan Multiple Range Test	DUNCAN	.01, .05 or .10
Student-Newman-Keuls	SNK	only .05 available
Tukey's Alternate Procedure	TUKEYB (BTUKEY)	only .05 available
Honestly Significant Difference	TUKEY	only .05 available
Modified LSD	LSDMOD (MODLSD)	Between 0 & 1, default = .05
Scheffe's Test	SCHEFFE	Between 0 & 1, default = .05

e. Trend Analyses (**Polynomial**):

The program can test for trends ranging from linear to a fifth degree polynomial. Basically you are testing to see if the differences in the means of the DV as defined by the IV follow a straight line or some higher order function such as:

$$Y = aX + bX^2 + ... + ex5 + C.$$

Note: T he groups must fall along a measurement continuum to use this procedure. If you have 5 groups, numbered 1 through 5, but the number stands for a categorical variable such as religion, then this analysis makes no sense to perform

Unfortunately, the program cannot supply the fitted equation. This can be done in other procedures in SPSS, such as CNLR/NLR.

<u>f. Tests of Assumptions-Homogeneity of Variance (**Homogeneity**):</u>

The program will calculate the Cochran's C, Bartlett-Box F and Hartley's F max test. Violations of homogeneity may lead to distortion of your Type I error rate. You might need corrective steps as outlined in some of our references (Howell, 1982; Wilcox, 1987). It also changes whether or not you would used pooled or separate variance estimates when using the Contrast subcommand. If this is mysterious to you, consult before it's too late.

Examples will be given of each.

EXAMPLE 1a: CALCULATING THE F-RATIO & GETTING DESCRIPTIVE STATISTICS (F IS SIGNIFICANT)

Most important is the conceptualization of the data. There are several groups of subjects. All subjects in each group are different or put another way, no subject is in more than one group. Also each subject only contributes one score.

The grouping factor is called the IV or independent variable and the scores are referred to as the dependent variable. We are looking to see if the means of each group's DV differ, telling us if there is an effect of the IV. In general, the data would look as follows:

$$IV_1 \ DV$$
$$IV_1 \ DV$$
$$IV_2 \ DV$$
$$IV_2 \ DV$$
.
.
DATA
.
.
$$IV_k \ DV$$
$$IV_k \ DV$$

Each line represents one subject. The first number is the IV or group number. IV_1 indicates membership in Group 1 and **DV** is the person's score. The next line is for the next person in the group.

For a real example, consider that we want to determine if the amount of time spent studying each week is different for Humanities, Social Sciences and Natural Science majors. A number of students in each group is questioned. We will indicate majors by the codes:

1 = Humanities

2 = Social Sciences

3 = Natural Sciences

The data might be:

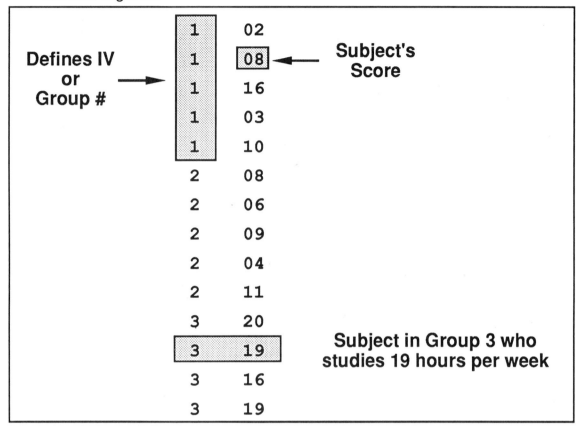

Given such an arrangement of data the basic command to calculate the oneway anova would be:

| oneway dv by iv (1,k) / statistics = descriptives . |

where:

oneway = the SPSS command name

dv = the name of the dependent variable

iv = the name of the independent variable

(1,k) defines the number of groups laid out by the iv

statistics = descriptives requests that means and standard deviation be calculated.

For our example, the command would be:

```
oneway hours by major (1,3) / statistics = descriptives .
```

where:

hours = dv

major = iv

(1,3) reflects that there are three groups based on the three majors

statistics = descriptives requests means and standard deviations of the variable hours for the three majors. The complete setup would be as follows:

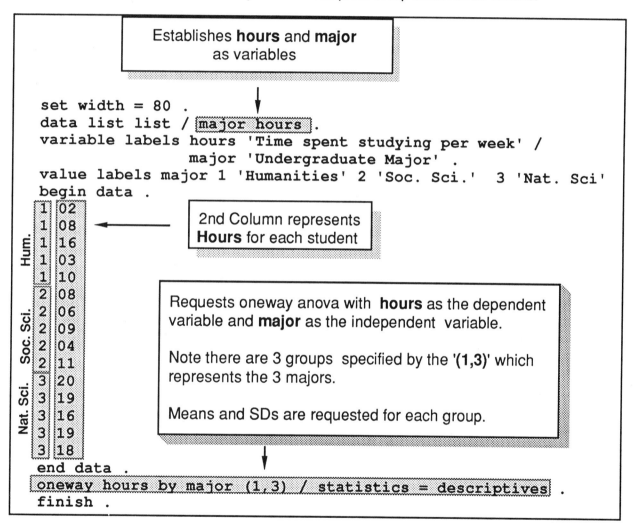

INTERPRETED OUTPUT FOR BASIC ONEWAY ANOVA AND DESCRIPTIVE STATISTICS.

Using the setup above, we will see that we have a significant oneway anova with $F(2,18) = 13.6986$ and p. = .0008. This is significant as with our $df_{bg} = 2$ and $df_{wg} = 12$, the probability of the F - ratio < .01. The means and the standard deviations for each group will be as follows:

Major	Mean	SD
Humanities	7.8000	5.6745
Social Sciences	7.6000	2.7019
Natural Sciences	18.4000	1.5166

The complete output is as follows:

```
1   0   set width = 80 .
    2   data list list / major hours .
    3   variable labels hours 'Time spent studying per week' /
    4                    major 'Undergraduate Major' .
    5   value labels major 1 'Humanities' 2 'Soc. Sci.'  3 'Nat. Sci' .
    6   begin data .
   21   end data .
   22   oneway hours by major (1,3) / statistics = descriptives .
```

- - - O N E W A Y - - - -

Variable HOURS   Time spent studying per week
By Variable MAJOR   Undergraduate Major

ANALYSIS OF VARIANCE

1.

SOURCE	D.F.	SUM OF SQUARES	MEAN SQUARES	F RATIO	F PROB.
BETWEEN GROUP	2	381.7333	190.866	13.6986	.0008
WITHIN GROUP	12	167.2000	13.9333		
TOTAL	14	548.9333			

2.   **3.**

GROUP	COUNT	MEAN	STANDARD DEVIATION	STANDARD ERROR	95 PCT CONF INT FOR MEAN		
Grp 1	5	7.8000	5.6745	2.5377	.7543	TO	14.8457
Grp 2	5	7.6000	2.7019	1.2083	4.2453	TO	10.9547
Grp 3	5	18.4000	1.5166	.6782	16.5170	TO	20.2830
TOTAL	15	11.2667	6.2618	1.6168	7.7990	TO	14.7343

GROUP	MINIMUM	MAXIMUM
Grp 1	2.0000	16.0000
Grp 2	4.0000	11.0000
Grp 3	16.0000	20.0000
TOTAL	2.0000	20.0000

1. Gray Box 1 contains the F ratio. As mentioned above, it significant as for an

   $F(2,18) = 13.6986$, p. = .0008.

2. Group numbers reflect the three groups (1 = Humanities Majors, 2 = Social

   Science Majors, 3 = Natural Science Majors).

3. <u>Gray Box 3</u> contains the means and standard deviations for each group.

SPSS/PC +™ 4.0 ONEWAY ANOVA SETUP

The SPSS/PC + ™ 4.0 setups are slightly different. To calculate the means and standard deviations for each group, the statistics command does not use a keyword but instead a numerical code (**statistics = 1**). This is shown below.

```
set width = 80 .
data list free / iv dv .
variable labels iv 'Independent Variable' /
            dv 'Dependent Variable' .          → optional
value labels iv, etc. .
IV₁ DV
IV₂ DV

  DATA                Each Line Represents One Subject
                   IV = Subject's Group; DV = Subject's Score
IVₖ DV
end data
oneway dv by iv (1,k) / statistics = 1
                  / other optional commands :polynomial
                                        contrast
                                        ranges
                                        format = labels.
finish .
```

REAL WORLD EXAMPLE:

```
set width = 80 .
data list free / major hours .
variable labels hours 'Time spent studying per week' /
           major 'Undergraduate Major' .
value labels major 1 'Humanities' 2 'Soc. Sci.'  3 'Nat. Sci' .
begin data .
1 02
1 08


etc.



3 16
3 19
3 18
end data .
oneway hours by major (1,3) / statistics = 1 .
finish .
```

Note that **statistics = 3** would be used for homogeneity of variance tests.

EXAMPLE 1b: F - RATIO IS NONSIGNIFICANT

In this example, we have altered the data (see means and standard deviations in Box 2) such that the F-ratio is not significant as F (2,12) = 2.1466 and p. = .1596 (see Box 1) which is > .05.

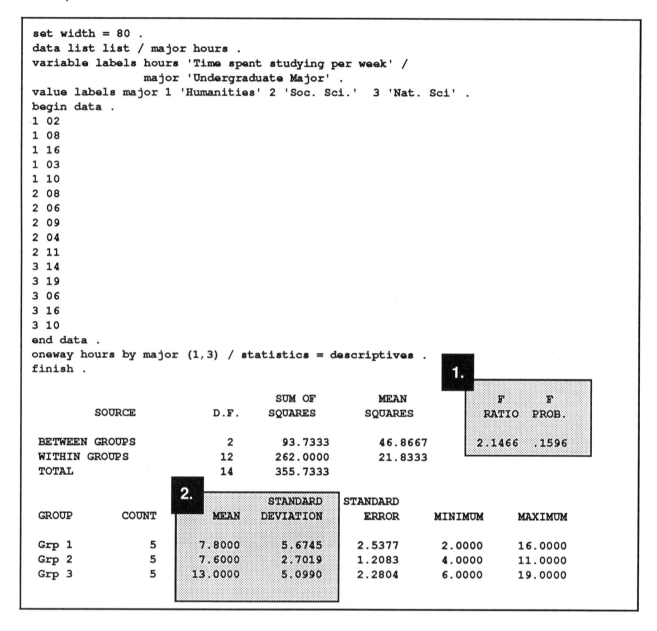

```
set width = 80 .
data list list / major hours .
variable labels hours 'Time spent studying per week' /
                major 'Undergraduate Major' .
value labels major 1 'Humanities' 2 'Soc. Sci.'  3 'Nat. Sci' .
begin data .
1 02
1 08
1 16
1 03
1 10
2 08
2 06
2 09
2 04
2 11
3 14
3 19
3 06
3 16
3 10
end data .
oneway hours by major (1,3) / statistics = descriptives .
finish .
```

1.

SOURCE	D.F.	SUM OF SQUARES	MEAN SQUARES	F RATIO	F PROB.
BETWEEN GROUPS	2	93.7333	46.8667	2.1466	.1596
WITHIN GROUPS	12	262.0000	21.8333		
TOTAL	14	355.7333			

2.

GROUP	COUNT	MEAN	STANDARD DEVIATION	STANDARD ERROR	MINIMUM	MAXIMUM
Grp 1	5	7.8000	5.6745	2.5377	2.0000	16.0000
Grp 2	5	7.6000	2.7019	1.2083	4.0000	11.0000
Grp 3	5	13.0000	5.0990	2.2804	6.0000	19.0000

EXAMPLE 2: APRIORI CONTRASTS

If the F ratio in the anova is significant, you may want to examine which differences among your means or sets of means are also significant. A significant F-ratio does not mean that each group differs from every other group. It is necessary to compare the individual pairings.

A crucial issue is how to control for Type I error as the more contrasts that are done, the higher the probability that the set of contrasts will contain at least one Type 1 error. You can fix the error rate at the alpha level used for the overall F-ratio by using a set of orthogonal contrasts. This means that the number of contrasts requested should not exceed dfbg. In other words, if you have 4 groups, your dfbg would be 3 (as dfbg = k-1, where k= the number of groups) and you should only request 3 contrasts.

However, the full use of apriori contrasts is beyond the scope of this book. We intend to show you how to set them up. For a fuller discussion of the issue, refer to Howell (1987), Keppel (1991), or Kirk, (1982)

Contrasts are request by the **contrast =** subcommand for the **oneway** command where **a b c d ...** refers to the coefficients of the contrasts. Let's use our example with three groups defined by major. The setup commands were:

```
set width = 80 .
data list list / major hours .
variable labels hours 'Time spent studying per week' /
                major 'Undergraduate Major' .
value labels major 1 'Humanities' 2 'Soc. Sci.'  3 'Nat. Sci' .
begin data .
     data
end data .
oneway hours by major (1,3) / statistics = descriptives .
finish .
```

We want to request two contrasts:

1. A comparison of the mean of the Humanities students with the Social Science and Natural Science majors combined into one group.

2. A comparison the Natural Science majors versus the Social Science majors.

   The groups are defined as 1 = Humanities, 2 = Social Science, and 3 = Natural Science.

Thus we will add the two contrast subcommands to the setup and it would look as follows:

```
set width = 80 .

etc.

oneway hours by major (1,3) / statistics = descriptives
                            / contrast = 2 -1 -1
                            / contrast = 0 1 -1 .
```

RULES FOR COEFFICIENT CONSTRUCTION

The coefficients mark the groups in the comparison. The rules are as follows:

1. Coefficients determine whether or not the group is used in the comparison.

2. Coefficient order follows the group order. Thus:

2 -1 -1 corresponds to a coefficient set of:

Group 1 (Humanities) = 2
Group 2 (Social Sciences) = -1
Group 3 (Natural Sciences) = -1

0 1 -1 corresponds to a coefficient set of:

Group 1 (Humanities) = 0
Group 2 (Social Sciences) = 1
Group 3 (Natural Sciences) = -1

3. Coefficients should sum to zero (if not, you will get an error message-see references for rationale). Thus:

2 + (-1) + (-1) = 0
and
0 + 1 + (-1) = 0

4. You can specify up to 50 contrasts.

5. Choosing the coefficients is easy if you just want to compare groups:

a. If just two groups are being tested, assign one group the coefficient **1** and the other group **-1.**
This was done for our second contrast. We wish to compare the means of Group 2 and Group 3.

b. If you are comparing a set of groups versus one group or another set of groups, then:

1. Define the sets and the groups that make them up.
2. Count the number of groups in each set.

3. Assign as coefficients to members of one set, the number of groups in the other set. Then assign the number of groups in the first set to as coefficients for the members of the second set *but make this a negative number.*

For example, we compared Group 1 (Humanities) versus the combination of Groups 2 and 3 (Social Sciences and Natural Sciences combined and the following illustration explains the coefficient process.

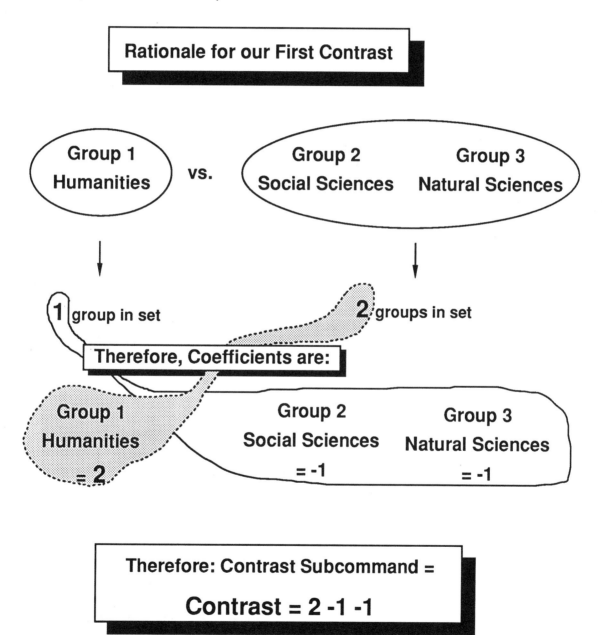

For another example, let's assume that we had problem with five groups defined by the independent variable. We want to compare Groups 2 and 3 versus groups 1, 4 and 5.

Thus, there are 2 groups in the first set of means and 3 in the second group of means. The contrast coefficients would look as follows:

```
Group              1    2    3    4    5
Coefficient        2   -3   -3    2    2
```

The ONEWAY command would look as follows:

```
oneway score by group (1,5) / statistics = descriptives
                            / contrast = 2 -3 -3 2 2
```

A complete example is as follows with an annotated output for two contrasts. In this case we want to compare:

1. The Humanities majors versus the combination of Social Science and Natural Science.
2. The Social Science majors versus the Natural Science majors.

We will see from the output that both contrasts are significant.

Setup

```
set width = 80 .
data list list / major hours .
variable labels hours 'Time spent studying per week' /
                major 'Undergraduate Major' .
value labels major 1 'Humanities' 2 'Soc. Sci.'  3 'Nat. Sci' .
begin data .
1 02
1 08
1 16
1 03
1 10
2 08
2 06
2 09
2 04
2 11
3 20
3 19
3 16
3 19
3 18
end data .
oneway hours by major (1,4) / statistics = descriptives
                / contrast = 2 -1 -1
                / contrast = 0 1 -1 .          1.

finish .
```

RELEVANT OUTPUT WITH ANNOTATIONS

```
 1  0  set width = 80 .
 2  data list list / major hours .
 3  variable labels hours 'Time spent studying per week' /
 4                   major 'Undergraduate Major' .
 5  value labels major 1 'Humanities' 2 'Soc. Sci.'  3 'Nat. Sci' .
 6  begin data .
21  end data .
22  oneway hours by major (1,4) / statistics = descriptives
23                                / contrast = 2 -1 -1
24                                / contrast = 0 1 -1 .
```

- - - - - - - - - - - - - - - O N E W A Y - - - - - - - - - - - - - - - -

```
     Variable  HOURS      Time spent studying per week
     By Variable  MAJOR   Undergraduate Major
```

ANALYSIS OF VARIANCE

1.

SOURCE	D.F.	SUM OF SQUARES	MEAN SQUARES	F RATIO	F PROB.
BETWEEN GROUPS	2	381.7333	190.8667	13.6986	.0008
WITHIN GROUPS	12	167.2000	13.9333		
TOTAL	14	548.9333			

2.

GROUP	COUNT	MEAN	STANDARD DEVIATION	STANDARD ERROR	95 PCT CONF INT FOR MEN		
Grp 1	5	7.8000	5.6745	2.5377	.7543	TO	14.847
Grp 2	5	7.6000	2.7019	1.2083	4.2453	TO	10.957
Grp 3	5	18.4000	1.5166	.6782	16.5170	TO	20.280
TOTAL	15	11.2667	6.2618	1.6168	7.7990	TO	14.733

3.

CONTRAST COEFFICIENT MATRIX

	Grp 1	Grp 2	Grp 3	Grp 4
CONTRAST 1	2.0	-1.0	-1.0	0.
CONTRAST 2	0.	1.0	-1.0	0.

4.

POOLED VARIANCE ESTIMATE

	VALUE	S. ERROR	T VALUE	D.F.	T PROB.
CONTRAST 1	-10.4000	4.0890	-2.543	12.0	0.026
CONTRAST 2	-10.8000	2.3608	-4.575	12.0	0.001

SEPARATE VARIANCE ESTIMATE

	VALUE	S. ERROR	T VALUE	D.F.	T PROB.
CONTRAST 1	-10.4000	5.2612	-1.977	4.6	**5.** 0.110
CONTRAST 2	-10.8000	1.3856	-7.794	6.3	0.000

1. <u>Gray Box 1</u> contains the F ratio. It significant as for an $F(2,18) = 13.6986$, p. = .0008.

2. <u>Gray Box 2</u> contains the means and standard deviations for each group. Group numbers reflect the three groups (1 = Humanities Majors, 2 = Social Science Majors, 3 = Natural Science Majors).

3. <u>Gray Box 3</u> contains the coefficients that you defined for each contrast. Note that **GRP stands for GROUP and that the group numbers on top of the display are staggered.**

4. <u>Gray Box 4</u> contains the t - statistic for each contrast using a pooled variance estimate. As in the T-TEST program (see Chapter 8), pooled variance assumes that the groups are not significantly unequal in variance. In other words, the standard deviations for each group are the same. We will discuss how to test for homogeneity of variance in a subsequent example.

   From Box 4, we would conclude that:

   a. Contrast 1 is significant as $p = .026$ and is $< .05$ (of course it would not be significant if we used an .01 significance level)

   b. Contrast 2 is significant as $p = .001$ and is $< .05$.

   Once again note that a $p = .000$ should be interpreted as $p. < .001$

5. <u>Gray Box 5</u> contains the t - statistic for each contrast using a separate variance estimate. As in the T-TEST program (see Chapter 8), separate variance estimates are used when the groups are not homogeneous in variance. In other words, the standard deviations for each group are not the same. We will discuss how to test for homogeneity of variance in a subsequent example.

EXAMPLE 3: APOSTERIORI CONTRASTS AND RANGES

Besides planned contrasts, it is useful to compare all possible combinations of means. There are several methods for these comparisons available in SPSS. In general, they are less powerful than apriori contrasts but do allow examination of all possible pairs. There is also debate as to which of the procedures is best. Please check our references and the literature. We will not enter the fray but simply document how to use the procedures and interpret significance.

The form of the subcommand to be added to the ONEWAY command is:

> ranges = name of procedure (alpha level desired)

One can request the following procedures. More than one can be requested at a time. Procedures differ in control of alpha level and SPSS/PC + ™ 4.0 names may be different.

PROCEDURE	SPSS NAME (PC+ NAME)	ALPHA LEVELS
Least Significant Difference	LSD	Between 0 and 1, default = .05
Duncan Multiple Range Test	DUNCAN	.01, .05 or .10
Student-Newman-Keuls	SNK	only .05 available
Tukey's Alternate Procedure	TUKEYB (BTUKEY)	only .05 available
Honestly Significant Difference	TUKEY	only .05 available
Modified LSD	LSDMOD (MODLSD)	Between 0 and 1, default = .05
Scheffe's Test	SCHEFFE	Between 0 and 1, default = .05

The following example, using our data, requests a Scheffe's test be conducted at the .05 alpha level. Note the highlighting of the needed subcommand.

```
set width = 80 .
data list list / major hours .
variable labels hours 'Time spent studying per week' /
                major 'Undergraduate Major' .
value labels major 1 'Humanities' 2 'Soc. Sci.'  3 'Nat. Sci' .
begin data .
        etc
end data .
oneway hours by major (1,3) / statistics = descriptives
                        / ranges = scheffe .
finish .
```

The additional output for the Scheffe's test is presented below. Note that the output for the other tests is similar.

R ELEVANT O UTPUT AND I NTERPRETATIONS

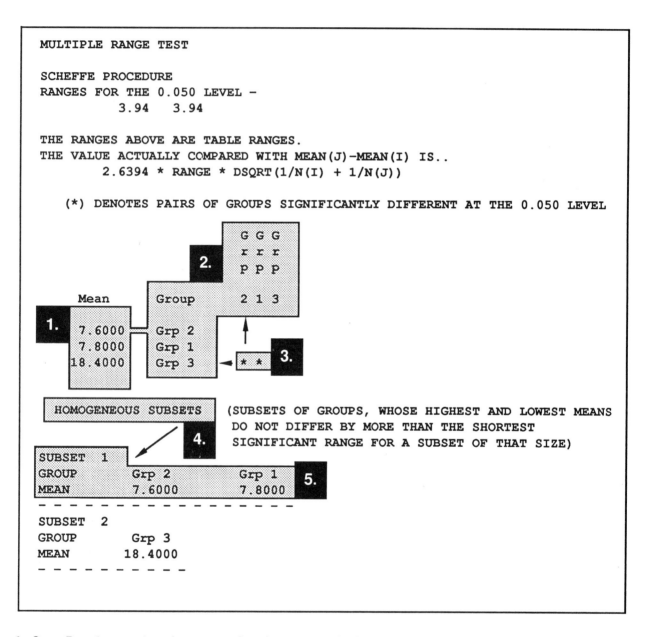

```
MULTIPLE RANGE TEST

SCHEFFE PROCEDURE
RANGES FOR THE 0.050 LEVEL -
        3.94    3.94

THE RANGES ABOVE ARE TABLE RANGES.
THE VALUE ACTUALLY COMPARED WITH MEAN(J)-MEAN(I) IS..
        2.6394 * RANGE * DSQRT(1/N(I) + 1/N(J))

   (*) DENOTES PAIRS OF GROUPS SIGNIFICANTLY DIFFERENT AT THE 0.050 LEVEL
```

```
                                  G G G
                                  r r r
                            2.    p p p

            Mean          Group   2 1 3

     1.     7.6000        Grp 2
            7.8000        Grp 1
           18.4000        Grp 3    * *   3.
```

```
       HOMOGENEOUS SUBSETS        (SUBSETS OF GROUPS, WHOSE HIGHEST AND LOWEST MEANS
                                   DO NOT DIFFER BY MORE THAN THE SHORTEST
                                   SIGNIFICANT RANGE FOR A SUBSET OF THAT SIZE)
                            4.

     SUBSET  1
     GROUP          Grp 2              Grp 1    5.
     MEAN           7.6000             7.8000
     - - - - - - - - - - - - - - - - -

     SUBSET  2
     GROUP          Grp 3
     MEAN          18.4000
     - - - - - - - - - - - -
```

1. <u>Gray Box 1</u> contains the means for the groups. **It is important to note that**
   they are listed in order of magnitude from lowest to highest.
   They are not listed in order of group number.
   For example, the first mean is 7.6 which is the actual mean from Group 2.
   This is noted by the gray connecting line between Gray Box 1 and Gray Box 2.

2. Gray Box 2 presents a matrix of means used to mark those which are significantly different. The order along the left side and across the top is determined by the magnitude of the means as listed in Gray Box 1.

3. Gray Box 3 **shows which mean pairs are significantly different** from each according to the Scheffe test at the .05 significance level. There is an asterisk at the intersection of Group 3 and Group 2. There is another asterisk for Group 3 and Group 1. Thus we conclude, that **Group 3 differs from Group 2.** Also, we conclude that that **Group 3 differs from Group 1.**
Note that the program only prints the lower left half of the matrix. The information would be identical in the top and half and thus redundant.

4. Gray Boxes 4 and 5 present an output style which may be confusing. It is interpreted as follows:

   a. Homogeneous subsets are groups of means that are not significantly different from each other.
   b. Group 2 and 3 are in the same group and are not significantly different.
   c. Group 3 has no other member of its group and so differs significantly from all other groups.

MARKING YOUR GROUPS WITH VALUE LABELS

You might want to label parts of your output by using the value labels for the independent variable rather than as GRP 1, etc. Do this by adding the **format = labels** subcommand after the **ranges** subcommand. Thus the oneway command would look like:

```
oneway hours by major (1,3) / statistics = descriptives
                            / ranges = scheffe
                            / format = labels .
```

The relevant output would look as follows:

```
   GROUP        COUNT        MEAN   DEVIATION      ERROR      MINIMUM      MAXIMUM

Humaniti         5        7.8000      5.6745      2.5377       2.0000      16.0000
Soc. Sci         5        7.6000      2.7019      1.2083       4.0000      11.0000
Nat. Sci         5       18.4000      1.5166       .6782      16.0000      20.0000

TOTAL           15       11.2667      6.2618      1.6168       2.0000      20.0000

                                 S H N
                                 o u a
                                 c m t
                                 . a .     ** Read this vertically!! **
                                   n
                                 S i S
                                 c t c
        Mean         Group       i i i

       7.6000       Soc. Sci
       7.8000       Humaniti
      18.4000       Nat. Sci     * *

SUBSET   1

GROUP         Soc. Sci      Humaniti
MEAN          7.6000        7.8000
- - - - - - - - - - - - - - - -
SUBSET   2

GROUP         Nat. Sci
MEAN          18.4000
- - - - - - - - - -
```

REQUESTING OTHER COMPARISON PROCEDURES

As noted before, you can ask for other procedures or request a different alpha level (see table above). The following command would request the Scheffe test at an alpha = .001 and the Modified LSD test at a default alpha level = .05:

```
oneway hours by major (1,3) / statistics = descriptives
                    / ranges = scheffe (.001)
                    / ranges = lsdmod .
```

EXAMPLE 4: TREND ANALYSIS THROUGH USE OF POLYNOMIAL COMMAND

As mentioned in the introduction, if you have the appropriately scaled independent variable (measurement data) then you can request a trend analysis which will test your data for significance of up to a fifth degree polynomial. Note you must have enough groups for such. You can't test for a trend higher than the value of your df_{bg}. The analysis is requested by adding a polynomial command to the setup as follows:

```
oneway dv by iv (1,k) / statistics = descriptives
                     / polynomial = n .
```

where **n** = the degree of the polynomial (linear, quadratic, cubic, fourth degree or up to fifth degree).

In this example, we have survey college freshpeople, sophomores, juniors, and seniors (**year**) as to how many hours they study per week (**hours**). The data indicate that as **year** increases, the number of hours spent studying increases. Thus **year** is our IV and **hours** will be our **DV**.

The analysis will indicate that there is a significant overall F - ratio and that **there are significant linear and quadratic trends**. Thus the data might be described as:

$$Y = aX + bX^2 + C$$

The setup is as follows (note the highlighting):

```
set  width = 80 .
data list list / year hours .
variable labels hours 'time spent studying per week' /
                year 'year in college' .
value labels year 1 'fresh.' 2 'soph' 3 'junior' 4 'senior' .
begin data .
1 01
        etc.
4 41
end data .
oneway hours by year (1,4) / statistics = descriptives
                         / polynomial = 3 .
finish .
```

The relevant output is as follows (note the highlighting):

```
        Variable  HOURS      time spent studying per week
     By Variable  YEAR       year in college

                                  SUM OF        MEAN        F        F
             SOURCE           D.F  SQUARES      SQUARE     RATIO    PROB.

     BETWEEN GROUPS            3   2754.7895    918.2632   56.2202  .0000[1]

UNWEIGHTED  LINEAR TERM   1   2407.2472   2407.2472   147.3825  .0000[2]
   WEIGHTED  LINEAR TERM   1   2240.0592   2240.0592    37.1465  .0000
DEVIATION FROM  LINEAR     2    514.7302    257.3651    15.7570  .0002

UNWEIGHTED  QUAD. TERM    1    456.5765    456.5765    27.9537  .0001[3]
   WEIGHTED  QUAD. TERM    1    447.5080    447.5080    27.3984  .0001
DEVIATION FROM  QUAD.      1     67.2222     67.2222     4.1156  .0606

UNWEIGHTED  CUBIC TERM    1     67.2222     67.2222     4.1156  .0606[4]
   WEIGHTED  CUBIC TERM    1     67.2222     67.2222     4.1156  .0606

WITHIN GROUPS             15    245.0000     16.3333
TOTAL                 18   2999.7895

                      STANDARD   STANDARD
GROUP  COUNT    MEAN[5]  DEVIATION    ERROR     95 PCT CONF INT FOR MEN

Grp 1    5     3.8000    2.9496     1.3191      .1377  TO     7.463
Grp 2    5     7.6000    2.7019     1.2083     4.2453  TO    10.957
Grp 3    5    13.0000    5.0990     2.2804     6.6688  TO    19.332
Grp 4    4    36.5000    5.0662     2.5331    28.4386  TO    44.564
```

The setup is as follows (note the highlighting):

1. The overall F - ratio is significant. That means significant differences exist in the data.

2. The **linear** trend is significant as it's p. < .0001.

3. The **quadratic** trend is significant as its p = .0001

4. The **cubic trend** is **not** significant as its p > .05.

5. Inspection of the means suggests the existence of the linear and quadratic trend as you can almost see the Senior mean sweep up!

EXAMPLE 5: TESTS FOR HOMOGENEITY OF VARIANCE

Having unequal variances is trouble for parametric statistics such as analyses of variance. This is a well researched topic not without controversy. We also mentioned it in our T-Test discussion (Chapter 8). Our references, among many others discuss the issue. We will present how to let ONEWAY conduct its test. If you are a novice and working with real and important data, we would suggest you consult with someone knowledgeable if the tests for homogeneity are significant.

The following example is based on our original data set. You may have noticed that the three majors had different standard deviations as well as different means. We test if these differences are significant by adding the keyword **homogeneity** to our **statistics = descriptives** command (see note for SPSS/PC + ™ 4.0) as seen below:

```
set width = 80 .
data list list / major hours .
variable labels hours 'Time spent studying per week' /
               major 'Undergraduate Major' .
value labels major 1 'Humanities' 2 'Soc. Sci.'  3 'Nat. Sci' .
begin data .
1 02
   etc .
3 18
end data .
oneway hours by major (1,3) / statistics = descriptives homogeneity .
finish .
```

In the following output, we have highlighted the standard deviations. They are different. We have also highlighted the new output of the **Tests for Homogeneity of Variances.** Cochrans C suggests the variances are significantly different as p = .034. However, the Bartlett-Box F is just over the .05 boundary for significance. Note, unlike T-TEST, ONEWAY does not evaluate the F_{max} test for significance.

NOTE FOR SPSS/PC + ™ 4.0 : Use **'statistics = 1, 3'** for the same analyses.

Given the significance of the Cochrans C, that might suggest using the SEPARATE VARIANCE ESTIMATES in evaluating the Contrasts. However, if you are a beginner, again, we suggest you consult.

```
                      ANALYSIS OF VARIANCE

                             SUM OF        MEAN         F       F
          SOURCE       D.F.  SQUARES       SQUARES      RATIO   PROB.

BETWEEN GROUPS          2    381.7333      190.8667    13.6986  .0008

WITHIN GROUPS          12    167.2000       13.9333

TOTAL                  14    548.9333

                                 STANDARD   STANDARD
GROUP       COUNT     MEAN       DEVIATION   ERROR     MINIMUM   MAXIMUM

Grp 1          5      7.8000      5.6745     2.5377     2.0000   16.0000
Grp 2          5      7.6000      2.7019     1.2083     4.0000   11.0000
Grp 3          5     18.4000      1.5166      .6782    16.0000   20.0000

TOTAL         15     11.2667      6.2618     1.6168     2.0000   20.0000
```

Tests for Homogeneity of Variances

```
Cochrans C = Max. Variance/Sum(Variances) =  .7703, P =  .034
                                                 (Approx.)
Bartlett-Box F =                             2.934 , P =  .055
Maximum Variance / Minimum Variance          14.000
```

OTHER SPSS ANOVA PROGRAMS

SPSS has several other programs that can calculate the oneway analysis of variance: ANOVA, MANOVA, MEANS. Each has its own special features. We find it most useful to use Manova because it can draw boxplots. However, Manova takes a significant investment in time to understand. For reference purposes, we present ANOVA, MEANS, and MANOVA setups using our data set. Note that MEANS and ANOVA cannot test for homogeneity of variance as ONEWAY and MANOVA can. MEANS does calculate a partial eta and eta^2 statistic (proportion of explained variance). MANOVA calculates partial eta^2.

ANOVA

```
set width = 80 .
data list list / major hours .
variable labels hours 'Time spent studying per week' /
                major 'Undergraduate Major' .
value labels major 1 'Humanities' 2 'Soc. Sci.'  3 'Nat. Sci' .
begin data .
1 02
     etc.
3 18
end data .
anova hours by major (1,3) / statistics.
finish .
```

MANOVA

```
set width = 80 .
data list list / major hours .
variable labels hours 'Time spent studying per week' /
                major 'Undergraduate Major' .
value labels major 1 'Humanities' 2 'Soc. Sci.'  3 'Nat. Sci' .
begin data .
     etc.
end data .
manova hours by major (1,3) / print = cellinfo (means)
                        homogeneity (bartlett cochran)
                        signif (efsize)
                    / plot = boxplots
                    / design .
finish .
```

MEANS

```
set width = 80 .
data list list / major hours .
variable labels hours 'Time spent studying per week' /
                major 'Undergraduate Major' .
value labels major 1 'Humanities' 2 'Soc. Sci.'  3 'Nat. Sci' .
begin data .
     etc.
end data .
means hours by major / statistics = anova .
finish .
```

OTHER SPSS/PC +™ 4.0 ANOVA PROGRAMS

ANOVA

```
set width = 80 .
data list free / major hours .
variable labels hours 'Time spent studying per week' /
                major 'Undergraduate Major' .
value labels major 1 'Humanities' 2 'Soc. Sci.'  3 'Nat. Sci' .
begin data .
1 02
      etc.
3 18
end data .
anova hours by major (1,3) / statistics = 3.
finish .
```

MANOVA

```
set width = 80 .
data list free / major hours .
variable labels hours 'Time spent studying per week' /
                major 'Undergraduate Major' .
value labels major 1 'Humanities' 2 'Soc. Sci.'  3 'Nat. Sci' .
begin data .
      etc.
end data .
manova hours by major (1,3) / print = cellinfo (means)
                             homogeneity (bartlett cochran)
                             signif (efsize)
                           / plot = boxplots
                           / design .
finish .
```

MEANS

```
set width = 80 .
data list free / major hours .
variable labels hours 'Time spent studying per week' /
                major 'Undergraduate Major' .
value labels major 1 'Humanities' 2 'Soc. Sci.'  3 'Nat. Sci' .
begin data .
      etc.
end data .
means hours by major / statistics = 1 .
finish .
```

CHAPTER 15: BETWEEN GROUPS FACTORIAL ANALYSIS OF VARIANCE

FACTORIAL ANOVA FOR INDEPENDENT GROUPS & INTERACTIONS

SUMMARY OF SPSS MINIMAL SETUP FOR MANOVA WITH K INDEPENDENT VARIABLES[1]

```
set  width = 80 .
data list list /  IV1 IV2 … IVK DV .
begin data .
IV1 IV2  …   IVk   DV
IV1 IV2  …   IVk   DV
IV1 IV2  …   IVk   DV

    .
    .
   DATA
    .
    .

IV1 IV2  …   IVk   DV
IV1 IV2  …   IVk   DV
end data .
manova DV by IV1 (1,?) IV2 (1,?) … IVk (1,?)
               / print = homogeneity signif (efsize)
               / plot = boxplots
               / omeans = tables (constant, IV1, IV2, … , IVk,
                              IV1 by IV2,
                              IV1 by IV3,
                              IV1 by IVk,
                                   .
                                   .
                              IVk-1 by IVk,
                              IV1 by IV2 by IV3
                                   .
                                   .
                              IVk-2 by IVk-1 by IVk,
                                   .
                              IV1 by IV2 by … IVk)
               / design .
finish .
```

---

[1] Use 'data list **free** / IV1 IV2 ... IVK DV .' for SPSS/PC +™ 4.0 .

REAL WORLD EXAMPLE OF TWO-WAY ANOVA[2]

```
set width = 80 .
data list list / sex age books .
value labels age 1 '20' 2 '25' 3 '30'
               / sex 1 'm' 2 'f' .
begin data .
1 1 5
1 1 2
1 1 0
1 1 2
1 2 6
1 2 4
1 2 1
1 2 2
1 3 5
1 3 1
1 3 1
1 3 4
2 1 1
2 1 6
2 1 5
2 1 5
2 2 6
2 2 10
2 2 10
2 2 8
2 3 18
2 3 19
2 3 14
2 3 19
end data .
manova books by  sex (1,2) age (1,3)
                / print =  homogeneity signif (efsize)
                / plot = boxplots
                / omeans = tables (constant, sex, age, sex by age)
                / design .
finish .
```

Requests 2-way Between Groups Anova
for :
  Dependent Variable = Books,
  Independent Variables = Sex , Age

Anova table, means, boxplots, tests for
  homogeneity of variance and partial eta ^{2}
  are printed.

---

[2] Use 'data list **free** / sex age books .' for SPSS/PC +™ 4.0 .

REAL WORLD EXAMPLE OF THREE-WAY ANOVA

```
set width = 80 .
data list list / ed state sex income .
value labels state 1 'OR' 2'WA' /
               ed 1 'college only' 2 'graduate degree'/
               sex 1 'male' 2 'female' .
begin data .
1 1 1 20
1 1 1 30
1 1 1 37
1 1 1 23
1 1 1 42
1 2 1 32
1 2 1 41
1 2 1 26
1 2 1 28
1 2 1 30
2 1 1 22
2 1 1 29
2 1 1 40
2 1 1 24
2 1 1 36
2 2 1 55
2 2 1 41
2 2 1 28
2 2 1 36
2 2 1 39
1 1 2 40
1 1 2 34
1 1 2 23
1 1 2 45
1 1 2 70
1 2 2 34
1 2 2 34
1 2 2 45
1 2 2 23
1 2 2 45
2 1 2 23
2 1 2 56
2 1 2 45
2 1 2 88
2 1 2 56
2 2 2 34
2 2 2 12
2 2 2  5
2 2 2 10
2 2 2 70
end data .
manova income by state (1,2) ed (1,2) sex (1,2)
                / print = homogeneity signif (efsize)
                / plot = boxplots
                / omeans = tables (constant, ed, state, sex,
                                  ed by state,
                                  ed by sex
                                  state by sex
                                  ed by state by sex)
                / design .
finish .
```

Requests 3-way Between Groups Anova for:

Dependent Variable = Income
Independent Variables = State, Age, Education

Anova table, means, boxplots, tests for homogeneity of variance and partial eta^2 are printed.

PURPOSE OF THE PROCEDURE AND STATISTICS

The Factorial analysis of variance is used to test for significance between the means of separate groups. Unlike the oneway analysis of variance, there are usually two or more independent variables when the anova is performed. Thus a group is classified according to more than one characteristic. It is not unusual to call the IVs as factors A, B, C, D, etc. Presenting all the formulas for the actual calculations goes beyond the scope of this book. They can be found in standard statistics texts (Howell, 1987; Keppel, 1991; Kirk, 1982; Winer, Brown, & Michels 1991). We will note some of the important equations when appropriate.

The basic idea of the factorial anova is to determine whether there is an effect of A, B, C, D, ... etc. and whether there are significant interactions between the Factors A, B, C, D, ... etc. Let's take some examples. Assume that we are interested in how many candy bars people eat per week according to their religion (Catholic, Jewish, Protestant). We ask a sample of each religion and compute the means.

Thus, our IV would be religion. Call it Factor A. Our dependent variable would be the number of candy bars eaten per week. We could perform a oneway anova on the data as seen in Chapter 14. There would be a separate group of subjects for each religion. Each group has different subjects in it. Schematically, our design would looks as follows:

One way Design

Factor A			Religions		
A_1	A_2	A_3	Catholic	Jewish	Protestant
S1 S2 S3	S4 S5 S6	S7 S8 S9	Barb Mike Sue	John Joan Ken	Tracy Terri Andy

In this instance, we would want to see if there are differences between the means of the three groups (A1, A2, and A3) which represent the three religions.

In our example, there were men and women mixed together in each group. Perhaps, we might be interested in whether or not each sex has a different mean for consuming candy. Also, it might be of interest to determine if each combination of sex and religion (i.e. Catholic Males or Protestant Females) differs from other combinations of sex and religion. Thus we would have a two-way design, with separate groups of subjects for each combination of sex and religion (2 x 3). It would look as follows:

Two way Factorial Designs

Religions

	A_1	A_2	A_3	Catholic	Jewish	Protestant	
B_1	S1 S2 S3	S4 S5 S6	S7 S8 S9	Barb Mary Sue	Jill Joan Kim	Tracy Terri Ann	Female
B_2	S10 S11 S12	S13 S14 S15	S16 S17 S18	Bob Jim Stan	Bill Mike Joe	Phil Otto Glen	Male

Sex

Such a design leads to three questions:

1. Is there an effect of A?

An effect of A means that if we consider only the means of the 6 people in each of the three A groups based on religion (i.e. A1(Catholic) = S1 - Barb, S2 - Mary, S3 - Sue, S10 - Bob, S11 - Jim and S12 - Stan), are there significant differences between them? Do the three religions differ? Sex is irrelevant.

2. Is there an effect of B or do the means of each sex differ? Religion is irrelevant as we wish to compare the mean of all the women (mean of B1) to the mean of all the men (mean of B2).

3. Is there an interaction of A and B?

It is rather complicated to fully explain in this context the idea of interactions. We would suggest that you refer to our references for a full explanation of the concept. However, let us offer a brief guide to interactions and their meaning.

A. THE GENERAL LINEAR MODEL:

The analysis of variance is based on a model of an individual's score which assumes the score is a sum of components. The components are the population mean, the effect of the various independent variables, the interactions of the independent variables, and an error term. There can also be covariates and there is a wide variety of error terms. If this is new to you, you need to consult our references. It is also good to know the Greek letters that we will be using. Here is a small table:

α = alpha

β = beta

γ = gamma

δ = delta

ε = epsilon

μ = mu

For a oneway design, the model would be conceived as:

$$X = \mu + \alpha + \varepsilon$$

Where:

X = your score
μ = the population mean
α = the effect of your IV or group Factor "A"
ε = error

Each group has its own α and the F ratio in a oneway anova tests if the α's are different. If the α's were nonexistant or equal to zero, the groups would be the same and the F would not be significant.

For a two-way design, the model would be:

$$X = \mu + \alpha + \beta + \alpha\beta + \varepsilon$$

Where:

X   = your score

μ = the population mean

α = the effect of your first IV or group Factor "A"

β = the effect of your second IV or group Factor "B"

$\alpha\beta$ = the interaction of "A" and "B"

ε = error

We can calculate an F - ratio to see if there is an effect of "A," and another to see if there is an effect of "B." In other words, we can check if the means of the religions (Factor A) contain significant differences and check if the means of Factor B (sex: female vs male) are different.

We can also calculate an F - ratio to see if each of the six individual groups as defined by both religion and sex (A and B) have nonzero $\alpha\beta$ terms. This would give us a significant F - ratio for the interaction.

B. INTERACTIONS IN TERMS OF NONPARALLEL LINES OR "ARE THE EFFECTS OF 'A' DEPENDENT OF THE LEVEL OF 'B' ?"

You might ask right now: What does this mean? What does nonzero $\alpha\beta$ terms have to do with the data. Good point! There are technical definitions but let's use a simple graphical approach. Let's look at the effect of Factor A. There may be an overall effect of Factor A. However, consider that the effect of Factor A might be different dependent on your B group membership. In other words, there is a pattern of differences among the means for three religions for the men. Is the pattern of differences for the women the same? If so, there is no interaction. If there is a difference in this pattern then there is an interaction. Inspect the following set of graphs with the two Factors A and B.

1. Main Effect of Factor "A"

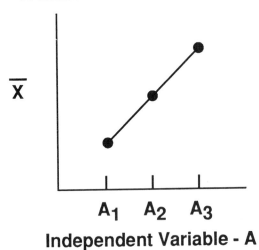

Independent Variable - A

2. No Main Effect of Factor "A"

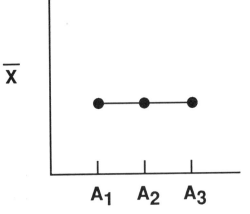

Independent Variable - A

3. Main Effect of "B", No Effect of "A" or Interaction of "A" and "B"

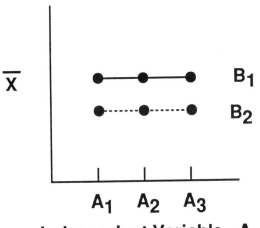

Independent Variable - A

4. Main Effect of Factor "A" & B, No Interaction of "A" and "B"

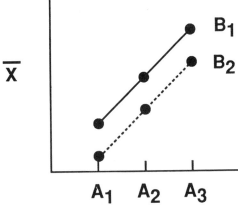

Independent Variable - A

5. Main Effect of Factor "A" & "B", Interaction of "A" and "B"

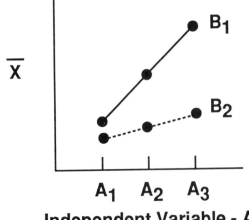

Independent Variable - A

6. Interaction of "A" and "B", No Main Effect of Factor "A" or "B"

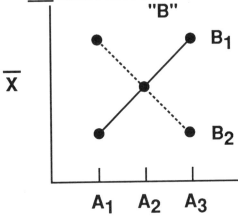

Independent Variable - A

Look at Example 1. In this case, there is only a oneway design with Factor A. As the means are different, there would be a significant F - ratio for this factor (let's assume all is well with sample size, etc. For these graphs, different means are to be taken as significantly different if well spaced). Compared to Example 2, there is no effect of Factor A.

Look at Example 3. We now have classified people by both A and B. There is a line for factor A for those in group B1 and another line for those in B2. There is no effect of A as both lines are flat. However, the B1 line is higher than the B2 line. There is an effect of B. Note, that the effect of B is the same for each condition of A. For A1, the difference between B1 and B2 is the same as for A2 and B2.

Look at Example 4, the B1 and B2 lines are different. Also as A changes, the means increase. Thus A has an effect and B has an effect. However, for each level of A, even though the means increase, the separation between the B1 and B2 lines stay the same!

In both examples (3 and 4), the B1 and B2 lines are parallel.

Look at Example 5. As A changes both B1 and B2 lines increase. Thus there is an effect of A. Note that the B1 line is higher than the B2 line. Thus, there is an effect of B. However, the B1 line is steeper than the B2 line. There is more of a change in A if you are in the B1 group. The lines are not parallel. The pattern of differences in the means for A for group B1 members is different from the pattern of means for A for group B2 members. **This is a two-way interaction!**

Last, look at the pattern of means in Example Six; B1 goes up and B2 goes down. If you averaged the three A groups for B1 and the three A groups for B2, these two means would have the same value (the dot at the center of the crossing point). There would be no effect of B. Similarly, if you computed the A means for each level of A (A1, A2, A3) combining B1 and B2, you would get a flat line as in Example 2 or no effect of A. However, if you plot the effect of A for B1 and the effect of A for B2, you see the lines are wildly different. There are different patterns for A depending on your B group. **Again, this is a two-way interaction!**

To summarize -

In a two-way design we test :

1. Is there an effect of A? (Are there α terms in the model?)

2. Is there an effect of B? (Are there β terms in the model?)

3. Does the effect of A change dependent on B, yielding an AB interaction? (Are there $\alpha\beta$ terms in the model?)

We test points 1, 2, and 3 by calculating an F - ratio for each. Each F - ratio will determine if the effect (A, B, AB) is significant.

The F-ratios are calculated as :

$$F_{effect} = \frac{MS_{effect}}{MS_{within\ groups}}$$

The general form of the **MS** or Mean Squares is:

$$MS_{effect} = \frac{Sum\ Squares_{effect}}{degrees\ of\ freedom_{effect}}$$

In a two-way design, with factors A and B, we would calculate three F - ratios. They would be:

$$F_A, \quad F_B, \quad and \quad F_{AB}.$$

The significance of the F-ratio informs us if there *is a significant effect. Note if it is significant, this does not mean that all the groups are significantly different from each other.* Determining which groups are different from each other is done by using planned and unplanned comparisons. These are not trivial and if not familiar with the procedure, you should consult the references.

THREE-WAY DESIGNS (FACTORS A, B, C)

There is no reason to limit a study to only two independent variables. Consider having three variables - Factors "A," "B," and "C" For a three-way design, the model would be:

$$X = \mu + \alpha + \beta + \gamma + \alpha\beta + \alpha\gamma + \beta\gamma + \alpha\beta\gamma + \varepsilon$$

Where:

X	= your score
μ	= the population mean
α	= the effect of your first IV or group Factor "A"
β	= the effect of your second IV or group Factor "B"
γ	= the effect of your third IV or group Factor "C"
$\alpha\beta$	= the interaction of "A" and "B"
$\alpha\gamma$	= the interaction of "A" and "C"
$\beta\gamma$	= the interaction of "B" and "C"
$\alpha\beta\gamma$	= the interaction of "A," "B" and "C"
ε	= error

The design of a three-way between groups anova would be similar to that of a two-way design. It might be easy to consider it as our original two-way design duplicated for different levels of the new third IV which is identified as **C**. This scheme is presented below with a new factor added to our study of whether or not candy consumption is related to religion and sex. Let's ask if the results would be different if we tested people in California and New York. Thus State = **C** and California = C1 and New York would equal C2.

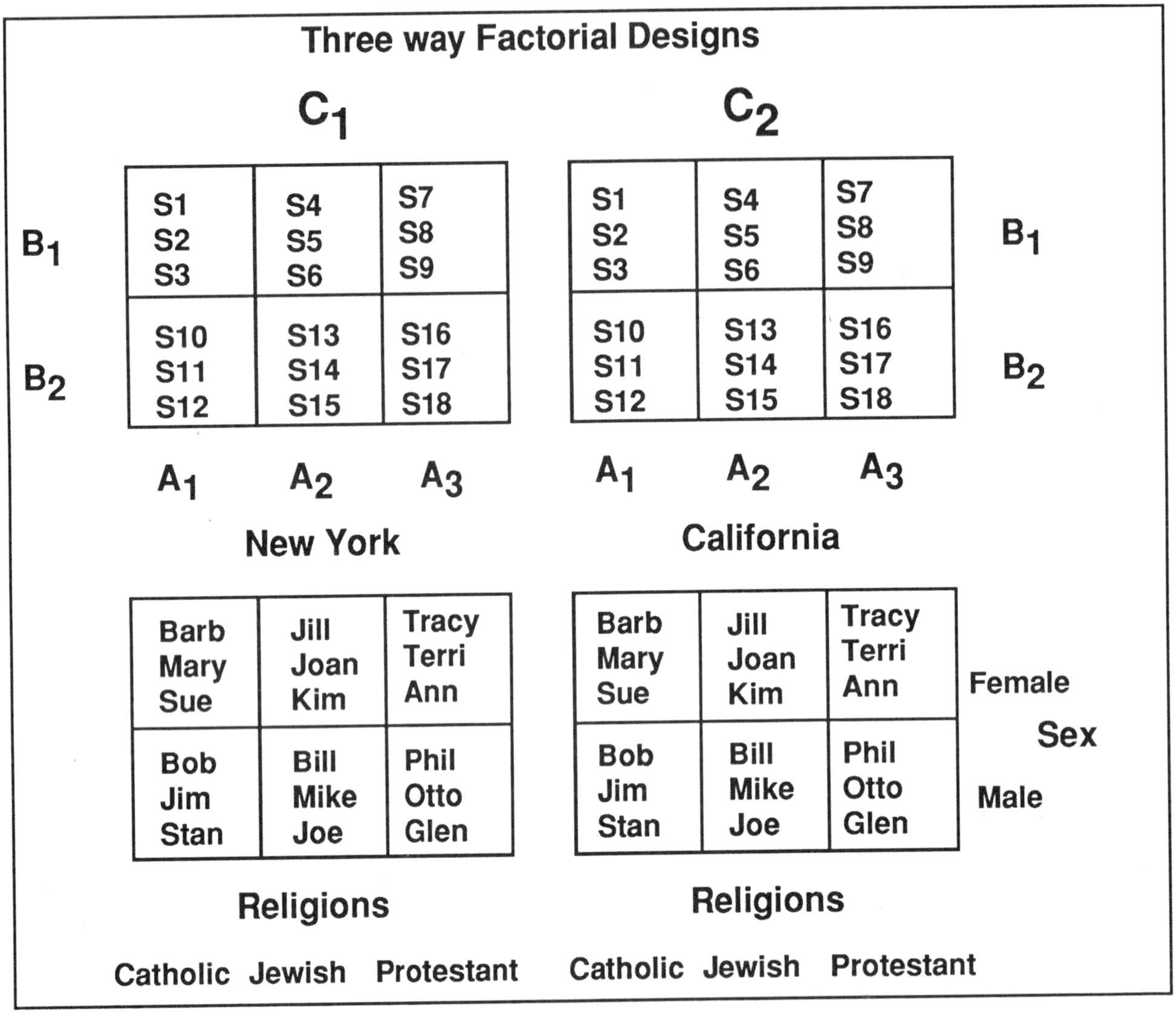

Three way Factorial Designs

C_1

S1 S2 S3	S4 S5 S6	S7 S8 S9
S10 S11 S12	S13 S14 S15	S16 S17 S18

B_1 (left of top row), B_2 (left of bottom row)

A_1 A_2 A_3

New York

C_2

S1 S2 S3	S4 S5 S6	S7 S8 S9
S10 S11 S12	S13 S14 S15	S16 S17 S18

B_1 (right of top row), B_2 (right of bottom row)

A_1 A_2 A_3

California

Barb Mary Sue	Jill Joan Kim	Tracy Terri Ann
Bob Jim Stan	Bill Mike Joe	Phil Otto Glen

Barb Mary Sue	Jill Joan Kim	Tracy Terri Ann
Bob Jim Stan	Bill Mike Joe	Phil Otto Glen

Female

Sex

Male

Religions   **Religions**

Catholic Jewish Protestant   Catholic Jewish Protestant

The crucial question is the significance of the three-way interaction and its interpretation. Let us argue as we did before for a two-way interaction. One way to look at it is that the $\alpha\beta\gamma$ terms exist in the linear model and are significant.

Another interpretation is like that for the two-way. Recall, that we have a two-way interaction if the effect "A" is different according to the level of the variable "B." Thus we had a significant two-way interaction when our "A" line for B1 was different from our "A" line for B2 as illustrated. For a three-way interaction consider that we have an AB interaction for each level of C as illustrated. We can look at AB for C1 and AB for C2. In terms of our illustration, we can examine the interaction of Religion and Sex for the California subjects and examine the interaction of Religion and Sex for our New York subjects. If those interactions **differ** in pattern then we might have a significant three-way ABC interaction. An example is as follows:

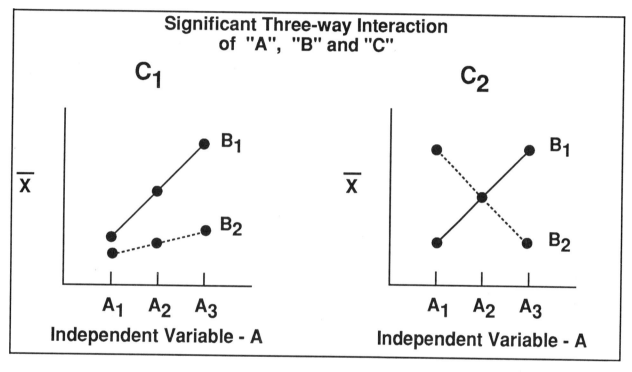

The AB patterns are different for C1 and C2!

Each of the terms in the model (A, B, C, AB, AC, BC, ABC) are independent and may or may not be significant. **Note that it does not have to be the case that the AB interactions have to differ according to C for the ABC interaction to be significant. It might be the case that the AC interactions differ according to B or BC differ according to A.** Probing the exact locus of the three-way interaction can be intense and is explained in our references. If you wanted to think of this in terms of parallelity, recall in a two-way interaction we had nonparallel lines. For a three-way interaction we would have nonparallel surfaces. Unfortunately, this exceeds SPSS's internal graphics capabilities. The issue is examined in our references.

FOUR-WAY DESIGNS (FACTORS A, B, C, D)

Consider having four variables - Factors "A," "B," "C," and "D". For a four-way design, the model would be:

$$X = \mu + \alpha + \beta + \gamma + \delta$$
$$+ \alpha\beta + \alpha\gamma + \alpha\delta + \beta\gamma + \beta\delta + \gamma\delta +$$
$$\alpha\beta\gamma + \alpha\beta\delta + \alpha\gamma\delta + \beta\gamma\delta +$$
$$\alpha\beta\gamma\delta + \varepsilon$$

Where:

X	= your score
μ	= the population mean
α	= the effect of your first IV or group Factor "A"
β	= the effect of your second IV or group Factor "B"
γ	= the effect of your third IV or group Factor "C"
$\alpha\beta$	= the interaction of "A" and "B"
$\alpha\gamma$	= the interaction of "A" and "C"
$\alpha\delta$	= the interaction of "A" and "D"
$\beta\gamma$	= the interaction of "B" and "C"
$\gamma\delta$	= the interaction of "C" and "D"
$\alpha\beta\gamma$	= the interaction of "A," "B," and "C"
$\alpha\beta\delta$	= the interaction of "A," "B," and "D"
$\alpha\gamma\delta$	= the interaction of "A," "C," and "D"
$\beta\gamma\delta$	= the interaction of "B," "C," and "D"
$\alpha\beta\gamma\delta$	= the interaction of "A," "B," "C," and "D"
ε	= error

It is important to note that now we have an effect for each of the individual IV's (A, B, C, D), five two-way interactions (one for each combination of the four IV's - AB, AC, BC, BD, CD), three three-way interactions (ABC, ABD, ACD, BCD) and one four-way interaction for all four IV's (ABCD). All will have to be tested for significance and thus there will be an F - ratio for each:

FA, FB, FC, FD
FAB, FAC, FAD, FBC, FBD, FCD
FABC, FABD, FACD,FBCD
FABCD

Interpretations of four-way interactions can get intense. You can consider a significant four-way interaction as indicating that $\alpha \beta \chi \delta$ terms exist in the model. Another way is that at least one set of three-way interactions differ according to the level of the fourth variable. If this is not clear to you, you really should consult the references.

Higher order designs are possible. Some argue that they become to complex to understand. However, the models and F -ratios just follow the same pattern as before.

Setting Up the Manova Program

We will adopt a different strategy for this section. To go through every possible combination of significant effects and interactions would make this chapter inordinately long. Thus we will give a theoretical setup and then examples of a two-way and three-way design. Also, we will introduce what we think is the most useful set of subcommands. If we did it command by command, we could write another book. Hopefully, you have gotten a feel for SPSS's style so this would be not too traumatic.

Our setups will:

1. Calculate the F -ratios for each effect and interaction.
2. Test for homogeneity of variance.
3. Present boxplots for each group as defined by the independent variables.
4. Present the means for the entire group, each effect and each cell mean based on the interactions and combinations of effects.
5. Calculate partial eta^2 for each effect and interaction.

MANOVA can do much more but this will suffice given our approach.

Most important is the conceptualization of the data. Each subject is marked by the set of independent variables as presented before. In general, the data would look as follows:

IV_1	IV_2	...	IV_k	DV
IV_1	IV_2	...	IV_k	DV
IV_1	IV_2	...	IV_k	DV

.
.
DATA
.
.

IV_1	IV_2	...	IV_k	DV
IV_1	IV_2	...	IV_k	DV
A	B	...	etc	DV

Each line represents one subject. The first number is the IV or group number. IV_1 indicates a level of treatment for the first independent variable. IV_2 indicates a level of treatment for the second independent variable. IV_k indicates a level of treatment for the last independent variable of the set used in the study and **DV** is the person's score. Thus, IV_1, IV_2, IV_3 would correspond to the **A B C** factors of a three-way factorial design. The next line is for the next person.

A TWO-WAY EXAMPLE (AB OR SEX BY AGE)

For a real example, consider that we want to determine if the number of books read per year depends on Sex or Age and if there is an interaction between sex and age. Groups are constructed of males and females who are grouped according to age: 20-year-olds, 25-year-olds, and 30-year-olds. For each age and gender combination we survey four people. The data could be conceptualized as follows:

Age

20		25		30		
5	2	6	4	5	1	**Male**
0	2	1	2	1	4	
						Sex
1	6	6	10	18	19	
5	5	10	8	14	19	**Female**

Each score represents an individual subject.

We want SPSS to produce:

F$_A$, F$_B$ and F$_{AB}$
or
F$_{Sex}$, F$_{Age}$ and F$_{Sex}$ by Age.

We also will request SPSS to calculate the means, test for homogeneity and calculate the partial eta^2. A generic AB setup would be as follows:

AB DESIGN

```
set width = 80 .
data list list / A B DV .
begin data .
A B score
  etc.
end data .
manova DV by A (1, a) B (1, b)
              / print = homogeneity signif (efsize)
              / plot = boxplots
              / omeans = tables (constant, A, B, A by B)
              / design .
finish .
```

a = number of groups for Factor **A**,

b = number of groups for Factor **B**, etc.

In the following figure, we will present an annotated archetypal setup next to the real one with equivalencies noted. Compare the lines! An annotated output follows.

The example sets out the **A B** anova laid out above with the dependent variable being the number of books read by the subject per year. The independent variables are sex and age. We will see the means and boxplots . Note that all three F-ratios are significant (p. < .001) and there is not significant heterogeneity of variance.

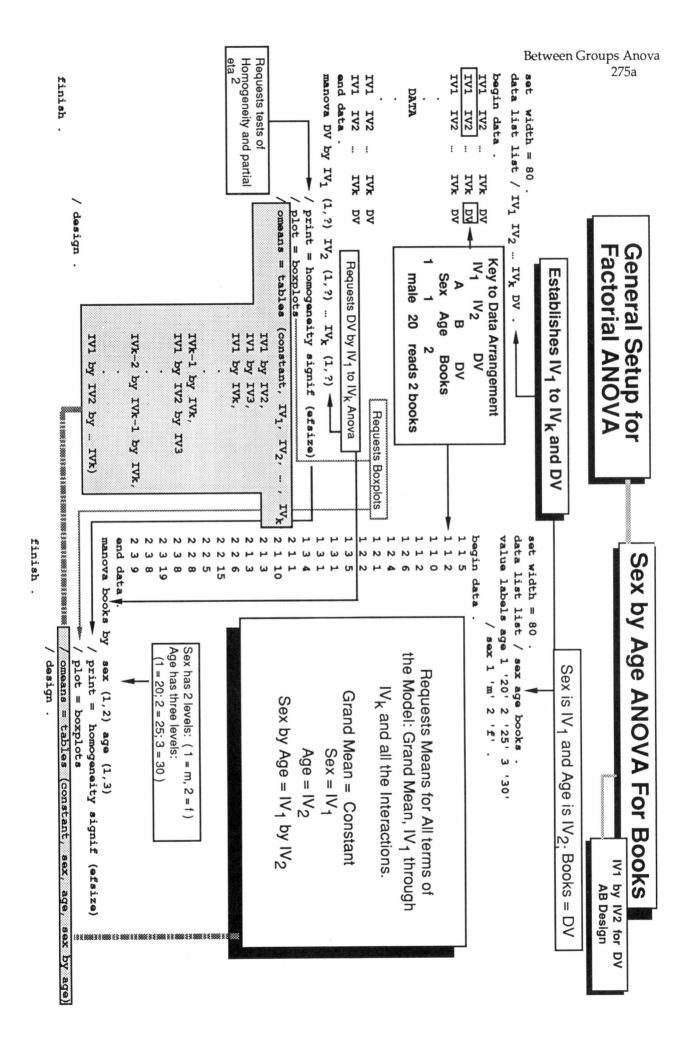

General Setup for Factorial ANOVA

Establishes IV1 to IVk and DV

```
set width = 80 .
data list list / IV1 IV2 ... IVk DV .

begin data .
IV1  IV2  ...  IVk  DV
IV1  IV2  ...  IVk  DV
IV1  IV2  ...  IVk  DV
     .        DATA
     .
IV1  IV2  ...  IVk  DV
IV1  IV2  ...  IVk  DV
IV1  IV2  ...  IVk  DV
and data .
manova DV by IV1 IV1 (1,?) IV2 (1,?) ... IVk (1,?)
  / omeans = tables (constant, IV1, IV2, ... , IVk,
             IV1 by IV2,
             IV1 by IV3,
             IV1 by IVk,
                 .
             IVk-1 by IVk,
             IVk-2 by IVk-1 by IVk,
                 .
             IV1 by IV2 by ... IVk)
  / print = homogeneity signif (efsize)
  / plot = boxplots
  / design .
finish .
```

Key to Data Arrangement

IV1	IV2		DV
A	B		DV
1	1		2
Sex	Age		Books
male	20		reads 2 books

Requests DV by IV1 to IVk Anova

Requests Boxplots

Requests tests of Homogeneity and partial eta 2

Sex by Age ANOVA For Books

IV1 by IV2 for DV
AB Design

Sex is IV1 and Age is IV2; Books = DV

```
set width = 80 .
data list list / sex age books .
value labels age 1 '20' 2 '25' 3 '30'
  / sex 1 'm' 2 'f' .
begin data .
1 1 5
1 1 2
1 1 0
1 1 2
1 2 4
1 2 6
1 2 1
1 2 2
1 3 5
1 3 1
1 3 1
2 1 10
2 1 1
1 3 4
1 3 1
1 3 1
2 1 3
2 1 3
2 2 6
2 1 3
2 2 8
2 2 8
2 2 5
2 2 15
2 3 19
2 3 8
2 3 8
2 3 9
and data .
manova books by sex (1,2) age (1,3)
  / print = homogeneity signif (efsize)
  / plot = boxplots
  / omeans = tables (constant, sex, age, sex by age)
  / design .
finish .
```

Requests Means for All terms of the Model: Grand Mean, IV1 through IVk and all the Interactions.

Grand Mean = Constant

Sex = IV1

Age = IV2

Sex by Age = IV1 by IV2

Sex has 2 levels: (1 = m, 2 = f)
Age has three levels:
(1 = 20; 2 = 25; 3 = 30)

AB Manova Output I

```
1  0  set width = 80 .
2  data list list / sex age books .
3  value labels age 1 '20' 2 '25' 3 '30'
4            / sex 1 'm' 2 'f .'
5  begin data .
6  end data .
30 manova books by  sex (1,2) age (1,3)
31              / print =  homogeneity signif (efsize)
32              / plot = boxplots
33              / omeans = tables (constant, sex, age, sex by age)
34              / design .
```

```
* * * * * * A N A L Y S I S    O F    V A R I A N C E * * * * * *
              CELL NUMBER
              1    2    3    4    5    6
Variable
   SEX        1    1    1    2    2    2
   AGE        1    2    3    1    2    3
```

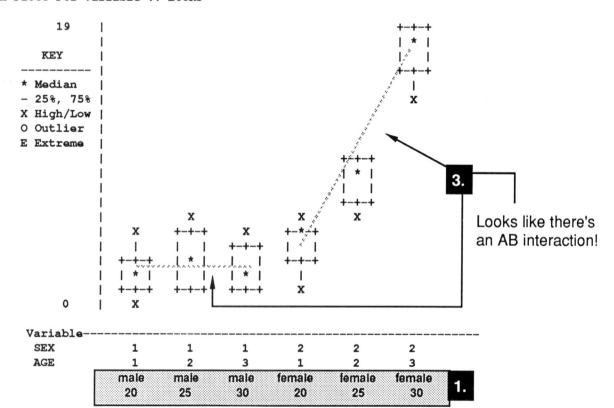

male	male	male	female	female	female
20	25	30	20	25	30

1.

```
Univariate Homogeneity of Variance Tests
   Variable .. BOOKS
```

```
      Cochrans C(3,6) =                        .20482, P = 1.000 (approx.)
      Bartlett-Box F(5,417) =                  .03038, P = 1.000
```

2.

```
- - - - - - - - - - - - - - - - - - - - - - - - - - - - - - - - - - - - - -
```

```
* * * * * * A N A L Y S I S    O F    V A R I A N C E -- DESIGN   1 * * * * * *
```

```
Box-Plots For Variable .. BOOKS
```

```
        19  |                                          +-+-+
            |                                          | * |
        KEY |                                          |   |
       ---------- |                                    +-+-+
        * Median  |                                      |
        - 25%, 75% |                                      X
        X High/Low |
        O Outlier  |
        E Extreme  |
            |                                   +-+-+
            |                                   | * |
            |                                   +-+-+
            |                 X        X        X
            |        X      +-+-+      X      +-*-+      X
            |        |      |   |      X      |   |      X
            |      +-+-+    |*|  |    +-+-+    |   |
            |      | * |    |   |    | * |    +-+-+
            |      +-+-+    +-+-+    +-+-+      |
         0  |        X                         X
```

3.

Looks like there's an AB interaction!

```
   Variable----------------------------------------------------------
      SEX        1        1        1        2        2        2
      AGE        1        2        3        1        2        3
```

male	male	male	female	female	female
20	25	30	20	25	30

1.

AB Manova Output II

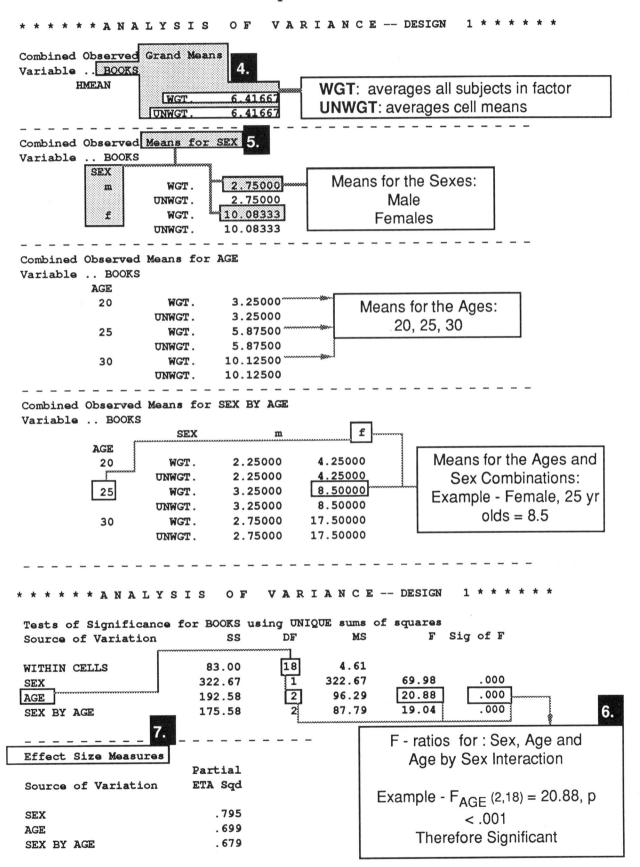

* * * * * * A N A L Y S I S   O F   V A R I A N C E -- DESIGN   1 * * * * * *

Combined Observed Grand Means **4.**
Variable .. BOOKS
    HMEAN

          WGT   6.41667
          UNWGT.   6.41667

> **WGT**: averages all subjects in factor
> **UNWGT**: averages cell means

- -

Combined Observed Means for SEX **5.**
Variable .. BOOKS
    SEX
     m   WGT.   2.75000
          UNWGT.   2.75000
     f   WGT.   10.08333
          UNWGT.   10.08333

> Means for the Sexes:
> Male
> Females

- -

Combined Observed Means for AGE
Variable .. BOOKS
    AGE
    20   WGT.   3.25000
          UNWGT.   3.25000
    25   WGT.   5.87500
          UNWGT.   5.87500
    30   WGT.   10.12500
          UNWGT.   10.12500

> Means for the Ages:
> 20, 25, 30

- -

Combined Observed Means for SEX BY AGE
Variable .. BOOKS
          SEX   m   f
    AGE
    20   WGT.   2.25000   4.25000
          UNWGT.   2.25000   4.25000
    25   WGT.   3.25000   8.50000
          UNWGT.   3.25000   8.50000
    30   WGT.   2.75000   17.50000
          UNWGT.   2.75000   17.50000

> Means for the Ages and
> Sex Combinations:
> Example - Female, 25 yr
> olds = 8.5

- -

* * * * * * A N A L Y S I S   O F   V A R I A N C E -- DESIGN   1 * * * * * *

Tests of Significance for BOOKS using UNIQUE sums of squares

Source of Variation	SS	DF	MS	F	Sig of F
WITHIN CELLS	83.00	18	4.61		
SEX	322.67	1	322.67	69.98	.000
AGE	192.58	2	96.29	20.88	.000
SEX BY AGE	175.58	2	87.79	19.04	.000

6.

> F - ratios for : Sex, Age and
> Age by Sex Interaction
>
> Example - $F_{AGE\ (2,18)} = 20.88$, p
> < .001
> Therefore Significant

- - - - - - - - - - - **7.** - - - - - - - - - - - -

Effect Size Measures

Source of Variation	Partial ETA Sqd
SEX	.795
AGE	.699
SEX BY AGE	.679

1. <u>Gray Box 1</u> explains the correspondence of the Cell Numbers to to our actual groups. The Cell Numbers are also used to mark the boxplots.

2. <u>Gray Box 2</u> contains tests for homogeneity of variance (the assumption that the cells have equal standard deviations or variances). In our example, there seems to be *no inhomogeneity of variance as the probability value is much greater than .05!*
   If these tests are significant (p. >05), you need to consider the appropriateness of the analysis of variance for your data.

3. <u>Box 3</u> presents a boxplot for each group. This is useful because it enables you to check for extreme scores and outliers which might suggest a problem in your sampling or something as mundane as an error of data entry. Also, the pattern of the medians (asterisk in box) gives you an indication of the patterns of the data. While Anovas are based on means, the medians should be reasonably close to them. In our example, we can see the reason for our significant **A B** interaction as the males vary very little across the three ages (20, 25, 30) while the females show a large increase from 20 to 30.

4. <u>Gray Box 4</u> presents the grand mean or the mean for all subjects considered as one large group, collapsed over all the conditions. This would be an estimate of μ in the model.

   Note that there are two means presented. You can average all subjects by just combining all subjects into one big group. This is done for the **WGT** figure. Another procedure would be to average the group means (each cell has a mean, so average them). This is the **UNWGT** figure. In our example, all cells have equal sample sizes. Thus there is no difference. However, if the sample sizes differed in cells, then the **WGT** and **UNWGT** figures would differ.

   An example showing how **WGT** and **UNWGT** works will follow this discussion.

5. <u>Gray Box 5</u> presented the means for the males and females, collapsed over the ages. The mean of 2.75 for the males includes the three groups (20-year-old males, 25-year-olds, and 30-year-olds). It is similar for the females.

Next, we present the means for each age. Each mean (20, 25, 30) combines both men and women.

Finally, we have the means for each combination of sex and age. The mean of 8.5 is the mean for 25 year old women.

Again, as the groups are equal, the **WGT** and **UNWGT** figures are the same.

6. <u>Box 6</u> presents the F - ratios for the AB design. Thus F_{sex}, F_{age}, and $F_{sex \, by \, age}$ are present with appropriate Sum of Squares (SS), Mean Squares(SS), Degrees of Freedom (DF), and Significance level (Sig of F) for each. Our example shows how to read the table.

For our data, we find that all three F -ratios are significant as the .000 should be interpreted as <u>p.</u> <.001.

7. <u>Box 7</u> presents partial eta^2 or effect sizes for three factors. Note that a partial eta^2 is not defined as SS_{effect}/SS_{total}. The latter is the typical eta^2. Partial eta^2 is defined as $SS_{effect} / (SS_{effect} + SS_{error})$. They do not sum to 1.0 as the typical eta^2 's would due. Thus in our example the partial eta^2 for sex is $SS_{sex} / (SS_{sex} + SS_{within \, cells})$ or $322.67/(322.67+83.00) = .795$.

WGT / UNWGT AND UNEQUAL CELL SIZES

```
set width = 80 .
data list list / sex age books .
value labels age 1'20' 2 '25' 3 '30'
              / sex 1 'm' 2 'f' .
begin data .
1 1 5
1 1 2        Typical Group is
1 1 0              4 people
1 1 2
1 2 6
1 2 4
1 2 1
1 2 2
1 3 5
1 3 1
1 3 1
1 3 4
2 1 1
2 1 6
2 1 5
2 1 5
2 2 6
2 2 10
2 2 10
2 2 8
2 3 18
2 3 19
2 3 14
2 3 19
2 3 18
2 3 19       Unequal Size Group
2 3 14         of 12 people
2 3 19
2 3 18
2 3 19
2 3 14
2 3 19
end data .
manova books by  sex (1,2) age (1,3)
 /print = homogeneity signif(efsize)
 /plot = boxplots
 /omeans = tables (constant,sex,age,
                sex by age)
 /design .
finish .
```

Note differences in highlighted means. **UNWGT is the same** as in AB Manova Output II figure but **WGT changes,** as they are based on total subjects, not cell means

```
Combined Observed Grand Means
  Variable .. BOOKS

HMEAN
     WGT.    9.18750  ↔ changes
    UNWGT.   6.41667  ↔ same

Combined Observed Means for SEX
  Variable .. BOOKS

 SEX
  m       WGT.      2.75000
          UNWGT.    2.75000
  f       WGT.     13.05000
          UNWGT.   10.08333

Combined Observed Means for AGE
  Variable .. BOOKS

AGE
 20       WGT.      3.25000
          UNWGT.    3.25000
 25       WGT.      5.87500
          UNWGT.    5.87500
 30       WGT.     13.81250
          UNWGT.   10.12500

Combined Observed Means for SEX BY AGE*
  Variable .. BOOKS

          SEX      m         f
AGE
 20      WGT.    2.25000   4.25000
         UNWGT.  2.25000   4.25000
 25      WGT.    3.25000   8.50000
         UNWGT.  3.25000   8.50000
 30      WGT.    2.75000  17.50000
         UNWGT.  2.75000  17.50000
```

* NO changes as cell means alone (without any combination of groups) are reported so WGT must equal UNWGT.

THREE-WAY BETWEEN GROUPS ANOVA

The following setup and and output are examples of an **A B C** or three-way anova. The dependent variable is Income and the independent variables are:

State :

     1 = Oregon

     2 = Washington

Education :

     1 = College

     2 = Graduate School

Sex :

     1 = Male

     2 = Female

A generic setup would be as follows:

```
set width = 80 .
data list list / A B C DV .
begin data .
A B C score
  etc.
end data  .
manova DV by A (1, a) B (1, b)
        C (1, c)  /
        print = homogeneity
        signif (efsize)
        / plot = boxplots
        / omeans = tables
          (constant, A, B, C,
          A by B, A by C,
          B by C, A by B by C)
        / design .
finish .
```

The actual setup and output are as follows:

ACTUAL SETUP (ABC DESIGN)

```
set width = 80 .
data list list / ed state sex income .
value labels state 1 'OR' 2'WA' /
    ed 1 'college only' 2 'graduate degree'/
    sex 1 'male' 2 'female' .
begin data .
1 1 1 20
1 1 1 30
1 1 1 37
1 1 1 23
1 1 1 42
1 2 1 32
1 2 1 41
1 2 1 26
1 2 1 28
1 2 1 30
2 1 1 22
2 1 1 29
2 1 1 40
2 1 1 24
2 1 1 36
2 2 1 55
2 2 1 41
2 2 1 28
2 2 1 36
2 2 1 39
1 1 2 40
1 1 2 34
1 1 2 23
1 1 2 45
1 1 2 70
1 2 2 34
1 2 2 34
1 2 2 45
1 2 2 23
1 2 2 45
2 1 2 23
2 1 2 56
2 1 2 45
2 1 2 88
2 1 2 56
2 2 2 34
2 2 2 12
2 2 2  5
2 2 2 10
2 2 2 70
end data .
manova income by state(1,2) ed(1,2) sex(1,2)
    / print = homogeneity signif (efsize)
    / plot = boxplots
    / omeans = tables (constant, ed, state,
        sex, ed by state, ed by sex,
        state by sex, ed by state by sex)
        / design .
finish .
```

OUTPUT
(ABC DESIGN)

```
1  0  set  width = 80 .
2  data list list / ed state sex income  .
3  value labels state 1 'OR' 2'WA' /
4              ed 1 'college only' 2 'graduate degree'/
5              sex 1 'male' 2 'female' .
6  begin data .
6  end data .
7  manova income by state (1,2) ed (1,2) sex (1,2)
8          / print = homogeneity signif (efsize)
8          / plot = boxplots
0          / omeans = tables (constant, ed, state, sex,
1                              ed by state,
2                              ed by sex
3                              state by sex
4                              ed by state by sex)
5          / design .
```

```
* * A N A L Y S I S   O F   V A R I A N C E * * * * * *
   40 cases accepted.
   0 cases rejected because of out-of-range factor values.
   0 cases rejected because of missing data.
   8 non-empty cells.

   1 design will be processed.

        CELL NUMBER
- - - - - - - - - - - - - - - - - - - - - - - - - -
* * * * * A N A L Y S I S  O F  V A R I A N C E -- DESIGN  1 * * * *

Box-Plots For Variable .. INCOME

   88 |                          E
      |
   KEY|
----------|
* Median  |          E                              O
- 25%, 75%|
X High/Low|
O Outlier |                    +-*-+
E Extreme |                    | |                   E
          |       +-+-+        | |
          |    X  | * |   X    +-+-+      O     | |  +-*-+
          | +-+-+ +-+-+ +-+-+               +-+-+  +-+-+ +-+-+
          | | * |       | * |     +-*-+     --*--  |   | |   |
          | +-+-+   X    +-+-+     +-+-+       X    | * |
          |    X                E                   | * |
    5     |                                        +-+-+
          |                                           X

Variable-------------------------------------------
STATE     1    1    1    1    2    2    2    2
ED        1    1    2    2    1    1    2    2
SEX       1    2    1    2    1    2    1    2
```

```
* * * * A N A L Y S I S   O F   V A R I A N C E -- DESIGN  1 * * * *

Combined Observed Grand Means
Variable .. INCOME
      HMEAN
                  WGT.    36.27500
                  UNWGT.  36.27500

- - - - - - - - - - - - - - - - - - - - - - - - - -
Combined Observed Means for ED
Variable .. INCOME
         ED
      college    WGT.    35.10000
                 UNWGT.  35.10000
      graduate   WGT.    37.45000
                 UNWGT.  37.45000
- - - - - - - - - - - - - - - - - - - - - - - - -
Combined Observed Means for STATE
Variable .. INCOME
         STATE
         OR      WGT.    39.15000
                 UNWGT.  39.15000
         WA      WGT.    33.40000
                 UNWGT.  33.40000
- - - - - - - - - - - - - - - - - - - - - - - - -
Combined Observed Means for SEX
Variable .. INCOME
         SEX
      male       WGT.    32.95000
                 UNWGT.  32.95000
      female     WGT.    39.60000
                 UNWGT.  39.60000
- - - - - - - - - - - - - - - - - - - - - - - - -
Combined Observed Means for STATE BY ED
Variable .. INCOME
                 STATE     OR       WA
      ED
      college    WGT.    36.40000  33.80000
                 UNWGT.  36.40000  33.80000
      graduate   WGT.    41.90000  33.00000
                 UNWGT.  41.90000  33.00000
```

```
* * * A N A L Y S I S   O F   V A R I A N C E -- DESIGN  1 * * *

Combined Observed Means for ED BY SEX
Variable .. INCOME
             ED      college   graduate
      SEX
      male      WGT.    30.90000  35.00000
                UNWGT.  30.90000  35.00000
      female    WGT.    39.30000  39.90000
                UNWGT.  39.30000  39.90000

- - - - - - - - - - - - - - - - - - - - - - - - - -
Combined Observed Means for STATE BY SEX
Variable .. INCOME
             STATE     OR        WA
      SEX
      male      WGT.    30.30000  35.60000
                UNWGT.  30.30000  35.60000
      female    WGT.    48.00000  31.20000
                UNWGT.  48.00000  31.20000

- - - - - - - - - - - - - - - - - - - - - - - - - -
Combined Observed Means for STATE BY ED BY SEX
Variable .. INCOME
                   STATE      OR        WA
      SEX     ED
      male    college  WGT.    30.40000  31.40000
                       UNWGT.  30.40000  31.40000
      male    graduate WGT.    30.20000  39.80000
                       UNWGT.  30.20000  39.80000
      female  college  WGT.    42.40000  36.20000
                       UNWGT.  42.40000  36.20000
      female  graduate WGT.    53.60000  26.20000
                       UNWGT.  53.60000  26.20000

- - - - - - - - - - - - - - - - - - - - - - - - -

* * * * * A N A L Y S I S   O F   V A R I A N C E -- DESIGN  1 * *

Tests of Significance for INCOME using UNIQUE sums of squares
Source of Variation      SS    DF      MS       F   Sig of F

WITHIN CELLS          7758.00  32   242.44
STATE                  330.62   1   330.62    1.36    .252
ED                      55.22   1    55.22     .23    .636
SEX                    442.23   1   442.23    1.82    .186
STATE BY ED             99.23   1    99.23     .41    .527
STATE BY SEX          1221.02   1  1221.02    5.04    .032
ED BY SEX               30.63   1    30.63     .13    .725
STATE BY ED BY SEX     555.02   1   555.02    2.29    .140

- - - - - - - - - - - - - - - - - - - - - - - - -
  Effect Size Measures
                        Partial
  Source of Variation   ETA Sqd

  STATE                   .041
  ED                      .007
  SEX                     .054
  STATE BY ED             .013
  STATE BY SEX            .136
  ED BY SEX               .004
  STATE BY ED BY SEX      .067
```

OTHER ANOVA PROGRAMS

SPSS has another program that can calculate the Between Groups Factorial analysis of variance (ANOVA). It is limited in its abilities as compared to MANOVA but may be easier to use. However, it cannot test for homogeneity of variance. A sample setup and output follows:

SETUP †.

```
set width = 80 .
data list list / sex age books .
value labels age 1 '20' 2 '25' 3 '30'
            / sex 1 'm' 2 'f' .
begin data .
1 1 5
1 1 2
1 1 0
1 1 2
1 2 6
1 2 4
1 2 1
1 2 2
1 3 5
1 3 1
1 3 1
1 3 4
2 1 1
2 1 10
2 1 3
2 1 3
2 2 6
2 2 15
2 2 5
2 2 8
2 3 8
2 3 19
2 3 8
2 3 9
end data .
anova books by sex (1,2) age (1,3)
      / statistics.
finish .
```

OUTPUT

```
 1   0  set width = 80
 2   data list list / sex age books
 3   value labels age 1 '20' 2 '25' 3 '30'
 4        / sex 1 'm' 2 'f'
 5   begin data .
29   end data .
30   anova books by sex (1,2) age (1,3)
31       / statistics  .
```

```
* * *  C E L L   M E A N S  * * *
              BOOKS
          BY SEX
             AGE

TOTAL POPULATION

       5.33
   (   24)

SEX
        1          2
       2.75      7.92
   (   12)  (   12)

AGE
        1          2          3

       3.25      5.88      6.88
   (    8)  (    8)  (    8)

         AGE
              1          2          3
SEX
         1    2.25      3.25      2.75
            (    4)  (    4)  (    4)

         2    4.25      8.50     11.00
            (    4)  (    4)  (    4)
```

```
* * *  A N A L Y S I S   O F   V A R I A N C E  * * *
               BOOKS
          by   SEX
               AGE
```

Source of Variation	Sum of Squares	DF	Mean Square	F	Sig of F
Main Effects	216.250	3	72.083	5.545	.007
SEX	160.167	1	160.167	12.321	.003
AGE	56.083	2	28.042	2.157	.145
2-Way Interactions	39.083	2	19.542	1.503	.249
SEX AGE	39.083	2	19.542	1.503	.249
Explained	255.333	5	51.067	3.928	.014
Residual	234.000	18	13.000		
Total	489.333	23	21.275		

---

† For SPSS/PC + ™ 4.0 :
data list free / sex age books .
  etc.
anova books by sex (1,2) age (1,3)
    / statistics = 3. '
finish.

SUMMARY OF FACTORIAL DESIGNS FOR SPSS [3]

AB DESIGN

```
set width = 80 .
data list list / A B DV .
begin data .
A B score
  etc.
end data  .
manova DV by A (1, a) B (1, b)
                / print = homogeneity signif (efsize)
                / plot = boxplots
                / omeans = tables (constant, A, B, A by B)
                / design .
finish .
```

a = number of groups for Factor **A**,
b = number of groups for Factor **B**, etc.

ABC DESIGN

```
set width = 80 .
data list list / A B C DV .
begin data .
A B C score
  etc.
end data .
manova DV by A (1, a) B (1, b) C (1, c)
                / print = homogeneity signif (efsize)
                / plot = boxplots
                / omeans = tables (constant, A, B, C,
                                   A by B,
                                   A by C,
                                   B by C,
                                   A by B by C)
                / design .
finish .
```

---

3. Use 'data list **free** / etc. ' for SPSS/PC +™ 4.0 .

A B C D D E S I G N

```
set width = 80 .
data list list / A B C D DV .
begin data .
A B C D score
  etc.
end data .
manova DV by A (1, a) B (1, a) C (1, c) D (1, d)
                / print = homogeneity signif (efsize)
                / plot = boxplots
                / omeans = tables (constant, A, B, C, D,
                            A by B,
                            A by C,
                            A by D,
                            B by C,
                            B by D,
                            C by D,
                            A by B by C,
                            A by B by D,
                            A by C by D,
                            B by C by D,
                            A by B by C by D)
                / design .
finish .
```

A B C D E D E S I G N

```
set width = 80  .
data list list / A B C D E DV  .
begin data .
A B C D E score
  etc.
end data  .
manova DV by A (1, a) B (1, b) C (1, c) D (1, d) E(1, e)
            / print = homogeneity signif (efsize) / plot = boxplots
            / omeans = tables (constant, A, B, C, D, E,
                            A by B,
                            A by C,
                            A by D,
                            A by E,
                            B by C,
                            B by D,
                            B by E,
                            C by D,
                            C by E,
                            D by E,
                            A by B by C,
                            A by B by D,
                            A by B by E,
                            A by C by D,
                            A by C by E,
                            A by D by E,
                            B by C by D,
                            B by C by E,
                            B by D by E,
                            C by D by E,
                            A by B by C by D
                            A by B by C by E
                            A by B by D by E
                            A by C by D by E
                            B by C by D by E
                            A by B by C by D by E)
                / design .
finish .
```

CHAPTER 16: REPEATED MEASURES ANALYSIS OF VARIANCE, LATIN SQUARES & ANCOVA

ANOVA DESIGNS WITH REPEATED TRIALS OR MATCHED GROUPS OR COVARIATES

I. PURPOSE OF THE PROCEDURE AND STYLES OF MANOVA

We do not start with examples as there are two ways of approaching the problem, referred to by us as **Method** I and **Method** II. You'll find the examples in front of each method's own section. First, it is a good idea to be familiar with the material in Chapters 14 and 15 before proceeding.

Using repeated measures designs in SPSS may entail a variety of approaches. We will try to make it as simple as possible. First, what is the basic idea of a repeated measures design? In factorial anovas (Chapter 15), there are usually two or more independent variables (IV) when the anova is performed. Thus a group is classified according to more than one characteristic. It is not unusual to call the IVs as factors A, B, C, D, etc. In each combination of the IVs, we find different people. The table below is taken from Chapter 15 and demonstrates, again that for each combination of A and B, there is a different group of people.

Two way Factorial Designs

	A₁	A₂	A₃
B₁	S1 S2 S3	S4 S5 S6	S7 S8 S9
B₂	S10 S11 S12	S13 S14 S15	S16 S17 S18

Religions

	Catholic	Jewish	Protestant	
	Barb Mary Sue	Jill Joan Kim	Tracy Terri Ann	Female
	Bob Jim Stan	Bill Mike Joe	Phil Otto Glen	Male

Sex

For a repeated measures designs, this is not the case. The same subject may be tested for the different levels of the IVs. This is an efficient technique as it is economical for the number of subjects consumed by the experiment. Also, the use of such repetitions may increase the statistical power of the design through the reduction of the error variance through the removal of the covariance. In other words, testing the same people several times removes (we hope) some of the random variability between the conditions. This yields more power.

Repeated measures designs can examine only one IV and thus be analogous to a Oneway between groups anova. All subjects would serve under all levels of the independent variable A. Such a design would look as follows:

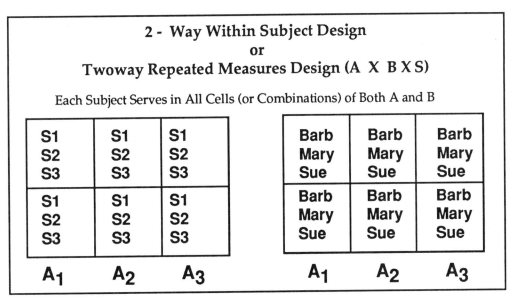

All subjects served in all three levels of the Factor A.

There is no reason why such designs cannot be fully factorial and have more than one IV. One can examine whether there is an effect of A, B, C, D, ... etc. and whether there are significant interactions between the Factors A, B, C, D, ... etc. Let's look at some examples.

Note that in the figure, we see these designs referred to as REPEATED MEASURES, WITHIN SUBJECTS or A X B X ... X S designs. All are acceptable.

3 - Way Within Subject Design
or
Threeway Repeated Measures Design (A X B X C X S)

Each Subject Serves in All Cells (or Combinations) of A, B and C

S1 S2 S3	S1 S2 S3	S1 S2 S3
S1 S2 S3	S1 S2 S3	S1 S2 S3

A_1 A_2 A_3

C_1

S1 S2 S3	S1 S2 S3	S1 S2 S3
S1 S2 S3	S1 S2 S3	S1 S2 S3

A_1 A_2 A_3

C_2

Barb Mary Sue	Barb Mary Sue	Barb Mary Sue
Barb Mary Sue	Barb Mary Sue	Barb Mary Sue

Barb Mary Sue	Barb Mary Sue	Barb Mary Sue
Barb Mary Sue	Barb Mary Sue	Barb Mary Sue

It also might be the case that the repetition only occurs for some of the variables and not the others. B might be repeated but different groups serve for levels of A. Thus a group of subjects gets assigned to an A level and this group runs through this level of A as combined with all the levels of B. This logic can extend to greater than two IVs. Examples follow.

1 Between; 1 Within Subject Design
A X (B X S)

Different Subjects for Each Level of A (A1 & A2).
Within Each Level of A ; All Subjects Serve in All Levels of B (B1, B2, B3)

	B1	B2	B3
A1	S1 S2 S3	S1 S2 S3	S1 S2 S3
A2	S4 S5 S6	S4 S5 S6	S4 S5 S6

1 Between; 2 Within Subject Design
A X (B X C X S)

Different Subjects for Each Level of A (A1 & A2).
Within Each Level of A ; All Subjects Serve in All Combinations of B and C

C_1

	B1	B2	B3
A1	S1 S2 S3	S1 S2 S3	S1 S2 S3
A2	S4 S5 S6	S4 S5 S6	S4 S5 S6

C_2

	B1	B2	B3	
	S1 S2 S3	S1 S2 S3	S1 S2 S3	A1
	S4 S5 S6	S4 S5 S6	S4 S5 S6	A2

A1	Barb Mary Sue	Barb Mary Sue	Barb Mary Sue
A2	Joan Kari May	Joan Kari May	Joan Kari May

	Barb Mary Sue	Barb Mary Sue	Barb Mary Sue	A1
	Joan Kari May	Joan Kari May	Joan Kari May	A2

2 Between; 1 Within Subject Design
A X B X (C X S)

Different Subjects for Each Combination of A and B
Within the AB Combinations; All Subjects Serve in All Levels of C (C1 & C2)

C_1

	B1	B2	B3
A1	S1 S2 S3	S4 S5 S6	S7 S8 S9
A2	S10 S11 S12	S13 S14 S15	S16 S17 S18

C_2

	B1	B2	B3	
	S1 S2 S3	S4 S5 S6	S7 S8 S9	A1
	S10 S11 S12	S13 S14 S15	S16 S17 S18	A2

A1	Barb Mary Sue	Babs Mona Sally	Lori Dale Lana
A2	Joan Kari May	Gail Alice Nan	Marsha Dot Lois

	Barb Mary Sue	Babs Mona Sally	Lori Dale Lana	A1
	Joan Kari May	Gail Alice Nan	Marsha Dot Lois	A2

Such designs as these can be called mixed, nested, split plot, 1 between/2 within, or noted by the factors A, B, C, etc with parentheses noting the repeated factors [i.e. A X B X (C X S)] .

There is one more important point about the general setup. In our examples, we used the same individuals for the factors that were repeated. This does not have to be the case. The individuals involved could be matched in some fashion. For example, if we had identical triplets, one of each set could serve in a three level repeated factor.

In all these designs, we are interested in the effects of A, B, ... ; AB, AC, ...; ABC...; etc. The issue is how to analyze the data. There are different opinions in the literature. We will present two approaches. Both approaches use the MANOVA program The first two analyze the design as a repeated measures anova. However, there are two ways to do this in SPSS. Each has advantages. There is a third way which treats the data as a multivariate analysis of variance. For more detailed discussion, we refer you to our references and a large literature. For the beginner, we would suggest a consultant. To be practical, most people can get by with one of the first two methods.

II. Method I: declaring the terms with 1 Score/Line

Summary of SPSS Minimal Setup Using Manova for a Completely Within Subject Factorial Design ($A \times B \times C \ldots \times IV_K \times S$)*

```
set  width = 80 .
data list list / A B C … IVₖ SUB Score .
begin data .
A   B   C …   IVₖ   DV SUB ¹
A   B   C …   IVₖ   DV SUB
A   B   C …   IVₖ   DV SUB
    .
  DATA
    .
A   B   C …   IVₖ   DV SUB
A   B   C …   IVₖ   DV SUB
end data .
manova Score by A (1,?) B (1,?) … IVₖ (1,?) SUB (1, s) ¹
        / omeans = tables (constant, A, B, ,… IVₖ,
            A by B,
            A by C,
            A by IVₖ,
            B by C,
              .
            IVₖ₋₁ by IVₖ,
            A by B by C ,
              .
            IVₖ₋₂ by IVₖ₋₁ by IVₖ,
              .
            A by B by C by … IVₖ)
      / design = A vs 1, A by SUB = 1,
         B vs 2, B by SUB = 2,
         C vs 3, C by SUB = 3,
              .
         IVk vs k, IVk by SUB = k,
         A by B vs k+1, A by B by SUB = k+1,
         A by C vs k+2, A by C by SUB = k+2,
         B by C vs k+3, B by C by SUB = k+3,
              .
         IVₖ₋₁ by IVₖ vs ?, IVₖ₋₁ by IVₖ by SUB = ? ² ,
              .
         A by B by C vs ? ², A by B by C by SUB = ? ²
              .
         A by B by … IVₖ vs ? ²,
         A by B by … IVₖ by SUB = ? ² .
finish   .
```

---

* Use **data list free / A B C … IVₖ**   for SPSS/PC + ™ 4. 0 .

[1] Please check the text for the numbering scheme for subjects. In general, it refers to the number of subjects within the repeated elements. *It does not represent the total number of individuals in the study!*

[2] We could continue with a crazy quilt of additions but they would be based on using a complicated set of combinations (nCr) and subscripts. Just try to keep count and check the examples in the text.

REAL WORLD EXAMPLE OF THREE-WAY A x B x C x S ANOVA

WITH 3 SUBJECTS (SUB) SERVING IN ALL CONDITIONS OF A (2 LEVELS), B (THREE LEVELS) & C (2 LEVELS)

```
set width = 80 .
data list list / A B C SUB score . [data list free /etc. for SPSS/PC+]
begin data .
1 1 1 1 37
1 1 2 1 43
1 2 1 1 39
1 2 2 1 45
1 3 1 1 31
1 3 2 1 41
2 1 1 1 42
2 1 2 1 44
2 2 1 1 30
2 2 2 1 45
2 3 1 1 21
2 3 2 1 58
1 1 1 2 33
1 1 2 2 36
1 2 1 2 29
1 2 2 2 37
1 3 1 2 31
1 3 2 2 45
2 1 1 2 30
2 1 2 2 59
2 2 1 2 53
2 2 2 2 54
2 3 1 2 35
2 3 2 2 56
1 1 1 3 39
1 1 2 3 45
1 2 1 3 42
1 2 2 3 48
1 3 1 3 32
1 3 2 3 54
2 1 1 3 44
2 1 2 3 68
2 2 1 3 33
2 2 2 3 54
2 3 1 3 24
2 3 2 3 65
end data .
manova    score by A (1, 2) B (1, 3) C (1, 2) SUB (1, 3)/
          omeans = tables (A, B, C,
                          A by B,
                          A by C,
                          B by C,
                          A by B by C)/
          design = A vs 1, A by SUB = 1,
                   B vs 2, B by SUB = 2,
                   C vs 3, C by SUB = 3,
                   A by B vs 4, A by C by SUB=4,
                   A by C vs 5, A by C by SUB=5,
                   B by C vs 6, B by C by SUB=6,
                   A by B by C vs 7,
                   A by B by C by SUB = 7 .

finish .
```

SUMMARY OF MIXED, NESTED, SPLIT PLOT, OR BETWEEN/WITHIN DESIGNS USING METHOD I (TERMS DECLARED WITH 1 SCORE/LINE)

A X (B X S) - see p.304 for Real World Example

```
set width = 80 .
data list list/ A B SUB Score  . [1]
comment A x ( B x S ) - B repeated.
begin data .
        a b sub score

end data .
manova Score by A (1, a) B(1, b) SUB (1, s)  /
        omeans = tables (A, B, A by B) /
        design = A vs 1,
                SUB w A = 1,
                B vs 2,
                A by B vs 2,
                B by SUB w A = 2  .
finish .
```

A X (B X C X S) - see p.310 for Real World Example

```
set width = 80 .
data list list / A B C SUB Score . [1]
comment A x ( B x C x S ) B & C repeated.
begin data .
        a b c sub score
end data .
manova Score by A (1, a) B (1, b) SUB (1, s) C (1, c)/
        omeans = tables (A, B, C, A by B, A by B,
                         B by C, A by B by C)/
        design = A vs 1,
                SUB w A  = 1,
                B vs 2, A by B vs 2,
                B by SUB w A = 2,
                C vs 3,
                A by C vs 3,
                C by SUB w A = 3,
                B by C vs  4,
                A by B by C vs 4,
                B by C by SUB w A  = 4 .
finish .
```

A X B X (C X S) - see p.306 for Real World Example

```
set width = 80 .
data list list / A B C SUB Score . [1]
comment A x B x (C x S) - just C repeated.
begin data .

a b c sub score

end data .
manova Score by A (1, a) B (1, b) SUB (1, s) C (1, c)/
        omeans = tables (A, B, C, A by B, A by B,
                         B by C, A by B by C) /
        design = A vs 1, B vs 1, A by B vs 1,
                SUB w A by B = 1,
                C vs 2,
                A by C vs 2, B by C vs 2,
                A by B by C vs 2,
                C by SUB w A by B = 2 .
finish .
```

[1] data list **free** / etc. for SPSS/PC + ™ 4.0

METHOD I: DECLARING THE ERROR TERMS FOR THE REPEATED MEASURES ANOVA WITH ONE SCORE PER CASE.

The issue is what to use as the error term in the F - ratios for the factors that have repeated levels. One approach is to use the interactions of the subjects' repeated scores (a factor noted as **S**) and the factors being tested - A, B, ... ; AB, AC, ...; ABC...; etc. (Kirk, 1982; Keppel, 1991). The exact layout of the error terms depends on the exact design. We will discuss the ones we have illustrated and then give general principles and examples for the setups.

A. Totally Within Subject Designs (A x S, A x B x S, A x B x C x S, etc.)

For the oneway design repeated measures design (A X S) , the linear model would be conceived as:

$$ X = \mu + \alpha + \pi + \alpha\pi + \varepsilon $$

Where:

X	= your score
μ	= the population mean
α	= the effect of your IV or group Factor "A"
π	= the subject effect (the repetitions) - Factor "S"
$\alpha\pi$	= the interactions of "A" and "S"
ε	= error

For a twoway totally within subject design (A x B x S) , the model would be:

$$ X = \mu + \alpha + \beta + \pi + \alpha\beta + \alpha\pi + \beta\pi + \alpha\beta\pi + \varepsilon $$

Where:

X	= your score
μ	= the population mean
α	= the effect of your first IV or group Factor "A"
β	= the effect of your second IV or group Factor "B"
π	= the subject effect (the repetitions) - Factor "S"
$\alpha\beta$	= the interaction of "A" and "B"
$\alpha\pi$	= the interaction of "A" and "S"

$\beta\pi$	= the interaction of "B" and "S"
$\alpha\beta\pi$	= the interaction of "A," "B" and "S"
ε	= error

For a three-way totally within subject design (A x B x C x S), the model would be:

$$X = \mu + \alpha + \beta + \gamma + \pi$$
$$+ \alpha\beta + \alpha\gamma + \alpha\pi + \beta\gamma + \beta\pi + \gamma\pi +$$
$$\alpha\beta\gamma + \alpha\beta\pi + \alpha\gamma\pi + \beta\gamma\pi +$$
$$\alpha\beta\gamma\pi + \varepsilon$$

Where:

x	= your score
μ	= the population mean
α	= the effect of your first IV or group Factor "A"
β	= the effect of your second IV or group Factor "B"
γ	= the effect of your third IV or group Factor "C"
π	= the subject effect (the repetitions) - Factor "S"
$\alpha\beta$	= the interaction of "A" and "B"
$\alpha\gamma$	= the interaction of "A" and "C"
$\alpha\pi$	= the interaction of "A" and "S"
$\beta\gamma$	= the interaction of "B" and "C"
$\gamma\pi$	= the interaction of "C" and "S"
$\alpha\beta\gamma$	= the interaction of "A," "B" and "C"
$\alpha\beta\pi$	= the interaction of "A," "B" and "S"
$\alpha\gamma\pi$	= the interaction of "A," "C" and "S"
$\beta\gamma\pi$	= the interaction of "B", "C" and "S"
$\alpha\beta\gamma\pi$	= the interaction of "A," "B," "C," and "S"
ε	= error

The pattern would be the same for an totally within subject ABCD, ABCDE, etc, set of designs. We can calculate an F - ratios for all the effects in the designs ("A" through the highest interaction "ABC..."). They would test if the appropriate terms (α through $\alpha\beta\chi$ ...) actually are statistically significant and exist in the model. In this first method the trick is to use the Mean Squares interaction of effect of interest (i.e. "A" or "ABC") and the subject factor ("S") for the error term in the ratio. The archetypal F -ratio and an example for F_A and F_{ABC} are as follows:

$$F_{Effect} = \frac{MS_{Effect}}{MS_{Effect\ by\ Subjects}} \; ; F_A = \frac{MS_A}{MS_{A\ by\ S}} \; ; F_{ABC} = \frac{MS_{ABC}}{MS_{A\ by\ B\ by\ C\ by\ S}}$$

We will use Manova commands to :

1. Declare the Effect by Subject Interactions for the F - ratios.

2. Request the means for the Independent Variables.

Benefits of Method I:

1. Easy to interpret Anova output.

2. Easy to Interpret Tables of Means.

Disadvantages of Method I:

1. Complicated and Long Manova Command.

2. Using 'Data list list / etc. ' with one score per line leads to very cumbersome files if you have a lot of data.

3. It is very memory intensive if working on a low-powered machine.

The general form of these setups are as follows for A x S, A x B x S and A x B x C x S designs. Full examples are given for A x S and A x B X C x S.

Key: A, B, C = Independent Variables

SUB = An Identification Number for Each Subject

Score = Dependent Variable

a = the number of levels of A

b = the number of levels of B

c = the number of levels of C

s = the number of subjects

manova, omeans: See Chapter 15 for fuller explanations. Manova is the command and omeans requests the means for the factors and interactions.

Totally Within Subjects Design (A x B x ... x S) - I

```
set width = 80
data list list /  A B C . . . IVK SUB Score
manova   Score by A (1, a) B (1, b) C (1, c) ...
         IVK (1, m) SUB (1, s) /
         omeans = tables (A, B, C, ... , IVK
                          A by B,
                          A by C,
                          B by C,
```

> **Requests Means for Main Effects and Interactions**

```
              add 2- way interactions with other IVs
                 until IVk (e.g. C by IVk) ,
                          A by B by C ,
              add 3- way interactions with other IVs
                 up to IVk  (e.g A by B by IVK),
              continue  higher order interactions until:
              A by B by C by IVk-1 by IVK /
```

$$F_c = \frac{MS_c}{MS_{c \text{ by Sub}}}$$

```
design = A vs 1, A by SUB = 1,
         B vs 2, B by SUB = 2,
         C vs 3, C by SUB = 3,
              . . .
         Contine until:
         IVK vs k, IVK by SUB = k
```

> **Defines Error Term : [Effect by S] Interaction for Each Effect**

```
         A by B vs k+1, A by B by SUB = k+1
         A by C vs k+2, A by C by SUB = k+2,
         B by C vs ?, B by C by SUB = ?,
              . . .
              add 2- way interactions with other IVs
                 until IVk :
                 (e.g. C by IVk vs ?, C by IVk by SUB = ?) ,
                   . . .
         A by B by C vs ?
         A by B by C by SUB = ? ,

              continue to add higher -order interactions until:
              A by B by C by ... IVK by SUB = ? ,
              A by B by C by ... IVK vs ? .
```

1. Score = Dependent Variable .
2. 'data list list / A B ...
   IVk SUB Score' defines how the
   data is arranged per line ;
3. Independent Variables:
   A = first IV, B = second IV,
   IVK = 'K'th and last IV.
4. SUB = the number of the
   Subject (1st, 2nd, etc.)
5. Little 'a', little 'b', etc.,
   little 's' = the # of
   levels for the IVs
   ('a' = levels of A,'
    b' = levels of B,etc.).
6. Litle 'm' = levels of IVK
7. Litle 's' = Number of
   subjects in a repeated block
   ('s' = number of subjects)

```
begin data
A1 B1 C1 . . . IVK1 1 Score
A1 B1 C2 . . . IVK1 1 Score
.
Aa Bb Cc        IVKm 1 Score
```
Subject 1

```
A1 B1 C1 . . . IVK1 2 Score
A1 B1 C2 . . . IVK1 2 Score
.
Aa Bb Cc . . . IVKm 2 Score
```
Subject 2

```
.
A1 B1 C1 . . . IVK1 S Score
A1 B1 C2 . . . IVK1 S Score
.
Aa Bb Cc . . . IVKm S Score
end data
finish
```
Subject # S

```
Aa     = last and highest level of A.
Bb     = last and highest level of B
IVKm = last and highest level of IVK
```

```
1-WAY WITHIN SUBJECT design (A x S)
EACH SUBJECT SERVES IN ALL CONDITIONS OF A
Source of Variance    Error
A                     A x S

set width = 80 .
data list list / A SUB score .
begin data .
A1 S1 Score
A2 S1 Score
.
Aa S1 Score
A1 S2 Score
.
.
Aa Ss Score
end data .
manova  score by A (1, a) SUB (1, s) /
        omeans = tables (A) /
        design = A vs 1, A by SUB = 1 .
finish .
```

A_1			A_2			A_3		
S1	Barb	5	S1	Barb	8	S1	Barb	10
S2	Mary	2	S2	Mary	3	S2	Mary	7
S3	Sue	16	S3	Sue	16	S3	Sue	24

Totally Within Subjects Oneway Design (A x S)

Setup

```
set width = 80 .
data list list / A SUB Score .
begin data .
1 1 5
2 1 8
3 1 10
1 2 2
2 2 3
3 2 7
1 3 16
2 3 16
3 3 24
end data .
manova score BY A(1,3) SUB(1,3 )/
  omeans = tables (A) /
  design  = A vs 1, A by  SUB = 1 .
finish .
```

$$F_A = \frac{MS_A}{MS_{A \times S}}$$

Error Term Defined, Used and F - Ratio Computed

Output

```
 1  0  set width = 80 .
 2  data list list / A SUB Score .
 3  begin data .
13  end data .
14  manova score BY A(1,3) SUB(1,3) /
15    omeans = tables (A)/
16    design  = A vs 1, A by  SUB = 1 .

Combined Observed Means for A
Variable .. SCORE
             A
             1        WGT.      7.66667
                    UNWGT.      7.66667
             2        WGT.      9.00000
                    UNWGT.      9.00000
             3        WGT.     13.66667
                    UNWGT.     13.66667

Tests of Sign. for SCORE using UNIQUE sums squares
Source of Variation          SS   DF     MS      F   Sig of F

Error 1                    9.78    4   2.44
A                         59.56    2  29.78  12.18     .020
```

TWO-WAY WITHIN SUBJECT DESIGN (A x B x S): EACH SUBJECT SERVES IN ALL CELLS OF BOTH A & B

SOURCE OF VARIANCE	ERROR
A	A x S
B	B x S
A x B	A x B x S

```
set width  = 80 .
data list list/  A B SUB Score .
begin data
A1 B1 S1 Score
A1 B2 S1 Score
.
Aa Bb S1 Score
A1 B1 C1 S2 Score
.
Aa Bb Ss Score
end data .
manova score by A (1, a) B(1, b) SUB (1, s)/
       omeans = tables (A, B, A by B) /
       design = A vs 1, A by SUB = 1,
       B vs 2, B by SUB = 2,
       A by B vs 3, A by B by SUB = 3 .
finish .
```

THREE-WAY WITHIN SUBJECT DESIGN (A x B x C x S): EACH SUBJECT IN ALL CELLS OF A, B & C

SOURCE OF VARIANCE	ERROR
A	A x S
B	B x S
C	C x S
A x B	A x B x S
A x C	A x C x S
B x C	B x C x S
A x B x C	A x B x C x S

```
set width = 80 .
data list list / A B C SUB Score .
begin data .
A1 B1 C1 S1 Score
A1 B1 C2 S1 Score
.
Aa Bb Cc S1 Score
A1 B1 C1 S2 Score
.
Aa Bb CC Ss Score
end data .
manova  score by A (1, a) B (1, b) C (1, c) SUB (1, s)/
        omeans = tables (A, B, C,
                      A by B,
                      A by C,
                      B by C,
                      A by B by C) /
        design = A vs 1, A by SUB = 1,
               B vs 2, B by SUB = 2,
               C vs 3, C by SUB = 3,
               A by B vs 4, A by B by SUB=4,
               A by C vs 5, A by C by SUB=5,
               B by C vs 6, B by C by SUB=6,
               A by B by C vs 7, A by B by C by SUB = 7 .
finish .        Examples and Output for an A x C x S Design Follows
```

Real Setup for A x B x C x S Design

```
set width = 80 .
data list list / A B C SUB score .
begin data .
1 1 1 1 37
1 1 2 1 43
1 2 1 1 39
1 2 2 1 45
1 3 1 1 31
1 3 2 1 41                    SUBJECT # 1
2 1 1 1 42
2 1 2 1 44
2 2 1 1 30
2 2 2 1 45
2 3 1 1 21
2 3 2 1 58
1 1 1 2 33
1 1 2 2 36
1 2 1 2 29
1 2 2 2 37                    SUBJECT # 2
1 3 1 2 31
1 3 2 2 45
2 1 1 2 30    2 LEVELS of A
2 1 2 2 59    3 LEVELS of B
2 2 1 2 53    2 LEVELS of C
2 2 2 2 54    3 SUBJECTS - Each Serves in All
2 3 1 2 35            Levels of A, B and C .
2 3 2 2 56
1 1 1 3 39
1 1 2 3 45
1 2 1 3 42
1 2 2 3 48
1 3 1 3 32
1 3 2 3 54                    SUBJECT # 3
2 1 1 3 44
2 1 2 3 68
2 2 1 3 33
2 2 2 3 54
2 3 1 3 24
2 3 2 3 65
end data .
manova   score by A (1, 2) B (1, 3) C (1, 2) SUB (1, 3)/
         omeans = tables (A, B, C,
                         A by B,
                         A by C,
                         B by C,
                         A by B by C)/
         design = A vs 1, A by SUB = 1,
                  B vs 2, B by SUB = 2,
                  C vs 3, C by SUB = 3,
                  A by B vs 4, A by B by SUB = 4,
                  A by C vs 5, A by C by SUB = 5,
                  B by C vs 6, B by C by SUB = 6,
                  A by B by C vs 7,
                  A by B by C by SUB = 7 .
finish .
```

Three - Way Within Subject Design (A X B X C X S)

Each Subject Serves in All Cells (or Combinations) of A, B and C

A1

C1	B1			B2			B3		
	S1 Barb	S2 Mary	S3 Sue	S1 Barb	S2 Mary	S3 Sue	S1 Barb	S2 Mary	S3 Sue

C2	B1			B2			B3		
	S1 Barb	S2 Mary	S3 Sue	S1 Barb	S2 Mary	S3 Sue	S1 Barb	S2 Mary	S3 Sue

A2

C1	B1			B2			B3		
	S1 Barb	S2 Mary	S3 Sue	S1 Barb	S2 Mary	S3 Sue	S1 Barb	S2 Mary	S3 Sue

C2	B1			B2			B3		
	S1 Barb	S2 Mary	S3 Sue	S1 Barb	S2 Mary	S3 Sue	S1 Barb	S2 Mary	S3 Sue

Schematic of (A x B x C x S)

```
set width = 80 .
data list list / A B C SUB score .
begin data.
A1 B1 C1 S1 Score
A1 B1 C1 S2 Score
A1 B1 C1 S3 Score
A1 B1 C2 S1 Score
A1 B1 C2 S2 Score
A1 B1 C2 S3 Score
   .
Aa Bb Cc S1 Score
Aa Bb Cc S2 Score
   .
A1 B1 C1 Ss Score
A1 B1 C2 Ss Score
Aa Bb Cc Ss Score
end data .
manova score by A (1, a) B (1, b) C (1, c) SUB (1, s) /
omeans = tables (A, B, C,
             A by B,
             B by C,
             A by B by C) /
design = A vs 1, A by SUB = 1,
         B vs 2, B by SUB = 2,
         C vs 3, C by SUB = 3,
         A by B vs 4, A by B by SUB=4,
         A by C vs 5, A by C by SUB=5,
         B by C vs 6, B by C by SUB=6,
         A by B by C vs 7,
         A by B by C by SUB = 7 .
finish .
```

Actual (A x B x C x S) Setup

```
set width = 80 .
data list list / A B C SUB score .
begin data
1 1 1 1 37
1 1 1 2 33
1 1 1 3 39
1 1 2 1 43
1 1 2 2 36
1 1 2 3 39
1 2 1 1 45
1 2 1 2 31
1 2 1 3 42
1 2 2 1 41
1 2 2 2 31
1 2 2 3 32
1 3 1 1 44
1 3 1 2 30
1 3 1 3 44
1 3 2 1 59
1 3 2 2 45
1 3 2 3 48
2 1 1 1 30
2 1 1 2 53
2 1 1 3 68
2 2 1 1 54
2 2 1 2 33
2 2 1 3 44
2 3 1 1 54
2 3 1 2 35
2 3 1 3 24
2 3 2 1 58  2 3 2 2 56  2 3 2 3 65
end data .
manova score by A (1, 2) B (1, 3) C (1, 2) SUB (1, 3) /
omeans = tables (A, B, C,
             A by B,
             B by C,
             A by B by C) /
design = A vs 1, A by SUB = 1,
         B vs 2, B by SUB = 2,
         C vs 3, C by SUB = 3,
         A by B vs 4, A by B by SUB=4,
         A by C vs 5, A by C by SUB=5,
         B by C vs 6, B by C by SUB=6,
         A by B by C vs 7,
         A by B by C by SUB = 7 .
finish.
```

OUTPUT FOR A x B x C x S DESIGN

```
etc.
 40   manova   score by A (1, 2) B (1, 3) C (1, 2) SUB (1, 3)/
 41            omeans = tables (A, B, C,
 42                             A by B,
 43                             A by C,
 44                             B by C,
 45                             A by B by C)/
 46         design = A vs 1, A by SUB = 1,
 47                  B vs 2, B by SUB = 2,
 48                  C vs 3, C by SUB = 3,
 49                  A by B vs 4, A by B by SUB=4,
 50                  A by C vs 5, A by C by SUB=5,
 51                  B by C vs 6, B by C by SUB=6,
 52                  A by B by C vs 7,
 53                  A by B by C by SUB = 7 .
```

> *Note:*
> 1. *Definition of Error Terms*
> 2. *F - Ratio and Use of These Errors*
> 3. *C effect and A x C interaction are*
>   *significant (p. < .05)*

* * A N A L Y S I S   O F   V A R I A N C E * * *

36 cases accepted.
36 cases rejected because of out-of-range factor
values.
 0 cases rejected because of missing data.
36 non-empty cells.

1 design will be processed.

Combined Observed Means for A
Variable .. SCORE

A		
1	WGT.	39.27778
	UNWGT.	39.27778
2	WGT.	45.27778
	UNWGT.	45.27778

Combined Observed Means for B
Variable .. SCORE

B		
1	WGT.	43.33333
	UNWGT.	43.33333
2	WGT.	42.41667
	UNWGT.	42.41667
3	WGT.	41.08333
	UNWGT.	41.08333

Combined Observed Means for C
Variable .. SCORE

C		
1	WGT.	34.72222
	UNWGT.	34.72222
2	WGT.	49.83333
	UNWGT.	49.83333

Combined Observed Means for A BY B
Variable .. SCORE

		A	
		1	2
B			
1	WGT.	38.83333	47.83333
	UNWGT.	38.83333	47.83333
2	WGT.	40.00000	44.83333
	UNWGT.	40.00000	44.83333
3	WGT.	39.00000	43.16667
	UNWGT.	39.00000	43.16667

Combined Observed Means for A BY C
Variable .. SCORE

		A	
		1	2
C			
1	WGT.	34.77778	34.66667
	UNWGT.	34.77778	34.66667
2	WGT.	43.77778	55.88889
	UNWGT.	43.77778	55.88889

Combined Observed Means for B BY C
Variable .. SCORE

		B		
		1	2	3
C				
1	WGT.	37.50000	37.66667	29.00000
	UNWGT.	37.50000	37.66667	29.00000
2	WGT.	49.16667	47.16667	53.16667
	UNWGT.	49.16667	47.16667	53.16667

Combined Observed Means for A BY B BY C
Variable .. SCORE

			A	
			1	2
C	B			
1	1	WGT.	36.33333	38.66667
		UNWGT.	36.33333	38.66667
1	2	WGT.	36.66667	38.66667
		UNWGT.	36.66667	38.66667
1	3	WGT.	31.33333	26.66667
		UNWGT.	31.33333	26.66667
2	1	WGT.	41.33333	57.00000
		UNWGT.	41.33333	57.00000
2	2	WGT.	43.33333	51.00000
		UNWGT.	43.33333	51.00000
2	3	WGT.	46.66667	59.66667
		UNWGT.	46.66667	59.66667

Tests of Significance for SCORE using
UNIQUE sums of squares

Source of Variation	SS	DF	MS	F	Sig of F
Error 1	224.00	2	112.00		
A	324.00	1	324.00	2.89	.231
Error 2	93.11	4	23.28		
B	30.72	2	15.36	.66	.565
Error 3	107.56	2	53.78		
C	055.11	1	2055.11	**38.21**	**.025 ***
Error 4	229.33	4	57.33		
A BY B	41.17	2	20.58	.36	.719
Error 5	30.89	2	15.44		
A BY C	336.11	1	336.11	**21.76**	**.043 ***
Error 6	121.78	4	30.44		
B BY C	376.06	2	188.03	6.18	.060
Error 7	205.11	4	51.28		
A BY B BY C	55.39	2	27.69	.54	.620

* Significant

COMPOSITE ERROR TERMS AND ADDED POWER

It is possible to use a composite error term and gain more statistical power in these designs if $MS_a = MS_b = MS_{a \times b}$. AB x S is used as this composite error term. Kirk (1982) refers to it as the RESIDUAL ERROR. It's SUM OF SQUARES = $SS_{a \times s}$ + $SS_{b \times s}$ + $SS_{a \times b \times s}$, with df = (s-1)(ab-1). See Kirk (1982, Chapter 9) for the appropriate conditions.

A by B Design

SOURCE	ERROR
A	AB x S
B	AB x S
A x B	AB x S

```
set width = 80 .
data list list/ A B SUB Score .
begin data .
… data as previously shown …
end data .
manova Score BY A( 1, a) B (1, b) SUB (1, s)/
       omeans = tables (A, B, A by B) /
       design = A vs 1,
       B vs 1,
       A by B vs 1,
       A by SUB + B by SUB + A by B by SUB = 1 .
finish .
```

For an ABC design, the design would use MS $_{abc \times s}$ as the error term as shown below:

Kirk's Method - One Error Term ($MS_{abc \times s}$)

SOURCE	ERROR
A	ABC x S
B	ABC x S
C	ABC x S
A x B	ABC x S
A x C	ABC x S
B x C	ABC x S
A x B x C	ABC x S

```
set width = 80 .
data list list/ A B C SUB Score .
begin data .
        … data as previously shown …
end data .
manova  Score by A (1, a) B(1, b) C (1, c) SUB (1, s)/
        omeans = tables (A, B, C, A by B, A by B,
                         B by C, A by B by C)/
        design = A vs 1, B vs 1, C vs 1,
                 A by B vs 1, A by C vs 1, B by C vs 1,
                 A by B by C vs 1,
        A by SUB + B by SUB + C by SUB +
        A by B by SUB + A by C by SUB +
        B by C by SUB + A by B by C by SUB = 1 .
finish .
```

B. MIXED, NESTED, SPLIT PLOT, BETWEEN/WITHIN DESIGNS
[A x (B x S), A x (B x C x S), A x B x (C x S) etc.]

The issue, again, is what to use as the error term in the F - ratios for the factors that have repeated levels. In these designs we now have two types of factors. One factor may be repeated and another may be totally between groups (different subjects for each group). This leads to there being different error terms for the factors and interactions dependent on whether or not the factor is repeated or not.

Basically:

1. A nonrepeated factor uses a Subject within Effect or Interaction error term.

2. An factor or interaction that is repeated uses the interaction of the repeated factor by subjects within the nonrepeated factors for the error term. All of this sounds confusing but the rationale can be found in Winer (1991), Kirk (1982) or Keppel (1991). It might be best to try to follow our examples. Some hints though:

a. SPSS uses Winer's notation.

b. When changing Keppel's (1991, p. 492) notation into SPSSX, the following transformations hold:

```
A x B = A by B      (Replace 'x' with 'by')
A / S   = A w S      (Replace '/' with 'w' for Within)
A B     = A by B
```

3. The term **S** refers to the number of the subject in the repeated block. It does not refer to the total number of subjects. Very carefully look at our examples where this is noted. We will present a map of the design, the generic SPSS setup for that design, and then complete example of an SPSS run and its output.

We will use examples with the factors A, B and C with 2 levels of A, 3 levels of B, and 2 levels of C. The repeated elements will have blocks with 3 subjects. Obviously, you can have more than just A, B, C and more subjects than three subjects in a block. However the principles would be them same. Now for the first example of an **A x (B X S)** design.

TWO-WAY DESIGN WITH ONE REPEATED FACTOR - A x (B x S)
DIFFERENT SUBJECTS FOR LEVELS OF A
EACH SUBJECT SERVES IN ALL LEVELS OF B

SOURCE	ERROR
A	S w A
B	B by S w A
A by B	B by S w A

```
set width = 80 .
data list list/ A B SUB Score  .
comment A x ( B x S ) .
begin data .
      a b sub score
end data .
manova Score by A (1, a) B(1, b) SUB (1, s)  /
      omeans = tables (A, B, A by B) /
      design = A vs 1,
               SUB w A = 1,
               B vs 2,
               A by B vs 2,
               B by SUB w A = 2  .
finish .
```

INSTRUCTIONS:

1. Layout all factors (including subjects): *Score by A (1, a) B(1, b) SUB (1, s)*

2. Request all means: *omeans = tables (A, B, A by B)*

3. Specify all effects and interactions: *design = A vs 1, etc.*

4. One line of data per score

5. The variable **SUB** does not represent total number of subjects
   but **number in the repeated block.**

   It is best to look at the examples!

1 Between; 1 Within Subject Design - A X (B X S)

Different Subjects for Each Level of A (A1 & A2).
Within Each Level of A ; All Subjects Serve in All Levels of B (B1, B2, B3)

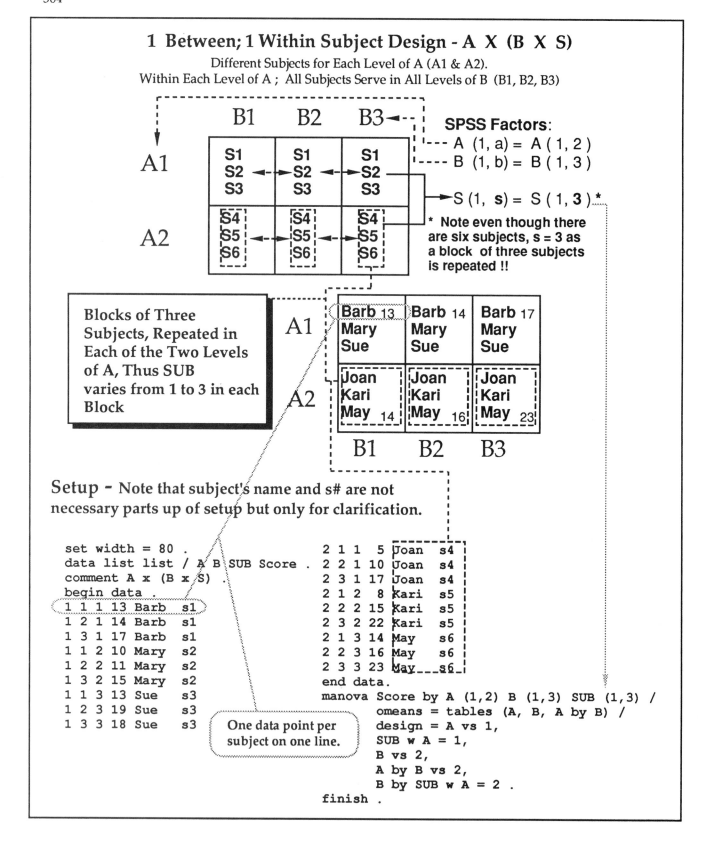

SPSS Factors:
- - - A (1, a) = A (1, 2)
- - - B (1, b) = B (1, 3)

S (1, **s**) = S (1, **3**).*

* Note even though there are six subjects, s = 3 as a block of three subjects is repeated !!

Blocks of Three Subjects, Repeated in Each of the Two Levels of A, Thus SUB varies from 1 to 3 in each Block

Setup - Note that subject's name and s# are not necessary parts up of setup but only for clarification.

```
set width = 80 .                        2 1 1  5 Joan  s4
data list list / A B SUB Score .        2 2 1 10 Joan  s4
comment A x (B x S) .                    2 3 1 17 Joan  s4
begin data .                            2 1 2  8 Kari  s5
1 1 1 13 Barb  s1                       2 2 2 15 Kari  s5
1 2 1 14 Barb  s1                       2 3 2 22 Kari  s5
1 3 1 17 Barb  s1                       2 1 3 14 May   s6
1 1 2 10 Mary  s2                       2 2 3 16 May   s6
1 2 2 11 Mary  s2                       2 3 3 23 May   s6
1 3 2 15 Mary  s2                       end data.
1 1 3 13 Sue   s3                       manova Score by A (1,2) B (1,3) SUB (1,3) /
1 2 3 19 Sue   s3                           omeans = tables (A, B, A by B) /
1 3 3 18 Sue   s3                           design = A vs 1,
                                            SUB w A = 1,
                                            B vs 2,
                                            A by B vs 2,
                                            B by SUB w A = 2 .
                                        finish .
```

One data point per subject on one line.

A x (B x S) Output

```
  1  0  set width = 80 .
  2  data list list / A B SUB Score .
  3  comment A x (B x S) .
  4  begin data .
 22  end data .
 23  manova Score by A (1,2) B (1,3) SUB (1,3) /
 24        omeans = tables (A, B, A by B) /
 25        design = A vs 1,
 26        Sub w A = 1,
 27        B vs 2,
 28        A by B vs 2,
 29        B by SUB w A = 2 .
```

* A N A L Y S I S   O F   V A R I A N C E *

Combined Observed Means for A
Variable .. SCORE
```
     A
              1    WGT.  14.44444
                 UNWGT.  14.44444
              2    WGT.  14.44444
                 UNWGT.  14.44444
```

Combined Observed Means for B
Variable .. SCORE
```
     B
              1    WGT.  10.50000
                 UNWGT.  10.50000
              2    WGT.  14.16667
                 UNWGT.  14.16667
              3    WGT.  18.66667
                 UNWGT.  18.66667
```

Combined Observed Means for A BY B
Variable .. SCORE
```
                  A       1         2
              B
              1   WGT.  12.00000   9.00000
                 UNWGT. 12.00000   9.00000
              2   WGT.  14.66667  13.66667
                 UNWGT. 14.66667  13.66667
              3   WGT.  16.66667  20.66667
                 UNWGT. 16.66667  20.66667
```

* A N A L Y S I S   O F   V A R I A N C E - DESIGN 1 *

Tests of Significance for SCORE using UNIQUE sums of squares

Source of Variation	SS	DF	MS	F	Sig of F	
Error 1	107.78	4	26.94			
A	.00	1	.00	.00	1.000	[1]
Error 2	18.89	8	2.36			
B	200.78	2	100.39	42.52	.000	[2]
A BY B	39.00	2	19.50	8.26	.011	[2]

---

1. 'A' effect not significant

2. 'B' and 'A by B' interaction are significant

THREE-WAY DESIGN WITH ONE REPEATED FACTOR - A x B x (C x S)
DIFFERENT SUBJECTS FOR THE A & B COMBINATIONS
EACH SUBJECT SERVES IN ALL LEVELS OF C

2 Between; 1 Within Subject Design
A X B X (C X S)

Different Subjects for Each Combination of A and B
Within the AB Combinations; All Subjects Serve in All Levels of C (C1 & C2)

C_1

	B1	B2	B3
A1	S1 S2 S3	S4 S5 S6	S7 S8 S9
A2	S10 S11 S12	S13 S14 S15	S16 S17 S18
A1	Barb Mary Sue	Babs Mona Sally	Lori Dale Lana
A2	Joan Kari May	Gail Alice Nan	Marsha Dot Lois

C_2

	B1	B2	B3
A1	S1 S2 S3	S4 S5 S6	S7 S8 S9
A2	S10 S11 S12	S13 S14 S15	S16 S17 S18
A1	Barb Mary Sue	Babs Mona Sally	Lori Dale Lana
A2	Joan Kari May	Gail Alice Nan	Marsha Dot Lois

SOURCE	ERROR
A	S w A by B
B	S w A by B
A by B	S w A by B
C	C by S w A by B
A by C	C by S w A by B
B by C	C by S w A by B
A by B by C	C by S w A by B

```
set width = 80 .
data list list / A B C SUB Score .
comment A x B x (C x S) .
begin data .
   a b c sub score
end data .
manova Score by A (1, a) B (1, b) SUB (1, s) C (1, c) /
      omeans = tables (A, B, C, A by B, A by B,
                       B by C, A by B by C)/
      design = A vs 1, B vs 1, A by B vs 1,
               SUB w A by B = 1,
               C vs 2,
               A by C vs 2, B by C vs 2,
               A by B by C vs 2,
               C by SUB w A by B = 2 .
finish .
```

SETUP FOR A X B X (C X S)

```
set width = 80 .
data list list / A B C SUB Score .
comment A x B x (C x S) .
begin data .
1 1  1 1 18    Barb   s1
1 1  2 1 14    Barb   s1
1 2  1 1 16    Babs   s4
1 2  2 1 12    Babs   s4
1 3  1 1 14    Lori   s7
1 3  2 1 15    Lori   s7
1 1  1 2 19    Mary   s2
1 1  2 2 12    Mary   s2
1 2  1 2 12    Mona   s5
1 2  2 2 08    Mona   s5
1 3  1 2 09    Dale   s8
1 3  2 2 09    Dale   s8
1 1  1 3 14    Sue    s3
1 1  2 3 10    Sue    s3
1 2  1 3 18    Sally  s6
1 2  2 3 10    Sally  s6
1 3  1 3 10    Lana   s9      Again note that the Names and s# are only
1 3  2 3 20    Lana   s9      for identification purposes & not needed
2 1  1 1 16    Joan   s10
2 1  2 1 10    Joan   s10     Also the s# refers to the specific
2 2  1 1 04    Gail   s13     subject by name! The variable SUB is
2 2  2 1 01    Gail   s13     used to identify the repeated blocks.
2 3  1 1 19    Marsha s16
2 3  2 1 16    Marsha s16     Barb, Mary & Sue are one repeated block.
2 1  1 2 08    Kari   s11     SUB is 1, 2 , 3 for them respectively.
2 1  2 2 04    Kari   s11
2 2  1 2 16    Alice  s14     Similarly Marsha, Dot and Lois are one
2 2  2 2 12    Alice  s14     repeated block and SUB is 1, 2, 3 for
2 3  1 2 10    Dot    s17     them respectively.
2 3  2 2 08    Dot    s17
2 1  1 3 18    May    s12
2 1  2 3 08    May    s12
2 2  1 3 06    Nan    s15
2 2  2 3 02    Nan    s15
2 3  1 3 16    Lois   s18
2 3  2 3 14    Lois   s18
end data .
manova Score by A (1, 2) B (1, 3) C (1, 2) SUB (1, 3) /
        omeans = tables (A, B, C, A by B, A by C,
                        B by C, A by B by C)/
        design = A vs 1, B vs 1, A by B vs 1,
                SUB w A by B = 1,
                C vs 2,
                A by C vs 2, B by C vs 2,
                A by B by C vs 2,
                C by SUB w A by B = 2 .
finish .
```

OUTPUT FOR A x B x (C x S)

```
... etc.
manova Score by A (1, 2) B (1, 3) C (1, 2) SUB (1, 3) /
        omeans = tables (A, B, C, A by B, A by C,
                    B by C, A by B by C)/
        design = A vs 1, B vs 1, A by B vs 1,
                SUB w A by B = 1,
                C vs 2,
                A by C vs 2, B by C vs 2,
                A by B by C vs 2,
                C by SUB w A by B = 2 .
        1 design will be processed.
```

```
** ANALYSIS OF VARIANCE -- DESIGN 1 **
Combined Observed Means for A
Variable .. SCORE
A
1       WGT.    13.33333
        UNWGT.  13.33333
2       WGT.    10.44444
        UNWGT.  10.44444
- - - - - - - - - - - - - - - - - - -
Combined Observed Means for B
Variable .. SCORE
B
1       WGT.    12.58333
        UNWGT.  12.58333
2       WGT.     9.75000
        UNWGT.   9.75000
3       WGT.    13.33333
        UNWGT.  13.33333
- - - - - - - - - - - - - - - - - - -
Combined Observed Means for C
Variable .. SCORE
C
1       WGT.    13.50000
        UNWGT.  13.50000
2       WGT.    10.27778
        UNWGT.  10.27778
- - - - - - - - - - - - - - - - - - -
Combined Observed Means for A BY B
Variable .. SCORE
            A       1           2
B
1       WGT.    14.50000    10.66667
        UNWGT.  14.50000    10.66667
2       WGT.    12.66667     6.83333
        UNWGT.  12.66667     6.83333
3       WGT.    12.83333    13.83333
        UNWGT.  12.83333    13.83333
- - - - - - - - - - - - - - - - - - -
Combined Observed Means for A BY C
Variable .. SCORE
            A       1           2
C
1       WGT.    16.16667    16.83333
        UNWGT.  16.16667    16.83333
2       WGT.    11.00000    12.00000
        UNWGT.  11.00000    12.00000
3       WGT.     7.83333     7.66667
        UNWGT.   7.83333     7.66667
```

```
4       WGT.     3.16667     5.33333
        UNWGT.   3.16667     5.33333
- - - - - - - - - - - - - - - - - - -
Combined Observed Means for B BY C
Variable .. SCORE
            B       1           2           3
C
1       WGT.    15.50000    12.00000    13.00000
        UNWGT.  15.50000    12.00000    13.00000
2       WGT.     9.66667     7.50000    13.66667
        UNWGT.   9.66667     7.50000    13.66667
- - - - - - - - - - - - - - - - - - -
Combined Observed Means for A BY B BY C
Variable .. SCORE
            A           1           2
C B
1 1     WGT.        17.00000    14.00000
        UNWGT.      17.00000    14.00000
1 2     WGT.        15.33333     8.66667
        UNWGT.      15.33333     8.66667
1 3     WGT.        11.00000    15.00000
        UNWGT.      11.00000    15.00000
2 1     WGT.        12.00000     7.33333
        UNWGT.      12.00000     7.33333
2 2     WGT.        10.00000     5.00000
        UNWGT.      10.00000     5.00000
2 3     WGT.        14.66667    12.66667
        UNWGT.      14.66667    12.66667
```

```
        Tests of Sig. for SCORE using
            UNIQUE sums of squares

Source of Variation
                SS      DF    MS      F    Sig of F

Error 1       382.67   12   31.89

A              75.11    1   75.11   2.36  .151
B              85.72    2   42.86   1.34  .297
A BY B         74.06    2   37.03   1.16  .346

Error 2        48.67   12    4.06

C              93.44    1   93.44  23.04  .000
A BY C          9.00    1    9.00   2.22  .162
B BY C         70.72    2   35.36   8.72  .005
A BY B BY C    22.17    2   11.08   2.70  .105
```

THREE-WAY DESIGN WITH ONE REPEATED FACTOR - A x (B x C x S)
DIFFERENT SUBJECTS FOR THE A LEVELS
EACH SUBJECT SERVES IN ALL COMBINATIONS OF B & C

1 Between; 2 Within Subject Design
A X (B X C X S)

Different Subjects for Each Level of A (A1 & A2).

Within Each Level of A ; All Subjects Serve in All Combinations of B and C

	C_1				C_2		
	B1	B2	B3		B1	B2	B3
A1	S1 S2 S3	S1 S2 S3	S1 S2 S3		S1 S2 S3	S1 S2 S3	S1 S2 S3	A1
A2	S4 S5 S6	S4 S5 S6	S4 S5 S6		S4 S5 S6	S4 S5 S6	S4 S5 S6	A2
A1	Barb Mary Sue	Barb Mary Sue	Barb Mary Sue		Barb Mary Sue	Barb Mary Sue	Barb Mary Sue	A1
A2	Joan Kari May	Joan Kari May	Joan Kari May		Joan Kari May	Joan Kari May	Joan Kari May	A2

SOURCE	ERROR	SOURCE	ERROR
A	S w A	A by C	C by S w A
B	B by S w A	B by C	B by C by S w A
A by B	B by S w A	A by B by C	B by C by S w A
C	C by S w A		

```
set width = 80 .
data list list / A B C SUB Score .
comment A x ( B x C x S ) .
begin data .
      a b c sub score
end data .
manova Score by A (1, a) B (1, b) SUB (1, s) C (1, c) /
        omeans = tables (A, B, C, A by B, A by B,
                    B by C, A by B by C)/
        design = A vs 1,
                SUB w A  = 1,
                B vs 2, A by B vs 2,
                B by SUB w A = 2,
                C vs 3,
                A by C vs 3,
                C by SUB w A = 3,
                B by C vs  4,
                A by B by C vs 4,
                B by C by SUB w A  = 4 .
finish .
```

SETUP FOR A x (B x C x S)
[OUTPUT WOULD BE SIMILAR TO PREVIOUS - SO OMITTED FOR BREVITY]

```
set width = 80 .
data list list / A B C SUB Score .
comment A x ( B x C x S ) .
begin data .
  1 1 1 1 45      Barb s1    Again note that the s# identifies the subject
  1 1 2 1 53      Barb s1      while the variable SUB is used for the
  1 2 1 1 40      Barb s1      repeated blocks.
  1 2 2 1 52      Barb s1
  1 3 1 1 28      Barb s1
  1 3 2 1 37      Barb s1
  1 1 1 2 35      Mary s2
  1 1 2 2 41      Mary s2
  1 2 1 2 30      Mary s2
  1 2 2 2 37      Mary s2
  1 3 1 2 25      Mary s2
  1 3 2 2 32      Mary s2
  1 1 1 3 60      Sue  s3
  1 1 2 3 65      Sue  s3
  1 2 1 3 58      Sue  s3
  1 2 2 3 54      Sue  s3
  1 3 1 3 40      Sue  s3
  1 3 2 3 47      Sue  s3
  2 1 1 1 50      Joan s4
  2 1 2 1 48      Joan s4
  2 2 1 1 25      Joan s4
  2 2 2 1 34      Joan s4
  2 3 1 1 16      Joan s4
  2 3 2 1 23      Joan s4
  2 1 1 2 42      Kari s5
  2 1 2 2 45      Kari s5
  2 2 1 2 30      Kari s5
  2 2 2 2 37      Kari s5
  2 3 1 2 22      Kari s5
  2 3 2 2 27      Kari s5
  2 1 1 3 56      May  s6
  2 1 2 3 60      May  s6
  2 2 1 3 40      May  s6
  2 2 2 3 39      May  s6
  2 3 1 3 31      May  s6
  2 3 2 3 29      May  s6
end data.
manova Score by A (1, 2) B (1, 3) SUB (1, s) C (1, 2) /
       omeans = tables (A, B, C, A by B, A by C,
                        B by C, A by B by C)/
       design = A vs 1,
                SUB w A  = 1,
                B vs 2, A by B vs 2,
                B by SUB w A = 2,
                C vs 3,
                A by C vs 3,
                C by SUB w A = 3,
                B by C vs  4,
                A by B by C vs 4,
                B by C by SUB w A  = 4 .
finish .
```

III. Method II: One Case per Line

Summary of SPSS Manova Setups for a Completely Within Subject Factorial Design
(A x B x C ...x x S)

A(i) x S (s) Design*

See page 315 for Real World Example

```
set width = 80 .
data list list / a1 a2 a3 a4 … ai. i levels of A
begin data .
a1 a2 a3 a4 … ai    > First subject
a1 a2 a3 a4 … ai

⬇ S subjects - Each variable typed is the actual score .

end data .
manova a1 to ai /
        wsfactor = a(i) /
        print = cellinfo (means) signif (avonly) /
        design .
finish .
```

A(i) x B (j) x S (s) Design *

See page 328 for Real World Example

```
set  width = 80 .
data list list / a1b1 a1b2 … a1bj a2b1 a2b2 … a2bj … aib1 aib2 … aibj .
                              i levels of A ; j levels of B
begin data .
a1b1 a1b2…a1bj a2b1 a2b2…a2b3 … aib1 aib2 … aibj … aib1 aib2 … aibj > 1st Subject

⬇ S subjects - Each variable typed is the actual score .

end data .
manova a1b1 to aibj / wsfactor = a(i) b(j)/
                  print = cellinfo (means) signif (avonly) /
                  design .
finish .
```

A(i) x B (j) x C (k) x S (s) Design *

```
set  width = 80 .
data list list / a1b1c1 … a1bjck … aibjck . i levels of A, j levels of B,
begin data .                         k levels of C
a1b1c1 … a1bjck … aibjck   > First subject

⬇ S subjects - Each variable typed is the actual score .

end data .
manova a1b1 to aibjck / wsfactor = a(i) b(j) c (k)/
                  print = cellinfo (means) signif (avonly) /
                  design .
finish .
```

---

* Use **data list free / etc.** for SPSS/PC + ™ 4. 0

SUMMARY OF MIXED, NESTED, SPLIT PLOT, OR BETWEEN/WITHIN DESIGNS USING METHOD II (ONE CASE PER LINE)

Real World Examples Will Be Given for C[AxBxS] Only

```
set  width = 80 .
data list list / b a1 a2 … ai . i levels of A
begin data .                    b levels of B
1 a1 a2 … ai        subjects for B₁
1 a1 a2 … ai
...                                   each 'a?' term = score
2 a1 a2 … ai        subjects for B₂
2 a1 a2 … ai
...
b a1 a2 … ai        subjects for Bᵦ
b a1 a2 … ai
...
end data .
manova a1 a2 … ai by b (1,b) / wsfactor = a(i) /
          print = cellinfo (means) signif (avonly)/
          design .
finish .
```

B[b] x C[c] x (A[i] x S) Design - 'A' IS REPEATED

```
set  width = 80 .
data list list / b c a1 … … ai . i levels of A, b levels of B
begin data .                          c levels of C
1 1   a1 … a1  a2 … a2 … ai    subjects for B₁ C₁

....
2 1   a1 … a1  a2 … a2 … ai    subjects for B₂ C₁

....
b 1   a1 … a1  a2 … a2 … ai    subjects for Bᵦ C₁

...
1 2   a1 … a1  a2 … a2 … ai    subjects for B₁ C₂

....
2 2   a1 … a1  a2 … a2 … ai    subjects for B₂ C₂

....
b 2   a1 … a1  a2 … a2 … ai    subjects for Bᵦ C₂

...
1 c   a1 … a1  a2 … a2 … ai    subjects for B₁ Cᵪ

....
2 c   a1 … a1  a2 … a2 … ai    subjects for B₂ Cᵪ

....
b c   a1 … a1  a2 … a2 … ai    subjects for Bᵦ Cᵪ
...                                  each 'a?' term = score
end data .
manova a1 to ai by b (1,b) c (1,c) / wsfactor = a(i) /
          print = cellinfo (means) signif (avonly)/
          design .
finish .
```

C[c] x (A[i] x B[j] x S) Design
'A' & 'B' are Repeated

see p.328 for Real World Example

```
set  width = 80 .
data list list / c a1b1 … a1bj  a2b1 … a2bj … aibj .
begin data .
1 a1b1 … a1bj  a2b1 … a2bj … aibj      subjects for C₁
1 a1b1 … a1bj  a2b1 … a2bj … aibj
....
2 a1b1 … a1bj  a2b1 … a2bj … aibj      subjects for C₂
...
c a1b1 … a1bj  a2b1 … a2bj … aibj      subjects for C_c
...                                    each 'a?b?' term = score
end data .
manova a1b1 to aibj by c (1,c) / wsfactor = a(i) b(j) /
          print = cellinfo (means) signif (avonly)/
          design .
finish .
```

Method II: One Line Per Case.

In this method, SPSS will automatically lay out the design and error terms based on the MANOVA command itself. Thus, the command setup is simpler. However output takes more interpretation. We will give examples of the MANOVA command and associated data setup and then a guide to interpreting the standard output. In summary:

Benefits of Method II:

1. Easy to set up.

2. Easy to test assumption.

3. Data setups aren't too long.

Disadvantages of Method II:

1. Somewhat complicated command.

2. Lots of intimidating output for novice.

3. Difficult to interpret tables of means.

We will start with a simple example of an **A X S Design** [A₁ A₂ A₃...A_a = Subject's Line].

Data:

The key to understanding the command is that the repeated factor is entered across the data line. Let's start simply. Assume an experiment with 4 conditions of Variable A.

Each subject is tested four times. We'll call the scores : A1, A2, A3, A4 for each trial. We would type them on a line as:

A1	A2	A3	A4

If the first subject was named Bob and his scores were A1 = 13 (first day), A2 = 9 (second day), A3 = 11(third day)< and A4 = 10 (fourth day). We would type his scores as:

13	9	11	10

Thus each subsequent subject would take up one line and have four scores typed across the line. We are interested if significant differences exist between the means of conditions A1 through A4. An entire set of data would look as follows:

```
13 9 11 10      -> Bob's Line of Data
8  8  7  4 -> Next subject
7  5  5  4
9  6  7  3
6  8  8  2
etc.
```

An appropriate data list command would be as follows:

```
data list list / a1 a2 a3 a4 .  ⇒ 4 levels of A
```

Note: We named each variable with a letter and number to note the repetition. (Remember the use of 'data list *free* '/ etc. for SPSS/PC +.)

MANOVA COMMAND:

An appropriate MANOVA command would be as follows:

```
manova a1 to a4 /
       wsfactor = a(4) /
       print = cellinfo (means) signif (avonly) /
       design .
```

Let's dissect the command so it can act as a template for further setups.

manova <u>a1 to a4</u> ➡   A1 to A4 are the scores to be analyzed.

wsfactor = <u>a(4)</u> ➡ Considers them as a repeated measures
design with 4 repetitions of a factor called 'A' .

print = cellinfo (means) signif (avonly) ➡ prints F tables
and means .

design ➡ This makes SPSS and MANOVA happy. <u>Just type it.</u>

A complete setup looks as follows:

A(k) X S DESIGN [A₁ A₂ A₃...Aᵢ = Subject's Line]

Where A_1 Identifies the score's level of the Independent Variable ' A ' . The actual score is the number typed in this position. 18 subjects in all.

EXAMPLE OF A(4) X S(18) DESIGN

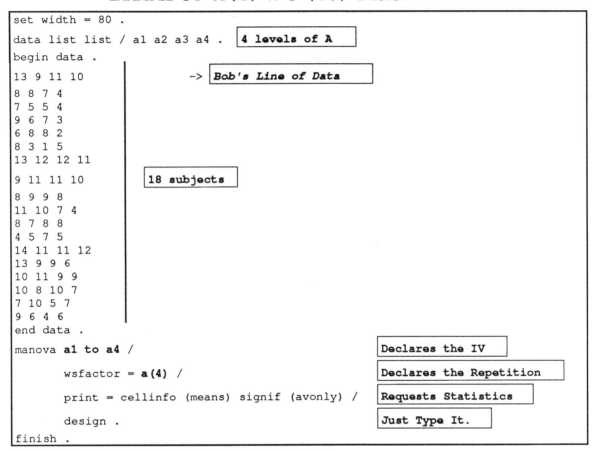

```
set width = 80 .
data list list / a1 a2 a3 a4 .      4 levels of A
begin data .
13 9 11 10               ->   Bob's Line of Data
8 8 7 4
7 5 5 4
9 6 7 3
6 8 8 2
8 3 1 5
13 12 12 11
9 11 11 10          18 subjects
8 9 9 8
11 10 7 4
8 7 8 8
4 5 7 5
14 11 11 12
13 9 9 6
10 11 9 9
10 8 10 7
7 10 5 7
9 6 4 6
end data .
manova a1 to a4 /                   Declares the IV
        wsfactor = a(4) /           Declares the Repetition
        print = cellinfo (means) signif (avonly) /   Requests Statistics
        design .                    Just Type It.
finish .
```

OUTPUT INTERPRETATION

Manova output can be a little dense. We are going to present two passes through it. In the first pass, we have highlighted the most important questions:

1. What are the group means for the four conditions of **A**.

2. Is the F - ratio significant?

Ignore the shrunken output until the second pass.

FIRST PASS: MEANS & F-RATIO

```
1  0  set width = 80 .
2  data list list / a1 a2 a3 a4.
3  begin data .
21 end data .
22 manova a1 to a4 /
23      wsfactor = a(4) /
24      print = cellinfo (means) signif (avonly) /
25      design .
```

```
* * * * * * A N A L Y S I S   O F   V A R I A N C E * * * * * *
       18 cases accepted.
        0 cases rejected because of out-of-range factor values.
        0 cases rejected because of missing data.
        1 non-empty cell.
        1 design will be processed.
```

- -

Cell Means and Standard Deviations   [1]

Variable .. A1

	Mean	Std. Dev.	N
For entire sample	9.278	2.697	18

- -

Variable .. A2

	Mean	Std. Dev.	N
For entire sample	8.222	2.487	18

- -

Variable .. A3

	Mean	Std. Dev.	N
For entire sample	7.833	2.834	18

- -

Variable .. A4

	Mean	Std. Dev.	N
For entire sample	6.722	2.886	18

- -

```
Tests of Between-Subjects Effects.

AVERAGED Tests of Significance for A using UNIQUE sums of squares
Source of Variation      SS      DF      MS        F  Sig of F

WITHIN CELLS           366.24    17    21.54
CONSTANT              4624.01     1  4624.01   214.64    .000

Tests involving 'A' Within-Subject Effect.

Mauchly sphericity test, W =      .85642
Chi-square approx. =            2.43685 with 5 D. F.
Significance =                   .786

Greenhouse-Geisser Epsilon =     .91864
Huynh-Feldt Epsilon =           1.00000
Lower-bound Epsilon =            .33333
```

AVERAGED Tests of Significance that follow are equivalent to
univariate or split-plot or mixed-model approach to repeated measures.
Epsilons may be used to adjust d.f. for the AVERAGED results.

Tests involving 'A' Within-Subject Effect.

AVERAGED Tests of Significance for A using UNIQUE sums of squares [2]

Source of Variation	SS	DF	MS	F	Sig of F
WITHIN CELLS	140.60	51	2.76		
A	60.15	3	20.05	7.27	.000

[1] Means and Standard Deviations for each condition of A.

[2] F - ratio for 'A' is significant as $F(3, 51) = 7.27$, p. <.001 .

SECOND PASS: CONSTANTS & ASSUMPTIONS

In this pass, we see MANOVA testing two things:

1. The constant term of the linear model - μ .

2. Some of the assumptions of the repeated measures design.

TEST OF THE CONSTANT

You may recall that the model for a repeated measure design is a version of the following:

$$X = \boxed{\mu} + \alpha + \pi + \alpha\pi + \textbf{\textit{etc.}} + \varepsilon$$

Your typical F - ratio as presented above tested for the significance of the effect of the independent variable **A** which is noted in the model as α . However the model also contains the term μ which represents the **population mean** of all subjects if summed over all conditions. The F -ratio noted as $\boxed{1}$ below tests whether the population mean for our data is equal to zero ($\mu = 0$). As the F- ratio is significant, we conclude that $\mu \neq 0$. The highlighted output is as follows:

```
 1   0   set width = 80 .
 2   data list list / a1 a2 a3 a4.
 3   begin data .
21   end data .
22   manova a1 to a4 /
23        wsfactor = a(4) /
24        print = cellinfo (means) signif (avonly) /
25        design .
* * * * * * A N A L Y S I S   O F   V A R I A N C E * * * * * *
     18 cases accepted.
      0 cases rejected because of out-of-range factor values.
      0 cases rejected because of missing data.
      1 non-empty cell.
      1 design will be processed.
- - - - - - - - - - - - - - - - - - - - - - - - - - - - - - - - - - - -
Cell Means and Standard Deviations
Variable .. A1
                              Mean   Std. Dev.        N
For entire sample            9.278    2.697           18
- - - - - - - - - - - - - - - - - - - - - - - - - - - - - - - - - - - -
Variable .. A2
                              Mean   Std. Dev.        N
For entire sample            8.222    2.487           18
- - - - - - - - - - - - - - - - - - - - - - - - - - - - - - - - - - - -
Variable .. A3
                              Mean   Std. Dev.        N
For entire sample            7.833    2.834           18
- - - - - - - - - - - - - - - - - - - - - - - - - - - - - - - - - - - -
Variable .. A4
                              Mean   Std. Dev.        N
For entire sample            6.722    2.886           18
- - - - - - - - - - - - - - - - - - - - - - - - - - - - - - - - - - - -
```

Tests of Between-Subjects Effects.

AVERAGED Tests of Significance for A using UNIQUE sums of squares

Source of Variation	SS	DF	MS	F	Sig of F	
WITHIN CELLS	366.24	17	21.54			
CONSTANT	4624.01	1	4624.01	214.64	.000	$\boxed{1}$

```
Tests involving 'A' Within-Subject Effect.

Mauchly sphericity test, W =         .85642
Chi-square approx. =               2.43685 with 5 D. F.
Significance =                       .786

Greenhouse-Geisser Epsilon =         .91864
Huynh-Feldt Epsilon =               1.00000
Lower-bound Epsilon =                .33333


AVERAGED Tests of Significance that follow are equivalent to
univariate or split-plot or mixed-model approach to repeated measures.

Epsilons may be used to adjust d.f. for the AVERAGED results.

Tests involving 'A' Within-Subject Effect.

AVERAGED Tests of Significance for A using UNIQUE sums of squares
Source of Variation         SS       DF       MS       F  Sig of F

WITHIN CELLS             140.60      51      2.76
A                         60.15       3     20.05     7.27    .000
```

1 TEST OF THE CONSTANT

As the F- ratio is significant, we conclude that $\mu \neq 0$ as **F(1, 17) = 214.64, p. <.001** .

TEST OF THE ASSUMPTIONS:

This is rather complicated for the novice. We will try to oversimplify. In repeated measures and mixed designs, one of the assumptions of the designs is basically that the correlations between the repeated variables are equal. **Thus in our design, the Pearson's correlation coefficients (r) between A1 to A4 should not be different from each other.** If they are different, then you increased your chance of Type I error (or reporting significance when there is none). The fancy name for this assumption is the *circularity assumption*. There is a fancy test for this based on evaluation of the variance-covariance matrix called the *Test for Sphericity* developed by Mauchley. Interested readers can refer to Kirk (1982, p. 257 - 258). In our example, this problem does not exist as the correlations are fairly close. We've printed the correlation matrix of A1 to A4 using CORRELATIONS see Chapter 12) .

```
               - -  Correlation Coefficients   - -
               A1         A2         A3         A4
A1          1.0000      .5868*     .5607*     .6076**
A2           .5868*    1.0000      .7653**    .6402**
A3           .5607*     .7653**   1.0000      .6413**
A4           .6076**    .6402**    .6413**   1.0000

* - Signif. LE .05       ** - Signif. LE .01        (2-tailed)
```

You can see that the correlation coefficients are quite close as they are between 0.5607 and 0.7653 . These differences are not large enough to give a significant violations of the assumption of sphericity as tested by Mauchley's method. You can see this as the chi - square value used for this test (**chi-square = 2.43685 with 5 d.f.**) does not reach significance as $p = .786$ which is much greater than .05. For this data set, don't worry.

etc.

Tests involving 'A' Within-Subject Effect.

Mauchly sphericity test, W =   .85642   [2]
Chi-square approx. =   2.43685 with 5 D. F.
Significance =   .786

Greenhouse-Geisser Epsilon =   .91864
Huynh-Feldt Epsilon =   1.00000
Lower-bound Epsilon =   .33333
etc.

[2] **Mauchly test is not significant.**

A SIGNIFICANT VIOLATION

In the following example, we have added a new variable **A5 (boldfaced)** which has a significantly differently correlation with our previous set of A1 to A4. This will be seen in the correlation matrix from CORRELATIONS and in the MANOVA output. After presenting the output we will discuss what one should do.

```
set width = 80 .
data list list / a1 a2 a3 a4 a5 .
begin data .
13 9 11 10    20
8 8 7 4        3
7 5 5 4        1
9 6 7 3        2
6 8 8 2        1
8 3 1 5        3
13 12 12 11    0
9 11 11 10     4
8 9 9 8        2       A5 added
11 10 7 4      2
8 7 8 8        2
4 5 7 5        20
14 11 11 12    1
13 9 9 6       6
10 11 9 9      5
10 8 10 7      2
7 10 5 7       1
9 6 4 6        3
end data .
manova a1 to a5 /
       wsfactor = a(5) /
       print = cellinfo (means) signif (avonly) /
       design .
correlations a1 to a4 a5.
```

RELEVANT OUTPUT

```
etc.

correlations a1 to a4 a5.

                - -  Correlation Coefficients   - -

         A1        A2        A3        A4        A5

A1    1.0000     .5868*    .5607*    .6076**   -.0691    Note the low values
A2     .5868*   1.0000     .7653**   .6402**   -.1740    of correlation as
A3     .5607*    .7653**  1.0000     .6413**    .1374    compared to A1 to A4.
A4     .6076**   .6402**   .6413**  1.0000      .0923
A5    -.0691    -.1740     .1374     .0923     1.0000

* - Signif. LE .05       ** - Signif. LE .01        (2-tailed)

etc.

Tests involving 'A' Within-Subject Effect.

 Mauchly sphericity test, W =       .04801
 Chi-square approx. =           46.81026 with 9 D. F.    Note the significant
 Significance =                    .000                   test as p. < .001 .
                                                         YOU VIOLATE THE
 Greenhouse-Geisser Epsilon =      .38042               ASSUMPTION!
 Huynh-Feldt Epsilon =             .41010
 Lower-bound Epsilon =             .25000               1/(5-1) = 1/4 = .25

* * * * * A N A L Y S I S   O F   V A R I A N C E -- DESIGN  1 * * * * * *
Tests involving 'A' Within-Subject Effect.

AVERAGED Tests of Significance for A using UNIQUE sums of squares
Source of Variation            SS     DF        MS        F  Sig of F
                                    ┌──────────────────────────────────────┐
                                    │ DF TO BE RECALCULATED - SEE DISCUSSION│
                                    └──────────────────────────────────────┘
WITHIN CELLS                684.38   68      10.06
A                           255.22    4      63.81    6.34   .000  - ? See below.
```

What to Do?

This is not straightforward. Here are the issues and problems.

❏   Your Type I error rate is too high.

❏   You can correct for the increase in error by decreasing your degrees of freedom by multiplying them by one of the Epsilon factors found in the output.

> **Greenhouse-Geisser Epsilon =**   .38042
>
> **Huynh-Feldt Epsilon =**   .41010
>
> **Lower-bound Epsilon =**   .25000

and then looking up the F value with these new df.

Decreasing the degrees of Freedom makes it harder to get significance as you need a bigger F value. This leads to less Type I error.

❑ WHICH EPSILON SHOULD YOU USE?

- There is an excellent discussion in Levine (1991).
- With no violations, the true epsilon factor is 1.0.
- The lower-bound estimate is the mathematical lower limit of the true epsilon and is equal to $1/(k-1)$ when K = the number of repeated measure or in our case = 5 as we have A1 to A5. Thus lower-bound epsilon is equal to $1/(5-1) = 1/4 = .25$.
- One cannot know the true epsilon so you must estimate it using the Huynh-Feldt or Greenhouse-Geisser methods.
- If these estimates are below 0.5 you have a severe violation of the assumption. Levine suggests that Huynh-Feldt be used in most situations and Greenhouse-Geisser when the assumption is strongly violated.

❑. LET'S USE IT!

Since our two epsilons are low (given the big difference in correlations), we would use the Greenhouse-Geisser correction and multiply our degrees of freedom by .38042.

Thus the corrected degrees of freedom would be:

Effect	**DF**		**EPSILON**		**New DF**
WITHIN CELLS	68	X.	.38042	=	25.86856
A	4	X.	.38042	=	1.52168

Use these to re-evaluate the F- ratio of 6.34. If we use the df as 1, 25 (the closest values rounded down), we would find that our F is significant at the .05 level as 6.34 > 4.24 (the tabled value - Beyer, 1968) but not at the .01 level as 6.34 < 7.77. **This is very different from the anova table which would have given us a significance level of <.001 if the df = 4, 68!**

❑. OH, NO! IT'S STILL NOT THAT EASY !

- There are doubts about the utility of the Mauchley test (Levine, 1991). It may be that this correction is not worth the trouble but since SPSS reports it, we interpreted for you. However, be warned that it is controversial!
- It is also suggested that the standard repeated measures anova be replaced by a true Manova design. It is you treat the repetitions as separate dependent variables, not as a repetition of the same dependent variable across the levels of the

independent variable. Such designs are less vulnerable to violation of assumptions.

- If you wish to engage this level of analysis, you are probably not a naive user and can follow the debates in the standard texts and the instructions in the SPSS Reference guide. Tabachnick and Fidell (1989) have a useful discussion of the issues and various setup examples.

MY OWN ADVICE TO THE BEGINNER OR CASUAL USER, IS THAT IF THE SPHERICITY ASSUMPTION IS VIOLATED - CHECK WITH A LOCAL EXPERT BEFORE GOING OFF INTO NEW DESIGNS OR TRANSFORMATIONS OF YOUR DATA!

FACTORIAL DESIGNS

It is now time to discuss factorial designs with more than one independent variable. As in our Method I discussion, these designs can be completely within subject with all subjects being in all conditions or they can be of a mixed nature with some independent variables being repeated and some defined separate groups. The two issues are :

1. Indicating the repetition.
2. Interpreting the output. Unfortunately the means are not well presented.

TOTALLY WITHIN SUBJECTS FACTORIAL DESIGNS.

The steps are as follows:

1. Determine the number of levels for the repeated variables. The product of these two numbers will be the number of scores for one subject. In our first example, we will have two repeated variables - A and B. A will have 4 levels and B will have 3 levels. Thus each subject will have 12 scores per line (4 x 3).

2. Create a data list with a hierarchical arrangement setting a level of A and then going through a level of B. In general, we let i = the number of levels of A and j = number of levels of B.

3. Name these variables with a combination of appropriate A and B levels as follows:

```
Levels of A:        A1              A2              A3              A4
Levels of B:  B1 B2 B3      B1 B2 B3      B1 B2 B3      B1 B4 B3
```

Data List and Variable Names:

data list list / a1b1 a1b2 a1b3 > A1 level, B from 1 to 3

                         a2b1 a2b2 a2b3 > A2 level, B from 1 to 3

> a3b1 a3b2 a3b3 > A3 level, B from 1 to 3

> a4b1 a4b2 a4b3 > A4 level, B from 1 to 3

4. Write the MANOVA command that indicates this structure. Pay attention to the **wsfactor** subcommand

```
manova a1b1 to a4b3 /
       wsfactor = a(4) b(3) /
       print = cellinfo (means) signif (avonly) /
       design .
```

Let's dissect the command so it can act as a template for further setups.

manova <u>a1b1 to a4b3</u> ➡ The 12 scores to be analyzed.

wsfactor = <u>a(4) b(3)</u> ➡ Considers them as a repeated measures design with 3 repetitions of a factor called 'A' and 3 repetitions of 'B'. <u>It also denotes that the levels of 'B' change within the levels of 'A' as 'a(4)' was typed first!</u>

print = cellinfo (means) signif (avonly) ➡ prints F tables and means .

design ➡ This makes SPSS and MANOVA happy. <u>Just type it</u>.

An example follows:

$$\boxed{A(i) \times B (j) \times S (s)}$$

{ $[A_1B_1\ A_1B_2\ ...\ A_1B_j]\ [A_2B_1\ A_2B_2\ ...\ A_2B_j]$ ...
  $[A_iB_1\ A_iB_2\ ...\ A_iB_j]$ = Subject's Line }

Where A_iB_j Identifies the score's levels of the Independent Variables ' A & B '. The actual score is the number typed in this position.

EXAMPLE OF A(4) X B (3) X S (12) DESIGN

```
set  width = 80 .
data list list / a1b1 a1b2 a1b3 a2b1 a2b2 a2b3      4 levels of A
                 a3b1 a3b2 a3b3 a4b1 a4b2 a4b3 .    3 levels of B
begin data .
13 13 14 9 12 11  11 12 11 10 11 12   -> Bob's Line of Data
 8  9 13 8 11  9   7 11  9  4 10  6    4 x 3 = 12 scores / subject
```

```
 7  8 10  5  9 11  5  9  9  4  8  9
 9 11 10  6 10  8  7  7 10  3  4  7
 6  8  7  8  7 10  8  8  5  2  8  7          12 Subjects
 8  4  9  3  5  6  1  7  4  5  5  6
12 11 13  8 12 11 11 12 11 10 11 12
 9  9 13  8 13  9  7 11  9  4 10  6
 7  8 10  5 10 11  5  9  9  4  8  9
 9 11 10  6 10  8  7  7 10  3  4  7
 6  8  7  8  7 10  9  8  5  3  8  7
 9  4 10  3  5  4  4  7  4 15  5  8
end data .
manova a1b1 to a4b3 / wsfactor = a(4) b(3)/
                      print = cellinfo (means) signif (avonly) /
                      design .
finish .
```

OUTPUT: THE MEANS & F-RATIOS ARE HARD TO READ!

Unfortunately, the output becomes cumbersome. Here are the important points:

1. Since the repeated variables entered for the design are a1b1 to a4b3, SPSS doesn't print the main effect means for A1, A2, A3 and A4 or the means for B1, B2 or B3. It just prints the means for a1b1 to a4b3. If you want the main effect means, you have to calculate them yourselves. This is not a problem if you have equal numbers of subjects. We will show you how to do the **'equal n'** calculation.

(Note: This is a big pain but I didn't write the program. Method II avoids this problems as it prints all the means. It is harder to set up. Win some, lose some. GM.)

2. A summarized F-table isn't presented. Each effect has its own sphericity test and then its F is reported.

We'll first show you an output and evaluate the F-ratios and sphericity tests. Then we will deal with means.

OUTPUT, F-RATIOS & SPHERICITY

```
 1   0  set  width = 80 .
 2   data list list / a1b1 a1b2 a1b3 a2b1 a2b2 a2b3
 3                     a3b1 a3b2 a3b3 a4b1 a4b2 a4b3 .
 4   begin data .
16   end data .
17   manova a1b1 to a4b3 / wsfactor = a(4) b(3)/
18                         print = cellinfo (means) signif (avonly) /
19                         design .
```

```
* * * * A N A L Y S I S   O F   V A R I A N C E * * *
- - - - - - - - - - - - - - - - - - - - - - - - - - - -
Cell Means and Standard Deviations
Variable .. A1B1
                        Mean   Std. Dev.      N
For entire sample       8.583    2.151       12
- - - - - - - - - - - - - - - - - - - - - - - - - - - -
Variable .. A1B2
                        Mean   Std. Dev.      N
For entire sample       8.667    2.708       12
- - - - - - - - - - - - - - - - - - - - - - - - - - - -
Variable .. A1B3
                        Mean   Std. Dev.      N
For entire sample      10.500    2.316       12
- - - - - - - - - - - - - - - - - - - - - - - - - - - -
Variable .. A2B1
                        Mean   Std. Dev.      N
For entire sample       6.417    2.065       12
- - - - - - - - - - - - - - - - - - - - - - - - - - - -
Variable .. A2B2
                        Mean   Std. Dev.      N
For entire sample       9.250    2.701       12
- - - - - - - - - - - - - - - - - - - - - - - - - - - -
Variable .. A2B3
                        Mean   Std. Dev.      N
For entire sample       9.000    2.216       12
- - - - - - - - - - - - - - - - - - - - - - - - - - - -
Variable .. A3B1
                        Mean   Std. Dev.      N
For entire sample       6.833    2.855       12
- - - - - - - - - - - - - - - - - - - - - - - - - - - -
Variable .. A3B2
                        Mean   Std. Dev.      N
For entire sample       9.000    2.000       12
- - - - - - - - - - - - - - - - - - - - - - - - - - - -
Variable .. A3B3
                        Mean   Std. Dev.      N
For entire sample       8.000    2.697       12
- - - - - - - - - - - - - - - - - - - - - - - - - - - -
Variable .. A4B1
                        Mean   Std. Dev.      N
For entire sample       5.583    3.942       12
- - - - - - - - - - - - - - - - - - - - - - - - - - - -
Variable .. A4B2
                        Mean   Std. Dev.      N
For entire sample       7.667    2.605       12
- - - - - - - - - - - - - - - - - - - - - - - - - - - -
Variable .. A4B3
                        Mean   Std. Dev.      N
For entire sample       8.000    2.132       12
- - - - - - - - - - - - - - - - - - - - - - - - - - - -
```

Explanation of F - Ratios and Sphericity Tests
(To the right - SEE BOLD-FACE)

1. Significant **constant** as $p. < .001$.

2. Main Effect of 'A':
   Nonsignificant violation of sphericity
   asp.= .110
   Significant effect of 'A' as $f(3,33) =$
   5.96 and $p. = .002$

3. Main Effect of 'B':
   Significant violation of sphericity as
   $p. = .001$
   Significant effect of 'B' as $f(3,33) =$
   14.27 and $p. < .001$

4. Main Effect of 'A by B Interaction':
   Significant violation of sphericity as
   $p. < .000$
   Nonsignificant effect of 'A by B' as
   $f(6,66) = 2.15$ and $p. = .054$ and thus
   $> .05$.

```
* * * * * * A N A L Y S I S   O F   V A R I A N C E --
DESIGN   1 * * *
Tests of Between-Subjects Effects.

AVERAGED Tests of Significance for MEAS.1 using
UNIQUE sums of square
Source of Variation    SS      DF      MS      F     Sig of F

WITHIN CELLS         432.08    11    39.28
CONSTANT            9506.25     1  9506.25   242.01   .000¹
```

Tests involving 'A' Within-Subject Effect.

```
Mauchly sphericity test, W =        .11942
Chi-square approx. =              20.66101 with 5 D. F.
Significance =                       .001²

Greenhouse-Geisser Epsilon =        .53444
Huynh-Feldt Epsilon =               .61156
Lower-bound Epsilon =               .33333
```

AVERAGED Tests of Significance that follow are equivalent to
univariate or split-plot or mixed-model approach to repeated
measures.
Epsilons may be used to adjust df for the AVERAGED results.

```
AVERAGED Tests of Significance for MEAS.1 using
UNIQUE sums of squares

Source of Variation    SS      DF      MS      F     Sig of F
WITHIN CELLS         158.86    33    4.01
A                     86.14     3   20.71    5.96   .002²
```

Tests involving 'B' Within-Subject Effect.

```
Mauchly sphericity test, W =        .64359
Chi-square approx. =               4.40696 with 2 D. F.
Significance =                       .110³

Greenhouse-Geisser Epsilon =        .73724
Huynh-Feldt Epsilon =               .82377
Lower-bound Epsilon =               .50000
```

AVERAGED Tests of Significance that follow are equivalent to
univariate or split-plot or mixed-model approach to repeated
measures.
Epsilons may be used to adjust df for the AVERAGED results.

Tests involving 'B' Within-Subject Effect.

```
AVERAGED Tests of Significance for MEAS.1 using
UNIQUE sums of squares

Source of Variation    SS      DF      MS      F     Sig of F
WITHIN CELLS          90.69    22    4.12
B                    117.54     2   50.77   14.27   .000³
```

Tests involving 'A BY B' Within-Subject Effect.

```
Mauchly sphericity test, W =        .00344
Chi-square approx. =              49.79017 with 20 D. F.
Significance =                       .000⁴

Greenhouse-Geisser Epsilon =        .43503
Huynh-Feldt Epsilon =               .58249
Lower-bound Epsilon =               .16667
```

AVERAGED Tests of Significance that follow are equivalent to
univariate or split-plot or mixed-model approach to repeated
measures.
Epsilons may be used to adjust df for the AVERAGED results.

Tests involving 'A BY B' Within-Subject Effect.

```
AVERAGED Tests of Significance for MEAS.1 using
UNIQUE sums of squares
Source of Variation    SS      DF      MS      F     Sig of F
WITHIN CELLS         199.43    66    3.02
A by B               117.54     6    6.51    2.15   .059⁴
```

CALCULATING A & B MEANS FROM AiBj CELL MEANS

```
* * ANALYSIS   OF   VARIANCE * * *
- - - - - - - - - - - -
Cell Means and Standard Deviations
Variable .. A1B1
                    Mean   Std. Dev.   N
For entire sample  8.583      2.151   12
- - - - - - - - - - - - -
Variable .. A1B2
                    Mean   Std. Dev.   N
For entire sample  8.667      2.708   12
- - - - - - - - - - - -
Variable .. A1B3
                    Mean   Std. Dev.   N
For entire sample 10.500      2.316   12
- - - - - - - - - - - -
Variable .. A2B1
                    Mean   Std. Dev.   N
For entire sample  6.417      2.065   12
- - - - - - - - - - - -
Variable .. A2B2
                    Mean   Std. Dev.   N
For entire sample  9.250      2.701   12
- - - - - - - - - - - -
Variable .. A2B3
                    Mean   Std. Dev.   N
For entire sample  9.000      2.216   12
- - - - - - - - - - - -
Variable .. A3B1
                    Mean   Std. Dev.   N
For entire sample  6.833      2.855   12
- - - - - - - - - - - -
Variable .. A3B2
                    Mean   Std. Dev    N
For entire sample  9.000      2.00    12
- - - - - - - - - - - -
Variable .. A3B3
                    Mean   Std. Dev.   N
For entire sample  8.000      2.697   12
- - - - - - - - - - - -
Variable .. A4B1
                    Mean   Std. Dev.   N
For entire sample  5.583      3.942   12
- - - - - - - - - - - -
Variable .. A4B2
                    Mean   Std. Dev.   N
For entire sample  7.667      2.605   12
- - - - - - - - - - - -
Variable .. A4B3
                    Mean   Std. Dev.   N
For entire sample  8.000      2.132   12
- - - - - - - - - - - -
```

Calculating the A and B Means:

1. Use Output to Create an **A by B** table.
2. Enter the means in the table.
3. Average across the rows for **A** means.
4. Average down the columns for **B** means.

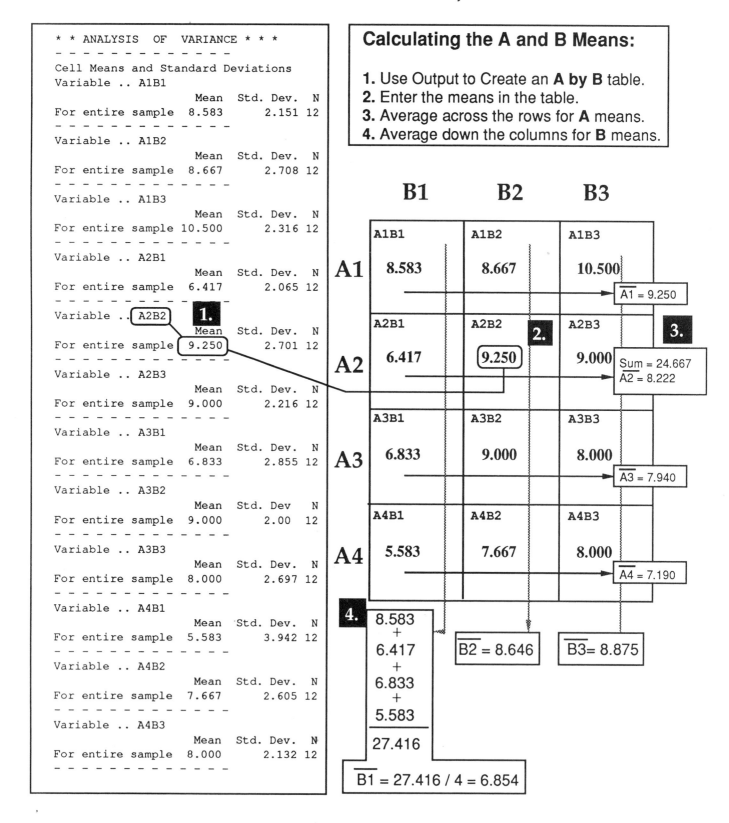

MIXED DESIGNS

With these designs, some factors are repeated and some are between groups. In your data list and manova commands you must indicate both relationships. Thus you have a combination of independent variables as in the between group designs in Chapter 15 and the repetition structure that we have been using in the preceding examples. Let's first look at a design where:

B is the between groups variables and A is repeated. The data list and subjects' data line reflect both respectively. In both SPSS lines, B is the IV and **a1 to ai** represents the repetitions of A.

❑ **data list list / b a1 a2 ... ai .**

❑ **b a1 a2 ... ai**

The MANOVA command reflects this setup where i = last repetition of A and (1,b) notes the levels of B.

```
manova a1 a2 … ai by b (1,b) / wsfactor = a(i) /
        print = cellinfo (means) signif (avonly)/
        design.
```

The entire setup would look like:

```
set   width = 80 .
data list list / b a1 a2 … ai . i levels of A
begin data .                    b levels of B
1 a1 a2 … ai       subjects for B₁
1 a1 a2 … ai
...                                 each 'a?' term = score
2 a1 a2 … ai       subjects for B₂
2 a1 a2 … ai
...
b a1 a2 … ai       subjects for B_b
b a1 a2 … ai
...
end data .
manova a1 a2 … ai by b (1,b) / wsfactor = a(i) /
        print = cellinfo (means) signif (avonly)/
        design .
finish .
```

A group of symbolic setups are found earlier on pages 321-313. For brevity's sake, one complete example follows:

C[c] x (A[i] x B[j] x S) DESIGN

$$C \{ [A_1B_1 \ A_1B_2 \ ... \ A_1Bj_b] \ [A_2B_1 \ A_2B_2 \ ... \ A_2Bj] \ ...$$
$$[A_iB_1 \ A_iB_2 \ ... \ A_iB_j] = Subject's \ Line \}$$

Where C = the levels of the Between Groups Independent Variable 'C' & A_aB_b Identifies the score's levels of the Independent Variables ' A & B ' . The actual score is the number typed in this position.

EXAMPLE OF A(3) X B (4) X C (2) DESIGN WITH 'A' AND 'B' REPEATED AND 2 BETWEEN GROUPS LEVELS OF 'C' WITH 6 SUBJECTS IN EACH REPEATED 'AB' BLOCK .

```
set  width = 80 .
data list list / c a1b1 a1b2 a1b3 a2b1 a2b2 a2b3    2 levels of C
                  a3b1 a3b2 a3b3 a4b1 a4b2 a4b3 .    4 levels of A
begin data .                                         3 levels of B
1 13 13 14 9 12 11 11 12 11 10 11 12
1  8  9 13 8 11  9  7 11  9  4 10  6
1  7  8 10 5  9 11  5  9  9  4  8  9     6 subjects for C₁
1  9 11 10 6 10  8  7  7 10  3  4  7
1  6  8  7 8  7 10  8  8  5  2  8  7
1  8  4  9 3  5  6  1  7  4  5  5  6

2  2  3  5 3  5  5  4  5  6  3  7  9
2  4 21  7 5  9  1  3 11  5  7  8 12
2  2  5  8 8  9 10  3  4  6 11 11 21
2  4  3  5 6  2  5  7  8  9  1 23 22     6 subjects for C₂
2  3  4  5 8 11 12 12 12  5  3  7  8
2  3  5  4 7 12 12 12 10  4  4  7  9
end data .
manova a1b1 to a4b3 by c (1,2) / wsfactor = a(4) b(3) /
            print = cellinfo (means) signif (avonly)/
            design .
finish .
```

OUTPUT

Again, Note the need to Calculate the Means for the Levels of A, B and C!
Make Sure You Can Find the F - Ratios for
A, B, C, AB, AC, BC & ABC!

```
 1  0  set width = 80 .
 2  data list list / c a1b1 a1b2 a1b3 a2b1 a2b2 a2b3
 3                    a3b1 a3b2 a3b3 a4b1 a4b2 a4b3 .
 4  begin data .
16  end data .
17  manova a1b1 to a4b3 by c (1,2) / wsfactor = a(4) b(3) /
18              print = cellinfo (means) signif (avonly)/
19              design .
```

* * * * * *A N A L Y S I S   O F   V A R I A N C E * * * * * *

Cell Means and Standard Deviations
Variable .. A1B1

FACTOR	CODE	Mean	Std. Dev.	N
C	1	8.500	2.429	6
C	2	3.000	.894	6
For entire sample		5.750	3.361	12

```
- - - - - - - - - - - - - - - - - - - - - - - - - - - - - - - - -
Variable .. A1B2
        FACTOR          CODE            Mean  Std. Dev.          N
  C                       1             8.833     3.061          6
  C                       2             6.833     6.998          6
For entire sample                      7.833     5.254         12
- - - - - - - - - - - - - - - - - - - - - - - - - - - - - - - - -
Variable .. A1B3
        FACTOR          CODE            Mean  Std. Dev.          N

  C                       1            10.500     2.588          6
  C                       2             5.667     1.506          6
For entire sample                      8.083     3.232         12
- - - - - - - - - - - - - - - - - - - - - - - - - - - - - - - - -
Variable .. A2B1
        FACTOR          CODE            Mean  Std. Dev.          N
  C                       1             6.500     2.258          6
  C                       2             6.167     1.941          6
For entire sample                      6.333     2.015         12
- - - - - - - - - - - - - - - - - - - - - - - - - - - - - - - - -
Variable .. A2B2
        FACTOR          CODE            Mean  Std. Dev.          N
  C                       1             9.000     2.608          6
  C                       2             8.000     3.795          6
For entire sample                      8.500     3.148         12
- - - - - - - - - - - - - - - - - - - - - - - - - - - - - - - - -
Variable .. A2B3
        FACTOR          CODE            Mean  Std. Dev.          N
  C                       1             9.167     1.941          6
  C                       2             7.500     4.506          6
For entire sample                      8.333     3.420         12
- - - - - - - - - - - - - - - - - - - - - - - - - - - - - - - - -
Variable .. A3B1
        FACTOR          CODE            Mean  Std. Dev.          N
  C                       1             6.500     3.332          6
  C                       2             6.833     4.262          6
For entire sample                      6.667     3.651         12
- - - - - - - - - - - - - - - - - - - - - - - - - - - - - - - - -
Variable .. A3B2
        FACTOR          CODE            Mean  Std. Dev.          N
  C                       1             9.000     2.098          6
  C                       2             8.333     3.266          6
For entire sample                      8.667     2.640         12
- - - - - - - - - - - - - - - - - - - - - - - - - - - - - - - - -
Variable .. A3B3
        FACTOR          CODE            Mean  Std. Dev.          N
  C                       1             8.000     2.828          6
  C                       2             5.833     1.722          6
For entire sample                      6.917     2.503         12


- - - - - - - - - - - - - - - - - - - - - - - - - - - - - - - - -
Variable .. A4B1
        FACTOR          CODE            Mean  Std. Dev.          N
  C                       1             4.667     2.805          6
  C                       2             4.833     3.601          6
For entire sample                      4.750     3.079         12
- - - - - - - - - - - - - - - - - - - - - - - - - - - - - - - - -
Variable .. A4B2
        FACTOR          CODE            Mean  Std. Dev.          N
  C                       1             7.667     2.733          6
  C                       2            10.500     6.317          6
For entire sample                      9.083     4.870         12
- - - - - - - - - - - - - - - - - - - - - - - - - - - - - - - - -
```

```
Cell Means and Standard Deviations   (Cont.)
Variable .. A4B3
        FACTOR              CODE                Mean    Std. Dev.         N

  C                          1                 7.833     2.317            6
  C                          2                13.500     6.348            6
  For entire sample                           10.667     5.433           12
```

- -

Tests of Between-Subjects Effects.

AVERAGED Tests of Significance for MEAS.1 using UNIQUE sums of squares
```
Source of Variation            SS       DF       MS        F  Sig of F

WITHIN CELLS                359.74      10     35.97
C                            21.01       1     21.01      .58    .462
```
- -

Tests involving **'A'** Within-Subject Effect.


```
Mauchly sphericity test, W =        .49801
Chi-square approx. =             6.08051 with 5 D. F.
Significance =                      .298

Greenhouse-Geisser Epsilon =        .72761
Huynh-Feldt Epsilon =              1.00000
Lower-bound Epsilon =               .33333
```

AVERAGED Tests of Significance that follow are equivalent to
univariate or split-plot or mixed-model approach to repeated measures.
Epsilons may be used to adjust d.f. for the AVERAGED results.

- -

Tests involving **'A'** Within-Subject Effect.

AVERAGED Tests of Significance for MEAS.1 using UNIQUE sums of squares
```
Source of Variation            SS       DF       MS        F  Sig of F

WITHIN CELLS                526.99      30     17.57
A                            18.30       3      6.10      .35    .791
C BY A                      221.47       3     73.82     4.20    .014
```

Tests involving **'B'** Within-Subject Effect.
```
Mauchly sphericity test, W =        .79135
Chi-square approx. =             2.10617 with 2 D. F.
Significance =                      .349

Greenhouse-Geisser Epsilon =        .82737
Huynh-Feldt Epsilon =              1.00000
Lower-bound Epsilon =               .50000
```

AVERAGED Tests of Significance that follow are equivalent to
univariate or split-plot or mixed-model approach to repeated measures.
Epsilons may be used to adjust d.f. for the AVERAGED results.
- -
Tests involving **'B'** Within-Subject Effect.

AVERAGED Tests of Significance for MEAS.1 using UNIQUE sums of squares
```
Source of Variation            SS       DF       MS        F  Sig of F

WITHIN CELLS                168.14      20      8.41
B                           222.26       2    111.13     13.22   .000
C BY B                        7.60       2      3.80       .45   .643
```
- -

Tests involving **'A BY B'** Within-Subject Effect.

```
Mauchly sphericity test, W =          .00989
Chi-square approx. =         35.90706 with 20 D. F.
Significance =                    .016

Greenhouse-Geisser Epsilon =     .42707
Huynh-Feldt Epsilon =            .64422
Lower-bound Epsilon =            .16667
```

AVERAGED Tests of Significance that follow are equivalent to
univariate or split-plot or mixed-model approach to repeated measures.
Epsilons may be used to adjust d.f. for the AVERAGED results.
- -
Tests involving **'A BY B'** Within-Subject Effect.

AVERAGED Tests of Significance for MEAS.1 using UNIQUE sums of squares

Source of Variation	SS	DF	MS	F	Sig of F
WITHIN CELLS	431.64	60	7.19		
A BY B	**105.68**	**6**	**17.61**	**2.45**	**.035**
C BY A BY B	**70.68**	**6**	**11.78**	**1.64**	**.153**

BOXPLOTS

The MANOVA program can also produce the same boxplot and stemleaf output as described in Chapter 15's anova designs. You would need to add the **/plot = boxplots** command to your setup. It would look as follows in one our our setups:

BOXPLOTS SETUP

```
set width = 80 .
data list list / a1 a2 a3 a4.
begin data .
13 9 11 10
 8 8 7 4
 7 5 5 4
 9 6 7 3
 6 8 8 2
 8 3 1 5
13 12 12 11
 9 11 11 10
 8 9 9 8
11 10 7 4
 8 7 8 8
 4 5 7 5
14 11 11 12
13 9 9 6
10 11 9 9
10 8 10 7
 7 10 5 7
 9 6 4 6
end data .
manova a1 to a4 /
       wsfactor = a(4) /
       print = cellinfo (means) signif (avonly) /
       plot = boxplots /
       design .

finish .
```

IV. LATIN SQUARE DESIGNS

Latin square designs control for nuisance variables. A good discussion of the design is found in Kirk (1982). The nuisance variables are assigned to the rows and columns of the design and the treatments to the appropriate places in the matrix. The number of subjects below is assumed to be ≥ 2. There must be equal numbers of levels for the rows, columns and treatments. The general scheme for the design looks as follows:

Nuisance Variable - Columns			
Treat 1	Treat 2	Treat 3	Treat 4
Treat 2	Treat 3	Treat 4	Treat 1
Treat 3	Treat 4	Treat 1	Treat 2
Treat 4	Treat 1	Treat 2	Treat 3

(with **Nuisance Variable - Rows** labeling the rows)

In the following example, we have four two nuisance variables and one treatment variable with four levels for each. There are two repetitions (n = 2).

ERROR TERMS

Our setup will contain three MANOVA commands. This is because there are options available for the appropriate error term. The standard error term for a Latin Square design is the $MS_{within\ cell}$ (#1 in setup) However, Kirk (1982, p. 314-315) suggests the use of a pooled term ($MS_{RES-pooled}$) if there are no treatment, row and column interactions (#3 MANOVA command). This can be tested by computing $F = MS_{RES}/MS_{WCELL}$ (#2 MANOVA command). These three commands will be:

Uses MS$_{within\ cell}$ for Error

```
1   manova   score by row (1,4) col (1,4) treat (1,4) /
           omeans  = tables (treat) /
           design = row col treat .
```

Generates Info for $F = MS_{RES}/MS_{WCELL}$

```
2   manova   score by row (1,4) col (1,4) treat (1,4) /
           omeans  = tables (treat) /
           design .
```

Uses MS$_{pooled\ cell}$ for Error

```
3   manova   score by row (1,4) col (1,4) treat (1,4) /
           omeans  = tables (treat) /
           error = w + r /
           design = row col treat .
```

The complete annotated setup is as follows:

SETUP

```
set width = 80 .
data list list / row col treat score .
begin data.
1 1 1 02
1 1 1 04
1 2 2 04
1 2 2 05
1 3 3 10
1 3 3 12
1 4 4 17
1 4 4 16
2 1 2 06
2 1 2 08
2 2 3 16
2 2 3 12
2 3 4 18
2 3 4 17
2 4 1 04
2 4 1 06
3 1 3 10
3 1 3 14
3 2 4 10
3 2 4 22
3 3 1 04
3 3 1 04
3 4 2 10
3 4 2 08
4 1 4 14
4 1 4 20
4 2 1 12
4 2 1 07
4 3 2 06
4 3 2 08
4 4 3 12
4 4 3 12
end data.
manova   score by row (1,4) col (1,4) treat (1,4) /
         omeans  = tables (treat) /
         design = row col treat .
manova   score by row (1,4) col (1,4) treat (1,4) /
         omeans  = tables (treat) /
         design .
manova   score by row (1,4) col (1,4) treat (1,4) /
         omeans  = tables (treat) /
         error = w + r /
         design = row col treat .
finish.
```

OUTPUT

```
┌─────────────────────────────────────────────────────────────┐
│    # 1. Conventional Within Cells Error Term -               │
│            Significant Treatment Effect                      │
└─────────────────────────────────────────────────────────────┘
```

```
->   manova   score by row (1,4) col (1,4) treat (1,4) /
->            omeans  = tables (treat) /
->            design = row col treat .
```

Combined Observed Means for TREAT Variable .. SCORE

TREAT		
1	WGT.	5.37500
	UNWGT.	5.37500
2	WGT.	6.87500
	UNWGT.	6.87500
3	WGT.	12.25000
	UNWGT.	12.25000
4	WGT.	16.75000
	UNWGT.	16.75000

Tests of Significance for SCORE using UNIQUE sums of squares

Source of Variation	SS	DF	MS	F	Sig of F
WITHIN CELLS	132.00	16	8.25		
ROW	31.13	3	10.38	1.26	.322
COL	8.63	3	2.88	.35	.791
TREAT	**651.12**	**3**	**217.04**	**26.31**	**.000**

```
┌─────────────────────────────────────────────────────────────┐
│           # 2. F = MSres/MSwcell =                           │
│  MSROW BY COL / MS WITHIN CELLS = 8.25 / 7.0 =1.18           │
│     Not Significant - Can use pooled term below in #3        │
└─────────────────────────────────────────────────────────────┘
```

2. $F = MS_{res}/MS_{wcell} = MS_{ROW\ BY\ COL} / MS_{WITHIN\ CELLS} = 8.25 / 7.0 = 1.18$
Not Significant - Can use pooled term below in #3

```
->   manova   score by row (1,4) col (1,4) treat (1,4) /
->            omeans  = tables (treat) /
->            design .
etc.
```

Tests of Significance for SCORE using UNIQUE sums of squares

Source of Variation	SS	DF	MS	F	Sig of F
WITHIN CELLS	132.00	16	**8.25**		
ROW	31.13	3	10.38	1.26	.322
COL	8.62	3	2.87	.35	.791
TREAT	179.21	3	59.74	7.24	.003
ROW BY COL	42.00	6	**7.00**	.85	.552
ROW BY TREAT	.00	0	.	.	.
COL BY TREAT	.00	0	.	.	.
ROW BY COL BY TREAT	.00	0	.	.	.

```
┌─────────────────────────────────────────────┐
│      #3. Pooled Error Term - Significant     │
│     Treatment Effect - Note F > than # 1.    │
└─────────────────────────────────────────────┘
```

```
->    manova   score by row (1,4) col (1,4) treat (1,4) /
->            omeans  = tables (treat) /
->            error = w + r /
->            design = row col treat .
```

```
etc.
 Tests of Significance for SCORE using UNIQUE sums of squares
 Source of Variation          SS      DF       MS        F  Sig of F

WITHIN+RESIDUAL             174.00    22      7.91
ROW                         31.13     3     10.38     1.31    .296
COL                          8.63     3      2.88      .36    .780
TREAT                      651.12     3    217.04    27.44    .000
```

If N = 1

If there is only one repetition (n= 1), Kirk (1982, p. 318) recommends using MS_{RES} for the error term. This would be requested as follows:

```
manova    score by row (1,4) col (1,4) treat (1,4) /
          omeans  = tables (treat) /
          error =  r /
          design = row col treat .
```

V. ANALYSIS OF COVARIANCE

(ANCOVA)

Analysis of Covariance is not necessarily a repeated measure design but it does use regression techniques. The basic idea is that there is a covariate or set of covariates. These are variables that are correlated with your dependent variable. Perhaps, then the effect of these covariates should be removed before your analysis of variance is calculated. For example, if your anova has four groups being tested on how different teaching methods influence arithmetic scores and your groups differ in IQ, the IQ differences would interfere with analyzing the effects of teaching method. Would the scores just reflect the basic ability differences in the groups and not the methods?

You, thus, can correlate the IQ variable with the arithmetic scores. If there is a significant correlation, you can thus predict the arithmetic scores from IQ. In an Ancova design, we will then compute the predicted arithmetic Score. We would subtract the predicted score from the original arithmetic score. This difference or residual score (Arithmetic - Arith. $_{pred}$) would then be the actual score used in our anova. Such an anova is an ancova. To repeat, an ancova is just an anova run on the residuals after predictions of the dependent variable have been made from a set of covariates. If there are more than one covariate, then the residual analysis will be based on a multiple regression. It would be wise to understand that process before using it. It is also the case that an appropriate ancova design will increase statistical power as the analysis based on residuals will have smaller error terms. Most anova designs that we presented can have covariates. There is a simple set of additions to the setups. We will present schematics for Between Groups and Within Groups Designs and then an example.

Between Groups Manova Setups
[Addition of *with Cov₁ ... Cov?* & / *pmeans* = evokes the ANCOVA]

With between group designs, you need to add covariates to the data list statement. The manova command has two important additions. First, you must add the `with Cov₁` ...

Cov? command in the beginning of the command. Second you may want to add the
/ pmeans = in order to see the means of the dependent variables after adjustments for
the covariates (means based on the residuals) and the mean as would predicted from the
regression model. The setup is very similar to the one used in Chapter 15.

GENERIC SETUP

```
set width = 80 .

data list list / DV IV₁  IV₂  … IVₖ cov₁ … cov? .

begin data .

          DV IV₁  IV₂  … IVₖ cov₁ … cov?

end data .

manova DV by IV₁ (1,?) IV₂ (1,?) … IVₖ (1,?)

        with Cov₁ … Cov?

        / omeans = tables (constant, IV₁, IV₂, … , IVₖ,

          etc. - see  Chapter 15

                                    IV₁ by IV₂ by … IVₖ)

        / pmeans = tables (constant, IV₁, IV₂, … , IVₖ,

          same as for omeans

                                    IV₁ by IV₂ by … IVₖ)

        / design .

finish .
```

Repeated Measures Ancova

There are many variants for the repeated measures designs depending on the way you choose to do them. Below you will find the generic setup for our **Method I**. It is similar to the Between Groups ancova just presented. This is because we are creating our own error terms. The situation is more complicated for **Method** II.

Method I

```
set width = 80 .
data list list / a b c … IVk Sub Score cov1 … cov? .
begin data .
          a b c IVk sub score cov1 … cov?
end data .
manova Score by A (1,?) B (1,?) … IVk (1,?) SUB (1, s)
        with Cov1 … Cov?
      / omeans = tables (constant, A, B, …, IVk,
          A by B,
          A by C,
          A by IVk,
          B by C,
              .
          IVk-1 by IVk,
          A by B by C ,
              .
          IVk-2 by IVk-1 by IVk,
              .
          A by B by C by … IVk)
    / pmeans = same as for omeans
        etc.
    / design = A vs 1, A by SUB = 1,
        B vs 2, B by SUB = 2,
        C vs 3, C by SUB = 3,
              .
        IVk vs k, IVk by SUB = k,
        A by B vs k+1, A by B by SUB = k+1,
        A by C vs k+2, A by C by SUB = k+2,
        B by C vs k+3, B by C by SUB = k+3,
              .
        IVk-1 by IVk vs ?, IVk-1 by IVk by SUB = ?    ,
              .
        A by B by C vs ? , A by B by C by SUB = ?
              .
        A by B by … IVk vs ? ,
        A by B by … IVk by SUB = ?   .
finish  .
```

Repeated Measures: Method II

For **Method II**, the situation is more complicated. You will need to enter redundant covariate entries for each dependent variable. These redundant variables must be renamed with the COMPUTE command (see Chapter 20). We will present one full generic command and then just give the MANOVA commands for some other designs.

EXAMPLE: A(i) X B (j) X S (s) COMPLETELY WITHIN DESIGN WITH ONE COVARIATE

```
set width = 80 .
data list list / a1b1 to aᵢbⱼ cov .
begin data .
     a1b1 to aᵢbⱼ cov    | - One line per subject .
end data .
compute cv1 = cov .
compute cv2 = cov .
 .
 .
 .
compute cv(axb) = cov .
manova a1b1 to aᵢbⱼ  with cv1 … cv(axb) *
        / wsfactor = a(i) b(j)  /
        print = cellinfo (means) signif (avonly) /
        design .
finish .
```

```
* You need to compute a set of variables (each equal to cov) for as many
times as there are cells in the design. In other words, if there are 2
levels of A and 3 levels of B, you would have to enter COV six times. It
would look like:
```

```
     compute cv1 = cov .
     compute cv2 = cov .
     compute cv3 = cov .
     compute cv4 = cov .
     compute cv5 = cov .
     compute cv6 = cov .
     manova a1b1 to a2b3  with cv1 cv2 cv3 cv4 cv5 cv6
             / wsfactor = a(2) b(3) /
             print = cellinfo (means) signif (avonly) /
             design .
```

A(i) x S (s) COMPLETELY WITHIN DESIGN WITH ONE COVARIATE

```
set width = 80 .
data list list / a1 a2 a3 a4 … aᵢ cov.  i levels of A
begin data .
a1 a2 a3 a4 … aᵢ   cov   > First subject
a1 a2 a3 a4 … aᵢ   cov
  ↓ S subjects - Each variable typed is the actual score .
end data .
compute cv1 = cov .
compute cv2 = cov .
  .
  .
  .
compute cvᵢ = cov .
manova a1 to aᵢ with cv1 to cvᵢ/
        wsfactor = a(i) /
        print = cellinfo (means) signif (avonly) /
        design .
finish .
```

A(i) x B (j) x C (k) x S (s) COMPLETELY WITHIN DESIGN WITH ONE COVARIATE

```
set width = 80 .
data list list / a1b1 to aᵢbⱼcₖ cov .
begin data .
     a1b1 to aᵢbⱼcₖ cov   | - One line per subject .
end data .
compute cv1 = cov .
compute cv2 = cov .
  .
  .
  .
compute cv(axbxc) = cov .
manova a1b1 to aᵢbⱼcₖ  with cv1 … cv(axbxc)
        / wsfactor = a(i) b(j) c (k) /
        print = cellinfo (means) signif (avonly) /
        design .
finish .
```

MIXED, NESTED, SPLIT PLOT, OR BETWEEN/WITHIN DESIGNS USING METHOD II

For the mixed designs, you will need to:

1. Add the covariate to the subjects' data and to the DATA LIST command as appropriate.

2. Add the appropriate number of COMPUTE statements depending on how many repeated trials there are in the design.

We will give one example for a **B[b] x C[c] x (A[i] x S) Design**. Other variants would follow the same pattern.

B[b] x C[c] x(A[i] x S) Design
'A' is Repeated & 1 Covariate

```
set  width = 80 .
data list list / b c a1 … ai cov.    i levels of A, b levels of B
begin data .                         c levels of C
1 1   a1 … a1  a2 … a2 … ai cov     subjects for B1 C1
. . . .
2 1   a1 … a1  a2 … a2 … ai cov     subjects for B2 C1
. . . .
b 1   a1 … a1  a2 … a2 … ai cov     subjects for Bb C1
. . .
1 2   a1 … a1  a2 … a2 … ai cov     subjects for B1 C2
. . . .
2 2   a1 … a1  a2 … a2 … ai cov     subjects for B2 C2
. . . .
b 2   a1 … a1  a2 … a2 … ai cov     subjects for Bb C2
. . .
1 c   a1 … a1  a2 … a2 … ai cov     subjects for B1 Cc
. . . .
2 c   a1 … a1  a2 … a2 … ai cov     subjects for B2 Cc
. . . .
b c   a1 … a1  a2 … a2 … ai cov     subjects for Bb Cc
. . .                              each 'a?' term = score
end data .
compute cv1 = cov .
   .
   .
   .
compute cvi = cov .
manova a1 to ai by b (1,b) c (1,c)
       with cv1 to cvi
           / wsfactor = a(i) /
             print = cellinfo (means) signif (avonly)/
             design .
finish .
```

An Example of a Simple ANCOVA with 1 Covariate

In the following example, we have added a dependent variable which is a test score (test). We wish to check for significance between 4 schools. However, we think the students may differ in basic ability which confounds our design. Since we have the students' IQ scores, we will use them as a covariate. In interpreting the ancova, check for the significance of the regression of iq and score, the F-ratio based on the residuals, and the adjusted means. The latter represent the means of the residuals.

Setup

```
set width = 80 .
data list list /  school test iq |            iq = covariate
variable labels school 'School'/
  test 'test score' / iq 'iq-covariate'  .
value labels school 1 'Able School' 2 'Bon School'
      3 'Cruise School' 4 'Down School' .
begin data .
1 4   62            ↓
1 6   87          3 7   84
1 3   53          3 7   76
1 5  107          3 5   72
1 1   52          3 5   78
1 2   45          3 5   73
1 2   53          3 6   64
1 2   59          4 7   85
2 4   67          4 8   94
2 6   69          4 9  100
2 3   62          4 8   93
2 3   61          4 9  125
2 2   58          4 11 102
2 3  103          4 9   78
2 4  108          4 10  99
2 3   65          end data .
3 7   81          manova test by  school (1,4) with iq | Requests Ancova
3 8   85                 / omeans = tables (school)
3 7   84                 / pmeans = tables (school)   | Requests Adjusted Means
                         / design .
└→
```

Output

```
CELL NUMBER       1    2    3    4
 Variable
   SCHOOL         1    2    3    4

Combined Observed Means for SCHOOL
Variable .. TEST
        SCHOOL
     Able Sch        WGT.    3.12500
                     UNWGT.  3.12500
     Bon Scho        WGT.    3.50000
                     UNWGT.  3.50000   | ORIGINAL MEANS FOR TEST
     Cruise S        WGT.    6.25000
                     UNWGT.  6.25000
     Down Sch        WGT.    8.87500
                     UNWGT.  8.87500
- - - - - - - - - - - - - - - - - - - - - - - -
Variable .. IQ
        SCHOOL
     Able Sch        WGT.   64.75000
                     UNWGT. 64.75000
     Bon Scho        WGT.   74.12500
                     UNWGT. 74.12500   | ORIGINAL MEANS FOR IQ
     Cruise S        WGT.   76.62500
                     UNWGT. 76.62500
     Down Sch        WGT.   97.00000
                     UNWGT. 97.00000
```

```
Tests of Significance for TEST using UNIQUE sums of squares
Source of Variation     SS     DF       MS        F  Sig of F

WITHIN CELLS          38.00    27     1.41
REGRESSION            13.25     1    13.25      9.41    .005
```

        ↳   TEST & IQ ARE SIGNIFICANTLY CORRELATED

```
SCHOOL               78.38     3    26.13     18.56    .000
```

        ↳   [EFFECT OF SCHOOL IS SIGNIFICANT
                      AFTER IQ COVARIED.]

- -

```
Correlations between Covariates and Predicted Dependent Variable
          COVARIATE
VARIABLE    IQ
TEST      1.000
```

- -

```
Averaged Squared Correlations between Covariates & Predicted Dependent Variable
VARIABLE   AVER. R-SQ
IQ          1.000
```

```
Regression analysis for WITHIN CELLS error term
--- Individual Univariate .9500 confidence intervals
```

        ↳   TEST & IQ REGRESSION MODEL

```
Dependent variable .. TEST              test score

COVARIATE          B      Beta   Std. Err.   t-Value   Sig. of t

IQ              .04185   .50839     .014      3.068      .005


COVARIATE   Lower -95%  CL- Upper

IQ              .014      .070
```

- -

```
Adjusted and Estimated Means
Variable .. TEST              test score
```

CELL	Obs. Mean	Adj. Mean [1]	Est. Mean [2]	Raw Resid. [3]	Std. Resid. [4]
1	3.125	3.685	3.125	.000	.000
2	3.500	3.667	3.500	.000	.000
3	6.250	6.313	6.250	.000	.000
4	8.875	8.085	8.875	.000	.000

```
Combined Adjusted Means for SCHOOL [1]
Variable .. TEST
     SCHOOL
     Able Sch   UNWGT.   3.68478
     Bon Scho   UNWGT.   3.66741
     Cruise S   UNWGT.   6.31278
     Down Sch   UNWGT.   8.08503
```

[1] ADJUSTED MEAN

  Mean DV calculated from the residuals. They can be quite different from the Obs. Means.

[2] ESTIMATED MEAN

  The mean for each cell predicted by the regression model.

[3] RAW RESIDUAL

  The difference between the actual and the predicted values of the DV.

[4] STANDARDIZED RESIDUAL

  The standardized difference between an observed value and the predicted value.

CHAPTER 17: MULTIPLE REGRESSION & PARTIAL CORRELATION

PREDICTION OF A Y SCORE FROM A SET OF X VARIABLES (X_1 TO X_K) & PARTIAL CORRELATION

SUMMARY OF SPSS MINIMAL REGRESSION SETUP [1]

```
set  width = 80 .
data list list/  var list .
begin data .
 data
end data .
regression     / descriptives / variables = var list
               / statistics =  default history
               / dependent = variable name (to be predicted)
               / enter var list / enter var list ... [2]
               / method = stepwise (var list)  ... [2]
               / method = forward (var list)   ... [2]
               / method = backward (var list)   ... [2]
               / method = remove (var list)   ... [2]
               / casewise = defaults all mahal
               / scatterplot (*res *pred) .
finish .
```

REAL WORLD EXAMPLE - PREDICT 'FIN' (GRADE ON A FINAL EXAM FROM 'T1' & 'T2' - TWO TEST SCORES)

```
set width = 80 .
data list list / t1 t2 fin .
variable labels t1 'test1' / t2 'test2'/ fin 'final grade'.
begin data .
43 61 129
        etc. (see later)          Predicts fin from t1 & t2
43 51 39
20 59 91
end data .
regression   / descriptives / variables = t1 t2 fin
             / statistics =  default history
             / dependent = fin
             / method = enter t1 t2 .   t1 & t2 must be used
finish .
```

---

1 Use **data list free /** *var list* . for SPSS/PC +™ 4.0 . Assume for all setups.

2 Pick one or more of these methods of variable selection.

PURPOSE OF THE PROCEDURE AND STATISTICS

Multiple regression is a complex topic and something of an art form. This section is primarily to give you a brief introduction into setting up a simple regression analysis. There are nuances and important points galore. I would not attempt such an analysis without first entering some serious study of the topic. However, we will show you some simple setups and examples. Please read a standard text to understand what all the statistics mean.

Multiple regression is like the linear regression we saw in Chapter 13. There we had two variables, **X** and **Y**. We attempted to see if **X** and **Y** were related in a linear fashion (straight line), whether the relationship was statistically significant, and the strength of the relationship. The discussion hinged around the equation for the regression line:

$$Y' = Slope \cdot X + Intercept$$

and the value of the Pearson's correlation coefficient :

$$r = \frac{\sum Z_x Z_y}{n}$$

In multiple regression, we have a similar situation except that there are several predictor variables or in other words, many Xs for our one Y variable. We want to develop an equation to predict Y from these Xs. The equation would look the following:

$$Y' = B_0 + B_1 X_1 + B_2 X_2 + B_3 X_3 + ... + B_k X_k$$

Where:

B_0 = Constant

B_1 = Regression coefficient for variable X_1

X_1 = First predictor variable

$B_2 X_2$ = Coefficient and variable for the ' 2nd ' predictor variable - X_2

$B_k X_k$ = Coefficient and variable for the ' kth ' predictor variable - X_k

B_o is similar to the Intercept term of the simple regression equation. B_1, B_2, ... , B_k are similar to the slope.

To determine the predictive strength of the relationship, you would compute a statistic referred to as the **Multiple R**. This statistic is just the Pearson's Correlation (r) coefficient between the subjects' real **Y** score and the **Y'** (prediction based on the equation $Y' = B_o + X_1B_1 + X_1B_1 + ... + X_kB_k$). Thus:

$$\boxed{\textbf{Multiple R} = \textbf{r}_{Y,Y'}}$$

If the Multiple R is high, then the equation predicts the real scores well. Our discussion will center around the following questions:

Questions:

1. Do we have a significant equation?

2. What variables should there be in the equation?

3. How should we test them?

4. How good is the equation?

5. How about outliers?

6. How about nonlinear relationships?

Our examples will be based on a simple data set, where we have two test scores (**t1**, **t2**) for each subject and a final exam score (**fin**). We wish to see if **fin** can be successfully predicted from **t1** and **t2** and develop an equation for this prediction. Thus 2 subjects' data would look like:

t1	t2	fin
43	61	129
50	47	60

We will present the simplest regression command with appropriate annotations just to get started. The command (**regression**) asks for or declares:

- Basic Descriptive Statistics (**descriptives**): means, standard deviations and a correlation matrix of the variables being used.
- Variables used in the analysis (**variables = t1 t2 fin**) .

- Regression statistics (**statistics = default history**): The regression equation and how it was developed, dependent of method of entry (see later).

- Dependent variables (**dependent = fin**): The variable to be predict or to serve as our Y'.

- Method of entry (**method = enter t1 t2**): SPSS gives you several options on how the predictor variables may be selected for the equation. We will discuss this in detail. In our first example, we will force both t1 and t2 to be used in the equation.

Put it all together and the command would look like:

regression / descriptives / variables = t1 t2 fin / statistics = default history / dependent = fin / method = enter t1 t2 .	Gives Basic Stats Variables to Be Used Regression Statistics Variable to Predict Method of Entry : Both t1 and t2 used

A complete setup would be:

SETUP WITH t1 & t2 AT ENTERING AT SAME TIME AND BEING USED

```
set width = 80 .
data list list / t1 t2 fin .
variable labels t1 'test1' / t2 'test2'/ fin 'final grade'.
begin data .
43 61 129
50 47 60
47 79 119
24 40 100
47 60 79
57 59 99
42 61 92
42 79 107
69 83 156
48 67 110
59 74 116
21 40 49
52 71 107
35 40 125
35 57 64
59 58 100
68 66 138
```

```
38  58  63
45  24  82
37  48  73
54  100 132
45  83  87
31  70  89
38  48  99
67  85  119
30  14  100
19  55  84
71  100 166
80  94  111
47  45  110
46  58  93
59  90  141
48  84  99
68  81  114
43  49  96
31  54  39
64  87  149
19  36  53
43  51  39
20  59  91
end data .
regression      / descriptives / variables = t1 t2 fin
                / statistics =  default history
                / dependent = fin
                / method = enter t1 t2 .
finish .
```

As we examine the output we will highlight the answers to our questions with gray boxes. We will see that there is a significant relationship. However, only one of the variables in the equation is statistically significant.

OUTPUT

```
    etc.
    45  regression / descriptives / variables = t1 t2 fin
    46       / statistics =  default history
    47       / dependent = fin
    48       / method = enter t1 t2 .


    * * * *   M U L T I P L E   R E G R E S S I O N   * * * *
```

1.

	Mean	Std Dev	Label
T1	46.025	15.408	test1
T2	62.875	20.087	test2
FIN	99.475	30.323	final grade

N of Cases =   40

2.

Correlation:

	T1	T2	FIN
T1	1.000	.672	.644
T2	.672	1.000	.585
FIN	.644	.585	1.000

Equation Number 1   Dependent Variable..   FIN   final grade

Block Number 1. Method: Enter   T1   T2

Variable(s) Entered on Step Number
    1..   T2   test2
    2..   T1   test1

3.

Multiple R	.67588
R Square	.45681
Adjusted R Square	.42745
Standard Error	22.94455

4.

Analysis of Variance

	DF	Sum of Squares	Mean Square
Regression	2	16381.23591	8190.61796
Residual	37	19478.73909	526.45241

F =   15.55814   Signif F =   .0000

5.

---------- Variables in the Equation -----------

Variable	B	SE B	Beta	T	Sig T
T2	.418835	.246951	.277454	1.696	.0983
T1	.900285	.321944	.457464	2.796	.0081
(Constant)	31.705103	12.831420		2.471	.0182

Equation Number 1   Dependent Variable..   FIN   final grade

6.

Summary table

Step	MultR	Rsq	F(Eqn)	SigF		Variable	BetaIn
1					In:	T2	.5848
2	.6759	.4568	15.558	.000	In:	T1	.4575

IMPORTANT INTERPRETATIVE POINTS OF THE OUTPUT

1. Black Box 1 contains the means and standard deviations of **fin, t1,** and **t2.**

2. Black Box 2 contains the correlation matrix for **fin, t1,** and **t2. Note that t1 has the highest Pearson's r with fin with a value of .644.** t2 and fin have a correlation of only .585.

3. Black Box 3 contains the Multiple R for the equation :

    a. The value is .67588. Multiple R can range between $\pm$ 1.0.

    b. Multiple R^2 (proportion of explained variance for the equation) = .45681.

    c. Adjusted R square = .42745. The Multiple R^2 is positively biased, meaning that when calculated from a sample, the value tends to be too big. Adjusted R square corrects for the bias. Note the adjusted value is less than Multiple R^2 (.42745 < .65681).

    d. The standard error of prediction = 22.94455. Roughly speaking this is the spread around the regression line.

4. Black Box 4 contains the *F*-test for the regression. Since $F_{(2,37)}$ = 15.55814 and *p.* < .0001, we have statistical significance. Remember that the **Signif F = .0000** is not really a probability of zero but is interpreted as less than .0001. As this is much less than .05 or .01, most people would say we have a significant result.

5. Black Box 5 presents the Regression Equation in the column **B** :

    a. The actual equation is of the form:
    $$Y' = B_0 + B_1 X_1 + B_2 X_2$$
    with SPSS referring to B_0 as the ' **(constant)** '. For our data, the equation would be:
    $$\text{Fin}' = 31.7705103 + .900285 \bullet T_1 + .418835 \bullet T_2$$

    b. The standard errors for B_0, B_1, B_2 are presented in the column **SE B.**

    c. Column **Beta** presents the standardized regression coefficients. These would be used to produce an equation to predict the **z score** (standardized score)   for **Y'** or in our case the **z score** predicted for **Fin**. The equation would be:

$$Z_{Y'} = \beta_1 Z_{X_1} + \beta_2 Z_{X_2}$$

with SPSS referring to **B$_0$** as the ' **(constant)** '. For our data, the equation would be:

$$Z_{Fin'} = .457464 \cdot Z_{T1} + .277454 \cdot Z_{T2}$$

It is arguable about how useful this equation is. **The Beta coefficients give some inkling as to how important each variable is to the equation. Note that this is not absolute. The situation is much more complicated than just examining the coefficients.** You must consult a regression text (see the References). We regret that we cannot fully discuss the issue here.

6. <u>Black Box 6</u> Presents t-tests for the significance of the B$_0$, B$_1$, B$_2$ terms. **This is most important.** Each term is compared against a null hypothesis of zero. If the term is not statistically significant, then it really shouldn't be used in the equation, despite its numerical value. Recall all the terms are in our equation because we forced them in with the '**method = enter t1 t2**' command.

For our equation, we see that T2 is not significant while T1 and the Constant are significant. Check the table below:

```
Variable        T     Sig T

T2            1.696   .0983    Not significant, p. > .05

T1            2.796   .0081    Significant
(Constant)    2.471   .0182    Significant
```

SELECTION OF VARIABLES WITH THE 'METHOD = ...' COMMAND

The equation developed is thus less than successful as it contains what seems to be a statistically insignificant term. If you have read about multiple regression then you know that there are several methods of variable entry or selection. It is (as always) controversial which method is better. Howell (1987) recommends either forced entry (you determine the order based on some apriori schema) or stepwise regression. We will give you the choices and show two examples. Please read more if you want to use one of these methods wisely. The various methods are listed as they would appear. You use one or more of them. We will show them one at a time.

```
regression      / descriptives / variables = var list
                / statistics =   default history
                / dependent = variable name (to be predicted)
                / enter var list / enter var list   ...
                / method = stepwise (var list)   ...
                / method = forward (var list)    ...
                / method = backward (var list)   ...
                / method = remove (var list).  ...
```

METHOD	DEFINITION
Enter	Forces Variables into equation in order and groups specified. Recommended if you have hypotheses about importance of variables. This is also called **Hierarchical** entry.
Forward	First variable entered as highest absolute correlation coefficient. Next entered is the variable with the highest partial correlation (see 17.26) coefficient, or, in order words, the one that adds the most to the Multiple R^2. You can set various statistical criteria for entry. Default is a p. $\leq$ .05 for the change or F = 3.84.
Backward	All variables are entered in the equation. Variables are dropped (the one with the smallest partial correlation first) and the equation recomputed. The process stops when a noticeable change from the full equation's Multiple R^2 is noted. There are criteria for removal. Minimal F-values ($<$ 2.71) and p values ($<$ .10) are used. In other words, the least significant are dropped first.
Stepwise	**The most commonly used and recommended method.** It is a combination of both Forward and Backward. A variable is entered in the manner of Forward selection, then another variable is entered. The first variable is examined in the manner of Backward selection for elimination. This continues until all variables are examined

and no more variables meet entry or elimination criteria. (*p* of entry must be < *p* of removal or F of entry must be > F for removal).

Remove   Eliminates Variables into equation in order and groups specified.

HIERARCHICAL REGRESSION with 'ENTER'

In our first example, we use ENTER = T1 T2 . Both variables were forced into the equation. In our next example, we use **enter** in a hierarchical fashion to force **t2** into the equation and then entered **t1**. Look at the changes in the sections called Blocks which we have highlighted . Note:

1. In Block One, t2 is a significant predictor.

2. In Block Two, with t1 entered, t2 again becomes nonsignificant.

SETUP FOR FORCED ENTRY: FIRST *t2*, THEN *t1*

```
set  width = 80 .
data list list/ t1 t2 fin .
variable labels t1 'test1' / t2 'test2'/ fin 'final grade' .
begin data .
43 61 129
        etc.
20 59 91
end data .
regression / descriptives / variables = t1 t2 fin
         / statistics =  default history
         / dependent = fin
         / enter t2 / enter t1 .
finish .
```

OUTPUT WHEN t2 FORCED TO ENTER FIRST

```
etc.
  45   regression / descriptives / variables = t1 t2 fin
  46           / statistics =  default history
  47           / dependent = fin
  48           / enter t2 / enter t1 .

         Mean  Std Dev  Label
etc.

N of Cases =     40

Correlation:
                 T1          T2          FIN

T1             1.000        .672        .644
T2              .672       1.000        .585
FIN             .644        .585       1.000
```

```
* * * *   M U L T I P L E   R E G R E S S I O N   * * * *
```

Equation Number 1   Dependent Variable..   FIN   final grade

Block Number 1. Method: Enter   T2

Variable(s) Entered on Step Number☞ **t2 entered first**
   1..   T2   test2

Multiple R	.58482
R Square	.34201 --- **strength of regression**
Adjusted R Square	.32469
Standard Error	24.91856

Analysis of Variance

	DF	Sum of Squares	Mean Square
Regression	1	12264.45628	12264.45628
Residual	38	23595.51872	620.93470

F =   19.75160   **Signif F = .0001 -> Significant Regressions**

-- Variables in the Equation --☞ **Equation for t2 [fin' = .882819 t2 + 43.967739]**

Variable	B	SE B	Beta	T	Sig T
T2	.882819	.198642	.584816	4.444	.0001 - t2 **significant**
(Constant)	43.967739	13.096318		3.357	.0018

------------ Variables not in the Equation ------------

Variable	Beta In	Partial	Min Toler	T	Sig T
T1	.457464	.417700	.548573	2.796	.0081

End Block Number 1   All requested variables entered.

Equation Number 1   Dependent Variable..   FIN   final grade

Block Number 2. Method: Enter   T1

Variable(s) Entered on Step Number ☞ **t1 added to equation**
   2..   T1   test1

Multiple R	.67588
R Square	.45681
Adjusted R Square	.42745
Standard Error	22.94455

Analysis of Variance

	DF	Sum of Squares	Mean Square
Regression	2	16381.23591	8190.61796
Residual	37	19478.73909	526.45241

F =   15.55814   Signif F = .0000

------------------ Variables in the Equation ------------------

Variable	B	SE B	Beta	T	Sig T
T2	.418835	.246951	.277454	1.696	.0983 - t2 **NOT SIGNIFICANT**
T1	.900285	.321944	.457464	2.796	.0081 - t1 **significant**
(Constant)	31.705103	12.831420		2.471	.0182

In summary, we get a different picture from each **method** command. An equation based on **t1** alone, looks like a better bet. In the next example, we let **Method = Stepwise** decide and develop it for us. Note that two variables examples are overly simplistic but we're trying to show the setup structure.

STEPWISE REGRESSION - LET THE PROGRAM FIGURE OUT THE BEST VARIABLES

```
set width = 80 .
data list list/ t1 t2 fin .
variable labels t1 'test1' / t2 'test2'/ fin 'final grade' .
begin data .
43 61 129

            etc.

20 59 91
end data .
regression  / descriptives / variables = t1 t2 fin
            / statistics =  default history
            / dependent = fin
            / method = stepwise .
finish .
```

OUTPUT

```
etc.
  45  regression / descriptives / variables = t1 t2 fin
  46           / statistics =  default history
  47           / dependent = fin
  48           / method = stepwise .

      * * * *   MULTIPLE   REGRESSION   * * * *

          Mean  Std Dev  Label
etc.

Correlation:
              T1          T2          FIN
T1         1.000        .672        .644
T2          .672       1.000        .585
```

FIN   **.644**   .585   1.00☞ | T1 and Fin have largest r |

```
Equation Number 1    Dependent Variable..   FIN    final grade

Block Number  1.  Method: Stepwise     Criteria   PIN  .0500    POUT  .1000

Variable(s) Entered on Step Number
```

1.. T1   test1   ☞ | t1 entered first as largest correlation with fin |

```
Multiple R          .64388
R Square            .41458
Adjusted R Square   .39918
Standard Error    23.50425
```

```
Analysis of Variance
                      DF        Sum of Squares       Mean Square
Regression             1          14866.88784        14866.88784
Residual              38          20993.08716          552.44966

F =      26.91085       Signif F =   .0000

------------------ Variables in the Equation ------------------

Variable              B        SE B        Beta        T    Sig T

T1             1.267152    .244267     .643880      5.188   .0000
(Constant)    41.154348  11.840718                  3.476   .0013

------------- Variables not in the Equation -------------

Variable     Beta In  Partial  Min Toler        T   Sig T

T2            .277454  .268581   .548573      1.696   .0983
```

┌───┐
│ ☞ Program produces 1 equation based only on t1 due to the   │
│   nonsignificance of t2.   │
│   │
│   Equation would be: Fin' = 1.267152 t1 + 41.154348   │
└───┘

```
End Block Number   1   PIN =      .050 Limits reached.
```

Finally, we get a different picture from each **method** command.

Stepwise   Fin' = 1.267152 • t1 + 41.154348

Enter t2 / Enter t1 Fin' = .882819 • t2 + 43.967739

Enter t1 t2   Fin' = 31.7705103 + .900285 • t1 +
$$.418835 \cdot t2$$

The equation based on t1 alone looks like a better bet as produced by **Stepwise**.

FURTHER EXAMINATIONS OF YOUR DATA

We've presented a simple set of regressions. However, there are many other interesting things that can be done with REGRESSION and many things your data should be checked for. Multiple regression is subject to various assumptions like all of the parametric statistics (normality, homogeneity of variance, homoscedasticity). SPSS can check for most. We will present two common problems. More thorough examinations of the topic can be found in our references.

OUTLIERS

One nasty problem is the existence of outliers in the data. Outliers are extreme scores that can radically distort your statistical analyses. We looked at outliers before in using EXAMINE. However useful, that program doesn't test for multivariate outliers. In other words, consider a set of scores for one person as defining a point in space or a place in a scattergram. Just as a univariate normal distribution has a *center* which is the mean, the scattergram has a center called the centroid. This is the point with coordinates that are the means of the variables being used. Thus if you only have a univariate distribution with scores called X, the mean is $\overline{X}$. If you have a scattergram with the variables X and Y, the centroid of the scattergram is the point with the coordinates ($\overline{X}$, $\overline{Y}$). In a three-dimensional scattergram (imagine a watermelon in space) defined by X, Y, and Z, the centroid would be ($\overline{X}$, $\overline{Y}$, $\overline{Z}$).

A multivariate outlier, to make a long story short, is an (X, Y, etc) point that is very far away from the centroid. "Very far away" should be defined statistically. We will show you the effects of an outlier on our regression data and also one way to spot one using **Mahalanobis' Distance.** Mahalanobis was a statistician from India who developed a method of measuring how far away a data point is from the centroid of a multivariate distribution.

In the following example:

- We will add an outlier to our data set. We will add a case with the following scores:

t1	t2	fin
200	300	36

- Show the effect on our regression
- Show how to find the outlier point with the addition of the REGRESSION subcommand :

```
/ casewise = defaults all mahal
```

Let's first look at the effects on our regression. We add the outlier to our setup.

```
set width = 80 .
data list list/ t1 t2 fin .
variable labels t1 'test1' / t2 'test2'/ fin 'final grade'
begin data   .
43 61 129
          etc.
20 59 91
200 300 36  [--> I'm the outlier]
end data .
regression  / descriptives / variables = t1 t2 fin
            / statistics = default history
            / dependent = fin
            / method = enter t1 t2 .
finish .
```

In the following output, look for the dramatic changes in the correlation matrix and regression equation - all generated by that one additional point. We will highlight the differences:

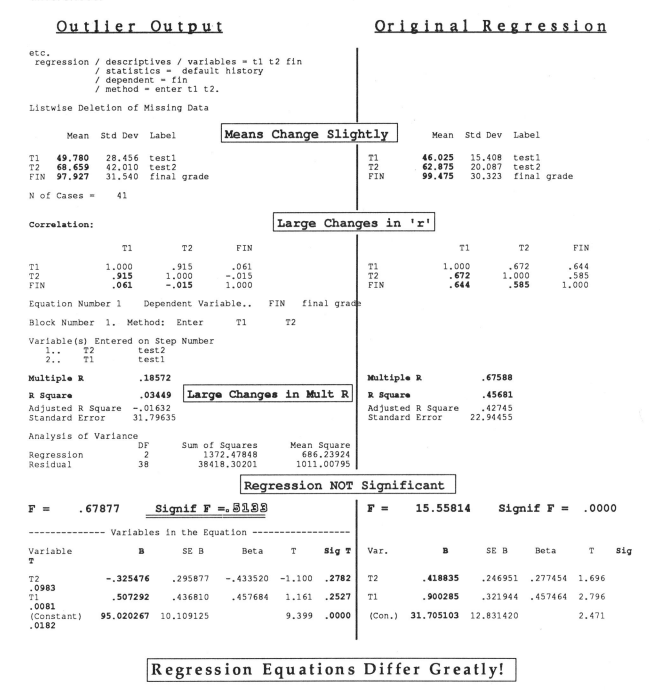

Outlier Output

Original Regression

```
etc.
 regression / descriptives / variables = t1 t2 fin
            / statistics =  default history
            / dependent = fin
            / method = enter t1 t2.

Listwise Deletion of Missing Data
```

Means Change Slightly

```
        Mean  Std Dev  Label                              Mean   Std Dev  Label

T1    49.780  28.456   test1                       T1    46.025  15.408   test1
T2    68.659  42.010   test2                       T2    62.875  20.087   test2
FIN   97.927  31.540   final grade                 FIN   99.475  30.323   final grade

N of Cases =   41
```

Correlation: **Large Changes in 'r'**

```
          T1       T2       FIN                          T1       T2       FIN

T1     1.000     .915     .061            T1         1.000     .672     .644
T2      .915    1.000    -.015            T2          .672    1.000     .585
FIN     .061    -.015    1.000            FIN         .644     .585    1.000
```

```
Equation Number 1    Dependent Variable..    FIN    final grade

Block Number  1.  Method: Enter    T1      T2

Variable(s) Entered on Step Number
     1..    T2        test2
     2..    T1        test1
```

```
Multiple R        .18572                    Multiple R        .67588
```

R Square   .03449 **Large Changes in Mult R** **R Square   .45681**

```
Adjusted R Square  -.01632                  Adjusted R Square  .42745
Standard Error   31.79635                   Standard Error   22.94455

Analysis of Variance
                  DF    Sum of Squares    Mean Square
Regression         2        1372.47848      686.23924
Residual          38       38418.30201     1011.00795
```

Regression NOT Significant

```
F =    .67877     Signif F =.5133          F =    15.55814     Signif F =  .0000

-------------- Variables in the Equation ------------------

Variable        B          SE B       Beta       T       Sig T      Var.         B         SE B      Beta       T      Sig
T
T2          -.325476    .295877    -.433520   -1.100    .2782      T2       .418835    .246951   .277454   1.696
.0983
T1           .507292    .436810     .457684    1.161    .2527      T1       .900285    .321944   .457464   2.796
.0081
(Constant)  95.020267  10.109125               9.399    .0000      (Con.)  31.705103  12.831420            2.471
.0182
```

Regression Equations Differ Greatly!

Fin' = 95.020267 + .507292•t1   Fin' = 31.7705103 + .900285•t1
       -.325476 •t2   + .418835•t2

We see that the addition of one point would totally change the regression situation. The point did not change the means of the variables very much, so how are we to detect the problem. One way to do this (there are others) is to request the Mahalanobis' Distance for, each case. This would detect the outlier. We would add the following subcommand to the REGRESSION command:

```
/ casewise = defaults all mahal
```

The entire setup would appear as:

LOOKING FOR OUTLIERS WITH MAHALANOBIS' DISTANCE

```
set width = 80 .
data list list/ t1 t2 fin .
variable labels t1 'test1' / t2 'test2'/ fin 'final grade'
begin data   .
43 61 129

        etc.

20 59 91
200 300 36   [--> I'm the outlier]
end data .
regression   / descriptives / variables = t1 t2 fin
        / statistics = default history
        / dependent = fin
        / method = enter t1 t2
        / casewise = defaults all mahal
finish .
```

The command will produce an additional chart and graph to our REGRESSION output. In the annotated output look for:

Case# -	Identifies the subject
Standardized Residual	

```
                          -3.0       0.0       3.0
              Case #    0:.......:.........:0
                  1  .          . *       .
```

(a Standardized or z score graph of *Resid - we will discuss this graph in the next section)

Fin	The Variable to Be Predicted
*Pred	The Predicted value for Fin
*Resid	The difference between Fin and the Predicted Value
*Mahal	The Mahalanobis' Distance (our outlier check) !
	See the big value (30.6855) for our outlier - Case 41

```
Y' or Predicted Value of Fin (Fin')
Fin' = 95.020267 + 0.507292X43 - 0.325476x61
     = 96.9788
```

etc. - See previous output for Outlier Data Set
Equation Number 1   Dependent Variable..   FIN   final gra
Casewise Plot of Standardized Residual

*: Selected   M: Missing

```
Y - Y'
Fin - Fin'
129 - 96.9798 =
32.0202
```

	-3.0 0.0 3.0			
Case #	O:........:........:O	FIN	*PRED	*RESID	*MAHAL
1	. . . *	129.00	96.9798	32.0202	.0645
2	. * . .	60.00	105.0875	-45.0875	1.6696
3	. . .*	119.00	93.1504	25.8496	.6977
4	. .*	100.00	94.1762	5.8238	.9518
5	. * .	79.00	99.3345	-20.3345	.0929
6	. *.	99.00	104.7328	-5.7328	1.3688
7	. *	92.00	96.4725	-4.4725	.1028
8	. . *	107.00	90.6140	16.3860	1.5800
9	. . *	156.00	103.0089	52.9911	.9229
10	. .*	110.00	97.5634	12.4366	.0058
11	. .*	116.00	100.8653	15.1347	.2799
12	. * .	49.00	92.6544	-43.6544	1.3833
13	. .*	107.00	98.2907	8.7093	.0076
14	. . *	125.00	99.7565	25.2435	.5321
15	. * .	64.00	94.2234	-30.2234	.5083
16	. *.	100.00	106.0729	-6.0729	1.9542
17	. . *	138.00	108.0347	29.9653	2.9834
18	. * .	63.00	95.4198	-32.4198	.2668
19	. * .	82.00	110.0370	-28.0370	5.0835
20	. *.	73.00	98.1672	-25.1672	.2418
21	. . *	132.00	89.8665	42.1335	2.2998
22	. *	87.00	90.8339	-3.8339	1.5261
23	. *	89.00	87.9630	1.0370	2.9045
24	. *	99.00	98.6745	.3255	.2496
25	. . *	119.00	101.3434	17.6566	.5315
26	. *.	100.00	105.6824	-5.6824	3.1892
27	. *	84.00	86.7577	-2.7577	3.8663
28	. . *	166.00	98.4904	67.5096	.5812
29	. .*	111.00	105.0089	5.9911	1.9557
30	. .*	110.00	104.2166	5.7834	1.3818
31	. *.	93.00	99.4781	-6.4781	.1245
32	. . *	141.00	95.6577	45.3423	.3789
33	. .*	99.00	92.0303	6.9697	1.0946
34	. .*	114.00	103.1526	10.8474	.9304
35	. *	96.00	100.8855	-4.8855	.4389
36	. * .	39.00	93.1706	-54.1706	.8320
37	. . *	149.00	99.1706	49.8294	.2523
38	. * .	53.00	92.9417	-39.9417	1.4445
39	. * .	39.00	100.2346	-61.2346	.3072
40	. *	91.00	85.9630	5.0370	4.3279
41	. * .	36.00	98.8360	-62.8360	30.6855
Case #	O:........:........:O	FIN	*PRED	*RESID	*MAHAL
	-3.0 0.0 3.0			

Distance From the Centroid

Our Outlier with a BIG MAHAL

We see that the output identifies **case # 41** as an outlier because it is so far way from the center of its multivariate scattergram. As we have seen the data analyzed without this case being present, we know that it completely changed the analyses. If we had just seen the output without checking for the Mahalanobis' distance, we would have been misled. Thus it is recommended to run such a check.

Case 41 could have been a typo. It could have been an individual that was inappropriate for the sample. Once identified and if justified, the case could be eliminated from the data set. One could use the selection procedures described in Chapter 20, such as the SELECT IF command, to remove case 41 from the analysis as follows:

```
set width = 80 .
data list list/ t1 t2 fin .
        etc.
20 59 91
200 300 36   [--> I'm the outlier]
end data .
select if ($casenum ne 41) .[$casenum is an internal
                            SPSS variable]
regression    / descriptives / variables = t1 t2 fin
              / statistics = default history
              / dependent = fin
              / method = enter t1 t2.
finish .
```

There are other ways to identify and deal with outliers. I've presented an extreme case to show you a simple setup and solution.

Note that we used an internal variable of SPSS called $casenum. When SPSS reads the data, it numbers them. Since we knew the case's position from the regression, we could remove it.

THE RELATIONSHIP IS NONLINEAR

Our last data-related problem will be a nonlinear relationship. Multiple regression assumes linear relationships (for the beginner - straight lines or planes, etc.). If the data are in some kind of curved relationship or other weird shape, you have trouble. In fact, such a nonlinear or not straight relationship can give you a pretty good Multiple R. The question is how to identify this problem. SPSS has two displays that can alert you to this risk. The first is the **graph of the standardized residuals** that we just saw. The second is a **graph of the residual values versus the predicted values** for your data. Nonlinear relationships can produce distinctive patterns.

We've generated a new data set with a dependent variable called FIN2. It depends on T1 and T2 because it is calculated by the following formula.

$$\mathbf{fin2} = \sqrt[3]{\mathbf{t1}} + (\mathbf{t2})^2.$$

We will regress FIN2 against T1 and T2. You will see that even though the relationship of the three variables is clearly nonlinear, the linear fit is pretty good. After presenting the regression, we will show how we could have detected the nonlinearity.

SETUP

```
set width = 80 .                         31.00    70.00    4903.14
data list list/t1 t2 fin2.               38.00    48.00    2307.36
begin data .                             67.00    85.00    7229.06
    43.00    61.00    3724.50            30.00    14.00     199.11
    50.00    47.00    2212.68            19.00    55.00    3027.67
    47.00    79.00    6244.61            71.00   100.00   10004.14
    24.00    40.00    1602.88            80.00    94.00    8840.31
    47.00    60.00    3603.61            47.00    45.00    2028.61
    57.00    59.00    3484.85            46.00    58.00    3367.58
    42.00    61.00    3724.48            59.00    90.00    8103.89
    42.00    79.00    6244.48            48.00    84.00    7059.63
    69.00    83.00    6893.10            68.00    81.00    6565.08
    48.00    67.00    4492.63            43.00    49.00    2404.50
    59.00    74.00    5479.89            31.00    54.00    2919.14
    21.00    40.00    1602.76            64.00    87.00    7573.00
    52.00    71.00    5044.73            19.00    36.00    1298.67
    35.00    40.00    1603.27            43.00    51.00    2604.50
    35.00    57.00    3252.27            20.00    59.00    3483.71
    59.00    58.00    3367.89         end data .
    68.00    66.00    4360.08         regression    / descriptives
    38.00    58.00    3367.36                       / variables = fin2 t1 t2
    45.00    24.00     579.56                       / statistics = default history
    37.00    48.00    2307.33                       / dependent = fin2
    54.00   100.00   10003.78                       / method = stepwise.
    45.00    83.00    6892.56         finish.
```

OUTPUT

```
set width = 80 .
data list list/ t1 t2 fin2 .
comment fin2 = (t1)**(1/3) + t2 ** 2 .
begin data .
end data .
regression  / descriptives
            / variables = fin2 t1 t2
            / statistics = default history
            / dependent = fin2
            / method = stepwise.
```

```
          * * * *   M U L T I P L E   R E G R E S S I O N   * * * *
Listwise Deletion of Missing Data

          Mean  Std Devi  Label

FIN2    4350.210  2534.755
T1        46.025    15.408
T2        62.875    20.087

N of Cases =    40

Correlation:

            FIN2        T1        T2

FIN2       1.000      .689      .980
T1          .689     1.000      .672
T2          .980      .672     1.000

Equation Number 1   Dependent Variable..  FIN2

   Descriptive Statistics are printed on Page   30

Block Number 1. Method: Stepwise    Criteria  PIN .0500   POUT .1000

Variable(s) Entered on Step Number
   1..   T2
```

NOTE: A VERY LARGE MULTIPLE R EVEN THOUGH THE DATA ARE NONLINEAR

Multiple R	.97973
R Square	.95986
Adjusted R Square	.95881
Standard Error	514.45441

Analysis of Variance

	DF	Sum of Squares	Mean Square
Regression	1	240517177.62406	240517177.62406
Residual	38	10057206.86014	264663.33842

F =   908.76651   Signif F =   .0000

```
----------------- Variables in the Equation -----------------

Variable              B        SE B       Beta        T  Sig T

T2          123.629098   4.101045    .979726    30.146  .0000
(Constant) -3422.969549  270.379107            -12.660  .0000
------------ Variables not in the Equation ------------

Variable    Beta In  Partial  Min Toler      T  Sig T

T1          .056450  .208695    .548573   1.298  .2023
End Block Number   1   PIN =     .050 Limits reached.
```

ADDING DISPLAYS TO DETECT NONLINEARITY

Thus, even though we have a nonlinear relationship, we have a very significant Multiple R of substantial value. With further analysis, we might miss the real relationship. As mentioned above, we will add two displays to our setup that would have indicated the possibility of nonlinearity. The REGRESSION setup will now look like:

```
Etc.
regression   / descriptives
             / variables = fin2 t1 t2
             / statistics = default history
             / dependent = fin2
             / method = stepwise
             / casewise = defaults all mahal
             / scatterplot (*res *pred)   .
finish .
```

The rest of the output will look the same as we just presented, so we will not repeat it. It would have the large Multiple R and be highly significant.

We have seen the `/ casewise = defaults all mahal` before. However, if there is nonlinear data, a pattern emerges in the plot of the standardized residuals. We will compare the display from our orginal regression of FIN versus T1 and T2 (fairly linear) versus the same display for FIN2 versus T1 and T1.

The thing to note is that in the left side of the figure (FIN), the standardized residuals seem fairly equally scattered on both sides of zero. This is not the case for the right side (FIN2). The scatter is not equal.

We will also present with the command `/ scatterplot (*res *pred)`, a scatterplot of the residual score versus the predicted score for both regressions. Again the right side is the nonlinear one. Note that the linear side has a random scatterplot. The nonlinear right side has a clear curve to it. It is the nature of this scatterplot that if nonlinearity exists, you may see a curved plot rather than a random scatter.

After we present these two plots, we will show a way to enhance the **casewise** plot with a **SORT CASES** command. It helps in detecting nonlinearity.

COMPARATIVE OUTPUTS FOR CASEWISE DISPLAY

Note Random Scatter For Fin Linear Relationship

Casewise Plot of Standardized Residual

*: Selected   M: Missing

```
           -3.0       0.0       3.0
Case #    O:......:......:O        FIN
    1     .      .     *   .    129.00
    2     .   *     .         .   60.00
    3     .       . *       .    119.00
    4     .       .   *     .    100.00
    5     .     *   .         .   79.00
    6     .       *.        .   99.00
    7     .       *         .   92.00
    8     .       .*        .   107.00
    9     .       .  *      .   156.00
   10     .       .*        .   110.00
   11     .       *         .   116.00
   12     .     * .         .   49.00
   13     .       *         .   107.00
   14     .       .     *   .   125.00
   15     .     * .         .   64.00
   16     .      *.        .   100.00
   17     .       . *       .   138.00
   18     .   *     .         .   63.00
   19     .       *         .   82.00
   20     .     * .         .   73.00
   21     .       .*        .   132.00
   22     .     * .         .   87.00
   23     .       *         .   89.00
   24     .       . *       .   99.00
   25     .      *.        .   119.00
   26     .       .    *    .   100.00
   27     .       . *       .   84.00
   28     .       .    *    .   166.00
   29     .     * .         .   111.00
   30     .       . *       .   110.00
   31     .      *.        .   93.00
   32     .       . *       .   141.00
   33     .      *.        .   99.00
   34     .     * .         .   114.00
   35     .       .*        .   96.00
   36     .  *     .         .   39.00
   37     .       .   *     .   149.00
   38     .      *.        .   53.00
   39     . *      .         .   39.00
   40     .       . *       .   91.00
Case #    O:......:......:O        FIN
           -3.0       0.0       3.0
```

Note Non- Random Scatter For Fin2 NonLinear Relationship

Casewise Plot of Standardized Residual

*: Selected   M: Missing

```
           -3.0       0.0       3.0
Case #    O:......:......:O       FIN2
    1     .     * .         .  3724.50
    2     .       *.        .  2212.68
    3     .       *.        .  6244.61
    4     .       . *       .  1602.88
    5     .     * .         .  3603.61
    6     .     * .         .  3484.85
    7     .     * .         .  3724.48
    8     .       *.        .  6244.48
    9     .       . *       .  6893.10
   10     .     * .         .  4492.63
   11     .       *.        .  5479.89
   12     .       . *       .  1602.76
   13     .     * .         .  5044.73
   14     .       . *       .  1603.27
   15     .     * .         .  3252.27
   16     .     * .         .  3367.89
   17     .     * .         .  4360.08
   18     .     * .         .  3367.36
   19     .       .     *   .   579.56
   20     .       *.        .  2307.33
   21     .       .     *   . 10003.78
   22     .       . *       .  6892.56
   23     .     * .         .  4903.14
   24     .     * .         .  2307.36
   25     .       . *       .  7229.06
   26     .       .       * .   199.11
   27     .     * .         .  3027.67
   28     .       .      *  . 10004.14
   29     .       .    *    .  8840.31
   30     .       *.        .  2028.61
   31     .     * .         .  3367.58
   32     .       . *       .  8103.89
   33     .       . *       .  7059.63
   34     .       . *       .  6565.08
   35     .     * .         .  2404.50
   36     .     * .         .  2919.14
   37     .       . *       .  7573.00
   38     .       . *       .  1298.67
   39     .     * .         .  2604.50
   40     .     * .         .  3483.71
Case #    O:......:......:O       FIN2
           -3.0       0.0       3.0
```

COMPARATIVE OUTPUTS FOR CASEWISE DISPLAY

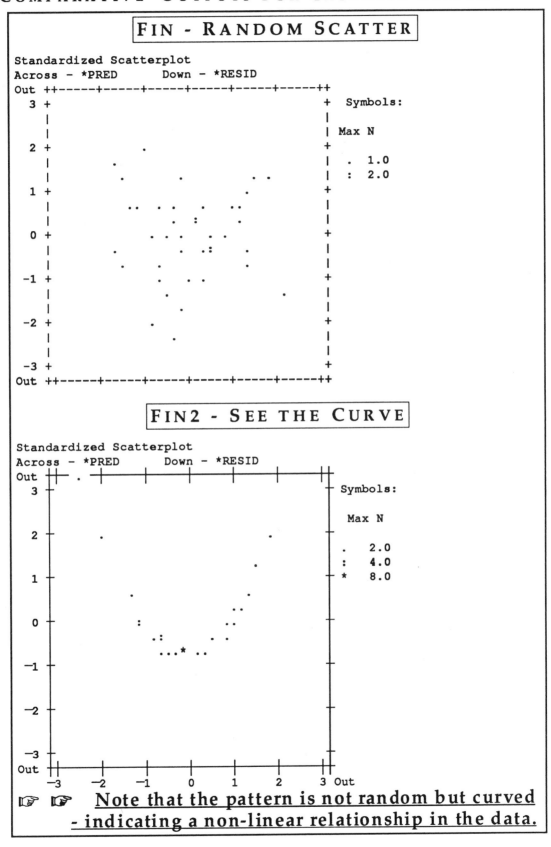

FIN - RANDOM SCATTER

Note that the pattern is not random but curved - indicating a non-linear relationship in the data.

It is possible to make the use of the casewise plot even clearer. If we sort the cases by the variable Fin or Fin2, a nonrandom scatter of the standardized residuals becomes even clearer. Sorting the cases is accomplished by adding the **SORT CASES** command before the REGRESSION command. It will restructure your file so that the cases are processed from highest to lowest (**SORT CASES** can be found in the *SPSS Reference Guide*). The setup would be slightly altered to appear as:

```
Etc.
sort cases by fin2 .
regression  / descriptives
            / variables = fin2 t1 t2
            / statistics = default history
            / dependent = fin2
            / method = stepwise
            / casewise = defaults all mahal
            / scatterplot (*res *pred)  .
finish .
```

Casewise Output

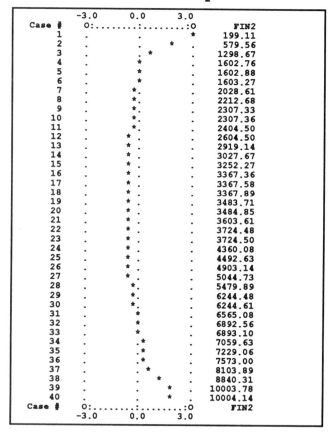

It is clear now that the standardized residuals are not scattered evenly about zero as the values of FIN2 increase. You can understand the plot as a visualization of the regression equation, which is straight, cutting through the curve or bowed shape of the actual relationship of FIN2 to T1 and T2. Below is an idealized schematic of the concept. See how the residuals in the ends of the curve differ from the center.

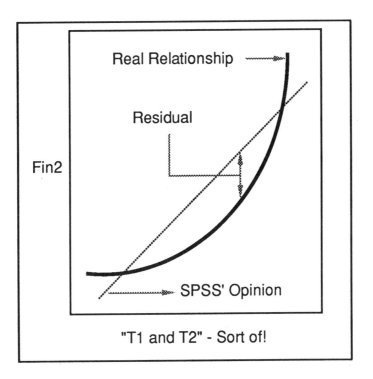

Real Relationship

Residual

Fin2

SPSS' Opinion

"T1 and T2" - Sort of!

Thus, if you look at such a casewise plot of the sorted cases' standardized residuals, and the pattern isn't random - look out! The casewise plot is an important tool for finding other problems in your data. Remember the pattern should be random. You can see other nasty things. For example, the sorted plot should be roughly the same width all the way across, meaning that for each value of FIN2, you have closely the same amount of positive and negative residuals of equal magnitude as FIN2 changes. If not you may violate an assumption of equal variances for the variables at the levels of the other variables (homoscedasticity). You don't want to see a casewise plot like this :

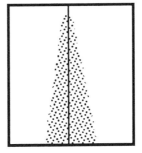

PARTIAL CORRELATION

SUMMARY OF SPSS PARTIAL CORRELATION SETUP

```
set width = 80 .
data list list/ y1 x1 x2 ...xj... xk . 1
begin data .

 y x1 x2 ... xk

end data .
partial corr variables = y1 with x1 by x2 ... xk (# up to k)2
        / significance = twotail
        / statistics  = all .
finish .
```

---

[1] Not available for SPSS/PC +™ 4.0 .

[2] # = level of partial correlation to be calculated (# of variables removed).

REAL WORLD EXAMPLE ($r_{y1x1.x21} = r_{fin,t1.t2}$)

```
set  width = 80 .
data list list/ t1 t2 fin .
variable labels t1 'test1' / t2 'test2'/ fin 'final grade' .
begin data
43 61 129
50 47 60
47 79 119
24 40 100
47 60 79
57 59 99
    etc. - see full data set in text
partial corr variables = fin with t1 by t2(1)
        / significance = twotail
        / statistics  = all .
finish .
```

REAL WORLD EXAMPLE ($r_{x3x4.y1y2y3}$)

```
set width = 80 .
data list list/ x1 to x6 y1 to y4 .
begin data .
3 0 3.10 500 1 15 21 040 049 1
1 1 3.08 410 0 24 52 071 107 5
    etc. - see full data set in text
end data .
partial corr variables = x3 with x4 by y1 to y3 (3)
        /significance = twotail
        /statistics = all .
finish .
```

PURPOSE OF THE STATISTIC

When examining regression data, one useful statistic is the partial correlation coefficient. It gives you an indication of how two variables are related if the effects of a third variable (or even more) are removed from their relationship. It is very helpful in understanding multiple regressions.

The idea is very simple. Let's assume we are interested in the relationship between the variables Y1 and X1. However, X2 is correlated with both of them. What would the correlation of Y1 and X1 be if we removed the variance predicted from X2 from both Y1 and X1? This is the information given in the partial correlation coefficient between Y1 and X1 with X2 **partialed out**. This would be called a **first order partial correlation** coefficient and can be written as:

$$r_{Y1X1.X2}$$

X2 (**called the control variable**) is removed from the correlation coefficient between Y1 and X1. The value is calculated by deriving the regression equations for Y1 as predicted from X2 (Y1' = BX2 +A) and X1 as predicted from X2 (X1' =bX2+a). The residuals for Y1 (Y1- Y1') and X1 (X1-X1') are then computed. A simple Pearson's product moment correlation coefficient is calculated for the residual's. In other words, (Y1- Y1') and (X1-X1') have their correlation coefficient computed. Since the predictions (Y1' and X1') are based on X2, this correlation coefficient (called the partial correlation coefficient) is based on how Y1 and X1 are related if X2 is removed from both of them.

There is no reason why more than one variable's variance cannot be removed from Y1 and X1. Assume that you want to correlate Y1 and X1 but remove X2 and X3. You would predict Y1 from X2 and X2 (Y1' = B_0 + B_1X2 + B_2X3) and X1 from X2 and X3 (X1' = b_0 + b_1X2 + b_2X3) using multiple regression. The residuals for Y1 and X21 based on the multiple regression would be calculated and correlated. The partial correlation coefficient with both X2 and X3 (second order partial) acting as control variables would be written as:

$$r_{Y1X1.X2X3}$$

We will show examples of these situations. SPSS's PARTIAL CORR command is quite simple. You need to identify the variables for which you want to calculate the partial correlation coefficient, which variable you want to remove, and how they should be removed. Do you want to remove just the effect of the variables one at a time, or more? The basic command looks as follows:

```
partial corr variables = Y1 with X1 by X2 ... Xk (# up to k)
        / significance = twotail
        / statistics   = all .
```

PARTIAL CORRELATION COEFFICIENTS WITH FIRST ORDER PARTIALS ($ry1x1.x2$)

In our first example, we have our two test scores, T1 and T2, and the final grade, FIN. We want to see the relationship between T1 and FIN, if T2 is removed or partialed from them. The PARTIAL CORR [partial corr] command would be:

```
partial corr variables = fin with t1 by t2 (1)
        / significance = twotail
        / statistics   = all .
```

Thus:

1. FIN is to be correlated with T1	`[variables = fin with t1]`
2. T2 is to be removed	`[by t2 (1)]`
3. 1 variable only is removed	`[(1)]`

4. Descriptive Statistics and Significance are requested .

Note in the output that:

- The normal Pearson's Correlation Coefficient between FIN and T1 = .6439 (called the Zero Order Partial)

- The Partial Correlation Coefficient between FIN and T1 = .4177 (called the Zero Order Partial) and is statistically significant ($p.$ = .008). Thus removal of T2 lessens the relationship between FIN and T1.

SETUP

```
set  width = 80 .
data list list/ t1 t2 fin .
variable labels t1 'test1' / t2 'test2'/ fin 'final grade' .
begin data
43 61 129
50 47 60
47 79 119
24 40 100
47 60 79
57 59 99
42 61 92
42 79 107
69 83 156
48 67 110
59 74 116
21 40 49
52 71 107
35 40 125
35 57 64
```

```
59 58 100
68 66 138
38 58 63
45 24 82
37 48 73
54 100 132
45 83 87
31 70 89
38 48 99
67 85 119
30 14 100
19 55 84
71 100 166
80 94 111
47 45 110
46 58 93
59 90 141
48 84 99
68 81 114
43 49 96
31 54 39
64 87 149
19 36 53
43 51 39
20 59 91
end data .
partial corr variables = fin with t1 by t2 (1)
              / significance = twotail
              / statistics   = all .
finish .
```

OUTPUT

```
       etc.
  45   partial corr variables = fin with t1 by t2(1)
  46               / significance = twotail
  47               / statistics   = all .

VARIABLE        MEAN      STANDARD DEV    CASES
FIN           99.4750        30.3230        40
T1            46.0250        15.4081        40
T2            62.8750        20.0872        40

ZERO ORDER PARTIALS
                 FIN          T1          T2
FIN           1.0000        .6439        .5848
              (    0)       (   38)      (   38)
              P= .          P= .000      P= .000
T1             .6439        1.0000        .6719
              (   38)       (    0)      (   38)
              P= .000       P= .         P= .000
T2             .5848         .6719       1.0000
              (   38)       (   38)      (    0)
              P= .000       P= .000      P= .
  (COEFFICIENT / (D.F.) / SIGNIFICANCE)


 -  PARTIAL  CORRELATION  COEFFICIENTS  -

CONTROLLING FOR..   T2  ☞ [r_fin,t1 . t2 ]
               T1
FIN            .4177
              (   37)
              P= .008
```

$[r_{fin,t1} \cdot t2]$

An Example of Arithmetic Score Correlated with Height with Grade Controlled

In our second example, we have constructed an artificial data set to demonstrate the concept. Let's say we want to correlate students' score on an arithmetic test with their height. Let's say we test three classes. One class is first-graders, the next is second-graders and the last is third-graders. It seems obvious to me that arithmetic score is strongly correlated with grade. However, as children get older and advance in grade, they also get taller. So if we just correlate height and arithmetic score, we might get a strong correlation but it's really just their grade level that's important.

In the following setup and output (see numbered annotations) , we will do two things to illustrate these relationships:

1 We will plot arithmetic score (ARITH) with HEIGHT but control for GRADE (using PLOT - see Chapter 13). PLOT will indicate a significant and strong relationship.

2 You will note that for each grade there is no relationship for ARITH with HEIGHT but that the three grades string together in a manner to give us a quite significant and powerful but spurious regression.

3 We will run PARTIAL CORR to show that if we remove GRADE from both ARITH and HEIGHT, their correlation disappears.

Setup With Output Following

```
set width = 80 .
data list list / arith height grade .
value labels grade 2 'second' 3 'third' 4 'fourth' .
begin data .
15 49 2
17 51 2
17 49 2
15 51 2
18 51 3
20 53 3
20 51 3
18 53 3
21 53 4
23 55 4
23 53 4
21 55 4
end data .
plot / format = regression / plot = arith with height by grade.
partial corr arith with height by grade (1)
        / significance = twotail
        / statistics = all .
finish .
```

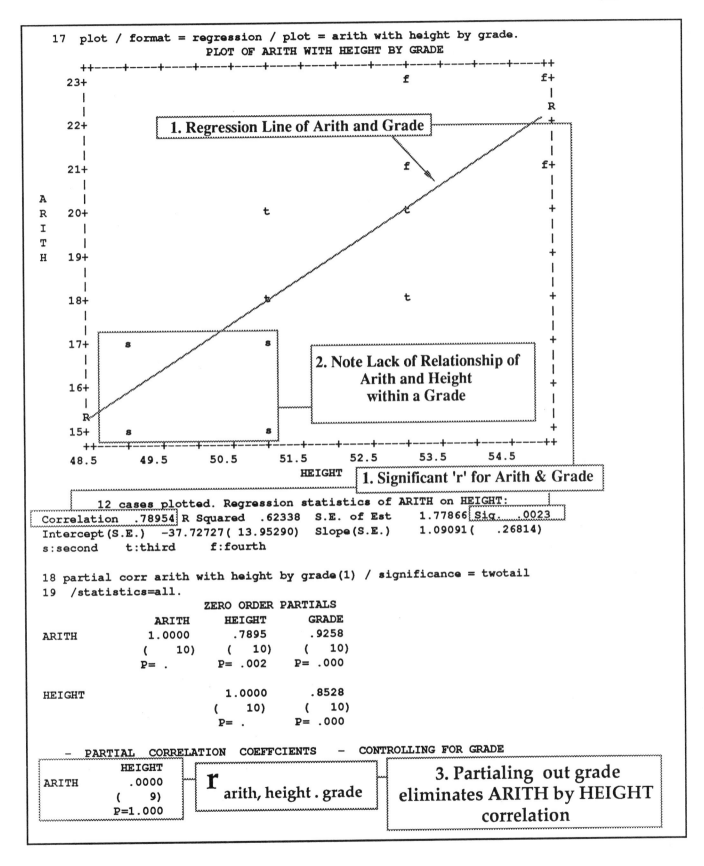

```
17  plot / format = regression / plot = arith with height by grade.
              PLOT OF ARITH WITH HEIGHT BY GRADE
```

1. Regression Line of Arith and Grade

2. Note Lack of Relationship of Arith and Height within a Grade

```
       HEIGHT
```

1. Significant 'r' for Arith & Grade

```
     12 cases plotted. Regression statistics of ARITH on HEIGHT:
 Correlation  .78954  R Squared  .62338  S.E. of Est   1.77866  Sig.   .0023
 Intercept(S.E.)  -37.72727( 13.95290)  Slope(S.E.)   1.09091(   .26814)
 s:second    t:third    f:fourth


18 partial corr arith with height by grade(1) / significance = twotail
19  /statistics=all.
                  ZERO ORDER PARTIALS
             ARITH       HEIGHT       GRADE
 ARITH       1.0000       .7895        .9258
            (   10)      (   10)      (   10)
             P= .         P= .002      P= .000


 HEIGHT                   1.0000       .8528
                         (   10)      (   10)
                          P= .         P= .000


  -  PARTIAL  CORRELATION  COEFFCIENTS  -  CONTROLLING FOR GRADE
             HEIGHT
 ARITH        .0000
            (    9)
             P=1.000
```

r arith, height . grade

3. Partialing out grade eliminates ARITH by HEIGHT correlation

USE OF VARIOUS LEVELS OF CONTROL VARIABLES
($r_{x3x4.y1}$ - etc.) ; ($r_{x3x4.y1y2}$ - etc.)
($r_{x3x4.y1y2y3}$)

In this set of examples, we have the variables X3 and X4; we want to test their correlation as we remove or partial out Y1, Y2, and Y3. However, we will enter several PARTIAL CORR commands to remove Y1 to Y3 separately, in pairs (Y1 & Y2, Y1 & Y3, Y2 & Y3) and finally Y1 to Y3 simultaneously. Note:

- How the number of variables to be removed or partialed out is entered in the PARTIAL CORR command:

      partial corr variables = x3 with x4 by y1 to y3 (1)
      partial corr variables = x3 with x4 by y1 to y3 (2)
      partial corr variables = x3 with x4 by y1 to y3 (3)

- How value of the correlation coefficient between X3 and X4 is reduced as more variables are partialed out.

SETUP

```
set width = 80 .
data list list/ x3 x4 y1 to y4 .
begin data .
 3.10 500   21 040 049 1
 3.08 410   52 071 107 5
 3.50 470   35 040 125 1
 3.43 210   35 057 034 5
 3.39 610   59 058 100 1
 3.76 510   68 066 138 2
 3.71 600   38 058 063 1
 3.00 470   45 024 082 3
 3.47 460   37 048 073 3
 3.69 800   54 100 132 2
 3.24 610   45 083 087 2
 3.46 490   31 070 089 2
 3.39 470   39 048 099 1
 3.90 610   67 085 119 2
 2.76 580   30 014 100 1
 2.70 410   19 055 084 2
 3.77 630   71 100 166 3
 4.00 790   80 094 111 2
 3.40 490   47 045 110 1
end data .
partial corr variables = x3 with x4 by y1 to y3 (1)   | One at a time
        /significance = twotail
        /statistics = all .
partial corr variables = x3 with x4 by y1 to y3 (2)   | All pairs removed
        /significance = twotail
        /statistics = all .
partial corr variables = x3 with x4 by y1 to y3 (3)   | All three at once
        /significance = twotail
        /statistics = all .
finish .
```

OUTPUT

```
1  0  set width = 80 .
2  data list list/ x1 to x6 y1 to y4 .
3  begin data .
22  end data .
23   partial corr variables = x3 with x4 by y1 to y3  (1)
24          /significance = twotail
25          /statistics = all .
```

VARIABLE	MEAN	STANDARD DEV	CASES
X3	3.4079	.3615	19
X4	532.6316	135.0655	19
Y1	45.9474	17.0765	19
Y2	60.8421	24.1759	19
Y3	98.3158	31.5807	19

ZERO ORDER PARTIALS

	X3	**X4**	Y1	Y2	Y3
X3	1.0000	.4698	.7215	.6653	.4077
	(0)	(17)	(17)	(17)	(17)
	P= .	P= .042	P= .000	P= .002	P= .083
X4	.4698	1.0000	.5651	.5219	.5290
	(17)	(0)	(17)	(17)	(17)
	P= .042	P= .	P= .012	P= .022	P= .020
Y1	.7215	.5651	1.0000	.6532	.6660
	(17)	(17)	(0)	(17)	(17)
	P= .000	P= .012	P= .	P= .002	P= .002
Y2	.6653	.5219	.6532	1.0000	.4655
	(17)	(17)	(17)	(0)	(17)
	P= .002	P= .022	P= .002	P= .	P= .045
Y3	.4077	.5290	.6660	.4655	1.0000
	(17)	(17)	(17)	(17)	(0)
	P= .083	P= .020	P= .002	P= .045	P= .

(COEFFICIENT / (D.F.) / SIGNIFICANCE)

- - - - P A R T I A L   C O R R E L A T I O N   C O E F F I C I E N T S - - -

CONTROLLING FOR..   Y1

	X4
X3	.1086
	P= .668

Note reduction of correlation from
r = .4698 to .1086 when Y1 removed

CONTROLLING FOR..   Y2

	X4
X3	.1924
	(16)
	P= .444

CONTROLLING FOR..   Y3

	X4
X3	.3279
	(16)
	P= .184

```
26   partial corr variables = x3 with x4 by y1 to y3 (2)
27           /significance = twotail
28           /statistics = all .
```

.etc

```
CONTROLLING FOR.. Y1    Y2


                    X4
X3                .0201
                (   15)
                 P= .939


CONTROLLING FOR.. Y1    Y3


                    X4
X3                .1497
                (   15)
                 P= .566


CONTROLLING FOR.. Y2    Y3


                    X4
X3                .1489
                (   15)
                 P= .569
```

```
29   partial corr variables = x3 with x4 by y1 to y3 (3)
30           /significance = twotail
31           /statistics = all .
```

etc.

- - - - P A R T I A L   C O R R E L A T I O N   C O E F F I C I E N T S - - -

```
CONTROLLING FOR.. Y1    Y2    Y3


                    X4          |  Note reduction of correlation from
X3                .0650         |  r = .4698 to .0650 when Y1, Y2 , Y3
                (   14)         |  are removed.
                 P= .811        |
```

CHAPTER 18: ASSORTED MULTIVARIATE STATISTICS

EXAMPLES OF SEVERAL POPULAR MULTIVARIATE PROCEDURES

SUMMARY OF MINIMAL SPSS COMMANDS FOR[1]

CANONICAL CORRELATION

manova X_1 to $X_?$ with Y_1 to $Y_?$ /
   print = signif (dimenr eigen)
          discrim (stan cor estim alpha (α)) /
   design .

REAL WORLD EXAMPLE

```
set width = 80 .
data list list/ ses sex gpa sat test1 test2 final eval .
begin data .
2 1 3.6 405 47 57 85 3
     etc.   Canonical Analysis of test1 to eval vs. ses to sat
1 2 3.0 485 22 55 87 1
end data .
manova   test1 to eval with ses to sat/
              print = signif (dimenr eigen)
                         discrim (stan cor estim alpha (.05))/
           design .
finish.
```

DISCRIMINANT ANALYSIS

compute case = $casenum .
discriminant groups = DV_1 (1,?)
   / variables = IV_1 (1,?) IV_2 (1,?) ...etc .
   / method = ? ♦ choose from *direct, wilks, mahal,*
                     maxminf, minresid,
                     rao   (**direct** or **mahal** recommended)
   / priors = size ♦ choose from *equal, size or value list with # of prob. =*
                        to number of DV groups.
   / save class=*var name* scores=*var name* probs=*var name*
   / statistics mean stddev univ raw coeff table
   / plot map cases.
list case *var name sets as in save class = etc. .*

REAL WORLD EXAMPLE

```
set width = 80 .
data list list/ ses sex gpa sat test1 test2 final eval .
    etc.
begin data .     Prediction of ses from gpa to eval
2 1 3.6 405 47 57 85 3
    etc.
1 2 3.0 485 22 55 87 1
end data .
compute case = $casenum | Subject number generated for listing
discriminant groups = ses (1,3) | We want to predict SES
    / variables = test1 test2 final eval | Use these IVs for prediction
    / method = mahal | Select IVs based on Mahalanobis criterion
    / priors = size | Use probabilities from data set for analysis
    / save class = prdses scores = prscore probs = prdprob
    / statistics mean stddev univ raw coeff table
    / plot combined map .| Helps understand functions
list case prdses drscore1 to prdprob3 . | Optional case info printed
finish.
```

FACTOR OR PRINCIPAL COMPONENT ANALYSIS

factor variables = X1 to X? / | variables to be analyzed

print = default fscore / | needed for appropriate statistical output

You might add **corr** for correlation matrix of X1 to X?

plot = eigen rotation (#, #) / | produces **Scree** & **factor loading plot**

#, # = factors to plot

extraction = ? / ♦ choose from **PC**, PAF, Alpha, Image, ULS, GLS, ML

rotation = ? / ♦ choose from **Varimax**, Equamax, Quartimax, Oblimin, Norotate

save reg (all *name*) . | Saves **factor scores** for all factors as name1 to name?

♦ **Bold face** = defaults if not specified.

REAL WORLD EXAMPLE

```
set width = 80 .
data list list/ ses sex gap sat test1 test2 final eval .
    etc.  Factor Analysis of Variable Set
begin data .
2 1 3.6 405 47 57 85 3
    etc.
1 2 3.0 485 22 55 87 1
end data .
compute case = $casenum . | Subject number generated for listing
factor variables = ses sex gap sat test1 test2 final eval /
    print = default fscore /
    plot = eigen   rotation (1,2) / | Factors 1 and 2 plotted
    extraction =  ALPHA / | Alpha extraction chosen
    rotation =   OBLIMIN / | Oblimin rotation chosen
    save reg (all fac) . | Factor scores saved
list case fac1 fac2 fac3 . | Factor scores printed
finish.
```

HOTELLING'S T^2 *

manova DV_1 to DV_k by IV (1,2) /
      print = cellinfo (means)
      homogeneity (cochran bartlett) signif (univ) /
      design .

---

* Note that Hotelling's T^2 is a special case of Manova with just two groups.

MULTIVARIATE ANALYSIS OF VARIANCE

manova DV_1 to DV_k by IV_1 (1,?) IV_2 (1,?) ...etc .
    with COV_1 to COV? /   ♦ For use with a MANCOVA.
    print = cellinfo (means)
    homogeneity (cochran bartlett) signif (univ) /
    design .

REAL WORLD EXAMPLE

```
set width = 80 .
data list list/ ses sex gpa sat test1 test2 final eval .
etc.
begin data .
2 1 3.6 405 47 57 85 3
etc .    Twoway Manova of final eval by SEX & SES
3 1 3.4 385 47 47 38 1
1 2 3.0 485 22 55 87 1
end data .
manova final eval by sex (1,2) ses (1,3) /
   print =   cellinfo (means)
    homogeneity (cochran bartlett) signif (univ) /
   design  .
finish .
```

INTRODUCTION

This chapter describes a group of procedures usually found in advanced texts or ones described as multivariate books. The techniques are a subset of many possibilities. Also the concepts are involved and need some study before application. We cannot cover every nuance or present data sets that show every possible set of variable relationships. The best we can do is present some straightforward and conventional approaches to these techniques. We recommend several texts that give a reasonable review of the theoretical underpinnings of these tests and their interpretations (Hair, Anderson, & Tatham, 1989; Marascuilo & Levin, 1983; Tabachnick, & Fidell, 1989). I'd read them before using a technique. They will also give you some insight into the more advanced options found in the various SPSS reference guides.

THE DATA SET

For our data, we will use nine variables as presented below. They are **ses** (socio-economic status), **sex** (male or female), **sat** (a Scholastic Aptitude Test score), two exams plus a final grade (**test1, test2, & final**), and class evaluation score (**eval**). We will add the appropriate commands to the data.

```
set width = 80 .
data list list/ ses sex gpa sat test1 test2 final eval .
variable labels ses 'Social-eco. status '/
                Eval ' Course Evaluation' .
value labels    ses 1 'High' 2 'Medium' 3 'Low' /
                sex 1 'Female' 2 'Male' /
                Eval 1 'Very Good '
                     2 'Good'
                     3 'So-So'
                     4 'Bad'
                     5 'Very Bad' .
begin data .
2 1 3.6 405 47 57 85 3          1 1 3.2 605 49 79 83 2
2 1 2.7 385 55 43 57 1          2 1 3.5 485 34 66 85 2
2 1 3.5 505 51 75 95 1          2 2 3.4 465 42 44 95 1
3 1 2.9 425 26 36 86 1          2 2 3.9 605 73 81 85 2
2 1 3.1 595 51 56 76 2          1 2 2.8 575 33 10 95 1
3 1 3.5 605 62 55 95 1          2 1 2.7 405 20 51 80 2
1 2 3.2 605 46 57 88 3          1 1 3.8 625 78 86 92 3
2 1 3.6 555 46 75 93 2          2 1 4.0 785 88 90 87 2
3 1 3.8 695 75 79 82 1          3 1 3.4 485 51 41 91 1
2 2 3.8 455 52 63 95 1          2 2 3.1 395 50 54 89 1
2 2 3.6 585 64 70 95 1          2 1 3.8 605 64 86 95 2
3 2 3.1 495 23 36 47 1          1 1 3.3 605 52 80 95 2
1 1 3.1 405 57 67 94 5          1 1 3.7 495 74 77 94 5
2 1 3.5 465 38 36 91 1          2 1 3.4 425 47 45 92 1
2 1 3.4 205 38 53 33 5          3 1 3.1 535 34 50 38 1
2 2 3.4 605 64 54 86 1          1 1 3.7 605 70 83 94 4
2 2 3.8 505 74 62 85 2          2 1 2.7 395 20 32 51 3
3 2 3.7 595 41 54 60 1          3 1 3.4 385 47 47 38 1
2 1 3.0 465 49 20 78 3          1 2 3.0 485 22 55 87 1
2 2 3.5 455 40 44 70 3          end data .
2 1 3.7 795 59 86 79 2              add appropriate analyses.
└┘     └┘    └┘    └┘
```

TESTING FOR SIGNIFICANCE IN MULTIVARIATE STATISTICS

If you are not familiar with multivariate statistics, then you may be in for some surprises when you look for the overall significance tests. With a simple t-test, the larger the *t* value, the more likely it is that you have a significant result. The same is true for *F*-tests. As *F* increases, your probability value decreases.

With multivariate tests, there isn't just one possible overall statistic (the *F* value for an anova) or the *t* in a *t*-test. There are several tests for overall significance. SPSS reports four: **Hotelling's** Trace, **Wilks' Lambda**, **Pillai's** Trace, **Roy's** largest root, **Wilks' Lambda**. They have different characteristics (see Tabachnick & Fidell,1989, pp. 398–399) for recommendations and discussion). Wilks' Lambda is commonly reported in studies. We will highlight it in our outputs. Pillai's Trace is robust and suggested for situations with small sizes, unequal sample sizes, and problems with the assumptions of the procedures (Tabachnick & Fidell, 1989).

The important thing to know is that unlike *F* or *t*, Wilks' Lambda gets smaller as you are more likely to get a significant result. The values range from 0 to 1. Smaller leads to significance. A value close to 1 is bad news. Wilks' Lambda is sort of like an inverted *F*- ratio. Its exact definition implies some knowledge of matrix algebra and can be found in the multivariate references. Just remember "small is good" if you are trying to reject the Null Hypothesis. We present two panels that you might find in the multivariate statistics programs. The first has a Wilks Lambda close to 1.0 (**.9972**) and no significance (**p. = .959**). The second has a smaller value (**.07076**) and significance (**p. < .001**).

WILK'S LAMBDA CLOSE TO 1.0 - NOT SIGNIFICANT

Test Name	Value	Exact F	Hypoth. DF	Error DF	Sig. of F
Pillais	.00228	.04233	2.00	37.00	.959
Hotellings	.00229	.04233	2.00	37.00	.959
Wilks	.99772	.04233	2.00	37.00	.959
Roys	.00228				

WILKS' LAMBDA CLOSE TO 0.0 - SIGNIFICANT RESULT

Test Name	Value	Approx. F	Hypoth. DF	Error DF	Sig. of F
Pillais	1.51449	5.33162	16.00	140.00	.000
Hotellings	5.79772	11.05190	16.00	122.00	.000
Wilks	.07076	8.48421	16.00	98.40	.000
Roys	.81417				

CANONICAL CORRELATION USING MANOVA
(CORRELATION BETWEEN A SET OF X [X_1 ... X_K] VARIABLES AND A SET OF Y [Y_1 ... Y_K] VARIABLES)

In Canonical Correlation, you have a set of X variables and Y variables. You wish to know which X variables are related to what Y variables. Let's look at a simple multiple regression with one Y variable and a set of X variables. We wanted, from the set of X variables, to come up with an equation of the form:

$$Y' = B_0 + B_1X_1 + B_2X_2 + ... + B_kX_k$$

which included the just the important X variables. You also wish a measure of the overall strength of the relationship (Multiple R). Now we want a **set of equations** as follows:

$$A_1Y_1 + A_2Y_2 + ... + A_kY_k$$
$$=$$
$$B_0 + B_1X_1 + B_2X_2 + ... + B_kX_k$$

The questions (and brief answers) are:

- **HOW MANY EQUATIONS ARE POSSIBLE OR, IN OTHER WORDS, WHAT SETS OF X VARIABLES ARE RELATED TO WHAT SETS OF Y VARIABLES?**

    This is also known as **dimensional reduction**. Maybe X_1 and X_3 are related to Y_3 and Y_5. Perhaps X_2 and X_4 are related to Y_1 and Y_2.

    The maximum number of possible equations is equal to the smallest number of variables for the X set and Y set. So if you have **three** X variables [X_1, X_2, X_3] and **five** Y variables [Y_1, Y_2, Y_3, Y_4, Y_5], you can have a maximum of **3** equations.

- **ARE THERE ANY SIGNIFICANT RELATIONSHIPS AT ALL; WHICH EQUATIONS ARE SIGNIFICANT AND WHAT IS THE STRENGTH OF THE RELATIONSHIP FOR EACH EQUATION?**

    Significance will be evaluated by a Wilks Lambda for the overall analysis and with a *F*-ratio for each equation. **Look for the following section in the output:**

    EFFECT .. WITHIN CELLS Regression

    The strength of the relationship is found in the Canonical Correlation Coefficient (**R**) which is simply the Pearson's Correlation Coefficient for the linear combination of Xs for one equation with the linear combination of the set of Ys for the equation. Thus each equation has its own **R**. **Look for the following section in the output:**

    Eigenvalues and Canonical Correlations

- **HOW MUCH DOES EACH VARIABLE CONTRIBUTE TO ITS EQUATION?**

1. **Pattern Interpretation** (Marascuilo & Levin, 1983, p.195): An indication of strength can be found in the standardized coefficients for each variable in its equation. **Look for the following in the output:**

Standardized canonical coefficients for DEPENDENT variables
Standardized canonical coefficients for COVARIATES

2. **Structure Matrix Approach** (Marascuilo & Levin, 1983, p.199): An indication of strength can be found in the correlations of the original variables with the canonical variates. **Look for the following in the output:**

Correlations between DEPENDENT and canonical variables
Correlations between COVARIATES and canonical variables

There is much more to a Canonical Correlation analysis and you should refer to our sources and references. Be that as it may, we will present a minimalist setup for an analysis with our data and an annotated output.

The basic setup for the MANOVA program to conduct the analysis is as follows:

Basic Setup

```
manova X₁ to X? with Y₁ to Y? /        defines sets of variables
    print = signif (dimenr eigen)      requests Canonical Corr.
    discrim ( stan cor estim alpha (α) ) /
    design .        α = significance level
```

For our data set we wish to examine the relationships of

[TEST1 TEST2 FINAL EVAL] vs. [SES SEX GPA SAT]

Our command will specify this analysis and request the **.05** significance level. It is as follows:

```
manova    test1 to eval with ses to sat /
          print = signif (dimenr eigen)
          discrim (stan cor estim alpha (.05))/
          design  .
```

The complete setup (*sans* all data and labels) would be:

SETUP

```
set width = 80 .
data list list/ ses sex gpa sat test1 test2 final eval .
     etc.
begin data .
2 1 3.6 405 47 57 85 3
     etc.
1 2 3.0 485 22 55 87 1
end data .
manova   test1 to eval with ses to sat/
         print = signif (dimenr eigen)
          discrim (stan cor estim alpha (.05))/
         design .
finish.
```

Output

```
* * * * A N A L Y S I S   O F   V A R I A N C E -- DESIGN  1 * * * * *

EFFECT .. WITHIN CELLS Regression
Multivariate Tests of Significance (S = 4, M = -1/2, N = 15 )


Test Name          Value  Approx. F Hypoth. DF   Error DF  Sig. of F


Pillais          1.51449    5.33162     16.00      140.00      .000
Hotellings       5.79772   11.05190     16.00      122.00      .000
Wilks             .07076    8.48421     16.00       98.40      .000
Roys              .81417
```

$\longrightarrow$ **Overall Significance as Wilks Lambda & Prob. are Small**

```
- - - - - - - - - - - - - - - - - - - - - - - - - - - - - - - - - - -
```

Eigenvalues and Canonical Correlations

R R^2

Root No.	Eigenvalue	Pct.	Cum. Pct.	Canon Cor.	Sq. Cor
1	4.381	75.567	75.567	.902	.814
2	1.254	21.629	97.196	.746	.556
3	.145	2.494	99.690	.355	.126
4	.018	.310	100.000	.133	.018

```
- - - - - - - - - - - - - - - - - - - - - - - - - - - - - - - - - - -
```

Dimension Reduction Analysis

Roots	Wilks L.	F	Hypoth. DF	Error DF	Sig. of F
1 TO 4	.07076	8.48421	16.00	98.40	.000
2 TO 4	.38077	4.35371	9.00	80.46	.000
3 TO 4	.85824	1.35035	4.00	68.00	.260
4 TO 4	.98236	.62841	1.00	35.00	.433

$\longrightarrow$ **Two Equations are Significant**

```
- - - - - - - - - - - - - - - - - - - - - - - - - - - - - - - - - - -
EFFECT .. WITHIN CELLS Regression (Cont.)
Univariate F-tests with (4,35) D. F.
```

Variable	Sq. Mul. R	Mul. R	Adj. R-sq.	Hypoth. MS	Error MS
TEST1	.62106	.78807	.57775	1725.77367	120.34301
TEST2	.68330	.82662	.64710	2466.94534	130.67410
FINAL	.35337	.59445	.27947	1077.75659	225.38782
EVAL	.50482	.71051	.44823	7.05484	.79088

Variable	F	Sig. of F
TEST1	14.34046	.000
TEST2	18.87861	.000
FINAL	4.78179	.003
EVAL	8.92028	.000

MEASURES OF THE STRENGTH OF THE CONTRIBUTION OF EACH VARIABLE TO EACH EQUATION FOLLOW

```
Standardized  canonical  coefficients  for  DEPENDENT  variables
              Function No.
```

Pattern Interpretation

Variable	1	2
TEST1	.286	-.578
TEST2	.539	-.199
FINAL	.294	.412
EVAL	.265	.937

- -

Correlations between DEPENDENT and canonical variables
        Function No.

Structure Matrix Approach

Variable	1	2
TEST1	.814	-.371
TEST2	.894	-.218
FINAL	.573	.077
EVAL	.440	.759

- -

Variance explained by canonical variables of DEPENDENT variables

CAN. VAR.	Pct Var DE	Cum Pct DE	Pct Var CO	Cum Pct CO
1	49.620	49.620	40.399	40.399
2	19.169	68.788	10.664	51.063

- -

Standardized canonical coefficients for COVARIATES
        CAN. VAR.

Pattern Interpretation

COVARIATE	1	2
SES	-.555	-.760
SEX	-.283	-.207
GAP	.716	-.117
SAT	.187	-.615

- -

Correlations between COVARIATES and canonical variables
        CAN. VAR.

Structure Matrix Approach

Covariate	1	2
SES	-.518	-.700
SEX	-.213	-.192
GAP	.763	-.458
SAT	.567	-.609

Variance explained by canonical variables of the COVARIATES

CAN. VAR.	Pct Var DE	Cum Pct DE	Pct Var CO	Cum Pct CO
1	24.767	24.767	30.420	30.420
2	15.407	40.174	27.693	58.113

Note : SPSS MANOVA produces a series of analyses which are not that useful for the basic Canonical Analysis. We will not reproduce them in their entirety but just note their presence .

- -

Regression analysis for WITHIN CELLS error term
--- Individual Univariate .9500 confidence intervals
Dependent variable .. TEST1
        Many, many tables, etc.
Variable   1

TEST1	*-.517*
TEST2	*-.389*
FINAL	*.334*
EVAL	*.432*

-> finish .

DISCRIMINANT ANALYSIS
(Predicting Group Membership From a Set of Variables)

In Discriminant Analysis, you have a dependent variable (DV) which is treated as categorical (e.g., Sex = female, male) and of variables (IVs) which you wish to use to predict the DV. The independent variables are usually measurement data (e.g., age, weight) but you can sneak in dummy coded categorical variables with some caution (check our multivariate references). In our example, we will try to predict someone's socio-economic status (ses) from two test scores, a final exam score, and their class evaluation.

Discriminant analysis works like an analysis of variance run backwards which crashes into a multiple regression. Since the goal is to predict group membership, we will see that the analysis goes through a series of steps:

I • **DO THE IVS SIGNIFICANTLY DIFFER ACCORDING TO THE DV?**

In other words, if you want to predict SES from a set of scores, then each SES group should have significantly different means for the scores. In our study, we would expect that the means of test scores, etc., would be different for each SES group, or how could they predict group membership? Significance will be evaluated by a Wilks Lambda for the overall analysis and with an *F* ratio for each IV.

♦ Look for the following section in the output:

<u>WILKS' LAMBDA (U-STATISTIC) AND UNIVARIATE F-RATIO</u>

II • **DERIVE LINEAR EQUATIONS (DISCRIMINANT FUNCTIONS) BASED ON THE IVS THAT CAN GIVE AN INDICATION OF HOW IMPORTANT THE IVS ARE TO GROUP PREDICTION.**

Deriving the Discriminant Functions:

Discriminant Analysis comes up with a set of discriminant functions (number of functions is equal to the Number of DV groups - 1). So if you have **three** levels of SES, you can have a maximum of **2** discriminant functions.

The functions are of the form:

$$D = B_0 + B_1 X_1 + B_2 X_2 + \ldots + B_k X_k$$

♦ Look for :

UNSTANDARDIZED CANONICAL
DISCRIMINANT FUNCTION COEFFICIENTS

The coefficients are chosen such that the Between Groups variance for this function is maximized for the DV groups. Once this function is computed, other orthogonal functions based on the remaining variance can be derived. The functions can be presented in standardized form also.

♦ Look for:

STANDARDIZED CANONICAL DISCRIMINANT FUNCTION COEFFICIENTS

Significance and Importance of Each Discriminant Functions:

Each function is analyzed for significance (Chi-square) and proportion of variance estimates and eigen values are computed.

♦ Look for:

CANONICAL DISCRIMINANT FUNCTIONS

Determining the Importance of Individual IVs or Predictor Variables:

Discriminant Analysis is similar to multiple regression. You can examine the magnitude of the **STANDARDIZED CANONICAL DISCRIMINANT FUNCTION COEFFICIENTS** as some indicator of strength. However, since variables can be correlated, this is ambiguous.

Another usual approach, like regression, is to use some method of statistical entry of variables.

♦ Look for the setup command:

/ m e t h o d = ? ♦ choose from *direct, wilks, mahal,maxminf,minresid, rao* (**direct** or **mahal** recommended)

and the output sections:

```
AT STEP ?, EVAL        WAS INCLUDED IN THE ANALYSIS.
--- VARIABLES NOT IN THE ANALYSIS AFTER STEP    ? ----
```

A third approach, like canonical correlation, uses the **Structure Matrix Approach** (Marascuilo & Levin, 1983, p.199). Thus, an indication of strength can be found in the correlations of the original variables with the discriminant scores.

♦ Look for the following in the output:

STRUCTURE MATRIX:

POOLED WITHIN-GROUPS CORRELATIONS BETWEEN DISCRIMINATING VARIABLES AND CANONICAL DISCRIMINANT FUNCTIONS

Determining the Importance of Each Discriminant Function into Assigning Group Membership.

SPSS gives you several outputs related to this problem. You can examine centroids for each group for each function. If they differ, then that discriminant function aids in distinguishing groups.

♦ Look for the chart entitled:

CANONICAL DISCRIMINANT FUNCTIONS EVALUATED AT GROUP MEANS (GROUP CENTROIDS)

You can also see this graphically in territorial maps that show the overlaps of the groups based on the discriminant values.

♦ Look for the graphs entitled:

TERRITORIAL MAP * INDICATES A GROUP CENTROID
ALL-GROUPS SCATTERPLOT – * INDICATES A GROUP CENTROID

III • DERIVE EQUATIONS BASED ON THE IVS THAT CAN : (1) PREDICT GROUP MEMBERSHIP & (2) GIVE AN INDICATION OF THE SUCCESS OF THESE GROUP PREDICTIONS.

Classifying the cases.

You might want a set of equations that can be used for new subjects to predict group membership. You will have one equation for each DV group. For a particular subject, you calculate the value for each group. The equation with the highest value then determines the group membership prediction. We will demonstrate this with the output and show how to get SPSS to do this for you with new data.

♦ Look for the coefficients in a table entitled:

CLASSIFICATION FUNCTION COEFFICIENTS (FISHER'S LINEAR DISCRIMINANT FUNCTIONS)

♦ The coefficients would appear as:

```
DV        =        1              2          ...          k

IV₁              numerical value   numerical value   numerical value
IV₂              numerical value   numerical value   numerical value
 ⋮
IV?              numerical value   numerical value   numerical value
(CONSTANT)       numerical value   numerical value   numerical value
```

Are these equations successful with current data?

One should see if the equations work well given the current data set. You can examine a table that indicates how many cases are misclassified. If you can't do better than chance then you have obvious trouble. You can choose probabilities based on equal distributions across groups or prior probabilities from the data or hypothesized by you. This choice determines the classification functions. We will present an example.

♦ Look for a table entitled:

CLASSIFICATION RESULTS

Printing a Case by Case Breakdown of Classification Results and Probabilities.

DISCRIMINANT can save a set of information for each case's classification. The information includes the predicted group, the discriminant scores for each function, and the probability of a cases being in each DV group. You can save the predicted group for each case, the discriminant score for each function and the probability of a score being assigned to a group. You have to assign a variable name for each requested. Discriminant will then generate the correct number of scores depending on the number of functions and groups.

♦ Look for DISCRIMINANT subcommand:

```
/ save class = var name scores = var name
       probs = var name
```

♦ Look for a table :

```
      NAME              LABEL
      --------          -------------------------------------

      Var  Name    ---  PREDICTED  GROUP  FOR  ANALYSIS      1
      etc.
```

♦ Look for LIST procedure:

```
list case var names from save class = etc.   .
```

BASIC SETUP

We are using DISCRIMINANT WITH added commands to print case information Look for:

1. Specification of the **DV** and of the **IV** set.

2. The **method** of entry of the IVs. You can use:

    a. Direct- -forcing entry of all variables

    b. A stepwise selection criterion (Mahal is recommended by Hair, et al, 1989)

3. The set of **prior(s)** probabilities used to determine the classification coefficients.

4. Information to be **save**d for each case (**class, scores, probs**). It is also **list**ed for each case. Similar information can be printed but not saved with **cases** .

5 **Statistics** requested (importantly including the classification **coef**ficients)

6. **Map**s and **plot**s to interpret the discriminant functions.

These points are indicated below:

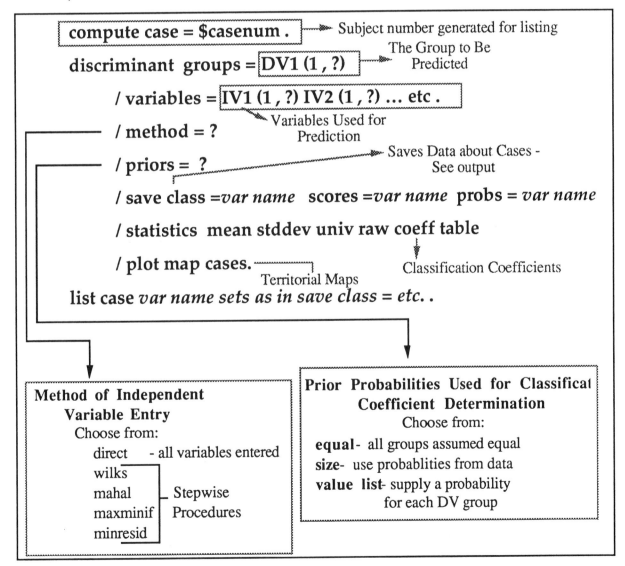

REAL WORLD EXAMPLE
[SES] predicted from [TEST1 TEST2 FINAL EVAL]

We are trying to predict SES (groups = 1 [high], 2 [medium], 3 [low]) from the students' two test scores (TEST1, TEST2), their final exam (FINAL), and their class evaluation score (EVAL). We will use the MAHAL method of data entry and base our classification on the probabilities from the data itself (PRIORS = SIZE). We will find that only one discriminant function is significant, that only FINAL and EVAL are selected for the equations, and that we classify correctly 75% of the time.

SETUP

```
set width = 80 .
data list list/ ses sex gpa sat test1 test2 final eval .
     labels, etc.
begin data .
2 1 3.6 405 47 57 85 3
     etc.
1 2 3.0 485 22 55 87 1
end data .
compute case = $casenum   | Subject number generated for listing
discriminant groups = ses (1,3) | We want to predict SES
   / variables = test1 test2 final eval | Use these IVs for prediction
   / method = mahal | Select IVs based on Mahalanobis criterion
   / priors = size | Use probabilities from data set for analysis
   / save class = prdses scores = prscore probs = prdprob
   / statistics mean stddev univ raw coeff table
   / plot combined map .| Helps understand functions
list case prdses drscore1 to prdprob3 . | optional case info printed
finish.
```

OUTPUT

```
->      discriminant groups = ses (1,3)
->          / variables = test1 test2 final eval
->          / method = mahal
->          / priors = size
->          / save class = prdses scores = prscore probs = prdprob
->          / statistics mean stddev univ raw coeff table
->          / plot combined map .
```

FOLLOWING VARIABLES HAVE BEEN CREATED:

NAME	LABEL	
PRDSES ---	PREDICTED GROUP FOR ANALYSIS 1	Predicted SES score for each case.
DRSCORE1 ---	FUNCTION 1 FOR ANALYSIS 1	Cases' discriminant score for Function 1.
DRSCORE2 ---	FUNCTION 2 FOR ANALYSIS 1	Cases' discriminant score for Function 2.
PRDPROB1 ---	PROBABILITY 1 FOR ANALYSIS 1	Cases' probability of being in SES group 1.
PRDPROB2 ---	PROBABILITY 2 FOR ANALYSIS 1	Cases' probability of being in SES group 1.
PRDPROB3 ---	PROBABILITY 3 FOR ANALYSIS 1	Cases' probability of being in SES group 1.

- - - - D I S C R I M I N A N T   A N A L Y S I S - - - -

ON GROUPS DEFINED BY SES   Social-eco. status

	NUMBER OF CASES		
SES	UNWEIGHTED	WEIGHTED	LABEL
1	9	9.0	High
2	23	23.0	Medium
3	8	8.0	Low
TOTAL	40	40.0	

GROUP MEANS

SES	TEST1	TEST2	FINAL	EVAL
1	53.44444	66.00000	91.33333	2.88889
2	50.69565	58.39130	81.60870	1.91304
3	44.87500	49.75000	67.12500	1.00000
TOTAL	50.15000	58.37500	80.90000	1.95000

GROUP STANDARD DEVIATIONS

SES	TEST1	TEST2	FINAL	EVAL
1	18.69566	23.75395	4.30116	1.53659
2	16.21008	18.39649	15.76169	0.99604
3	17.77187	13.95657	24.13319	0.00000
TOTAL	16.88202	19.24296	17.68644	1.19722

**WILKS' LAMBDA (U-STATISTIC) AND UNIVARIATE F-RATIO
WITH   2 AND   37 DEGREES OF FREEDOM**

Tests whether significant differences exist
for each IV broken down by DV (SES) .

VARIABLE	WILKS' LAMBDA	F	SIGNIFICANCE
TEST1	0.97057	0.5610	0.5754
TEST2	0.92256	1.553	0.2251
FINAL	0.79432	4.790	0.0141
EVAL	0.72835	6.900	0.0028

Significant differences in **Final** are found for SES groups
Significant differences in **Eval** are found for SES groups

- - - - - - - - D I S C R I M I N A N T   A N A L Y S I S - - - - -

ON GROUPS DEFINED BY SES   Social-eco. status

ANALYSIS NUMBER   1
STEPWISE VARIABLE SELECTION

**SELECTION RULE: MAXIMIZE MINIMUM MAHALANOBIS
   DISTANCE (D SQUARED) BETWEEN GROUPS**

```
MAXIMUM NUMBER OF STEPS.................       8
MINIMUM TOLERANCE LEVEL.................. 0.00100
MINIMUM F TO ENTER......................  1.0000
MAXIMUM F TO REMOVE.....................  1.0000
```

CANONICAL DISCRIMINANT FUNCTIONS

```
MAXIMUM NUMBER OF FUNCTIONS.............          2
MINIMUM CUMULATIVE PERCENT OF VARIANCE... 100.00
MAXIMUM SIGNIFICANCE OF WILKS' LAMBDA....  1.0000
```

PRIOR PROBABILITIES | Based on the numbers of each SES category in the Data .

GROUP	PRIOR	LABEL
1	0.22500	High
2	0.57500	Medium
3	0.20000	Low
TOTAL	1.00000	

```
┌────────────────────────────────────────────────────────────────────┐
│ Record of Variablle Entry Into Analysis based on Method = Mahal     │
└────────────────────────────────────────────────────────────────────┘
```

AT STEP   1, EVAL   WAS INCLUDED IN THE ANALYSIS. | *Eval enters Equation*

```
                            DEGREES OF FREEDOM  SIGNIF.   BETWEEN GROUPS
WILKS' LAMBDA      0.72835       1    2      37.0
EQUIVALENT F       6.89974            2      37.0   0.0028

MINIMUM D SQUARED  0.757583                                   2         3
EQUIVALENT F       4.49662            1      37.0   0.0407
```

--------------- VARIABLES IN THE ANALYSIS AFTER STEP   1 ---------------

```
VARIABLE   TOLERANCE  F TO REMOVE     D SQUARED      BETWEEN GROUPS

EVAL       1.0000000  6.8997
```

--------------- VARIABLES NOT IN THE ANALYSIS AFTER STEP   1 ---------------

```
                     MINIMUM
VARIABLE  TOLERANCE  TOLERANCE  F TO ENTER    D SQUARED     BETWEEN GROUPS

TEST1     0.9843778  0.9843778  0.15518
TEST2     0.9841300  0.9841300  0.60710
FINAL     0.8665620  0.8665620  8.0974        1.886609        1         2
```

* *

AT STEP   2, FINAL   WAS INCLUDED IN THE ANALYSIS. | *Final enters Equation*

```
                            DEGREES OF FREEDOM  SIGNIF.   BETWEEN GROUPS
WILKS' LAMBDA      0.50236       2    2      37.0
EQUIVALENT F       7.39589            4      72.0   0.0000

MINIMUM D SQUARED  1.88661                                    1         2
EQUIVALENT F       5.93708            2      36.0   0.0059
```

--------------- VARIABLES IN THE ANALYSIS AFTER STEP   2 ---------------

```
VARIABLE   TOLERANCE  F TO REMOVE     D SQUARED      BETWEEN GROUPS

FINAL      0.8665620  8.0974
EVAL       0.8665620  10.461
```

--------------- VARIABLES NOT IN THE ANALYSIS AFTER STEP   2 ---------------

```
                     MINIMUM
VARIABLE  TOLERANCE  TOLERANCE  F TO ENTER    D SQUARED     BETWEEN GROUPS

TEST1     0.7947318  0.6996139  0.69458
TEST2     0.8895061  0.7832423  0.83370E-02
```

F LEVEL OR TOLERANCE OR VIN INSUFFICIENT FOR FURTHER COMPUTATION.

SUMMARY TABLE

```
           ACTION     VARS  WILKS'          MINIMUM
STEP ENTERED REMOVED   IN    LAMBDA  SIG.    D SQUARED  SIG.   BETWEEN GROUPS

 1  EVAL               1    .72835  .0028    .75758    .0407     2        3
 2  FINAL              2    .50236  .0000   1.88661    .0059     1        2
```

```
┌────────────────────────────────────────────────────────────────────┐
│ Coefficients to Generate Predictions - See Below                    │
└────────────────────────────────────────────────────────────────────┘
```

CLASSIFICATION FUNCTION COEFFICIENTS
(FISHER'S LINEAR DISCRIMINANT FUNCTIONS)

```
SES    =         1           2           3
              High        Medium       Low

FINAL      0.4741655   0.4070857   0.3205960
EVAL       5.297456    4.032622    2.715476
(CONSTANT) -30.79709  -21.02154  -13.72718
```

Significance and Importance of Discriminant Functions

CANONICAL DISCRIMINANT FUNCTIONS

	FCN	EIGENVALUE	PCT OF VARIANCE	CUM PCT	CANONICAL CORR	:	AFTER FCN	WILKS' LAMBDA	CHISQUARE	DF	SIG	
						:	0	0.5024	25.128	4	0.0000	
1*		0.9838	99.66	99.66	0.7042	:	1	0.9966	0.124	D	.7249	*Function 2 is Not Useful!*
2*		0.0034	0.34	100.00	0.0582	:						

   * MARKS THE   2 CANONICAL DISCRIMINANT FUNCTIONS REMAINING IN THE ANALYSIS.

STANDARDIZED CANONICAL DISCRIMINANT FUNCTION COEFFICIENTS

	FUNC 1	FUNC 2
FINAL	0.84795	0.65952
EVAL	0.92369	-0.54843

STRUCTURE MATRIX:
POOLED WITHIN-GROUPS CORRELATIONS BETWEEN DISCRIMINATING VARIABLES
                                      AND CANONICAL DISCRIMINANT FUNCTIONS
(VARIABLES ORDERED BY SIZE OF CORRELATION WITHIN FUNCTION)

	FUNC 1	FUNC 2
TEST1	0.42048*	0.16870
TEST2	0.32015*	0.08942
FINAL	0.51053	0.85986*
EVAL	0.61395	-0.78935*

UNSTANDARDIZED CANONICAL
DISCRIMINANT FUNCTION COEFFICIENTS

	FUNC 1	FUNC 2
FINAL	0.5239619E-01	0.4075318E-01
EVAL	0.8805458	-0.5228106
(CONSTANT)	-5.955916	-2.277452

CANONICAL DISCRIMINANT FUNCTIONS EVALUATED
AT GROUP MEANS (GROUP CENTROIDS)

GROUP	FUNC 1	FUNC 2
1	1.37340	-0.06567
2	0.00459	0.04820
3	-1.55828	-0.06471

TERRITORIAL MAP   * INDICATES A GROUP CENTROID

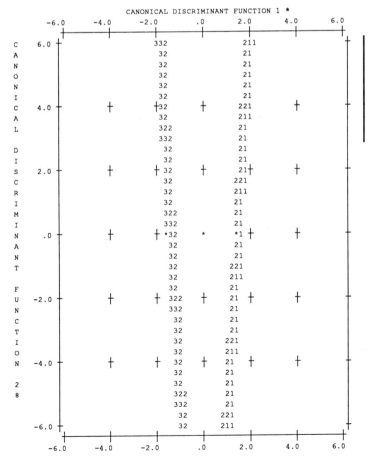

SYMBOLS USED IN TERRITORIAL MAP

SYMBOL	GROUP	LABEL
1	1	High
2	2	Medium
3	3	Low
*		GROUP CENTROIDS

Note that Function 1 is useful as the centroids differ. .
They are too close for Function 2 .

```
            ALL-GROUPS SCATTERPLOT - * INDICATES A GROUP CENTROID

                    CANONICAL DISCRIMINANT FUNCTION 1
            OUT   -4.0      -2.0       .0       2.0       4.0   OUT
          X-------+---------+---------+---------+---------+-------X
      OUT X                                                      X    CLASSIFICATION RESULTS -
  C
  A                                                                                NO. OF    PREDICTED GROUP MEMBERSHIP
  N                                                                  ACTUAL GROUP  CASES      1         2        3
  O                                                                  ------------  ------    -------   -------  -------
  N
  I   4.0 +                                          +             GROUP     1       9         4         5        0
  C                                                                High                     44.4%     55.6%    0.0%
  A
  L                                                                GROUP     2      23         0        22        1
                                                                  Medium                     0.0%     95.7%    4.3%
  D
  I   2.0 +                                          +             GROUP     3       8         0         4        4
  S                                                                Low                        0.0%     50.0%   50.0%
  C
  R                             321                                PERCENT  OF  "GROUPED"  CASES  CORRECTLY  CLASSIFIED: 75.0%
  I                           312     1
  M                             22
  I    .0 +              *      *2    *1            +             SYMBOLS  USED  IN  PLOTS
  N                          3     2    1
  A                               2      1                         SYMBOL  GROUP  LABEL
  N                       3      2         1                       ------  -----  ----------------
  T                      3                                          1       1     High
                                                                    2       2     Medium
  F  -2.0 +               2                          +              3       3     Low
  U                                                                 *             GROUP CENTROIDS
  N
  C
  T
  I                         2
  O  -4.0 +                                          +
  N
  2
      OUT X                                                      X
          X-------+---------+---------+---------+---------+-------X
            OUT   -4.0      -2.0       .0       2.0       4.0   OUT
```

```
->    compute case = $casenum .  | We generate an ID number for each case.
->    list   variables = case prdses drscore1 to prdprob3 .
```

┌───┐
│ We list the scores computed by the **SAVE** subcommand   │
└───┘

CASE	PRDSES	DRSCORE1	DRSCORE2	PRDPROB1	PRDPROB2	PRDPROB3
1.00	2.00	1.13940	-.38186	.42623	.56354	.01023
2.00	3.00	-2.08879	-.47733	.00239	.25912	.73849
3.00	2.00	-.09773	1.07129	.09627	.81672	.08701
4.00	2.00	-.56930	.70451	.04971	.77132	.17897
5.00	2.00	-.21271	-.22583	.09233	.79092	.11675
		etc.				
35.00	2.00	-.25492	.94903	.07808	.81006	.11186
36.00	3.00	-3.08431	-1.25164	.00016	.06352	.93632
37.00	1.00	2.49151	-.53790	.83020	.16942	.00038
38.00	2.00	-.64207	-1.76747	.05440	.70374	.24186
39.00	3.00	-3.08431	-1.25164	.00016	.06352	.93632
40.00	2.00	-.51690	.74526	.05377	.78020	.16603

USING THE CLASSIFICATION FUNCTIONS TO ASSIGN GROUP MEMBERSHIP

Once the analysis is completed, you may want to classify another set of data. There are two ways to do this. There is a method to include another set of data with the original set and then analyzing them together. This may be inefficient. Thus we present a small separate run that takes the classification functions and uses COMPUTE and IF statements to assign new cases to groups. Our strategy is to compute a group score for each function, pick the highest value, and then output the group number based on the highest value. Check Chapter 20 for use of COMPUTE, IF, and LIST.

OUTPUT FROM ORIGINAL DISCRIMINANT RUN

```
CLASSIFICATION  FUNCTION  COEFFICIENTS
(FISHER'S  LINEAR  DISCRIMINANT  FUNCTIONS)

SES       =        1              2              3
                   High           Medium         Low

FINAL              0.4741655      0.4070857      0.3205960
EVAL               5.297456       4.032622       2.715476
(CONSTANT)         -30.79709      -21.02154      -13.72718
```

SETUP TO USE FUNCTIONS ON NEW CASES

```
set width = 80 .
data list list / sex gpa sat test1 test2 final eval .
begin data .
1 3.6 405 47 57 85 3
2 3.0 485 22 55 87 1
end data .
compute case = $casenum .
compute  ses1  =   0.4741655*final  +  5.297456*eval  -  30.79709  .
compute  ses2  =   0.4070857*final  +  4.032622*eval  -  21.02154  .
compute  ses3  =   0.3205960*final  +  2.715476*eval  -  13.72718  .
compute  grp  =  max  (ses1  to  ses3)  .
if  (grp  eq  ses1)  grpnum  =  1  .
if  (grp  eq  ses2)  grpnum  =  2  .
if  (grp  eq  ses3)  grpnum  =  3  .
list  case  grpnum  grp  ses1  to  ses3  .
finish .
```

Thus, GRPNUM will be the group predicted for each case. Our output also contains the highest value (GRP) from the classification functions set (SES1 to SES3).

OUTPUT FROM COMPUTATION RUN

```
etc.
->    list case grpnum grp ses1 to ses3 .

 CASE    GRPNUM       GRP      SES1      SES2      SES3

1.00       2.00     25.68     25.40     25.68     21.67
2.00       2.00     18.43     15.75     18.43     16.88
Number of cases read:  2     Number of cases listed:   2
```

FACTOR AND PRINCIPAL COMPONENTS ANALYSIS

(Dimensional Reduction or Relationships

Among a Set of X [X$_1$ ... X$_K$] Variables)

In Factor and Principal Components Analysis, you have a set of X variables. You suspect that there is really a smaller set of underlying common factors. Each of your variables may contribute something to this underlying set of factors. You want to determine what are these underlying factors and how does each of your variables from the X set contribute. The procedures basically come up with a set of linear equations that are made of combinations of your variables. Each equation is a factor. An example of such an equation for Factor 1 (Y$_1$) would look as follows:

$$Y_1 = B_1^{(1)}X_1 + B_2^{(2)}X_2 + ... + B_K^{(K)}X_k$$

A similar equation might be noted as Y$_2$. A subject can thus have a factor score produced by such an equation. Thus the techniques reduce a large set of variables into a smaller set and can tell you how each subject fairs on these new factors. You could also apply these equations to new subjects to determine how they would score on these new variables.

Obviously, there is much more to it. We need to determine significance of the factors and importance of variables. There are rather large books and chapters on this. We will show 2 simple setups and explain the command structure but we recommend a good deal of reading before attempting a serious use of the techniques.

OPTIONS FOR THE FACTOR PROCEDURE

When using Factor you have several things to decide. They are:

1. What method of **extraction** should be used? Choices are:

CODE	METHOD
ALPHA	ALPHA FACTORING
GLS	GENERALIZED LEAST SQUARES
IMAGE	IMAGE FACTORING
ML	MAXIMUM LIKELIHOOD EXTRACTION
PAF	PRINCIPAL AXIS FACTORING
PC	PRINCIPAL COMPONENTS ANALYSIS
ULS	UNWEIGHTED LEAST SQUARES EXTRACTION METHOD

2. What method of **rotation** should be used? Choices are:

CODE	METHOD
EQUAMAX	COMBINES QUARTIMAX & VARIMAX
NOROTATE	NO ROTATION
OBLIMIN	OBLIQUE ROTATION, NONORTHOGONAL AXES
QUARTIMAX	QUARTIMAX
VARIMAX	VARIMAX ROTATION

3. You can also decide the criteria to extract the factors. We will use the SPSS defaults described in the manuals.

We will also add some useful printing options and ones to save the factor scores. The general form of the command is as follows.

```
factor variables = X1 to X? /   | variables to be analyzed

    print = default fscore /   | needed for appropriate statistical output
                               You might add corr for correlation matrix of X1 to X?

    plot = eigen rotation (#,#) / | produces Scree plot & factor loading plot
                                    #, # = factors to plot

    extraction = ? /   ♦ choose from PC, PAF, Alpha, Image, ULS, GLS, ML

    rotation = ? /   ♦ choose from Varimax, Equamax, Quartimax, Oblimin, Norotate

    save reg (all name) .  | Saves factor scores for all factors, calls them name1 to name?

                    ♦ Bold face = defaults if not specified.
```

REAL EXAMPLE

In this example, we will run a factor analysis on our variables. We will first present an annotated Alpha Extraction and Oblimin rotation. We will then present an Equamax for comparison. We will use the default Kaiser rule (eigenvalue > 1) to determine the number of factors. There will be three. We will also save and print the factor scores for the subjects.

SETUP

```
set width = 80 .
data list list/ ses sex gap sat test1 test2 final eval .
    etc.
begin data .
2 1 3.6 405 47 57 85 3
    etc.
1 2 3.0 485 22 55 87 1
end data .
compute case = $casenum .
factor variables = ses sex gap sat test1 test2 final eval /
    print = default fscore /
    plot = eigen  rotation (1,2) /
    extraction =  Alpha /
    rotation =    Oblimin /
    save reg (all fac) .
list case fac1 fac2 fac3 .
```

OUTPUT

```
->   compute case = $casenum .
->   factor variables = ses sex gap sat test1 test2 final eval  /
->       print = default fscore /
->       plot = eigen  rotation (1,2)/
->       extraction =  Alpha /
->       rotation =    Oblimin /
->       save reg (all fac) .
```

- - - - - - - - - - - F A C T O R   A N A L Y S I S - - - - - - - - - - -

ANALYSIS NUMBER 1   LISTWISE DELETION OF CASES WITH MISSING VALUES
EXTRACTION 1 FOR ANALYSIS 1, ALPHA FACTORING (ALPHA)

INITIAL STATISTICS:

VARIABLE	COMMUNALITY	*	FACTOR	EIGENVALUE	PCT OF VAR	CUM PCT
		*	3 Factors with Eigenvalues > 1, Selected by Kaiser Rule.			
SES	.67911	*	1	3.17497	39.7	39.7
SEX	.32288	*	2	1.61272	20.2	59.8
GAP	.72410	*	3	1.25269	15.7	75.5
SAT	.50185	*	4	.78393	9.8	85.3
TEST1	.63817	*	5	.51122	6.4	91.7
TEST2	.69345	*	6	.31727	4.0	95.7
FINAL	.48799	*	7	.22444	2.8	98.5
EVAL	.60233	*	8	.12275	1.5	100.0

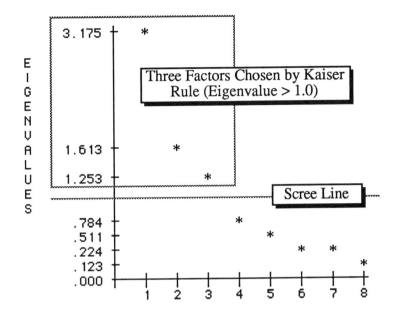

ALPHA ATTEMPTED TO EXTRACT   3 FACTORS.

MORE THAN   25 ITERATIONS REQUIRED. CONVERGENCE =   .02884

FACTOR MATRIX:

Factor Loadings - Coefficients Relating Standardized Variable Scores to Factor Scores For Orthogonal Case (Before Rotation), Coefficients = Correlation between Variables & Factor Scores, Can Used to Calculate Factor Scores

	FACTOR 1	FACTOR 2	FACTOR 3
SES	-.36114	-.24988	1.31053
SEX	-.04135	-.39095	-.11509
GAP	.74237	-.07119	.18542
SAT	.66331	-.25138	.08091
TEST1	.85426	.09150	.11308
TEST2	.85813	.29542	.14172
FINAL	.49676	-.19134	-.24359
EVAL	.12456	.79091	-.19997

FINAL STATISTICS:

VARIABLE	COMMUNALITY	*	FACTOR	SS LOADINGS	PCT OF VAR	CUM PCT
		*				
SES	1.91034	*	1	2.85164	35.6	35.6
SEX	.16780	*	2	1.04134	13.0	48.7
GAP	.59056	*	3	1.90385	23.8	72.5
SAT	.50971	*				
TEST1	.75091	*				
TEST2	.84374	*				
FINAL	.34272	*				
EVAL	.68105	*				

OBLIMIN ROTATION 1 FOR EXTRACTION 1 IN ANALYSIS 1 - KAISER NORMALIZATION.

Note: Following set of matrices   (Pattern, Structure) for Oblimin Rotation

OBLIMIN CONVERGED IN   5 ITERATIONS.

PATTERN MATRIX:

Unique relationships for between Factors and Variables		
FACTOR 1	FACTOR 2	FACTOR 3
SES .06561	-.12994	1.38354
SEX -.03381	-.40279	-.07693
GAP .77894	-.00806	.09203
SAT .69017	-.20263	.01304
TEST1 .84877	.15228	-.00923
TEST2 .84001	.35802	.00180
FINAL .42702	-.18709	-.29495
EVAL -.02043	.77131	-.28380

STRUCTURE MATRIX:

Correlation of Factor Scores and Variables after Rotation		
FACTOR 1	FACTOR 2	FACTOR 3
SES -.17338	-.15314	1.37460
SEX -.02767	-.40203	-.06406
GAP .76305	.00390	-.04110
SAT .68441	-.19084	-.10148
TEST1 .85300	.16723	-.15713
TEST2 .84594	.37262	-.14823
FINAL .47423	-.17446	-.36472
EVAL .04157	.77595	-.29388

FACTOR CORRELATION MATRIX:

Documents Rotation		
FACTOR 1	FACTOR 2	FACTOR 3
FACTOR 1 1.00000		
FACTOR 2 .01742	1.00000	
FACTOR 3 -.17110	-.01760	1.00000

HORIZONTAL FACTOR 1   VERTICAL FACTOR 2

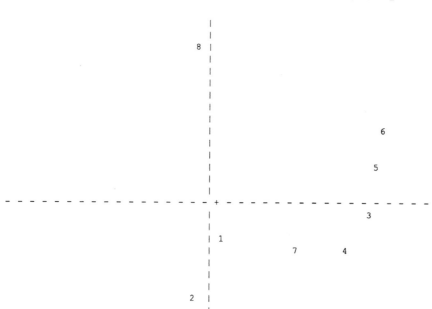

SYMBOL	VARIABLE	COORDINATES	SYMBOL	VARIABLE	COORDINATES
1	SES	(.06561, -.12994)	2	SEX	(-.03381, -.40279)
3	GAP	(.77894, -.00806)	4	SAT	(.69017, -.20263)
5	TEST1	(.84877, .15228)	6	TEST2	(.84001, .35802)
7	FINAL	(.42702, -.18709)	8	EVAL	(-.02043, .77131)

FACTOR SCORE COEFFICIENT MATRIX:

> **Use to Calculate Factor Scores After Rotation - Multiply
> Z score of Each Variable by Z score and Sum**

	FACTOR 1	FACTOR 2	FACTOR 3
SES	.03326	.72796	3.01753
SEX	.07242	.13959	.72046
GAP	.04678	-.75653	-1.48048
SAT	.10421	-.14600	.14778
TEST1	.42945	.11815	-.02736
TEST2	.48618	.81999	1.09373
FINAL	.09541	.15557	1.04317
EVAL	-.10216	1.01517	1.42689

COVARIANCE MATRIX FOR ESTIMATED REGRESSION FACTOR SCORES:

	FACTOR 1	FACTOR 2	FACTOR 3
FACTOR 1	.91785		
FACTOR 2	.10315	.94320	
FACTOR 3	-.11575	.54244	3.18999

3 REGRESSION FACTOR SCORES WILL BE SAVED WITH ROOTNAME: FAC

FOLLOWING FACTOR SCORES WILL BE ADDED TO THE ACTIVE FILE:

NAME	LABEL
FAC1	REGR FACTOR SCORE 1 FOR ANALYSIS 1
FAC2	REGR FACTOR SCORE 2 FOR ANALYSIS 1
FAC3	REGR FACTOR SCORE 3 FOR ANALYSIS 1

->   list case fac1 fac2 fac3 .

> **Produces a listing of the Individual Factor Scores per Subject**

CASE	FAC1	FAC2	FAC3
1.00	-.30609	.46293	-.00700
2.00	-.57398	-.06775	-1.10639
3.00	.55271	-.26322	-.23646
4.00	-1.21888	.31042	4.04075
5.00	-.08632	.34963	.54646
6.00	.46851	-.06241	3.31166
7.00	-.08426	.27481	-.94997
etc.			
38.00	-1.93619	.84892	.36779
39.00	-.63587	-.51548	-.34529
40.00	-.71557	-1.10213	-2.78422

Number of cases read: 40   Number of cases listed: 40

EQUAMAX ROTATION PRODUCES DIFFERENT OUTPUT

In this example, we switch to an Equamax rotation. The big difference is that we no longer get the STRUCTURE and PATTERN Matrices after the rotation.

```
->      factor variables = ses sex gap sat test1 test2 final eval   /
->          print = default fscore /
->          plot = eigen   rotation (1,2)/
->          extraction =  Alpha /
->          rotation =  equamax /
->          save reg (all fac) .
```

Etc.

EQUAMAX   ROTATION 1 FOR EXTRACTION 1 IN ANALYSIS 1 - KAISER NORMALIZATION.

EQUAMAX CONVERGED IN   5 ITERATIONS.

ROTATED FACTOR MATRIX:

	FACTOR 1	FACTOR 2	FACTOR 3
SES	.00108	1.37254	-.16274
SEX	-.02722	-.07544	-.40170
GAP	.76841	-.00485	.00911
SAT	.68537	-.07407	-.18571
TEST1	.84134	-.11352	.17370
TEST2	.83075	-.09998	.37894
FINAL	.43868	-.34885	-.16908
EVAL	-.01215	-.27547	.77783

FACTOR TRANSFORMATION MATRIX:

	FACTOR 1	FACTOR 2	FACTOR 3
FACTOR 1	.96350	-.25376	.08532
FACTOR 2	-.10481	-.06431	.99241
FACTOR 3	.24635	.96513	.08856

```
                    HORIZONTAL FACTOR   1   VERTICAL FACTOR   2
                                         I
                                         I
                                         I
                                         I
                                         I
                                         I
- - - - - - - - - - - - - - - - - - - - -+- - - - - - - - - - - - - - -
                                         I                         3
                                       2 I                   4         6
                                         I                             5
                                         I
                                       8 I
                                         I
                                         I                 7
                                         I
```

SYMBOL	VARIABLE	COORDINATES	SYMBOL	VARIABLE	COORDINATES
1	SES	(.00108, 1.37254)	2	SEX	(-.02722, -.07544)
3	GAP	(.76841, -.00485)	4	SAT	(.68537, -.07407)
5	TEST1	(.84134, -.11352)	6	TEST2	(.83075, -.09998)
7	FINAL	(.43868, -.34885)	8	EVAL	(-.01215, -.27547)

FACTOR SCORE COEFFICIENT MATRIX:

	FACTOR 1	FACTOR 2	FACTOR 3
SES	.39839	3.05819	.70929
SEX	.16125	.73243	.13556
GAP	-.12263	-1.50695	-.74685
SAT	.12755	.15034	-.14620
TEST1	.42936	-.00422	.12108
TEST2	.61280	1.14440	.81615
FINAL	.22494	1.05894	.14969
EVAL	.05397	1.45650	1.00539

COVARIANCE MATRIX FOR ESTIMATED REGRESSION FACTOR SCORES:

	FACTOR 1	FACTOR 2	FACTOR 3
FACTOR 1	.95758		
FACTOR 2	.32244	3.25382	
FACTOR 3	.15633	.55323	.93748

MANOVA - MULTIVARIATE ANALYSIS OF VARIANCE
(A SET OF DEPENDENT VARIABLES $[DV_1 ... DV_K]$ AND A SET OF INDEPENDENT VARIABLES $[IV_1 (1,?)... IV_K (1,?)]$)

We will present a simple explanation and example of Manova. The basic situation is one in which you have more than one dependent variable with a set of independent variables arranged in a design similar to the many kinds of Anova designs. It would be possible to several separate anovas. However, this has two problems. First, the more separate anovas you do, the higher the probability of Type I error. Second, separate anovas don't take into account or give you any information about the inter-relationships of the dependent variable set. A manova can help you.

An anova compares the means of a set of univariate distributions. The issue is whether or not there is separation between some of the group means. This can be portrayed graphically in the hypothetical oneway anova for three groups found in following figure:

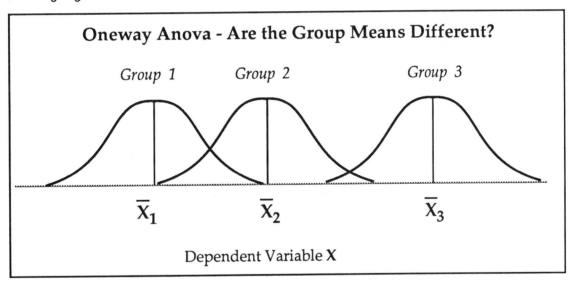

It looked like Groups 1, 2, and 3 are different. This would be tested by computing an *F*-ratio. Of course, one might follow up with appropriate comparison techniques to localize the differences.

A manova is similar except that it doesn't compare univariate distributions, it compares multivariate distributions. Consider having two dependent variables per subject (X and Y). Thus our three groups define three (X,Y) scattergrams. A scattergram is a multivariate distribution as we record the frequency not of an X value but of a (X,Y) pair. Thus we get a frequency distribution that looks like a little mound. Its footprint is an ellipse and its mounded shape is that of the normal curve. Each scattergram has a measure of central tendency called a centroid. The centroid is the point with coordinates being that of the Mean of X and the Mean of Y ($\overline{X}$, $\overline{Y}$). We can graph our three groups and see if they differ. The basic operation of the Manova is to see if the centroids of three differ significantly. If they do, then it would be appropriate to examine the differences between the X means and the Y means. This rationale is laid out in the following figure which contains the three groups' multivariate distributions for X and Y. It is possible that you can have a significant manova and not significant differences between X means or Y means. The distance between the centroids can be bigger than any difference between X and Y means due to the Pythagorean theorem. If this occurs, you may need to examine the data using the canonical variates as we demonstrated in Canonical Correlation.

One can extend this logic to factorial designs, repeated measures designs, and analyses of covariance. Also, a well known multivariate extension of the *t* - test known as Hotelling's T^2 can be done with MANOVA. In this case you would have an independent variable with just two levels.

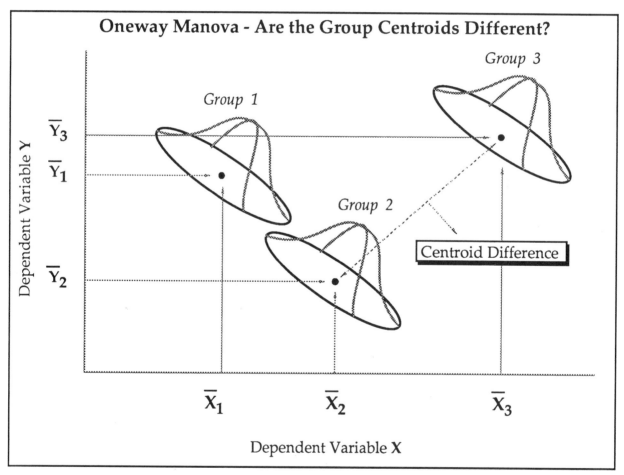

The basic manova setup is quite easy. It is similar to the manova setups that we used for Anovas in our earlier chapters. You need to:

Declare the Dependent Variables. (There must be more than one for a manova.)

Declare the Independent Variables with Appropriate Levels.

Request the Means for the Dependent Variables.

Request the Univariate *F*-ratios to be examined if the Manova itself is significant.

The univariate *F* - ratios are just anovas conducted separately on each dependent variable. It is important to note that the univariate *F*-ratios do not have their probabilities based on the overall set of anovas. Thus, be aware of Type I error.

The general setup is as follows:

BASIC SETUP

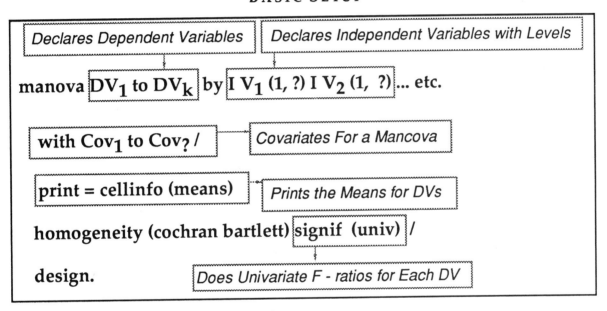

Declares Dependent Variables | Declares Independent Variables with Levels

manova DV$_1$ to DV$_k$ by I V$_1$ (1, ?) I V$_2$ (1, ?) ... etc.

with Cov$_1$ to Cov$_?$ / — Covariates For a Mancova

print = cellinfo (means) — Prints the Means for DVs

homogeneity (cochran bartlett) signif (univ) /

design. — Does Univariate F - ratios for Each DV

In our example, we will conduct a manova on the final grade (FINAL) and class evaluation (EVAL). The independent variables are SEX and SES. In the output that follows, look for the MANOVA significance tests (Wilks' Lambda, etc.) for the centroids of the effects: SEX, SES and SES BY SEX interaction. Then look for the univariate *F*-ratios for these same effects but presented separately for each dependent variable — EVAL and FINAL. We will see that: we do not have multivariate significance for the SEX by SES interaction and the univariate interactions (see notes 1 & 2); we do have have multivariate and univariate significance for SES (see notes 3 & 4); and multivariate significance for SEX but only univariate significance for the effect of SEX on EVAL.

SETUP

```
set width = 80 .
data list list/ ses sex gpa sat test1 test2 final eval .
etc.
begin data .
2 1 3.6 405 47 57 85 3
etc.
3 1 3.4 385 47 47 38 1
1 2 3.0 485 22 55 87 1
end data .
manova final eval by sex (1,2) ses (1,3) /
   print = cellinfo (means)
   homogeneity (cochran bartlett) signif (univ) /
   design .
```

OUTPUT

```
-> manova final eval by sex (1,2) ses (1,3) /
->    print = cellinfo (means)
->    homogeneity (cochran bartlett) signif (univ) /
->    design .
```

* * * * * * A N A L Y S I S   O F   V A R I A N C E * * * * * *
- -

Cell Means and Standard Deviations
Variable .. FINAL

FACTOR	CODE	Mean	Std. Dev.	N
SEX	Female			
SES	High	92.000	4.517	6
SES	Medium	78.467	18.023	15
SES	Low	71.667	26.447	6
SEX	Male			
SES	High	90.000	4.359	3
SES	Medium	87.500	8.384	8
SES	Low	53.500	9.192	2
For entire sample		80.900	17.686	40

- -

Variable .. EVAL   Course Evaluation

FACTOR	CODE	Mean	Std. Dev.	N
SEX	Female			
SES	High	3.500	1.378	6
SES	Medium	2.133	1.060	15
SES	Low	1.000	.000	6
SEX	Male			
SES	High	1.667	1.155	3
SES	Medium	1.500	.756	8
SES	Low	1.000	.000	2
For entire sample		1.950	1.197	40

- -

Univariate Homogeneity of Variance Tests
Variable .. FINAL

Cochrans C(6,6) =   .57404, P = .001 (approx.)
Bartlett-Box F(5,362) =   3.61551, P = .003

Variable .. EVAL   Course Evaluation

Cochrans C(6,6) =   .38551, P = .099 (approx.)
2 Cells have zero variance, Bartlett-Box test cannot be done.

```
EFFECT .. SEX BY SES
```

Note that SEX by SES is NOT Significant Multivariately [1]

Multivariate Tests of Significance (S = 2, M = -1/2, N = 15 1/2)

Test Name	Value	Approx. F	Hypoth. DF	Error DF	Sig. of F [1]
Pillais	.20057	1.89492	4.00	68.00	.121
Hotellings	.22408	1.79266	4.00	64.00	.141
Wilks	.80906	1.84394	4.00	66.00	.131
Roys	.12075				

Note.. F statistic for WILK'S Lambda is exact.

Univariate F-tests with (2,34) D. F.

SEX by SES is NOT Significant Univariately for FINAL & EVAL [2]

Variable	Hypoth. SS	Error SS	Hypoth. MS	Error MS	F	Sig. of F [2]
FINAL	899.85727	8761.56667	449.92864	257.69314	1.74599	.190
EVAL	3.24048	31.90000	1.62024	.93824	1.72690	.193

- -

```
EFFECT .. SES        Note that SES is Significant Multivariately [3]
```

Multivariate Tests of Significance (S = 2, M = -1/2, N = 15 1/2)

Test Name	Value	Approx. F	Hypoth. DF	Error DF	Sig. of F [3]
Pillais	.50197	5.69644	4.00	68.00	.001
Hotellings	.97771	7.82171	4.00	64.00	.000
Wilks	.50308	6.76295	4.00	66.00	.000
Roys	.49170				

Note.. F statistic for WILK'S Lambda is exact.

Univariate F-tests with (2,34) D.F.

SES is Significant Univariately for FINAL and EVAL [4]

Variable	Hypoth. SS	Error SS	Hypoth. MS	Error MS	F	Sig. of F [4]
FINAL	2913.73259	8761.56667	1456.86629	257.69314	5.65349	.008
EVAL	8.66027	31.90000	4.33013	.93824	4.61519	.017

```
EFFECT .. SEX        Note that SEX is Significant Multivariately [5]
```

Multivariate Tests of Significance (S = 1, M = 0, N = 15 1/2)

Test Name	Value	Exact F	Hypoth. DF	Error DF	Sig. of F [5]
Pillais	.17592	3.52239	2.00	33.00	.041
Hotellings	.21348	3.52239	2.00	33.00	.041
Wilks	.82408	3.52239	2.00	33.00	.041
Roys	.17592				

Note.. F statistics are exact.

Univariate F-tests with (1,34) D. F.

Note that SEX is Significant only for EVAL Univariately [6]

Variable	Hypoth. SS	Error SS	Hypoth. MS	Error MS	F	Sig. of F [6]
FINAL	91.25235	8761.56667	91.25235	257.69314	.35411	.556
EVAL	4.47935	31.90000	4.47935	.93824	4.77422	.036

CHAPTER 19: NONPARAMETRIC STATISTICS

ASSORTED NONPARAMETRIC STATISTICS (USED FOR RANKS, CATEGORICAL DATA OR WHEN MEASUREMENT DATA DOESN'T MEET THE ASSUMPTIONS)

This chapter describes sets of procedures that allow you to use various nonparametric techniques. Nonparametrics are usually used when data sets do not meet the assumptions of the parametric techniques or the data are of a type not appropriate to parametric techniques. Several texts review the theoretical underpinnings of these tests and concepts (Daniel, 1990; Everitt, 1977; Siegel & Castellan, 1988). Note that nonparametric are generally thought to be less powerful (less likely to find true significance) than a parametric test when the latter is appropriate and correctly applied. We will present a series of tests and examples of simple data sets to illustrate their use.

GROUP DIFFERENCES

The first set of procedures to be presented uses NPAR TESTS to look for differences between groups. The archetypal setup is:

> ### npar test *test name = variable description*

The exact form is specific to the tests. You will need fill in the test and variable description.

BINOMIAL TEST
(USING THE BINOMIAL DISTRIBUTION- $[P + Q]^n$)

We wish to determine whether the distribution of a variable comes from a binomial distribution with a probability of *p*. The test is performed as two-tailed test. Our setup is the simplest and assumes that:

1. The variable SUSHI is dichotomous.

2. The probability of the first category (p) is 0.5.

We wish to determine if a sushi tester faced with good or bad fish (50% each) would be likely to identify 7 pieces of fish correctly. We used the weight command to our advantage to enter the number correct and incorrect (1 wrong = **0 1**; 7 correct = **1 7**) Thus we need only to say:

> npar tests binomial = sushi .

One can change the probability for p and specific values of a variable to be used in the test. Thus if we wanted the two values to be tested (with the first assumed to have a probability of .4) to be 3 and 4, we would use:

npar tests binomial (.4) = variable (3,4).

Setup and output for our sushi example follow:

SETUP

```
set width = 80 .
data list list / sushi freq .
value labels sushi 0 'wrong' 1 'correct' .
weight by freq .
begin data .
0  1
1  7
end data .
npar tests binomial = sushi .
finish .
```

OUTPUT

```
          - - - Binomial Test

           SUSHI
Cases
                        Test Prop. =    .5000
     1    =  .00        Obs. Prop. =    .1250
     7    = 1.00
     -                  Exact Binomial
     8    Total         2-Tailed P  =   .0703
```

Note this is a two-tailed probability. Divide by two (2-Tailed P = .0703) to determine the probability of getting 7 choices correct (1-Tailed P = .0703/2 = .3515). Two-tailed probabilities are calculated when p = .5. If *p* didn't equal .5, a one-tail probability would be computed as seen below with a *p* = .4 .

```
npar tests binomial (.4) = sushi .

           SUSHI
     Cases
                        Test Prop. =    .4000
     1    =  .00        Obs. Prop. =    .1250
     7    = 1.00
     -                  Exact Binomial
     8    Total         1-Tailed P  =    .1064
```

CHI-SQUARE
(See Chapters 10 and 11 for a Fuller Presentation)

COCHRAN'S Q
(Difference Between Repeated Proportions)

You have dichotomous data over several trials. Do the proportions differ? In this example, we have 4 trials and 15 subjects. The outcomes are coded as 0 and 1. You don't have to use 0 and 1; you could have used, for example, 2 and 3. However, there must be only two values for the variables tested. In our example, the differences between proportions are significant. Note this test is an extension of the McNemar test to more than two variables. The general form is:

```
npar tests cochran = var list .
```

SETUP

```
set  width  =  80  .
data  list  list/  x1  to  x4  .
begin  data  .
1  0  1  1
1  0  1  1
1  0  1  1
1  0  1  1
1  0  1  1
1  0  1  1
1  0  1  1
1  0  1  1
1  0  1  1
1  0  1  1
1  1  1  1
1  0  1  1
1  1  1  1
1  1  1  1
1  0  0  0
end  data  .
npar  tests  cochran  =  x1  to  x4  .
finish  .
```

OUTPUT

```
- - - - Cochran  Q  Test

    Cases

  =  1.00  =  .00    Variable

        15       0   X1
         3      12   X2
        14       1   X3
        14       1   X4

   Cases          Cochran Q      D.F.    Significance
     15            32.3333         3         .0000
```

FRIEDMAN TWO-WAY ANOVA

(Differences Between Repeated Ranks)

This is similar to a repeated measures oneway anova but based on ranks. See p. 16.30 for the comparison. We have the variables a1 to a4 representing the repeated factor. We simply need to note this is the command whose general form is:

> npar tests friedman = *var list* .

Our example will be significant.

SETUP

```
set width = 80 .
data list list / a1 a2 a3 a4 .
begin data .
13 9 11 10
8 8 7 4
7 5 5 4
9 6 7 3
6 8 8 2
8 3 1 5
13 12 12 11
9 11 11 10
8 9 9 8
11 10 7 4
8 7 8 8
4 5 7 5
14 11 11 12
13 9 9 6
10 11 9 9
10 8 10 7
7 10 5 7
9 6 4 6
end data .
npar tests friedman = a1 to a4.
finish .
```

OUTPUT

```
- - - - - Friedman  Two-Way  Anova

Mean Rank    Variable

   3.17      A1
   2.61      A2
   2.47      A3
   1.75      A4

Cases      Chi-Square     D.F.    Significance
  18         11.0167        3          .0116
```

Note there is significance.

KOLMOGOROV-SMIRNOV TEST / ONE SAMPLE
(Goodness of Fit of a Distribution Against Specified Distribution)

We check whether a sample comes from a specific distribution. The choices are UNIFORM or rectangular, NORMAL, or POISSON. You can specify the characteristics of the distribution. Thus the command has several variations (we will call our variable 'X'):

nonpar tests k-s (**uniform**) = x .	Use range of '**X**'.
nonpar tests k-s (uniform, **min** , **max**) = x .	Use **min** to **max** values.
nonpar tests k-s (**normal**) = x .	Use mean and std. dev of '**X**'.
nonpar tests k-s (normal, **mean**, **std. dev.**) = x .	Use **mean** and **std. dev** values .
nonpar tests k-s (**poisson**) = x .	Use mean of '**X**'.
nonpar tests k-s (poisson, **mean**) = x .	Use **mean** value supplied.

SETUP

```
set width = 80 .
data list list / x wt .
weight by wt .
begin data .
1 0
2 10
3 20
4 33
5 40
6 50
7 35
8 20
9 12
10 2
end data
nonpar  tests  k-s  (uniform,1,10)  =  x  . Uniform  from  1  to  10
nonpar  tests  k-s  (normal)  =  x  .    Normal  with  mean,  SD   of  X
finish .
```

OUTPUT

```
- - - - - Kolmogorov - Smirnov Goodness of Fit Test
->    nonpar tests k-s (uniform,1,10) = x .
      X
      Test distribution - Uniform      Range:   1.00 to 10.00
                  Cases:  223

      Most extreme differences
Absolute       Positive        Negative     K-S Z      2-Tailed P | Significant
   .19432        .18087         -.19432      2.902         .000    | Difference

->    nonpar tests k-s (normal) = x .
      X
      Test distribution - Normal                 Mean:  5.5874
                                   Standard Deviation:  1.8430
                  Cases:  223
         Most extreme differences
Absolute       Positive        Negative     K-S Z      2-Tailed P | Significant
   .12220        .10202         -.12220      1.825         .003    | Difference
```

KOLMOGOROV SMIRNOV TEST / TWO SAMPLE
(Compare One Distribution Against Another Distribution)

We check whether one distribution differs from another in location and dispersion. Thus the test picks up shape, variability and/or central tendency differences. Data must be at least ordinal. We will compare the variable SCORE for group 1 versus group 2. We indicate the group with the variable GROUP (values = 1 or 2). You could use another two values (say 3 or 4), you just have to specify them. We will not find a significant difference. The command specifies the target variable (SCORE) and the grouping factor (GROUP) :

---

npar tests k-s = score by group (*value ,value*) .

SETUP

```
set width = 80 .
data list list /group score .
begin data
  1   100
  1   110
  1   125
  1   140
  1   120
  1   130
  1   115
  1    95
  1   145
  1   120
  2    85
  2    95
  2   110
  2   125
  2   105
  2   115
  2   100
  2    80
  2   130
  2   105
end data .
npar tests k-s = score by group (1,2) .
finish .
```

OUTPUT

```
Kolmogorov  -  Smirnov  2-Sample  Test

      SCORE
   by GROUP


        Cases

         10   GROUP = 1.00
         10   GROUP = 2.00
         --
         20   Total

      Most extreme differences
 Absolute    Positive     Negative     K-S Z    2-Tailed P
  .40000      .00000       -.40000      .894        .400

      Note:  Nonsignificant  Difference
```

KRUSKAL-WALLIS ONE-WAY ANOVA
(Differences Between Ranks for ≥ 2 Groups)

This is a nonparametric equivalent of an one-way ANOVA which is based on mean ranks. Our dependent variable is hours and is broken down by major with values from 1 to 3. We will find a significant difference. See Chapter 14 for the equivalent anova on these data.

SETUP

```
set width = 80 .
data list list / major hours .
variable labels hours 'Time spent studying per week' /
               major 'Undergraduate Major' .
value labels major 1 'Humanities' 2 'Soc. Sci.' 3 'Nat. Sci'.
begin data .
1 02
1 08
1 16
1 03
1 10
2 08
2 06
2 09
2 04
2 11
3 20
3 19
3 16
3 19
3 18
end data .
npar tests k-w = hours by major (1,3)    .
finish .
```

OUTPUT

```
- - - - - Kruskal-Wallis 1-Way Anova

    HOURS      Time spent studying per week
 by MAJOR      Undergraduate Major

   Mean Rank    Cases

        5.40        5   MAJOR =   1   Humanities
        5.70        5   MAJOR =   2   Soc. Sci.
       12.90        5   MAJOR =   3   Nat. Sci
                   --
                   15   Total
                                      Corrected for ties
   Cases    Chi-Square  Significance    Chi-Square   Significance
      15      9.0150       .0110          9.0636        .0108
```

MCNEMAR'S TEST
(Test of Repeated 2 $\times$ 2 Categories)

Basically a Cochran's Q (see previous) for only two repetitions. We will test whether political party affiliation changes for students from high school to college. We've entered the number of students (63) who are Democrats in both (1,1), Democrats and then Republicans (21 for the 1,2), etc. We will find significance. For the command you just need to specify the two variables.

> ## npar tests mcnemar = var1 var2 .

SETUP

```
set width = 80 .
data list list / partyhs partycol wt .
variable labels partyhs 'High School' / partycol 'College' .
value labels partyhs partycol 1 'dem' 2 'rep' .
weight by wt .
begin data .
1 1 63
1 2 21
2 1 4
2 2 12
end data .
npar tests  mcnemar  =  partyhs  partycol  .
finish .
```

OUTPUT

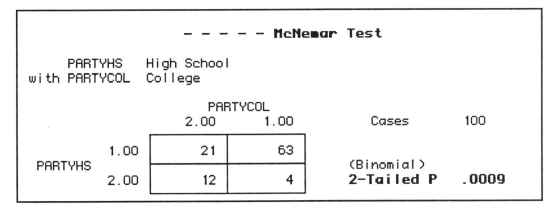

```
- - - - - McNemar Test

    PARTYHS     High School
with PARTYCOL   College

                    PARTYCOL
                2.00    1.00        Cases       100

        1.00      21      63
PARTYHS                             (Binomial)
        2.00      12       4        2-Tailed P   .0009
```

MANN-WHITNEY U
(Difference in Mean Rank Between Two Groups)

We test whether two groups differ in mean rank. This is similar to a t-test in intent. You need to specify the two groups. We will compare the variable SCORE for group 1 versus group 2. We indicate the group with the variable GROUP (values = 1 or 2). You could use another two values (say 3 or 4); you just have to specify them. We will not find a significant difference. The command specifies the target variable and the grouping variable.

---

npar tests m-w = score by group (*value , value*) .

S E T U P

```
set width = 80 .
data list list / group score .
begin data
    1  100
    1  110
    1  125
    1  140
    1  120
    1  130
    1  115
    1   95
    1  145
    1  120
    2   85
    2   95
    2  110
    2  125
    2  105
    2  115
    2  100
    2   80
    2  130
    2  105
end data .
npar tests m-w = score by group (1,2)  .
finish   .
```

O U T P U T

Mann-Whitney U - Wilcoxon Rank Sum W Test

          SCORE
     by GROUP

Mean Rank   Cases

      12.90   10 GROUP = 1.00
       8.10   10 GROUP = 2.00
                  --
                  20 Total

                Exact   Corrected for ties
  U   W   2-Tailed P   Z   **2-Tailed P**
26.0   129.0   .0753   -1.8197   .0688

Note: Nonsignificant Difference

MEDIAN TEST
(Differences Between Ranks)

This is a nonparametric equivalent of an oneway ANOVA which is based comparing medians. Our dependent variable is hours and is broken down by major with values from 1 to 3. We will find a significant difference. See Chapter 14 for the equivalent anova on these data.

S E T U P

```
set width  =  80 .
data list list / major hours .
        etc.
           data  same  as  for  Kruskal-Wallis  above
npar tests median = hours by major (1,3)      .
finish
```

OUTPUT

```
- - - - - Median Test
        HOURS        Time spent studying per week
   by MAJOR          Undergraduate Major

                              MAJOR
                         1        2        3

              GT Median    1        1        5
   HOURS
              LE Median    4        4        0


   Cases        Median     Chi-Square     D.F.   Significance
    15          10.00        8.5714         2       .0138
```

MOSES TEST OF EXTREME REACTIONS
(Difference in Ranges Between Two Groups)

We are comparing the ranges of a variable for two groups (specified by the values of another variable) for significance. A one-tailed probability is computed and recomputed after dropping a specified number (default = 5%) of the first group. The command specifies the target variable and the grouping variable.

> **npar tests moses = score by group (*value* , *value*) .**

You can specify the **number of cases** to be dropped, if not wanting to use the default. This is the actual number and not a percent figure. If you want to base the exclusion on a percent value, you will have to calculate it from the number of cases that you have. The specification would appear as:

> **npar tests moses (n) = score by group (*value* , *value*) .**

In our example, we use the default and divide the variable SCORE up into two groups using the variable GROUP. The range will not differ significantly.

SETUP	**OUTPUT**
| ```
set width = 80 .
data list list / group score .
begin data
  1  100
  1  110
  1  125
  1  140
  1  120
  1  130
  1  115
  1   95
  1  145
  1  120
  2   85
  2   95
  2  110
  2  125
  2  105
  2  115
  2  100
  2   80
  2  130
  2  105
end data .
npar tests moses = score by group (1,2) .
finish .
``` | ```
- -  Moses  Test  of  Extreme  Reactions

        SCORE
     by GROUP


              Cases

       (Control)  10  GROUP = 1.00
    (Experimental) 10  GROUP = 2.00
                   --
                   20  Total

1-Tailed P    Span of Control Group
   .5000          18   Observed
   .6858          15   After removing 1 outlier(s)
                       from each end

    Note: Not significant
``` |

SIGN TEST
(Difference Between 2 Repeated Groups)

This is similar to a repeated, matched, or correlated t-test. See p. 162 for correspondence. You simply need to specify the variables to be compared as follows:

> **npar tests sign =** *var list* **.**

Our example compares SCORE1 and SCORE2 . The difference is significant.

SETUP	**OUTPUT**
| ```
set width = 80 .
data list list / score1 score2 .
begin data .
    100  116
    110  127
    125  139
    140  153
    120  138
    130  143
    115  130
     95  102
    145  158
    120  138
end data .
npar test sign=score1 score2.
finish .
``` | ```
- - - - - Sign Test

      SCORE1
  with SCORE2


Cases

    0  - Diffs (SCORE2 LT SCORE1)
   10  + Diffs (SCORE2 GT SCORE1)
    0    Ties
   --
   10    Total
                (Binomial)
            2-Tailed P =    .0020
    Note: Significant
``` |

CORRELATIONAL TECHNIQUES

KENDALL COEFFICIENT OF CONCORDANCE
(AGREEMENT AMONG RANKS)

The coefficient (**W**) measures agreement between raters. Each line of data is one rater and each variable is an item to be rated.

> **npar tests kendall = *var list* .**

W can have values from 0 to 1 (perfect agreement). In our case, we have three variables (R1 to R3) and 8 judges (eight lines of data). There will be significance.

SETUP

```
set width = 80 .
data list list / r1 to r3 .
begin data .
2 3 1
2 3 1
3 2 1
2 3 1
3 2 1
1 2 3
2 3 1
2 3 1
end data .
npar tests   kendall = r1 to r3 .
finish .
```

OUTPUT

```
- - - - - Kendall  Coefficient  of  Concordance

    Mean Rank      Variable

         2.13      R1
         2.63      R2
         1.25      R3

Cases         W              Chi-Square    D.F.    Significance
   8        .4844              7.7500        2         .0208
```

NONPAR CORR
(Correlation Between Ranks)

NONPAR CORR can calculate both the Spearman Correlation Coefficient and the Kendall Correlation Coefficient (tau-b) based on ranks. One simply lists the variables to be correlated. We will request a two-tailed significance test and both coefficients to be printed. If omitted, a one-tail level would be used and only the Spearman would be reported. The command structure is:

```
nonpar corr var list / print = twotail both .
```

In our example, both coefficients are significant.

SETUP

```
set width = 80 .
data list list / rank1 rank2 .
begin data
1 2
2 1
3 5
4 3
5 4
6 6
7 7
8 9
9 8
10 10
end data .
nonpar corr rank1 rank2 / print = twotail both .
finish .
```

OUTPUT

```
  -   KENDALL   CORRELATION   COEFFICIENTS   -

RANK2                 .8667
                   N(   10)
                   SIG .000


                     RANK1

  -   SPEARMAN   CORRELATION   COEFFICIENTS   -

RANK2                 .9515
                   N(   10)
                   SIG .000


                     RANK1
```

CHAPTER 20: DATA MANIPULATION

VARIOUS WAYS OF MANIPULATING, PRINTING, ENTERING & SAVING DATA

This chapter describes sets of commands that allow you to manipulate your data and have more flexibility in how data is entered and set up for SPSS. The topics will be:

- Printing Data: **LIST, PRINT**

- Selecting Data: **SELECT IF, TEMPORARY**

- Transforming variables or creating new variables: **COMPUTE, RECODE**

- Conditional transformation: **IF, DO IF, ELSE IF, ELSE, END IF**

- External Data Sets: **DATA LIST FILE = 'FILENAME' ... etc.**

- Formatting Data :

    ❑ Columns

    ❑ Multiple records DATA LIST RECORDS = #

    ❑ Errors in formatting.

    ❑ Fortran-like formats (**'a', 'f', 'x', 't'**)

- System Files:

    ❑ **SAVE FILE, GET FILE, DISPLAY**

    ❑ SPSS® 4.0 FOR UNIX™ and SPSS ® for the Macintosh ®

    ❑ SPSS/PC ™ + 4.0.

PRINTING DATA

SUMMARY OF SPSS COMMANDS:

```
LIST Variable List .
                    OR
PRINT {OUTFILE = ?} / Variable List .¹
EXECUTE .
_____

1    PRINT Not Available for SPSS/PC ™ + 4.0
```

EXAMPLE: PRINTS 'X' SCORES IN LISTING

```
set width = 80 .
data list list / x . { data list free / etc. for SPSS/PC ™ + }
begin data.
1
2
3
end data .
list x.
finish .
```

EXAMPLE: PRINTS 'X' SCORES ON EXTERNAL FILE
'DATA. 1' - (Not Available for SPSS/PC ™ + 4.0)

```
set width = 80 .
data list list / x .
file handle = ? - check your local installation if
    needed.
begin data.
1
2
3
end data .
print outfile = 'data.1' / x .
execute .
finish .
```

EXAMPLE OF LIST SETUP

This setup will read the three scores and produce a list of the three.

```
set width = 80 .
data list list / x .
begin data.
1

2

3
end data .
list x.
finish .
```

EXAMPLE OF PRINT SETUP

This setup will read the three scores and produce a list of the three on the external file 'data. 1'. It contains 1,2,3 .

```
set width = 80 .
data list list / x .
begin data .
1
2
3
end data .
print outfile = 'data.1' / x .
execute .
finish .
```

LIST OUTPUT (MACINTOSH VERSION)

```
Note the list of scores.
-> set width = 80 .
-> data list list / x .
-> begin data.
-> 1
-> 2
-> 3
-> end data .
-> list x .
```
_____

SPSS Release 4.0 for Macintosh
Page 2

```
        X
```

```
      1.00
      2.00  | Listed   Scores
      3.00  |
```

Number of cases read   3   Number of cases listed:3

PRINT OUTPUT (UNIX VERSION)

```
1   0   set width = 80 .
2   data list list / x .
3   begin data .
6   end data .
7   print outfile = 'data.1' / x .
8   execute .
9   finish .
```

UNIX DIRECTORY ('data.1' ADDED BY PRINT COMMAND)

```
% ls
data.1          print
% cat data.1
      1.00
      2.00  | >  3 scores in data.1
      3.00  |
%
```

PRINT RESULTS IN MACINTOSH WINDOW
(USES SAME COMMANDS)

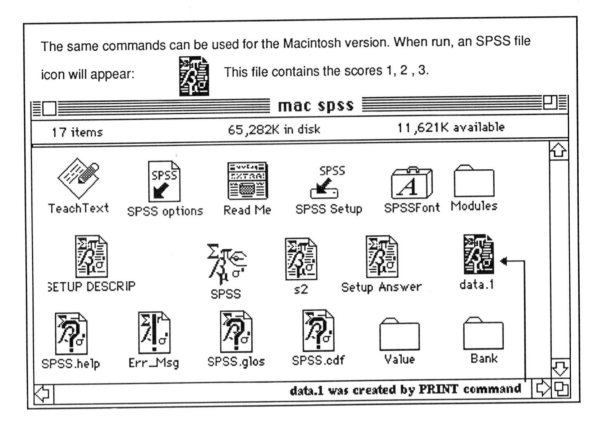

The same commands can be used for the Macintosh version. When run, an SPSS file icon will appear: This file contains the scores 1, 2 , 3.

It could be opened by SPSS again or other application. Below is **data.1** opened from Microsoft® Word. As you can see it contains the three scores.

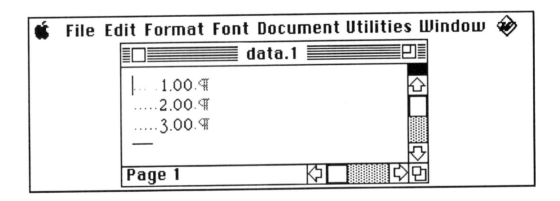

SELECTION OF DATA

SUMMARY OF SPSS 'SELECT IF' COMMANDS:

COMMAND STRUCTURE

select if (*logical expression*) .
temporary - if used before 'select if', the
selection lasts for only one procedure.

LOGICAL TERMS:

gt -	greater than	lt - less than
ge -	greater than or =	le - less or =
eq -	equal to	ne - not equal
and		
not		
or		

QUICK EXAMPLE: SELECTS 'X' SCORES GE 2 AND COMPUTES THE MEAN.

```
set width = 80 .
data list list / x . ¹
begin data.
1          WON'T BE IN CALCULATION
2          WILL BE IN CALCULATION
3          WILL BE IN CALCULATION
end data .
select if (x ge 2) .
descriptives x .
finish .
```

---

¹ Use 'data list **free** / etc. for SPSS/PC+™ 4.0 .

Purpose of the 'Select IF' Command:

The purpose of the SELECT IF command is to allow analyses of just parts of the data set. You construct a logical expression that is inserted in your setup. Once this is executed, only cases that meet this logical test will be analyzed from that point on in your setup. The other cases which are not chosen no longer can or will be processed.

Note:

1. This does not eliminate the cases from a stored setup file. The selection only is true for current SPSS session. The command is positioned before its use.

2. It is possible to make a selection procedure have a temporary effect such that all data can still be worked with later. We will show you this procedure later.

Structure of the 'Select IF' Command:

The command is made of up of the key words 'select if' plus a logical expression inclosed in parentheses as follows:

select if (*logical expression*) .

The logical expressions are constructed using variable names and the following abbreviations. The expression must follow the rules of logic to be successful.

Logical Terms:

gt -	greater than	lt - less than
ge -	greater than or =	le - less or =
eq -	equal to	ne - not equal
and		
not		
or		

The following examples will demonstrate the usage and effects of such commands. We have a data set that has for each person:

1. The hospital in which they were treated (hospital).

2. The length in days of their three stays in the hospital (stay1 to stay3)

3. The total cost in $1000 (costk).

We will pick groups, print them, and analyze them using **SELECT IF** commands. Note we use the **LIST** command to demonstrate our results.

BASIC SETUP

```
set width = 80 .
data list list / hospital stay1 to stay3 costk . 1
variable labels costk 'total cost of stay in $1000'.
value labels hospital 1 'Happy Dale'
                       2 ' Sunnyvale'
                       3 ' Arborview'
                       4 ' Meadowlane'
                       5 'Bedlam' .
begin data .
1 78 65 90        60
3 67 65 56        58
4 77 89 78        63
5 98 67 99        65
1 78 67 89        84
3 89 67 89        52
2 56 34 20        72
5 77 98 50        67
4 55 99 34        59
3 66 78 98        67
2 89 80 89        60
1 67 80 56        58
3 77 89 89        63
5 98 67 99        65
1 78 33 88        84
1 89 45 89        52
3 56 34 20        72
4 77 98 50        15
2 55 99 34        59
2 66 78 98        67
3 89 65 89        60
2 45 80 56        58
1 77 89 89        63
4 98 67 99        65
1 78 45 89        84
5 89 67 89        52
4 56 34 20        72
3 77 98 42        45
2 55 99 34        59
1 66 78 98        67
3 89 65 89        60
2 45 65 56        58
3 77 89 89        63
2 98 45 99        65
2 78 45 89        84
3 89 67 89        52
2 56 34 20        72
4 77 98 50        67
5 55 99 34        59
2 66 78 98        45
end data .
select if (?) .
list all .
frequencies variables = ?.
finish .
```

_____

1 Use 'data list **free** / etc. for SPSS/PC+[TM] 4.0 .

Select Only Those Cases Where Hospital = Five
(Note there are **5** cases.)

```
set width = 80 .
data list list / hospital stay1 to stay3
                costk . 1
variable labels costk 'total cost in $1000'.
value labels hospital 1 'Happy Dale'
                       2 'Sunnyvale'
                       3 'Arborview'
                       4 'Meadowlane'
                       5 'Bedlam' .
begin data .
1 78 65 90       60
3 67 65 56       58
4 77 89 78       63
5 98 67 99       65
1 78 67 89       84
3 89 67 89       52
2 56 34 20       72
5 77 98 50       67
4 55 99 34       59
3 66 78 98       67
2 89 80 89       60
1 67 80 56       58
3 77 89 89       63
5 98 67 99       65
1 78 33 88       84
1 89 45 89       52
3 56 34 20       72
4 77 98 50       15
2 55 99 34       59
2 66 78 98       67
3 89 65 89       60
2 45 80 56       58
1 77 89 89       63
4 98 67 99       65
1 78 45 89       84
5 89 67 89       52
4 56 34 20       72
3 77 98 42       45
2 55 99 34       59
1 66 78 98       67
3 89 65 89       60
2 45 65 56       58
3 77 89 89       63
2 98 45 99       65
2 78 45 89       84
3 89 67 89       52
2 56 34 20       72
4 77 98 50       67
5 55 99 34       59
2 66 78 98       45
end data .
select if (hospital eq 5) .
list all .
frequencies variables = costk .
finish .
```

Output Based on The Selected FIVE Cases

Note how all values of HOSPITAL = 5 .

```
etc.
->    select if (hospital eq 5) .
->    list all .

HOSPITAL    STAY1    STAY2    STAY3    COSTK

    5.00    98.00    67.00    99.00    65.00
    5.00    77.00    98.00    50.00    67.00
    5.00    98.00    67.00    99.00    65.00
    5.00    89.00    67.00    89.00    52.00
    5.00    55.00    99.00    34.00    59.00
N
umber of cases read:  5    Number of cases listed:  5

->    frequencies variables = costk .

COSTK      total cost in $1000

Value                          Valid    Cum
Label    Value  Frequency  Percent  Percent  Percent

         52.00       1      20.0     20.0     20.0
         59.00       1      20.0     20.0     40.0
         65.00       2      40.0     40.0     80.0
         67.00       1      20.0     20.0    100.0
                 -------  -------  -------
         Total       5     100.0    100.0

Valid cases     5        Missing cases      0
```

Our next example will use **ge**, **and** & **eq** commands.

---

[1]   Use 'data list **free** / etc. for
      SPSS/PC+™ 4.0 .

Select Only Those Cases Where:
'costk ge 72 and hospital eq 2'

```
set width = 80 .
data list list / hospital stay1 to
               stay3 costk . 1
variable labels costk 'total cost in $1000'.
value labels hospital 1 'Happy Dale'
                      2 'Sunnyvale'
                      3 'Arborview'
                      4 'Meadowlane'
                      5 'Bedlam' .

begin data .
1 78 65 90     60
3 67 65 56     58
4 77 89 78     63
5 98 67 99     65
1 78 67 89     84
3 89 67 89     52
2 56 34 20     72
5 77 98 50     67
4 55 99 34     59
3 66 78 98     67
2 89 80 89     60
1 67 80 56     58
3 77 89 89     63
5 98 67 99     65
1 78 33 88     84
1 89 45 89     52
3 56 34 20     72
4 77 98 50     15
2 55 99 34     59
2 66 78 98     67
3 89 65 89     60
2 45 80 56     58
1 77 89 89     63
4 98 67 99     65
1 78 45 89     84
5 89 67 89     52
4 56 34 20     72
3 77 98 42     45
2 55 99 34     59
1 66 78 98     67
3 89 65 89     60
2 45 65 56     58
3 77 89 89     63
2 98 45 99     65
2 78 45 89     84
3 89 67 89     52
2 56 34 20     72
4 77 98 50     67
5 55 99 34     59
2 66 78 98     45
end data .
select if (costk ge 72 and hospital
          eq 2) .
list all .
frequencies variables = costk .
finish .
```

Output Based on The Selected THREE Cases

Note how all values of HOSPITAL = 2 and COSTK ≥ 72.

```
etc.
50  select if (costk ge 72 and hospital
              eq 2) .
51  list all .

HOSPITAL   STAY1    STAY2    STAY3    COSTK

  2.00     56.00    34.00    20.00    72.00
  2.00     78.00    45.00    89.00    84.00
  2.00     56.00    34.00    20.00    72.00

Number of cases read:  3   Number of cases listed:  3

  52  frequencies variables = costk .


COSTK      total cost of stay in $1000

                                    Valid    Cum
Value Label  Value Frequency Percent Percent Percent

            72.00      2      66.7    66.7    66.7
            84.00      1      33.3    33.3   100.0
                     ------- ------- -------
            Total      3     100.0   100.0

Valid cases      3    Missing cases     0
```

---

1   Use 'data list **free** / etc. for
    SPSS/PC+^{TM} 4.0 .

USE OF 'TEMPORARY' SELECTIONS

The previous examples selected a subset of the data. An analysis following the SELECT IF command would only operate on the selected data. It would be as if the other cases did not exist. Sometimes, one wants to select a set of data, conduct an analysis and then select a different set of data for another analysis. This can be done by pairing a TEMPORARY command with the SELECT IF. If this is done, then the selection process only holds for one procedure. The data 'returns' so to speak in its entirety for the next analysis.

We will set up a data set for three groups and then pick each one for a procedure. First, we will also show how if we did not use a TEMPORARY command, we would eliminate all our data.

Eliminating All Your Data with SELECT IF

In this example, we have people classified by **RACE**. We have also entered their weight. First we want to list the people with **RACE** = 1 (African-Americans). Then we want to run examine on the Asian-Americans (**RACE** = 2). It won't work as the first SELECT IF [**select if (race eq 1)**] eliminates the Asian-Americans and the EXAMINE run crashes.

SETUP

```
set width = 80 .
data list list / race weight .  1
value labels race 1 'African-amer.'  2 'Asian-Amer.'
                       3 'Cauc.' .
begin data .
1 120
1 134
1 125
2 147
2 110
2 123
3 124
3 131
3 125
end data .
select if (race eq 1) .   ⇒ Selects   African-Americans
list race weight .
select if (race eq 2 ) .  ⇒ Try to  select  Asian-Americans
examine weight .
finish .
_____
1  Use 'data list free / etc. for SPSS/PC+™ 4.0 .
```

OUTPUT

```
SPSS Release 4.0 for Macintosh
->    set width = 80 .
->    data list list / race weight .
->    value labels race 1 'African-amer.' 2 'Asian-Amer.'
->                     3 'Cauc.' .
->    begin data .
->    end data .
->    select if ( race eq 1) .
->    list   race weight .

    RACE    WEIGHT

    1.00    120.00
    1.00    134.00                  ⟹  AFRICAN - AMERICANS SELECTED
    1.00    125.00

Number of cases read:  3    Number of cases listed:   3

->    select if (race eq 2 ) .
->    examine weight  .

>Warning # 17470.   Command name: EXAMINE
>The number of non-missing cases for this split group is
equal to ZERO.   No analysis for this split group will be
provided.
              NOTE THERE ARE NO LONGER ANY RACE = 2 FOLKS!
->    finish .
```

Use of the TEMPORARY Command

In this example, we have have put a TEMPORARY command in front of each select if. Thus, the **race = 1** selection is made and then goes away. We then select for **race = 2** and can do our EXAMINE run.

Setup with TEMPORARY Command

```
set width = 80 .
data list list / race weight . ¹
value labels race 1 'African-amer.' 2 'Asian-Amer.'
                    3 'Cauc.' .
begin data . _____
1 120          ¹ Use 'data list free / etc. for SPSS/PC+ᵀᴹ 4.0 .
  etc.
3 125
end data .
temporary  .
select if (race eq 1) .
list race weight .
temporary  .
select if (race eq 2) . .
examine weight  .
finish .
```

Output with TEMPORARY Command

```
->     set width = 80 .
->     data list list / race weight .
->     value labels race 1 'African-amer.' 2 'Asian-Amer.'
->                      3 'Cauc.' .
->     begin data .
->     end data .
->     temporary .
->     select if (race eq 1) .
->     list   race weight .
```

╔══════════════════════════════════════╗
║ Race = 1 only for the LIST run   ║
╚══════════════════════════════════════╝

```
    RACE    WEIGHT


    1.00    120.00
    1.00    134.00
    1.00    125.00
Number of cases read:  3     Number of cases listed:  3
```

╔══════════════════════════════════════╗
║ All Races (1,2,3) return to data.   ║
╚══════════════════════════════════════╝

```
->     temporary .
->     select if (race eq 2) .
->     examine  weight .
```

╔══════════════════════════════════════╗
║ Race = 2 only for the EXAMINE run   ║
╚══════════════════════════════════════╝

```
    WEIGHT

Valid cases:      3.0   Missing cases:     .0   Percent missing:      .0
Mean    126.6667  Std Err   10.8372  Min   110.0000  Skewness   .8455
Median  123.0000  Variance 352.3333  Max   147.0000  S E Skew  1.2247
5% Trim    .      Std Dev   18.7705  Range  37.0000  Kurtosis    .
                                     IQR    37.0000  S E Kurt    .


Frequency     Stem & Leaf
    3.00        1  *  124

Stem width:     100.00
Each leaf:        1 case(s)
```

```
Variables       WEIGHT
N of Cases       3.00
Symbol Key:         *   - Median   (O) - Outlier   (E)  - Extreme
```

COMPUTE STATEMENTS

SELECTIVE SET OF SPSS ' COMPUTE ' COMMANDS:

COMMAND STRUCTURE

> **compute** *variable* * = *expression* .

* Variable can be already existing or a new name.

ARITHMETIC TERMS & FUNCTIONS:

+	add	*	multiply
-	subtract	**	exponentiation
/	divide		(raise expression to a power)

abs	*(var or expression)*	- absolute value
rnd	*(var or expression)*	- round
exp	*(var or expression)*	- e $^{(var\ or\ exp)}$
ln	*(var or expression)*	- natural logarithm
lg10	*(var or expression)*	- base$_{10}$ logarithm
trunc	*(var or expression)*	- truncation (10.3 = 10)
sqrt	*(var or expression)*	- square root
sin	*(var or expression)*	- sine*
cos	*(var or expression)*	- cosine*

---

* The value of the expression is in radians, not degrees! The relationship is 1 radian $\approx 57°17'44.8''$ or $360 = 2\pi$ radians.
    There is no tangent function but tan $(x) = \sin (x)/\cos (x)$.

STATISTICAL FUNCTIONS:

sum	*(variables)*	- $\sum X$
mean	*(variables)*	- $\sum X / N$
sd	*(variables)*	- Standard Deviation = $\sqrt{[\sum x^2 / (N-1)]}$
var	*(variables)*	- Variance = $\sum x^2 / (N-1)$
cfvar	*(variables)*	- Coefficient of Variation = SD/Mean
min	*(variables)*	- Minimum of Variables
max	*(variables)*	- Maximum of Variables

Note: There are many other functions dealing with alphanumeric strings, dates and random numbers available. See the SPSS® Reference Guide (1990).

QUICK EXAMPLE: MULTIPLIES EACH 'X' BY 3.2.

```
set width = 80 .
data list list / x . ¹
begin data.
1      becomes 3.2
2      becomes 6.4
3      becomes 9.6
end data .
compute x = x*3.2 .
list x .
descriptives x . based on {3.2, 6.4 , 9.6}
finish .
```

QUICK EXAMPLE: COMPUTES MEAN OF X1, X2 & X3 FOR EACH SUBJECT AND ADDS NEW VARIABLE 'AVER'.

```
set width = 80 .
data list list / x1 to x3 . ¹
begin data.
1 4 5   aver would = 3.33
2 1 2   aver would = 1.67
3 1 3   aver would = 2.33
end data .
compute aver = mean (x1 to x3) .
list x1 to x3 aver .
frequencies variables = aver .
finish .
```

¹ Use 'data list **free** / etc. for SPSS/PC+™ 4.0 .

PURPOSE OF THE 'COMPUTE' COMMAND:

It is sometimes the case that you need to transform a variable or wish to create a new variable that is based on the already existing variables. You can do this with the COMPUTE statement. It allows you to:

- Transform old variables either on a permanent basis for the length of a session or just for one analysis (use of TEMPORARY).
- Create new variables.
- Save the transform or new variables in a new SPSS file (use of SAVE statement to be described later .

The form of the COMPUTE statement is :

compute variable = expression .

where 'variable' can be an old variable or a new variable being added. The expression is made up of arithmetic, statistical or other functions. An abbreviated list of what we find most useful for the novice is found on p. 437. We will not repeat it for brevity's sake.

Note that expression construction follows the normal rules of algebraic preference and use of parentheses. Thus, terms in parentheses are evaluated first. Exponentiation comes before division and multiplication (of equal precedence) and they have precedence over addition and subtraction (of equal precedence). The command is positioned in the setup before you wish it to take effect.

We will give four examples. The first will transform an old variable, print the new values, and use them in an analysis. The second will do the same but on a temporary basis to demonstrate the use of the temporary command in conjunction with compute statements. The third will create a new variable, list it and use it in an analysis. The fourth will compute the Pythagorean Theorem.

---

1. Compute Setup - Multiplies ' x ' score by 3.2

```
set width = 80 .
data list list / x .¹
begin data.
1       becomes 3.2
2       becomes 6.4
3       becomes 9.6
end data .
compute  x = x*3.2  .
list x .
descriptives x  .
finish  .
```
------

¹ Use 'data list free / x .' for
    SPSS/PC+^{TM} 4.0 .

Output

```
etc.

SPSS Release 4.0 for Macintosh
compute x = x*3.2 .
list x .
  X

3.20 Transformed score
6.40 Transformed score
9.60 Transformed score

descriptives x .

Valid
Variable  Mean Std Dev Min.  Max.    N

X           6.40 *    3.20  3.20  9.60    3
     * Mean of {3., 6.4, 9.60}
```

2. TEMPORARY Compute Setup - Multiplies ' x ' score by 3.2 ONLY for DESCRIPTIVES command. Data returns to original for LIST command.

```
set width = 80 .
data list list / x .
begin  data.
1
2
3
end data .
temporary . COMPUTE holds for next
compute x = x*3.2 .     procedure
descriptives  x .
list x . Data returns to original.
finish  .
```

Output

```
etc.
->    temporary .
->    compute x = x*3.2 .
->    descriptives x .

SPSS Release 4.0 for Macintosh


Valid
Variable  Mean  Std Dev   Min.   Max.   N

X         6.40     3.20    3.2   9.60   3
              ↳ Based on x*3.2
->    list x .

          X

     1.00        Original Data returns
     2.00         for next procedure
     3.00            (LIST)
```

3. Creation of New Variable Based on COMPUTE Command. Mean of x1, x2 & x3 will be calculated for each case, listed & used.

```
set width = 80 .
data list list / x1 to x3 .
begin data.
1 4 5
2 1 2
3 1 3
end data .
compute aver = mean (x1 to x3) .  Computes the mean
list aver .                        of x1, x2 and x3
frequencies variables = aver .
```

OUTPUT

```
SPSS Release 4.0 for Macintosh
etc.
->    compute aver = mean (x1 to x3) .
->    list  x1 to x3 aver .

   X1     X2    X3    AVER

 1.00   4.00   5.00   3.33  Average for each person's scores
 2.00   1.00   2.00  1.67
 3.00   1.00   3.00  2.33
Number of cases read: 3    Number of cases listed:  3

->    frequencies variables = aver .
          Frequency Distribution of New Variable 'AVER'
AVER                                Valid    Cum
Value    Value Frequency  Percent  Percent  Percent
Label
         1.67      1       33.3     33.3     33.3
         2.33      1       33.3     33.3     66.7
         3.33      1       33.3     33.3    100.0
                 -------  -------  -------
         Total     3      100.0    100.0
```

CONDITIONAL COMPUTATIONS

SUMMARY OF SPSS ' IF ' COMMAND:

COMMAND STRUCTURE

if (*logical expression*) *computation*.

LOGICAL TERMS:

gt -	greater than	lt - less than	
ge -	greater than or =	le - less or =	
eq -	equal to	ne - not equal	
and	not	or	

ARITHMETIC TERMS & FUNCTIONS:
see list on p. 437

QUICK EXAMPLE: IF 'X' SCORE IS GREATER OR EQUAL TO 2 THEN ADD 5 TO 'Y' SCORE.

```
set width = 80 .
data list list / x y . ¹
begin data.
1     2     Y remains unchanged at 2
2     4     5 will be added to Y (4+5 = 9)
3     3     5 will be added to Y (3+5 = 8)
end data .
if (x ge 2)  y = y + 5.
list y .
finish .
```

---

¹ Use 'data list **free** / x y. for SPSS/PC+^{TM} 4.0 .

PURPOSE OF THE 'IF' COMMAND:

The purpose of the IF command is to allow changes or computations depending on whether a condition is satisfied. You construct a logical expression about a variable or set of variables. The syntax is the same as that for the SELECT IF statement. Then you add a computation as done with a COMPUTE statement. The point is that the computation is only done if the logical expression is true.

IF statements can be used in conjunction with the TEMPORARY command as described before for COMPUTE and SELECT IF. Again, the command is positioned before its use.

STRUCTURE OF THE 'IF' COMMAND:

The command is made of up of the key words 'if' plus a logical expression inclosed in parentheses and a computation as follows:

if (*logical expression*) computation.

Let's look at a simple example where we will add 5 to one variable (Y) if another variable (X) has a value greater than equal to 2. Then we will print the new values to demonstrate the effect of the IF statement

```
            SETUP

set width = 80 .
data list list / x y . ¹
begin data.
1       2       Y will remain unchanged
2       4       5 will be added to Y
3       3       5 will be added to Y
end data .
if (x ge 2)   y = y + 5.
list x y .
finish .
```

```
¹   Use 'data list free / x y. for
      SPSS/PC+™ 4.0 .
```

```
           OUTPUT

SPSS Release 4.0 for Macintosh

->    set width = 80 .
->    data list list / x y .
->    begin data.
->      1       2
->      2       4
->      3       3
->    end data .
->    if (x ge 2)   y = y + 5.
->    list  x y .

       X        Y

     1.00     2.00    Unchanged
     2.00     9.00    5 added (4+5)
     3.00     8.00    5 added (3+5)

Number of cases read:   3
Number of cases listed:   3
```

SUMMARY OF SPSS 'DO IF ' COMMAND:

COMMAND STRUCTURE

>   do if (*logical expression*) .
>   compute* *variable* = *expression* .
>   else .
>   compute* *variable* = *expression* .
>   end if .

OR

>   do if (*logical expression*) .
>   compute* *variable* = *expression* .
>
>   else if (*logical expression*) .
>
>   compute* *variable* = *expression* .
>
>   else .
>
>   compute* *variable* = *expression* .
>
>   end if .

Logical Terms, Arithmetic Terms & Functions:
see previous lists

---

* RECODE statements could be used instead of COMPUTEs. See RECODE description that follows.

PURPOSE OF THE ' DO IF ' COMMAND:

The purpose of the DO IF command is to allow a series of changes or computations depending on whether a set of conditions is satisfied. You construct the logical expressions about a variable or set of variables. The syntax of the expression is the same as that for the SELECT IF or IF statements. However, you also add more expressions to be tested and statements such as COMPUTEs which are to be executed if the previous logical expression is not true.

DO IF statements can be used in conjunction with the TEMPORARY command as described before for COMPUTE, IF and SELECT IF. Again, the command is positioned before its use.

STRUCTURE OF THE 'DO IF' COMMAND:

The command is made of up of the key words 'do if' , 'else if', 'else ', logical expressions, compute statements and an 'end if'. Statements can have one branch or choice or more than one. Both cases are illustrated.

ONE BRANCH - TESTS FOR ONE LOGICAL CONDITION

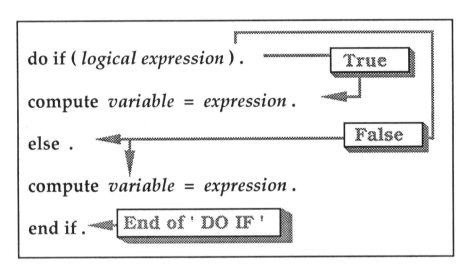

EXAMPLE (see previous footnotes for SPSS/PC+™ 4.0):

IF 'X' SCORE IS GREATER OR EQUAL TO 2 , ADD 5 TO 'Y' SCORE. IF THIS IS NOT TRUE, ADD 3 TO 'Y' SCORE.

```
set width = 80 .
data list list / x y .
begin data.
1       2       3 will be added to Y (1+3 = 4)
2       4       5 will be added to Y (4+5 = 9)
3       3       5 will be added to Y (3+5 = 8)
end data .
do if (x ge 2) .
y = y + 5 .
else    .
```

```
y = y + 3 .
end if .
list y .
finish .
```

OUTPUT

```
 etc.
->   end data .
->   do if (x ge 2) .
->   compute y = y + 5 .
->   else .
->   compute y = y + 3 .
->   end if .
->   list y .
       Y
    5.00
    9.00    --------> Transformed Y Scores
    8.00
Number of cases read:  3
Number of cases listed:  3
->   finish .
```

TWO BRANCH - TESTS FOR TWO LOGICAL CONDITIONS

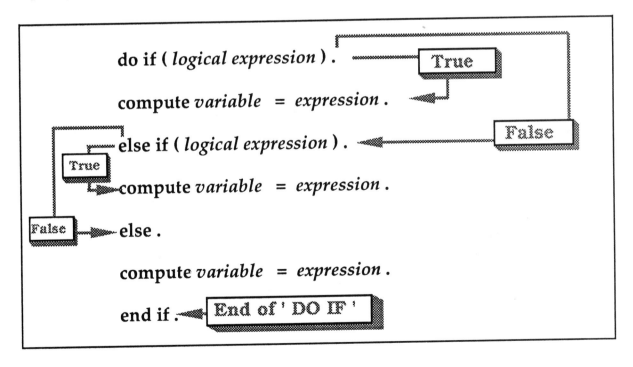

EXAMPLE (see previous footnotes for SPSS/PC+™ 4.0):

1. IF 'X' SCORE IS EQUAL TO 1 , CREATE A NEW SCORE CALLED 'Z' WHICH EQUALS 'Y' SCORE TIMES 5.0 .

2. IF THIS IS NOT TRUE, CHECK IF X EQUALS 2. IF SO, THEN CREATE A 'Z' WHICH EQUALS 'Y' TIMES 3.0

3. IF 'X' IS NOT EQUAL TO 1 OR 2, CREATE A 'Z' SCORE WHICH IS EQUAL TO 'Y' TIMES 4.0 .

SETUP *

```
set width = 80 .
data list list / x y .
begin data.
1 2        Z will be equal to 10 ( 2 x 5 )
2 4        Z will be equal to 12 ( 4 x  3 )
3 3        Z will be equal to 12 ( 3 x 4 )
end data .
do if (x eq 1) .
compute z = y * 5 .
else if ( x eq 2) .
compute z = y * 3 .
else .
compute z = y*4 .
end if .
list x y z .
finish .
```

---

* Note that RECODE statements could be used instead of COMPUTE statements.

OUTPUT

```
etc.

->      do if (x eq 1) .
->      compute z = y * 5 .
->      else if ( x eq 2) .
->      compute z = y * 3 .
->      else .
->      compute z = y*4 .
->      end if .
->      list  x y z.

      X           Y           Z

   1.00        2.00       10.00
   2.00        4.00       12.00
   3.00        3.00       12.00
```

RECODING DATA

SUMMARY OF SPSS COMMANDS:

```
COMMAND:

RECODE VAR LIST ( RANGE = VALUE )
  ( RANGE = VALUE ) ... INTO VAR LIST

RANGE = LIST OF VALUES ( #, #, ETC,
  OR USES KEY WORDS

KEY WORDS FOR RANGE:

LO = LOWEST SCORE
HI = HIGHEST SCORE
THRU  - Used to set the range.
INTO - Recoded values put into new
        variable or variables.
```

PURPOSE OF THE 'RECODE' COMMAND

Again you might need to transform a variable or wish to create a new variable that is based on the already existing variables. You could use COMPUTEs if a calculation is needed but sometimes a straight substitution into an old variable or creation of a new variable can be done without calculation just using a list of substitutions. In these cases, it is easier to use the RECODE statement. RECODE allows you to:

- Substitute a new value for a previous value, set of values, or range of values for the length of a session or just for one analysis (use of TEMPORARY) .

- Create new variables whose values are based on a previous value, set of values, or range of values.

- Save the transform or new variables in a new SPSS file (use of SAVE statement to be described later).

Example 1: **● BASIC RECODE SETUP**
(see previous footnotes for SPSS/PC+™ 4.0)

```
set width = 80 .
data list list /  major gpa sat .
value labels  major 1 'humanities'
                    2 'science'
                    3 'social science'   .
begin data .
2      3.6 410
3      2.9 430        ' 3 ' becomes a ' 2 '
2      3.1 600
3      3.5 610
1      3.2 610
2      3.6 560
1      3.8 700
2      3.8 460
1      3.6 590
3      3.1 500        ' 3 ' becomes a ' 2 '
1      3.1 410
2      3.5 470
2      3.8 510
3      3.7 600        ' 3 ' becomes a ' 2 '
2      3.0 470
1      3.2 610
end data .
recode major (2,3 = 2) .        '2 & 3 ' becomes a ' 2 '
value labels major 1 'Humanities'
                   2 'Not Human.'.  ' 2 ' relabeled .
list major .
frequencies variables = major .
finish .
```

OUTPUT - NOTE CHANGES OF ' ' TO '2'

```
etc.
-> recode major (2,3 = 2) .
-> value labels major  1 'Humanities'
->                     2 'Not Human.' .
-> list major .

   MAJOR

    2.00
    2.00
    2.00
    2.00
    1.00
    2.00
    1.00
    2.00
    1.00
    2.00
    1.00
    2.00
    2.00
    2.00
    2.00
    1.00

-> frequencies variables = major .

MAJOR
                                      Valid    Cum
Value Label  Value  Frequency  Percent  Percent  Percent

Humanities   1.00        5      31.3    31.3     31.3
Not Human.   2.00       11      68.8    68.8    100.0
                       -------  -------  -------
             Total      16     100.0   100.0
```

Example 2 :   ● **Use of Ranges with THRU**

(see previous footnotes for SPSS/PC+™ 4.0)

```
set width = 80 .
data list list /  score1 to score3 .
begin data .
 90 80 90      score1 becomes 4
 67 80 56        "        1
 77 89 90        "        2
 98 67 99        "        4
 78 67 89        "        2
 89 67 89        "        3
 56 34 20        "        0
 77 98 50        "        2
 45 99 34        "        0
 66 78 98        "        1
end data .
recode score1 (0 thru 59 = 0) (60 thru 69 = 1)
       (70 thru 79 = 2) (80 thru 89 = 3)
       (90 thru 100 = 4) .    Note the use of
list score1 to score3.        of a range .
finish .
```

OUTPUT - NOTE CHANGES OF SCORE1 TO {0,1,2,4}

```
etc.

->   recode score1 (0 thru 59 = 0) (60 thru 69 = 1)
->          (70 thru 79 = 2) (80 thru 89 = 3)
->          (90 thru 100 = 4) .
->  list sex score1 to score3.

  SCORE1    SCORE2    SCORE3

    4.00     80.00     90.00
    1.00     80.00     56.00
    2.00     89.00     90.00
    4.00     67.00     99.00
    2.00     67.00     89.00
    3.00     67.00     89.00
     .00     34.00     20.00
    2.00     98.00     50.00
     .00     99.00     34.00
    1.00     78.00     98.00
```

Example 3 * :
- Use of Ranges with LO, HI and THRU
- Creation of New Variables With INTO
- New Value Labels for New Variables

```
set width = 80 .
data list list / score1 to score3 .
begin data .
90 80 90
67 80 56
77 89 90
98 67 99        Note the use of LO, HI and THRU
78 67 89        Note that score1 to score3 will be
89 67 89              unchanged but new recoded values
56 34 20              will be put into pf1 to pf3
77 98 50
45 99 34
66 78 98
end data .
recode score1 to score3 (lo thru 59 = 0)
      (60 thru hi = 1) into pf1 to pf3 .
value labels pf1 to pf3 1 'tops' 2 'bottoms' .
list score1 to score3 pf1 to pf3 .
frequencies variables = pf1 .
finish .
```

* See previous footnotes for SPSS/PC+™ 4.0

OUTPUT - NOTE GENERATION OF PF1 TO PF2

```
etc.

->recode score1 to score3 (lo thru 59 = 0)
->       (60 thru hi = 1)  into pf1 to pf3 .
->value labels pf1 to pf3  0 'bottoms' 1 'tops'  .
->list score1 to score3 pf1 to pf3 .
```

SCORE1	SCORE2	SCORE3	PF1	PF2	PF3
90.00	80.00	90.00	1.00	1.00	1.00
67.00	80.00	56.00	1.00	1.00	.00
77.00	89.00	90.00	1.00	1.00	1.00
98.00	67.00	99.00	1.00	1.00	1.00
78.00	67.00	89.00	1.00	1.00	1.00
89.00	67.00	89.00	1.00	1.00	1.00
56.00	34.00	20.00	.00	.00	.00
77.00	98.00	50.00	1.00	1.00	.00
45.00	99.00	34.00	.00	1.00	.00
66.00	78.00	98.00	1.00	1.00	1.00

```
->      frequencies  variables  =  pf1  .
```

PF1

Value Label	Value	Frequency	Percent	Valid Percent	Cum Percent
bottoms	.00	2	20.0	20.0	20.0
tops	1.00	8	80.0	80.0	100.0
	Total	10	100.0	100.0	

THE DATA LIST & FORMATTING

SUMMARY OF SPSS COMMANDS:

1. EXTERNAL DATA

DATA LIST FILE = 'FILENAME' / ETC.

2. FORMATTED DATA

DATA LIST / VARIABLE LIST + FORMAT (EITHER COLUMNS OR FORTRAN - SEE TEXT)

3. MULTIPLE RECORDS OR LINES PER CASE

DATA LIST RECORDS = # / VARIABLE LIST + FORMAT.

EXTERNAL DATA

Up till now, all of our setups have contained the data for the analysis. This may be inconvenient when using very large data sets. SPSS (Mac, Unix and PC) version offer you the option of having the data in another file on your system. This way you can manipulate the command structure without having to see the data or use the same set of commands on different sets of data. The crucial subcommand will be inserted in the data list command. You will add a FILE = 'FILENAME' as seen below. This will indicated where SPSS should find the data. We give examples for the three systems after describing the basic situation which is common to all three.

Original Setup with Internal Data	Setup with External Data	Data File - Named 'data.1'

set width = 80 .
data list list / x .
begin data .
1
2
3
end data .
descriptive = x .
finish.
	set length = 80 .
	data list file = **'data.1'**
	    list / x . [1]
	descriptives x .
	finish.
	
	―――――――――
	[1] data list file = **'data.1'**
	    free / x . [1]
	
	for SPSS/PC+™ 4.0
		1
		2
		3

Note the crucial differences:

- There are no data in the setup.
- The BEGIN DATA, DATA itself, and END DATA statements are missing
- The addition of **file = 'data.1'**
  'data.1' is the file that contains the data. This file can be named according to the conventions of the system under use. I chose 'data.1'. It is not a required SPSS name

We will present examples from :

S P S S® 4.0 FOR UNIX™

S P S S / P C + ™ 4.0

S P S S® for the Macintosh®

SPSS® 4.0 FOR UNIX™

The data is contained in a file 'data.1'. The setup refers to this file. Below you will find an annotated Unix session that lists the relevant files, demonstrates that 'data.1' contains the actual set of data (done for your edification but not necessary) and then runs the job.

```
% ls                        Lists our directory
data.1          ext         data.1 = data, ext = setup
sun% cat data.1             Shows the data
1
2
3
% spss < ext                        Runs the setup
                            - answer follows

    1   0   set length = 80 .
    2   0   data list file = 'data.1 list / x .
    3   0   descriptives x .

Number of valid observations (listwise) =       3.00
                                                Valid
Variable    Mean   Std Dev Minimum    Maximum     N
X           2.00     1.00    1.00        3.00      3
```

SPSS/PC+™ 4.0

The data is contained in a file **'data.1'**. The setup will request this file. Below you will find an annotated DOS session that lists the relevant files, demonstrates that **'data.1"** contains the actual set of data (done for your edification but not necessary), and then calls up SPSS/PC+™ 4.0 where I typed a setup to use **'data.1'**.

```
C:\SPSS>dir d*                      Lists our directory
 Directory of  C:\SPSS

DEMOTEST INC   674   1-31-91  12:17p
DATA     1      10   2-25-92   5:31p    data.1 = data
    2 File(s)   1536000 bytes free

C:\SPSS>type data.1                 Shows the data
1
2
3

C:\SPSS> spsspc                     Evokes  SPSS/PC  Window
```

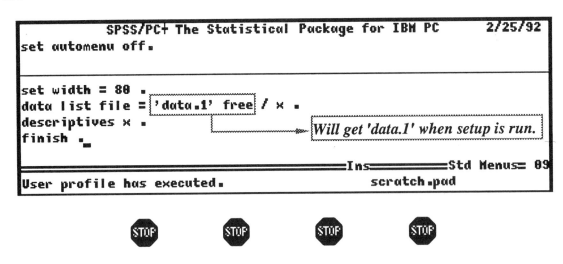

Important point: Make sure the file 'data.1' is a text file with line breaks and not in a word processing format. See Chapter 2 - SPSS/PC + ™ 4.0. If this is not the case, the file will not be read correctly and the program might crash.

SPSS® for the Macintosh®

The setup will again request the file containing the data. However, there are several nuances as there are different ways to create data files. One way is to create a pure data file in the SPSS input window and then save it. Alternatively, one could create the file in a word processor and save it as text with line breaks. We discussed this in Chapter 2:: SPSS® for the Macintosh®.

Examples of both scenarios are given below:

Creation of External Data File with SPSS ® for the Macintosh ®

1. Open program

See Chapter 2: SPSS® for the Macintosh® , pp. 76-77

2. Enter Data in Input Window

See Chapter 2: SPSS® for the Macintosh® , pp. 78 for details. It should look as follows:

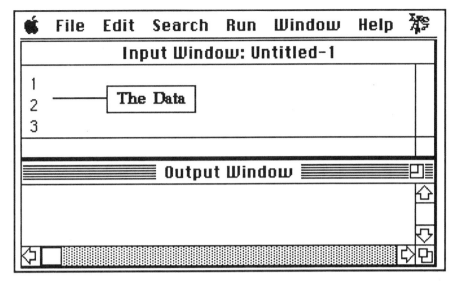

3. Save the data .

See Chapter 2: SPSS® for the Macintosh® , pp. 89-90

Creation of External Data File with a Word Processor

Obviously, there are a lot of word processing programs available. The basic principle is to create the data and then save the data in a format that is text only with line breaks. You don't want to open a file full of the word processor's internal formatting commands. Below is one example from Microsoft® Word 4.0. Note:

- The File format as (**File Format...**)**Text w/breaks** marked as **1.** .

- The data in the window ≣ **Untitled1** ≣ marked as **2.** .

Microsoft® Word 4.0

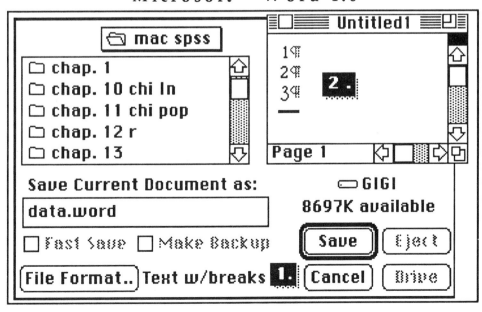

These procedures created two data files. **DATA.1** is from SPSS and **DATA.WORD** is from Microsoft® Word. Both can be seen on the Macintosh® desktop below.

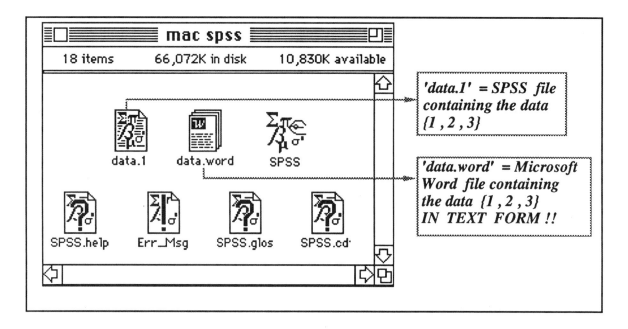

Either file could be accessed by naming them in the DATA LIST command as seen in the following SPSS® for the Macintosh® **Input Windows**:

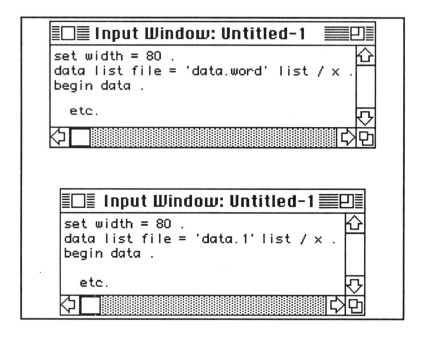

Note that the 'DATA LIST FILE = ' can be used in conjunction with the formatting commands that follow.

FORMATTING DATA

SUMMARY OF SPSS COMMANDS

DATA LIST / *Variable List column-column*[1]
Variable List column-column [1] ....

---

[1] Column refers to the starting and end position of the variable
and may also include information as to implied decimals places
by use of a ' (#) ' or whether or not the variable is alphanumeric
' (a) ' .

OR

DATA LIST / *Variable List (fortran-like
formats) ....*

FORTRAN FORMAT (abridged set)

f a . b	**numeric variable where:** **a = number of places; b = implied decimal**
a #	**alphanumeric variable of # spaces**
# x	**# blank spaces**
t #	**tab to column #**

PURPOSE OF FORMATTING

In our previous data sets and setups, we have deliberately used one of the simplest methods of entering our data. This was a 'data list list' (or 'data list free') format where all our data were numbers, separated by one or more blank spaces and all a subject's or case's data could fit on one line.

It is possible that you might have data where there are no spaces between scores. After all, each space takes time to type and memory. With a large file, the blanks take up unnecessary room. Also, you might want to enter letters as well as numbers. What about people's names? Last, you might have so much data that you have to use more than one line per subject. SPSS can handle these situations (and even more complicated data structures). This section will deal with some of the simpler contingencies.

We will demonstrate and explain formatting. The data will be in fixed places on the line. It may contain letters or numbers, have decimals, implied decimals and blanks spaces. If you have used a computer language like Fortran or some others, these concepts may be familiar to you. There are two styles of formatting which we will explain by example.

This style works on all versions of SPSS. You no longer need to type 'DATA LIST ⌶⌶⌷⌷' or 'DATA LIST ⌵⌵⌵⌵'.

Column Oriented FORMATTING

This is a very simple method. Assume that for each case, the variables are typed in the same place. You must tell SPSS the columns in which the data are located. If the data are plain numbers, then nothing else need be done. If the data are characters or have implied decimals then this has to be indicated. The general style is:

data list / variable starting column #- ending column #
variable list sc # - ec# (no. of implied decimals)
variable list sc # - ec# (a) .

This is a generic setup. You can have any order.

Example 1. Just Some Numbers.

In this example:

We have 4 people.

We have three variables: sex, age, wt.

Sex is typed in column **1.** [data list / **sex 1** age 2-4 wt 5-7 .]

Age is typed in columns **2** through **4.** [data list / sex 1 **age 2-4** wt 5-7 .]

Wt is typed in columns **5** through **7.** [data list / sex 1 age 2-4 **wt 5-7** .]

Setup

```
set width = 80 .
data list / sex 1 age 2-4 wt 5-7
begin data .
1100170
2045120
2045120
1056230
end data .
frequencies variables = age .
finish .
```

KEY TO COLUMNS

__Se x__
```
1100170
2045120
2045120
1056230
```

__Age__
```
1100170
2045120
2045120
1056230
```

__WT__
```
1100170
2045120
2045120
1056230
```

Output

```
->    set width = 80 .
->    data list / sex 1 age 2-4 wt 5-7 .

This command will read 1 records
           from the command file
```

Variable	Rec	Start[1]	End[1]	Format[2]
SEX	1	1	1	F1.0
AGE	1	2	4	F3.0
WT	1	5	7	F3.0

```
->    begin data .
->    end data .
->    frequencies variables = age .

AGE
```

Value Label	Freq	Percent	Valid Percent	Cum Percent
45	2	50.0	50.0	50.0
56	1	25.0	25.0	75.0
100	1	25.0	25.0	100.0
Total	4	100.0	100.0	

_____

[1] SPSS interprets your format. Check it!!

[2] We will explain this below.

It is important to note that SPSS prints an interpretation of the data arrangement for you. Each variable is listed with its starting and ending columns. Also given is the **format** of the variable. **Format** refers to the type of information the variable contains. SPSS uses a version of the Fortran language formatting scheme In our examples, we will see only **f** and **a** formats.

An **F** format is interpreted:

$$f_{a \cdot b} \qquad a = \text{number of places; } b = \text{implied decimal}$$

Thus we know how many spaces the variable takes up and how many decimal places are implied. We will see examples of each. The above example assumes the data are whole numbers. We will present use of implied decimals later.

Example 2. Alphanumeric Variables.

In this example: We have 4 people.

We have 4 variables: name, sex, age, wt.

The important addition to this data set are the N A M E S which are obviously letters. We need to tell SPSS or trouble will ensue. This is done by putting the letter **a** in parentheses after the column declaration as follows: │ variable # - # (a) │. In our next example we will start each data line with the subjects' names in columns 1 through 20. We will list the names. Note:

Name is typed in column **1 through 20**. [data list / **name 1 – 20(a)** … .]

Sex is typed in column **21**. [data list / … **sex 21** … .]

Age is typed in columns **22** through **24** . [data list / … **age 22–24** … .]

Wt is typed in columns **25** through **27** . [data list / … **wt 25–27** .]

SETUP

```
set width = 80 .
data list / name 1-20 (a) sex 21
          age 22-24 wt 25-27 .
begin data .
Smith              1100170
Manoogianodell     2045120        Twenty  spaces  for  Names.
Joe                2045120        Sex  starts  in  21.
Herman             1056230
end data .
list name age.
finish .
```

OUTPUT

```
->   set width = 80 .
->   data list / name 1-20 (a) sex 21 age 22-24 wt 25-27 .

This command will read 1 records from the command file
Variable   Rec   Start     End     Format

NAME        1     1        20       A20      │ Names are read in ! │

SEX         1     21       21       F1.0
AGE         1     22       24       F3.0
WT          1     25       27       F3.0

->   begin data .
->   end data .
->    list name age.


NAME                     AGE               │ Names are printed ! │


Smith                    100
Manoogianodell            45
Joe                       45
Herman                    56
```

A warning! Be careful not to attempt a statistical procedure on an alphanumeric variable. How could you compute the mean of a set of names? Watch what happens if we do! The program alerts you to the fact.

```
->    descriptives name age.
                                              Valid
Variable      Mean    Std Dev  Minimum   Maximum    N  Label

NAME          This  is  a  string  (alphanumeric)  variable.
AGE           61.50   26.19      45       100       4
```

Example 3. Use of the Var# to Var# Convention.

If you have repeated variables, such as exam1 to exam3 specified in your data list, you can simply mark out the entire range for the set of variables. SPSS will correctly divide the number of columns by the number of variables. It must be a whole number, of course. It is assumed that each variable of the subset takes up the same amount of space.

In this example: We have three exam scores of 3 digits each.

They start in column 8 and go to 16 (9 total spaces).

Note how SPSS interprets the **'exam1 to exam3 8-16'**.

SETUP AND INTERPRETATION

```
set width = 80 .
data list / sex 1 age 2-4 wt 5-7
              exam1 to exam3 8-16 .
begin data .
1100170100100100
2 45120056067089
                        |
2045120088084086        | ┌─────────────────────┐
                        | │ Columns 8 through 16 │
1056230032060056        | └─────────────────────┘
end data .              |
frequencies variables = exam1 .
finish .

->    set width = 80 .
->    data list / sex 1 age 2-4 wt 5-7
->              exam1 to exam3 8-16 .

This command will read 1 records from the command file
Variable      Rec     Start   End     Format

SEX           1       1       1       F1.0
AGE           1       2       4       F3.0
WT            1       5       7       F3.0
EXAM1         1       8       10      F3.0      |
                                                | ┌─────────┐
EXAM2         1       11      13      F3.0      | │ 8 to 16 │
                                                | └─────────┘
EXAM3         1       14      16      F3.0      |
         etc.
```

Example 4. Use of Implied Decimals

If a variable or set of variables has a fixed decimal place, it is a waste of space to type it. The . just takes up room, memory, and offers another chance for a typing error. It is possible to have SPSS read data with decimals and then correctly evaluate the magnitude of the numbers. This is done by putting an implied decimal number after the column description. The digits will be read and then the implied decimal number will be counted in from the right of the digits.

DATA LIST / *Variable List column-column (#)*
Variable List column-column (#)....

In the below example, we enter a body temperature as **0986**. It will be interpreted as **98.6** .

We have added a set of temperatures (temp1 to temp3) in columns 17–28. After the 17-28 we added a (1) . Thus 12 columns will be read. They will be divided into 3 variables of 4 digits each. A decimal will be inserted one place in from the right of each number.

SETUP

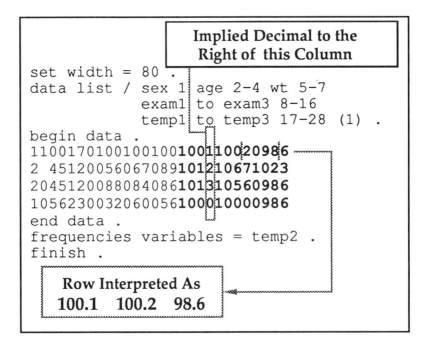

OUTPUT

In the following output, you will see that SPSS has interpreted the data such that: (1) temp1 to temp3 has an implied decimal one place to the right (**f4.1**); (2) numbers type as **1002** have becomes **100.2**. This is seen in the FREQUENCIES for temp2

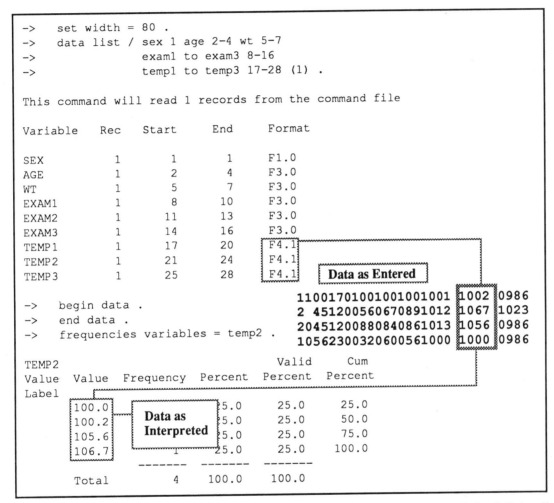

```
->      set width = 80 .
->      data list / sex 1 age 2-4 wt 5-7
->                  exam1 to exam3 8-16
->                  temp1 to temp3 17-28 (1) .

This command will read 1 records from the command file

Variable    Rec    Start    End    Format

SEX          1       1       1     F1.0
AGE          1       2       4     F3.0
WT           1       5       7     F3.0
EXAM1        1       8      10     F3.0
EXAM2        1      11      13     F3.0
EXAM3        1      14      16     F3.0
TEMP1        1      17      20     F4.1
TEMP2        1      21      24     F4.1
TEMP3        1      25      28     F4.1
```

Data as Entered

```
->      begin data .           11001701001001001001 1002 0986
->      end data .             2 451200560670891012 1067 1023
->      frequencies variables = temp2 .   20451200880840861013 1056 0986
                                10562300320600561000 1000 0986
```

```
TEMP2                                    Valid    Cum
Value   Value   Frequency   Percent   Percent   Percent
Label
        100.0                  5.0      25.0      25.0
        100.2    Data as       5.0      25.0      50.0
        105.6    Interpreted   5.0      25.0      75.0
        106.7        1        25.0      25.0     100.0
                 -------    -------   -------
        Total        4        100.0    100.0
```

What would happen if we had typed our setup so temp1 to temp3 had 2 implied decimals. The example and output follow:

SETUP

```
set width = 80 .
data list / sex 1 age 2-4 wt 5-7
            exam1 to exam3 8-16
            temp1 to temp3 17-28 (2) .
begin data .
11001701001001001001 10020986
2 451200560670891012 10671023
20451200880840861013 10560986
10562300320600561000 10000986
end data .
frequencies variables = temp2 .
finish .
records
```

ABRIDGED OUTPUT

```
etc.
TEMP1     1    17      20  F4.2
TEMP2     1    21      24  F4.2
TEMP3     1    25      28  F4.2


TEMP2
Value Label    Value   Frequency

               10.00        1
               10.02        1
               10.56        1
               10.67        1
```

Example 5. More than One Line per Case or Subject

It is possible that an individual subject has more data than can fit on one line. This is easily handled by SPSS. You will need to add a **records = #** notation to the data list and a series of '/1 *format* '/2 *format* ... '/# *format* ' for the number of lines described. # = the number of lines per case. We will present an example with 4 cases of two lines of data for each case. **RECORDS = 2** indicates there are two lines per case.

SETUP

```
set width = 80 .
data list records = 2 / 1 sex 1 age 2-4 wt 5-7
                        / 2 day1 to day7 1-7 .
begin data .
1100170          First   case
1111111
2 45120          Second  case
1000000
2045120          Third   case
1111000
1056230          Fourth  case
0000000
end data .
frequencies variables = age .
finish .
```

INTERPRETATION

```
->      data list records = 2 / 1 sex 1 age 2-4 wt 5-7
->                             / 2 day1 to day7 1-7 .

This  command  will  read  2  records  from  the  command  file

Variable    Rec    Start    End      Format

SEX          1       1        1       F1.0
AGE          1       2        4       F3.0
WT           1       5        7       F3.0
DAY1         2       1        1       F1.0
DAY2         2       2        2       F1.0
DAY3         2       3        3       F1.0
DAY4         2       4        4       F1.0
DAY5         2       5        5       F1.0
DAY6         2       6        6       F1.0
DAY7         2       7        7       F1.0
```

Example 6. Errors in the Format

Errors in the format can be disastrous. The DATA LIST statement will not be processed. If this occurs, the variables do not exist. **Every command that follows and contains the variables will be marked as in error.** This usually terrifies the novice. **So, if the data list is not correct, don't worry about the other errors messages until the data list is correct.** Check the following annotated example.   **See how the initial mistake in the data list causes a slew of irrelevant errors. Ignore the slew! Fix the data list and run again.**

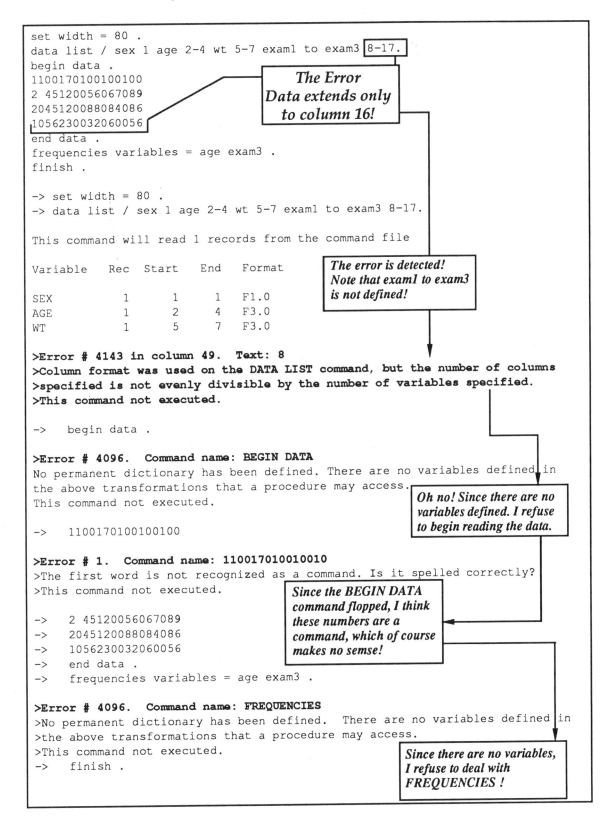

```
set width = 80 .
data list / sex 1 age 2-4 wt 5-7 exam1 to exam3 8-17.
begin data .
1100170100100100
2 45120056067089
2045120088084086
1056230032060056
end data .
frequencies variables = age exam3 .
finish .
```

The Error
Data extends only
to column 16!

```
-> set width = 80 .
-> data list / sex 1 age 2-4 wt 5-7 exam1 to exam3 8-17.


This command will read 1 records from the command file


Variable    Rec    Start    End    Format


SEX          1       1       1      F1.0
AGE          1       2       4      F3.0
WT           1       5       7      F3.0
```

The error is detected!
Note that exam1 to exam3
is not defined!

```
>Error # 4143 in column 49.  Text: 8
>Column format was used on the DATA LIST command, but the number of columns
>specified is not evenly divisible by the number of variables specified.
>This command not executed.

->    begin data .
```

```
>Error # 4096.   Command name: BEGIN DATA
No permanent dictionary has been defined. There are no variables defined in
the above transformations that a procedure may access.
This command not executed.

->    1100170100100100
```

Oh no! Since there are no
variables defined. I refuse
to begin reading the data.

```
>Error # 1.   Command name: 110017010010010
>The first word is not recognized as a command. Is it spelled correctly?
>This command not executed.

->    2 45120056067089
->    2045120088084086
->    1056230032060056
->    end data .
->    frequencies variables = age exam3 .
```

Since the BEGIN DATA
command flopped, I think
these numbers are a
command, which of course
makes no semse!

```
>Error # 4096.   Command name: FREQUENCIES
>No permanent dictionary has been defined.  There are no variables defined in
>the above transformations that a procedure may access.
>This command not executed.
->    finish .
```

Since there are no variables,
I refuse to deal with
FREQUENCIES !

FORTRAN-LIKE FORMATTING

It is also possible to use formatting in the style of the Fortran computer language. This technique is useful for more sophisticated data arrangements. We will present only a very small subset of possibilities to read simple numeric and alphanumeric data.

The basic idea is not to describe column locations but to give a set of instructions on how to read the case. It's like the game of Giant Steps or Mother, May I? You tell SPSS to read a set of numbers, now read a set of letters, now skip three spaces, now read another set of numbers. You don't have to explicitly mention the column locations.

We will use four type of Fortran formats:

f a . b   numeric variable where:
a = number of places; b = implied decimal

a #   alphanumeric variable of # spaces

 # x   # blank spaces

t #   tab to column #

They are used in a DATA LIST command by putting a format description in parentheses, after a variable list like so:

data list / variable list   (fortran format) .

The format is a combination of elements, separated by commas. The element may be repeated. This is indicated by a number in front of the element. Let's look at several examples.

Example 1. One 2-Digit Number and Two 3-Digit Numbers.

Given the following setup:

```
set width = 80 .
data list / sex age wt (f1,2f3) .
begin data .
1100170
2 45120
2045120
1056230
end data .
frequencies variables = age .
finish .
```

The four lines of data are to be read as follows:

sex = 1   age = 100   wt = 170

sex = 2   age = 45   wt = 120

sex = 2   age = 45   wt = 120

sex = 1   age = 56   wt = 230

as the format (f1, 2f3) implies:

f1 - read a numeric variable of 1 digit length.

2f3 - read two numeric variables of 3 digit length.

The output shows the effect of the format. We've highlighted the variable **age**.

```
->     set width = 80 .
->     data list / sex age wt (f1, 2f3) .

This command will read 1 records from the command file

Variable   Rec    Start    End    Format

SEX          1      1        1     F1.0
AGE          1      2        4     F3.0
WT           1      5        7     F3.0

->    begin data .
->    end data .
->    frequencies variables = age .

                                    Valid     Cum
     Value  Frequency  Percent    Percent   Percent

        45       2       50.0       50.0      50.0
        56       1       25.0       25.0      75.0
       100       1       25.0       25.0     100.0
               -------  -------    -------
    Total        4      100.0      100.0
```

Example 2. Implied Decimals.

By adding a decimal to an **f** format, we can use implied decimals similar to the column formats. In the following, we have added the variables **temp1 to temp3**. As before, the data are type without a decimal. We will add to the format **3f4.1** . Our setup would be:

```
set width = 80 .
data list / sex age wt exam1 to exam3
         temp1 to temp3 (f1,5f3,3f4.1) .
begin data .
11001701001001001001100020986
2 451200560670891012120671023
20451200880840861013105600986
10562300320600561000100000986
end data .
frequencies variables = temp2 .
finish .
```

The **3f4.1** would be interpreted as follows:

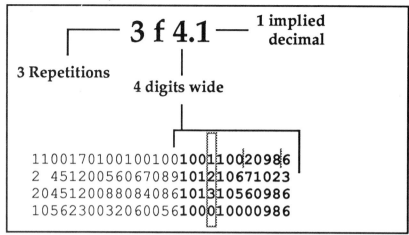

Output

```
-> set width = 80 .                              ->    begin data .
-> data list /sex age wt exam1 to exam3          ->    end data .
->      temp1 to temp3 (f1,5f3,3f4.1) .          ->    frequencies variables = temp2 .

This command will read 1 record                  TEMP2

                                                                       Valid     Cum
Variable  Rec Start  End    Format               Value  Freq.  Percent Percent  Percent

SEX        1    1     1     F1.0                  100.0    1     25.0    25.0     25.0
AGE        1    2     4     F3.0                  100.2    1     25.0    25.0     50.0
WT         1    5     7     F3.0                  105.6    1     25.0    25.0     75.0
EXAM1      1    8    10     F3.0                  106.7    1     25.0    25.0    100.0
EXAM2      1   11    13     F3.0                        ----   -------  -------
EXAM3      1   14    16     F3.0                  Total    4    100.0   100.0
TEMP1      1   17    20     F4.1
TEMP2      1   21    24     F4.1
TEMP3      1   25    28     F4.1
```

Example 3. Use of Tabs (t#)

It may be the case that you want to skip to a specific place on the record to read the next variable or set of variables. To do this use **t#**. SPSS will start reading at the **#'** specified. In the following example we wish to skip to COLUMN 22 after reading SEX, AGE, WT, AND EXAM1 TO EXAM3. We have highlighted column 22 below where temp1 starts. Note the setup on the left and the output on the right.

```
set width = 80 .                                 This command will read 1 record
data list / sex age wt exam1 to exam3            Variable Rec   Start     End   Format
   temp1 to temp2 (f1, 5f3, t22, 3f4.1) .
begin data .                                     SEX       1      1        1    F1.0
11001701001001 00.....100110020986 1             AGE       1      2        4    F3.0
2 45120056067089       101210671023              WT        1      5        7    F3.0
2045120088084086       101310560986              EXAM1     1      8       10    F3.0
1056230032060056       100010000986              EXAM2     1     11       13    F3.0
end data .                                       EXAM3     1     14       16    F3.0
etc.                                             TEMP1     1     22       25    F4.1
                                                 TEMP2     1     26       29    F4.1
  1 '.....' are not typed but for clarity.       TEMP3     1     30       33    F4.1
```

Example 4. Use #X to Skip Spaces

You can also skip spaces by typing **#x**. SPSS will then move its position over by the number specified. In the following example, VARIABLE X is in column 1 and we want to skip to column 4 for VARIABLE Y. Thus we type **2x** in the format as shown and highlighted below. We marked the two blank spaces with **..** . You don't need to type these! They are added for clarity.

SETUP AND FORMAT INTERPRETATION

```
set width = 80 .
data list / x y (f1, 2x, f2) .
begin data .
1..23
2..34
3..45
end data.
list x y .
finish .
```

Variable	Rec	Start	End	Format
X	1	1	1	F1.0
Y	1	4	5	F2.0

Example 5. Combination of Elements

You can combine all these elements into one data list if need be. In the following, we have: 1) external data in a " file = 'ext.mixed' "; 2) Two records per case - 'records = 2' ; 3) a mixture of columns and fortran with alphanumeric data and implied decimals.

SETUP

```
set width = 80 .
data list file = 'ext.mixed' records = 2
  / 1 name (a20) iq 30-32
  / 2 sex 1 age 2-4 wt 5-7  exam1
  to exam3  temp1 to temp3 (3f3,3f4.1) .
frequencies variables = temp2 .
finish .
```

EXT.MIXED

```
smith, rashid                 150
11001701001001001001100200986
kornblatt, nancy              130
2 4512005606708910121061010671023
jones, glenn                  120
20451200880840861013105600986
```

SPSS INTERPRETATION

```
This command will read 2 records from ext.mixed
Variable    Rec   Start   End   Format

NAME         1      1      20    A20
IQ           1     30      32    F3.0
SEX          2      1       1    F1.0
AGE          2      2       4    F3.0
WT           2      5       7    F3.0
EXAM1        2      8      10    F3.0
EXAM2        2     11      13    F3.0
EXAM3        2     14      16    F3.0
TEMP1        2     17      20    F4.1
TEMP2        2     21      24    F4.1
TEMP3        2     25      28    F4.1
```

SYSTEM OR SAVE FILES

SUMMARY OF SPSS COMMANDS:

> SPSS® 4.0 FOR UNIX™ & SPSS® for the Macintosh®
>
> CREATION -
>
>   SAVE OUTFILE = 'FILENAME' / MAP .
>
> DOCUMENTING A SYSTEM FILE'S CONTENTS
>
> DISPLAY DICTIONARY .
>
> SPSS/PC™ + 4.0
>
> CREATION -
>
>   SAVE OUTFILE = 'FILENAME' .
>
> DOCUMENTING A SYSTEM FILE'S CONTENTS
>
> DISPLAY ALL .
>
> USING - ALL SYSTEMS
>
> GET FILE = 'FILENAME' .

PURPOSE OF SYSTEM FILES:

The setups that we have used for examples are rather small. However, it is not uncommon to have much larger data sets. Also, you can modify significantly your data through use of selection and transformation procedures (SELECT IF, COMPUTE, RECODE, etc.). If each time you wanted to use your data, you had to rerun the original setup it would take a fair amount. It would be nice to save the data, variable labels, value labels, missing values, new variables, transformed variables, etc., in a way in which they can be quickly and easily accessed. If you have 30,000 cases, who wants to mess with the original setup. Thus, we will show the use of SYSTEM OR SAVE FILES.

A system file is sort of like a dehydrated meal. All the ingredients are there and ready to go. You cook the meal, you dehydrate it. You store it. You add water and then you eat it. The comparisons for SPSS are:

Food	Spss
Prepare the Meal	Write a setup
Dehydrate	SAVE command
Add water	GET command
Eat	Do some more analyses

The archetypal command structure to create a system file would be:

```
set width ...
data list  ...
transformations  (if  any):
        if ...
        select if ...
        recode ...
        compute, etc.
variable labels ... .
value labels ... .
missing values ... .
begin data (note data could be external) ... .
end data ... .
analyses ... .
save outfile = 'filename' ... .
finish ... .
```

There are nuances in commands for the various versions of SPSS. This will be dealt with in turn. The archetypal setup to use a system file would be (again specific nuances will be shown later):

```
set width ...
get file = 'filename'  .
analyses, transformations, ... , etc.
finish ... .
```

We will now show examples of creating, using, and documenting system files. First will be for SPSS® 4.0 FOR UNIX™ & SPSS ® for the Macintosh ®. The setup will contain variables and labeling information for the subject's SEX, three test scores (SCORE1 TO SCORE3), and their height in inches (HTIN). We will compute the average of the test score as a new variable (AVER) and create a second new variable which will be their height in feet (HTFT). Then we will create the system file as a file called 'GM.SAV' using the command **save outfile = 'gm.sav' / map** . The addition of the optional word **map** will give us a confirmation of the saved variables.

SPSS® 4.0 FOR UNIX™ & SPSS® for the Macintosh®

```
set width = 80 .
data list list / sex score1 to score3 htin .
value labels sex 1 'male' 2 'female' .
variable labels sex 'gender' .
missing value sex (3) .
compute htft = htin/12 .
compute aver = mean(score1 to score3) .
begin data.
1 90 80 90  56
1 67 80 56  70
1 77 89 90  52
1 98 67 99  63
1 78 67 89  56
2 89 67 89  60
2 56 34 20  71
2 77 98 50  67
2 45 99 34  89
2 66 78 98  48
2 66 89 100 56
end data.
descriptives aver htft .
save outfile = 'gm.sav'/ map .
finish .
```

New variables created.
AVER & HTFT

Creates the system file.

Below is an SPSS® 4.0 FOR UNIX™ output. The SPSS® for the Macintosh® is similar.

```
1   0  set width = 80 .
2   data list list / sex score1 to score3 htin  .
3   value labels sex 1 'male' 2 'female' .
4   variable labels sex 'gender' .
5   missing value sex (3) .
6   compute htft = htin/12 .
7   compute aver = mean(score1 to score3) .
8   begin data.
19  end data.
20  descriptives aver  htft .

Number of valid observations (listwise) =        11.00
Variable   Mean     Std Dev   Minimum   Maximum    N
AVER       74.91      15.38     36.67     88.00    11
HTFT        5.21        .95      4.00      7.42    11

  21    save  outfile = 'gm.sav'/ map  .
```

gm.sav is
created .

```
OUTPUT FILE MAP
Result     Input1
------     ------
SEX        SEX
SCORE1     SCORE1
SCORE2     SCORE2          'MAP' LISTS THE STORED VARIABLES.
SCORE3     SCORE3
HTIN       HTIN
HTFT       HTFT
AVER       AVER


Time stamp on saved file:    16 MAR 92 12:10:13
File contains  7 variables,
56 bytes per case before compression
11 cases saved
```

Creation time
is noted.

# of Cases

After running this setup on a Unix system or Macintosh, the file **'gm.sav'** would be seen in our directories or on our desktop.

Let's look at a Unix example. Assume that our setup is in a file called **'saving'** and we will send the output (seen above) to **'sav.1'**. The process would look as follows:

```
% ls
  saving   [SAVING is the setup.]

% spss < saving > sav.1
End of job:  22 command lines  0 errors  0 warnings  0 CPU seconds

% ls
  gm.sav   saving   sav.1 [GM.SAV appears.]
```

If the same setup is run on the Macintosh, the following icon containing the system file 'gm.sav' would appear on our desktop.

gm.sav

USING SYSTEM FILES:

To use the file and the information it contains, you need to use the **get** command. It has the form:

> **get file = 'filename' .**

This will evoke your setup in the configuration it had when saved. In the following example, we will use the variables AVER and HTFT. Recall that these were new variables that we created and saved. We will also use the variable SEX to show that the value labels were saved.

SETUP

set width = 80. get file = 'gm.sav' . correlations aver htft . frequencies variables = sex . finish .	**Opens the system file 'gm.sav'.** **Uses the new variables.** **Watch for value labels.**

OUTPUT

```
1  0   set width = 80.
    2  get file = 'gm.sav'  .          GM.SAV is opened.
File gm.sav
   Created:  16 MAR 92 12:10:13 - 7 variables

   3   correlations aver htft .        Created  variables
   - - Correlation Coefficients  - -       used.

            AVER        HTFT
AVER      1.0000      -.6586*
HTFT      -.6586*      1.0000

* - Signif. LE .05  ** - Signif. LE .01 (2-tailed)

   4   frequencies variables = sex .

SEX        gender
Value                             Valid     Cum
Label       Value  Freq. Percent  Percent   Percent

male        1.00    5    45.5      45.5      45.5     Labels  from  Setup
female      2.00    6    54.5      54.5     100.0        Used
                   ------- -----    -----
       Total       11    100.0    100.0

Valid cases    11      Missing cases      0
```

INTERROGATING A SYSTEM FILES
USE OF 'DISPLAY':

Sometimes we create a system file like 'GM.SAV' and forget what is in it. You can't easily read the file as it is in a machine specific non-text form. I've done this too many times myself to laugh it off as an uncommon mistake. Also, someone might create the file for you to use but not send any documentation. While you can easily write a setup that opens the file using a 'GET FILE = ...' command, it would be nice to see a list of variables with associated types, formats, and assigned labels. We can do this with the command:

display dictionary .

We will get a listing that will document the file for us. In the following example setup and output, we will interrogate 'GM.SAV'. Note in the output that the original variables and the new ones are described.

SETUP

```
set width = 80.
get file = 'gm.sav' .        Gets GM.SAV
display dictionary .         Interrogates  the
file
finish .
```

OUTPUT

```
   1  0  set width = 80.
   2  get file = 'gm.sav' .

File gm.save
   Created:  16 MAR 92 12:10:13 - 7 variables

   3  display dictionary .

         List of variables on the active file

                                                    Position
Name                                                   1
SEX       gender
          Print Format: F8.2       Write Format: F8.2
          Missing Values: 3.00

          Value     Label
          1.00      male
          2.00      female

                                                       2
SCORE1
          Print Format: F8.2       Write Format: F8.2

                                                       3
SCORE2
          Print Format: F8.2       Write Format: F8.2

                                                       4
SCORE3
          Print Format: F8.2       Write Format: F8.2

                                                       5
HTIN
          Print Format: F8.2       Write Format: F8.2

                                                       6
HTFT
          Print Format: F8.2       Write Format: F8.2

                                                       7
AVER
          Print Format: F8.2       Write Format: F8.2
```

SPSS/PC ™ + 4.0 and System Files

The command structure is slightly different. The **MAP** subcommand is not available for the **SAVE** command and the form of the **DISPLAY** command is different. Respectively, they would be :

```
save file = 'filename' .
```

and

```
display all .
```

The 'GET FILE = ... ' command is the same. The following SPSS/PC ™ + 4.0 setup called 'SAVE.PC' would create a system file called 'gm.sav'. You will see it on the directory after the setup. 'SAVE.PC' was run using **c:> spsspc save.pc** as described in Chapter 2.

PC Setup

```
set width = 80 .
data list free/ sex score .
begin data .
1 10
2 20
2 30
end data .
save outfile = 'gm.sav' .
finish .
```

Directory With 'gm. save' Created

```
C:\>dir

 Directory of  C:\

GSS   SYS   68136      1-10-91     2:10p
GM    BAK   951        8-15-91     3:18p
GM    ANS   624        8-16-91     9:11a
GM1   ANS   624        8-16-91     9:14a
GM    SAV   2656       3-16-92     4:54p
SAVE  PC    123        3-16-92     4:42p
```

If we wanted to interrogate 'gm.sav', we could also use **display**. However, the command is **display all.** as below:

```
set width = 80 .

get file = 'gm.sav'

display  all .

finish .
```

References

Beyer, W. H. (Ed.) (1968). *CRC Handbook of Tables for Pprobability and Statistics, 2nd ed.* Boca Raton, FL : CRC Press, Inc..

Daniel, W.W. (1990). *Applied Nonparametric Statistics, 2nd ed.* Boston:PWS-Kent.

Everitt, B. S. (1977). *The Analysis of Contingency Tables.* London: Chapman and Hall.

Hair, J. F., Jr., Anderson, R. E., & Tatham, R. L. (1989). *Multivariate Data Analysis with Readings, 2nd. ed.,* New York: Macmillan.

Howell, D. C. (1987). *Statistical Methods for Psychology, 2nd. ed.* Boston: Duxbury Press.

Keppel, G. (1991). *Design and Analysis, 3rd ed.* Prentice-Hall, 1982.

Kirk, R.E. (1982). *Experimental Design, 2nd ed.* Brooks/Cole, 1982.

Levine, G. (1991). *A Guide to SPSS for the Analysis of Variance.* Hillsdale, NJ: Lawrence Erlbaum Associates.

Marascuilo, L.A., & Levin, J. R. (1983). *Multivariate Statistics in the Social Sciences.* Belmont, CA: Wadsworth, Inc.

Marascuilo, L.A., & Levin, J. R. (1983). *Multivariate Statistics in the Social Sciences.* Belmont, CA: Wadsworth, Inc.

Norusis, M. J. (1990). *SPSS/PC +™ 4.0 Base Manual.* Chicago: SPSS, Inc..

Seigel, S., & Castellan, N.J. (1988). *Nonparametric Statistics for the Behaviorial Sciences, 2nd ed.* New York:McGraw-Hill.

SPSSX Statistical Algorithms.. (1983). Chicago: SPSSX.

SPSS® for the Macintosh®: Operations Guide. (1990). Chicago: SPSS, Inc..

SPSS® for Unix™: Operations Guide. (1990). Chicago: SPSS, Inc..

SPSS® Reference Guide. (1990). Chicago: SPSS, Inc..

SPSS® Reference Guide. (1990). Chicago: SPSS, Inc..

Tabachnick, B.G., & Fidell, L.S. (1989). *Using Multivariate Statistics, 2nd ed.* New York: Harper & Row.

Wilcox, R. R. (1987). New designs in analysis of variance. *Annual Review of Psychology, 38,* 29–60.

Winer, B.J., Brown, D.R., & Michels, K. M. (1991). *Statistical Principles in Experimental Design, 3rd ed.* New York: McGraw-Hill.

Index

D

E

F

G

L

M

N

O

P

Index
488

T

U

V

W

X

Y

Z